Allen
.65

157
h35

121

D1597005

THE CONTEMPORARY SCIENCE SERIES.

Edited by HAVELOCK ELLIS.

THE PSYCHOLOGY OF THE EMOTIONS.

THE PSYCHOLOGY OF
THE EMOTIONS

BY

TH. RIBOT

PROFESSOR AT THE COLLEGE OF FRANCE, EDITOR OF THE
"REVUE PHILOSOPHIQUE."

THE WALTER SCOTT PUBLISHING CO., LTD.
PATERNOSTER SQUARE, LONDON, E.C.
CHARLES SCRIBNER'S SONS
597 FIFTH AVENUE, NEW YORK

PREFACE.

———◆———

THE psychology of states of feelings, it is generally recognised, is still in a confused and backward condition. Although it has benefited in some measure by the contemporary allurement of psychological research, it must be acknowledged that it has only exerted a moderate seduction upon workers; the preference has been given to other studies, such as those of perception, of memory, of images, of movement, of attention. If any proof is necessary we may find it in the bibliographies, now published in Germany, America, and France, which give the psychological inventory of each year; of the whole number of books, memoirs, and articles which appear, less than the twentieth part, on an average, relates to the feelings and emotions. It is a very small part compared to the part played by the emotions and passions in human life, and this region of psychology is not deserving of such neglect. It is true that in recent years W. James and Lange seem to have brought this state of stagnation to an end. Their thesis, paradoxical in appearance, has aroused, especially in America, many discussions, criticisms, defences, and, what is of more value, observations and researches.

b

9489

It must be acknowledged that for those who have any care for precision and clearness the study of the feelings and emotions presents great difficulties. Internal observation, always an uncertain guide which leads us but a little way, is here especially questionable. Experiment has given some very useful results, but they are much less important and numerous than in other regions of psychology. Detailed researches and monographs are lacking, so that the subject abounds with questions on which little light has yet been thrown. Finally, the dominant prejudice which assimilates emotional states to intellectual states, considering them as analogous, or even treating the former as dependent on the latter, can only lead to error.

We have, in fact, in every study of the psychology of feeling to choose between two radically distinct positions, and this choice involves a difference in method. Concerning the final and essential nature of states of feeling there are two contrary opinions. According to one, they are secondary and derived, the qualities, modes, or functions of knowledge; they only exist through it; they are "confused intelligence": that is the *intellectualist* thesis. According to the other, they are primitive, autonomous, not reducible to intelligence, able to exist outside it and without it; they have a totally different origin: that is the thesis which under its present form may be called *physiological*. These two doctrines exhibit variations which I ignore, as I am not writing their history, but they all come into one or the other of these two great currents.

The intellectualist theory, which is of considerable age, has found its most complete expression in

Herbart and his school, for whom every state of feeling only exists through the reciprocal relation of representations; every emotion results from the co-existence in the mind of ideas which agree or disagree; it is the immediate consciousness of the momentary elevation or depression of psychic activity, of a free or impeded state of tension. But it does not exist by itself; it resembles musical harmonies and dissonances, which differ from elementary sounds though only existing through them. Suppress every intellectual state, and feeling vanishes; it only possesses a borrowed life, that of a parasite. The influence of Herbart still persists in Germany, and, with some exceptions (Horwicz, Schneider, etc.), complete or mitigated intellectualism predominates.

The doctrine which I have called physiological (Bain, Spencer, Maudsley, James, Lange[1]) connects all states of feeling with biological conditions, and considers them as the direct and immediate expression of the vegetative life. It is the thesis which has been adopted, without any restriction, in this work. From this standpoint feelings and emotions are no longer a superficial manifestation, a simple efflorescence; they

---

[1] It may be doubted whether all the English writers here mentioned can be strictly classed with the physiological school as understood by M. Ribot. With regard to Mr. Spencer, for instance, this is indicated by a brief summary of his own position in a private letter to the Rev. Angus Mackay, who had presented a statement of the " confused intelligence " theory, " which I conceive to be a part of the truth," wrote Mr. Spencer, adding that "joined with the dimly aroused association of ideas derived from the experiences of the individual, I hold that the body of the emotion consists more largely of the inherited associations of experiences and still more vague states of consciousness which result from excitement of them." It is clear that the evolutionary view does not necessarily fall wholly into the "physiological " group. —ED.

plunge into the individual's depths; they have their
roots in the needs and instincts, that is to say, in
movements. Consciousness only delivers up a part
of their secrets; it can never reveal them completely;
we must descend beneath it. No doubt it is awkward
to have to invoke an unconscious activity, to call in
the intervention of an obscure and ill-determined
factor; but to wish to reduce emotional states to
clear and definite ideas, or to imagine that by this
process we can fix them, is to misunderstand them
completely and to condemn ourselves beforehand to
failure.

For the rest, this is neither the place to criticise
the intellectualist thesis, nor to justify the other
in passing; the whole work is devoted to this task.

The book consists of two parts. The first studies
the more general manifestations of feeling : pleasure
and pain, the characteristic signs of this form of
psychic life, everywhere diffused under manifold
aspects; then the nature of emotion, a complex
state which in the order of feelings corresponds to
perception in the order of knowledge.

The second deals with the special emotions. This
detailed study is of great importance for reasons
which will be explained later on, especially because
we must not rest in generalities; it furnishes a means
of control and verification. The nature of the emotional life cannot be understood unless we follow it
in its incessant transformations—that is to say, in
its history. To separate it from social, moral, and
religious institutions, from the æsthetic and intellectual movements which translate it and incarnate
it, is to reduce it to a dead and empty abstraction.
Thus an attempt has been made to follow all the

emotions one after the other in the progress of their development, noting the successive movements of their evolution or their retrogression.

The pathology of each emotion has been sketched to complete and throw light on the study. I have tried to show that beneath an appearance of confusion, incoherence, and promiscuity, there is, from the morbid to the normal, from the complex to the simple, a conducting thread which will always bring us back to the point of origin.

A work which has for its aim to set forth the present situation of the psychology of feeling and emotion .might have been made very long. By eliminating every digression and all historical exposition, it has been made as short as possible.

TH. RIBOT.

CONTENTS.

———◆———

Part I.—GENERAL PSYCHOLOGY.

CHAPTER I.

CHAPTER II.

CHAPTER III.

CHAPTER IV.

CHAPTER V.

CHAPTER VI.

CHAPTER VII.

CHAPTER VIII.

CHAPTER IX.

CHAPTER X.

CHAPTER XI.

CHAPTER XII.

Part II.—SPECIAL PSYCHOLOGY.

CHAPTER IV.

CHAPTER V.

CHAPTER VI.

CHAPTER VII.

The complex emotions are derived from the simple (1) by way
of complete evolution; in a homogeneous form: Examples—
In a heterogeneous form: Examples—(2) by arrest of development—(3) by composition; two forms—Composition by
mixture; with convergent elements; with divergent elements
—Composition by combination (sublimity, humour)—Modesty
—Is it an instinct?—Hypotheses as to its origin.

CHAPTER VIII.

Origin of the Social Feelings—Animal societies—Nutritive
societies—The individual and society—Domestic societies—
Social instinct has its source neither in sexual nor in maternal
love—Gregarious societies—Attraction of like for like—Origin
of social tendencies—Accidental and transitory unions, of
variable duration, and voluntary—The social tendencies arise
from the conditions of existence—Social life does not spring
from domestic life—The higher societies among animals: they
exclude family relations—Human societies—Two opposite
theories of their origin: the family, the horde—Evolution of
the family—Evolution of social life—The family and the clan
not similar institutions—The moral sense. Two views of its
origin: (a) the intellectual, (b) the emotional—They correspond to two stages in its development—Its innateness and its
necessity belong to the motor, not the intellectual order—
Genesis of the benevolent feeling. Psychological analysis of
its generative elements. Facts in support of this—Discoverers
in morality—Genesis of the sense of justice—Phases of its
development—Conclusion: complexity of the moral sense—
Pathology. Elimination of the questions of criminal anthropology. Moral insensibility.

CHAPTER IX.

Importance of the subject—Its Divisions. First Period:
origin of the religious feeling—Primitive notions of the Infinite
(Max Müller); Ancestor-worship (H. Spencer)—Fetichism,
animism; Predominance of fear—Practical, utilitarian, social,
but not moral character—Second period: (1) Intellectual
evolution; Conception of a Cosmic Order first physical, then
moral—Function of increasing generalisation; its stages; (2)
Emotional evolution; Predominance of love; addition of the

CHAPTER X.

CHAPTER XI.

CHAPTER XII.

CHAPTER XIII.

CHAPTER XIV.

INTRODUCTION.

THE EVOLUTION OF THE AFFECTIVE LIFE.

In all affective manifestations there are two elements: the motor states or impulses, which are primary; the agreeable or painful states, which are secondary— Unconscious organic protoplasmic sensibility; micro-organisms—Chemical interpretation; psychological interpretation—Are there pure states of feeling?— Affirmative facts—The period of needs, the instinct of conservation—The period of primitive emotions— How they may be determined; the genetic or chronological method—Fear, anger, affection, the self-feeling, sexual emotion—Are joy and grief emotions?—The abstract emotions and their conditions—The passions are the equivalent in feeling of an intellectual obsession.

AT the outset it may be useful to sketch in rough outline the general evolution of the life of feeling from its humble origin in organic sensibility to its highest and most complex forms. Afterwards we shall present the corresponding and inverse picture, that of its dissolution.

If we take at random, in the form in which daily experience gives them to us, the states known under the vague names of "sentiments," "emotions," "passions": joy and sorrow, a toothache, a pleasurable perfume, love or anger, fear or ambition, æsthetic enjoyment or religious emotion, the rage of gambling or benevolence, the shudder of the sublime or the discomfort of disgust, and so on, for they are innumerable, one first observation is obvious even on a superficial examination: all these states, whatever they may be, offer a double aspect, objective or external, subjective or internal.

We note in the first place the *motor* manifestations: movements, gestures, and attitude of the body, a modification in the voice, blushing or pallor, tremors, changes in the secretions or excretions, and other bodily phenomena, varying in different cases. We may observe them in ourselves, in our fellows, and in animals. Although they may not always be motor in the strict sense, we may so call them, since they are all the result of a centrifugal action.

We note also, in ourselves directly and by the evidence of consciousness, in others indirectly and by induction, the existence of certain states which are agreeable, painful, or mixed, with their modes or shades, extremely variable in quality and in intensity.

Of these two groups—the motor manifestations on one side, the pleasures, pains, and their compounds on the other side—which is fundamental? Can we put them on the same level, and if we cannot, which is that which supports the other?

My reply to this question is clear: it is the motor manifestations which are essential. In other words, what are called agreeable or painful states only constitute the superficial part of the life of feeling, of which the deep element consists in tendencies, appetites, needs, desires, translated into movements. Most classical treatises (and even some others) say that sensibility is the faculty of experiencing pleasure and pain. I should say, using the same terminology, that sensibility is the faculty of tending or desiring, and *consequently* of experiencing pleasure and pain. There is nothing mysterious in the tendency; it is a movement or an arrest of movement in the nascent stage. I employ this word "tendency" as synonymous with needs, appetites, instincts, inclinations, desires; it is the generic term of which the others are varieties; it has the advantage over them of embracing at the same time both the psychological and physiological aspects of the phenomenon. All the tendencies suppose a motor inner-vation; they translate the needs of the individual, whatever they may be, physical or mental; the basis, the root of the affective life is in them, not in the consciousness of pleasure and pain which accompanies them according as they are satisfied or opposed. These agreeable or painful states are only signs and indications; and just as symptoms reveal to us the existence of a disease, and not its essential nature, which must be sought in the hidden lesions of the tissues, organs, and functions, so pleasure and pain are only *effects* which must guide us in the search and determination of causes hidden in the region of the instincts. If the contrary opinion has generally prevailed, and priority been accorded to the study of agreeable and painful manifestations considered as the essential element in the emotional life and serving to define it, that is the result of a bad method, of an exclusive faith in the evidence of consciousness, of a common illusion which consists in believing that the conscious portion of an event is its principal portion, but especially the consequence of the radically false idea that the bodily phenomena which accompany all states of feeling are factors that are negligible and external, foreign to psychology, and without interest for it.

For the present what has just been said is only an affirmation; the proofs will come later, and will occupy the whole of this book; at the outset it is only necessary to indicate clearly the position taken up. We may now follow the evolution of the life of feeling in its chief stages, which are—pre-conscious sensibility, the appearance of the primitive emotions, their transformation either into complex and abstract emotions or into that stable and chronic state which constitutes the passions.

I.

The first period is that of protoplasmic, vital, organic pre-conscious sensibility. We know that the organism has its memory; it preserves certain impressions, certain normal or morbid modifications; it is capable of adaptation: this point has been well established by Hering (who had been preceded by Laycock and Jessen). It is the outline of the superior form of psychic conscious memory. In the same way there exists an inferior unconscious form—organic sensibility—which is the preparation and the outline of superior conscious emotional life. Vital sensibility is to conscious feeling what organic memory is to memory in the ordinary sense of the word.

This vital sensibility is the capacity to receive stimuli and to re-act to them. In a well-known memoir, now of ancient date,[1] Claude Bernard wrote : "Philosophers generally only know and admit conscious sensibility, that which their ego bears witness to. It is for them the psychic modification, pleasure or pain, determined by external modifications. . . . Physiologists necessarily place themselves at another point of view. They have to study the phenomenon objectively, under all the forms which it puts on. They observe that at the moment when a modifying agent acts on man, it not only provokes pleasure and pain, it not only affects the soul : it affects the body, it determines other re-actions besides the psychic re-actions, and these automatic re-actions, far from being an accessory part of the phenomenon, are on the contrary its essential element." Then he showed experimentally that the employment of anæs-thetics, pushed to an extreme, first abolished conscious sensibility, then the unconscious sensibility of the intestines and glands, then muscular irritability, finally the lively movements of the epithelial tissue. In the same way among plants : under the influence of ether the sensitive plant loses its singular properties, seeds cease to germinate, yeast to ferment, etc. Whence follows the conclusion that sensibility resides, not in the organs or tissues, but in their anatomical elements.

Since then these investigations into protoplasmic sensibility have been pursued with much ardour among micro-organisms. These beings, sometimes animal, sometimes vegetable, are simple masses of protoplasm, generally mono-cellular, appearing homogeneous, without differentiation of tissues. Now very varied *tendencies* have been found among these organisms. Some seek light, others flee from it per-sistently. The protoplasmic mass of myxomycetes which live in the bark of the oak, if placed in a watch-glass full of water, remain there in repose ; but if sawdust is placed around them they immediately emigrate towards it as if seized by home-sickness. The actynophrys acts in

---

[1] "La sensibilité dans le règne animal et le règne végétal" (1876, in *Science expérimentale*, pp. 218 *et seq.*).

the same way with regard to starch. Bacteria can discover even the trillionth part of a milligram of oxygen in a neighbouring body. Certain sedentary ciliated creatures appear to choose their food. Some also have thought that they detected an elective tendency in the movement which draws the male ovule towards the female ovule. I have only recalled a few of the many facts which have been enumerated.

If it is necessary to mention other examples, I may refer to the case studied in our own days under the name of "phagocytosis." The struggle for life goes on, not only among individuals, but also among the anatomical elements which constitute the individual. Every tissue—muscular, connective, adipose, etc.—possesses phagocytes (devouring cells), of which the duty consists in devouring and destroying old or enfeebled cells of the same kind. Besides these special phagocytes there are general phagocytes, such as the white corpuscles of the blood, which come to the help of the others when they are not equal to their task. They stand against the pathogenic microbes, waging upon them an internal struggle, and opposing the invasion of infectious germs. This apparently teleological property seems at first very surprising. Later investigations have shown that the phagocytes are endowed with a sensibility (called chemio-taxic), owing to which they are able to distinguish the chemical composition of their environment and to approach it or leave it accordingly; deteriorated tissues attract certain of them which incorporate the feeble or dead cells, while the healthy and vigorous elements are perhaps able to defend themselves by secreting some substance which preserves them from phagocytosis.

These facts, taken from among many others to which I shall again have to refer when dealing with the sexual instinct, have been interpreted in two very different ways: one psychological, the other chemical.

For some there is in all these phenomena a rudiment of consciousness. Since the movements are adapted and appropriate, varying according to circumstances, there must be choice they say, and choice involves a psychic element; the mobility is the revelation of an obscure "psyche" endowed with attractive and repulsive tendencies.

For the others (whose opinion I adopt), the whole may be explained on physico-chemical grounds. No doubt

there is affinity, attraction and repulsion, but only in the
scientific sense; these words are metaphors derived from
the language of consciousness which should be purged of
all anthropomorphic elements. Several authors have shown
by numerous observations and experiments the chemical
conditions which determine or prevent this pretended
choice (Sachs, Verworn, Löb, Maupas, Bastian, etc.).

On this point, as on all questions of origin, we must
decide according to probabilities, and the probabilities
appear to be all in favour of the chemical hypothesis. In
any case, this matter has only a secondary interest for us
here. If we admit conscious tendencies, then the origin
of the emotional life coincides with the very origin of
physiological life. If we eliminate all psychology, there
still remains the physiological tendency, that is to say the
motor element, which in some degree, from the lowest
to the highest, is never quite wanting.

This excursion into the pre-conscious period—since we
so regard it—puts us in possession of one result. At the
end of this investigation we find two well-defined tendencies,
physico-chemical and organic—the one of attraction, the
other of repulsion; these are the two poles of the life of
feeling. What is attraction in this sense? Simply assimilation; it blends with nutrition. With sexual attraction,
however, we must note that we already reach a higher
grade; the phenomenon is more complex, the monocellular
being no longer acts to preserve itself but to maintain the
species. As to repulsion, we may remark that it is
manifested in two ways. On one side it is the opposite
of assimilation : the cell or the tissue rejects what does not
suit it. On another side, at a somewhat superior stage, it
is in some degree already defensive.

We have thus gained a basis for our subject by finding
that beneath the conscious life of feeling there exists a
very low and obscure region, that of vital or organic sensibility, which is an embryonic form of conscious sensibility
and supports it.

II.

We now pass from darkness to light, from the vital to
the psychic. But before entering into the conscious

period of the life of feeling and following it in the progress
of its evolution, this is perhaps the place to examine
a sufficiently important question which has usually been
wrongly answered in the negative : Are there *pure* states of
feeling—that is to say, states empty of any intellectual
element, of every representative content, not connected
either with perceptions or images or concepts, simply subjective, agreeable, disagreeable, or mixed? If we reply in
the negative, it follows that without exception no kind
of feeling can ever exist by itself; it always requires a
support; it is never more than an accompaniment. This
proposition is held by the majority; it has naturally been
adopted by the intellectualists, and Lehmann has recently
maintained it in its most radical form; a state of emotional
consciousness is never met with ; pleasure and pain are
always connected with intellectual states.[1] If we reply in
the affirmative, then the state of feeling is considered as
having at least sometimes an independent existence of its
own and not as condemned to play for ever the part of
acolyte or parasite.

This is a question of fact, and observation alone can
settle it.   Although there are other reasons to give in
favour of the autonomous and even primordial character of
the life of feeling, I reserve them for the conclusion of this
book, to remain at present in the region of pure and simple
experience.   There can be no doubt that, as a rule,
emotional states accompany intellectual states, but I deny
that it can never be otherwise, and that perceptions and
representations are the necessary condition of existence,
absolutely and without exception, of every manifestation of
feeling.

There is a first class of facts which I only refer to in
order not to ignore them.   Although they have been
invoked they seem to me to carry little weight.   I refer
to the emotions which suddenly break out in animals and
are not explicable by any anterior experience.   Gratiolet
having presented to a very young puppy a fragment of
wolf's skin so worn that it resembled parchment, the animal
on smelling it was seized with extreme fright.   Kröner, in

---

[1] " Ein rein emotionneller Bewusstseinszustand kommt nicht vor ;
Lust und Unlust sind stets an intellektuelle Zustände geknüpft,"
Die Hauptgesetze der menschlichen Gefühlslebens (1892), p. 16.

his book on cœnæsthesia,[1] has collected similar facts. It is,
however, so difficult to know what passes in the consciousness of an animal, and to ascertain the part of instinct and
of hereditary transmission, that I do not insist. Moreover,
in all these cases the emotion is excited by an *external*
sensation which touches a spring and sets the mechanism
of instinct at work; so that it might be argued that
we are not here concerned with a pure and independent state of feeling. To remove all doubt, we require
cases in which the state of feeling precedes the intellectual
state, not being provoked by, but, on the contrary, provoking it.

The child at the beginning can only possess a purely
affective life. During the intra-uterine period he neither
hears nor sees nor touches; even after birth it is some
weeks before he learns to localise his sensations. His
psychic life, however rudimentary it may be, must consist
in a vague state of pleasure and pain analogous to ours.
He cannot connect them with perceptions, because he is
still unable to perceive. It is a widely accredited opinion
that the infant enters into life by pain; Preyer has questioned this; we shall see later on what grounds. At present
we need not insist upon these facts, since we cannot interpret
them except by induction. Adults will furnish us with unquestionable and abundant evidence.

As a general rule, every deep change in the *internal*
sensations is translated in an equivalent fashion into the
cœnæsthesia and modifies the tone of feeling. Now the
internal sensations are not representative, and this factor,
of capital importance, has been forgotten by the intellectualists. Of this purely organic state, which afterwards becomes
a state of feeling, and then an intellectual state, we shall
later on find numerous examples in studying the genesis of
the emotions; it is enough for the moment to note a few
of them. Under the influence of haschisch, says Moreau
(de Tours), who has studied it so well, "the feeling which
is experienced is one of happiness. I mean by this a state
which has nothing in common with purely sensual pleasure.
It is not the pleasure of the glutton or the drunkard, but is
much more comparable to the joy of the miser or that

---

[1] *Das Körperliche Gefühl* (1887), pp. 80, 81.

caused by good news." I once knew well a man who for
ten years constantly took haschisch in large doses; he with-
stood the drug better than might be expected, and finally
died insane. I received his oral and written confidences,
often to a greater extent than I desired. During this long
period I have often noted his feeling of inexhaustible satisfaction, translated now and again into strange inventions or
commonplace reflections, but in his opinion invaluable. At
the epoch of puberty, when it follows its normal development, we know that there is a profound metamorphosis.
Certain conditions, known or unknown, act on the organism
and modify its state (first moment); translated into consciousness, these organic conditions give birth to a particular
tone of feeling (second moment); this state of feeling produces corresponding representations (third moment). The
representative element appears in the last place. Similar
phenomena are produced under other conditions, in which
the cœnæsthesia is modified by the state of the sexual organs
(menstruation, pregnancy). The emotional state is produced first, the intellectual state afterwards. But the most
abundant source from which we may draw examples at will
is certainly the period of incubation which precedes the
appearance of mental diseases. In most cases it is a state
of vague sadness. Sadness without a cause, it is commonly
said, and rightly, if by that is meant that it is produced
neither by an accident nor by bad news nor by ordinary
causes; but not causeless, if we take into consideration the
internal sensations which in such a case play a part which is
unperceived but not the less effective. This inclination to
melancholy is also the rule in the neuroses. Sometimes it
happens that the state of feeling, instead of being a slow
incubation, is an *aura* of emotional character and short
duration (a few minutes to at most a few hours). Some
patients, by repeated experience, are aware of this; they
know by the change that the attack is approaching. Féré
(*Les Epilepsies*) gives several examples; among others, that
of a young man who under these circumstances became
totally changed in character, which he expressed in an
original manner by saying, "I feel that my heart changes."
That is because *in the last stage* this state of feeling takes
form and becomes fixed in an idea, as may best be seen in
persecutional insanity.

Without insisting, as would be easy, on any further enumeration of facts, we may reduce these pure states of feeling to four principal types :

1. Agreeable state (pleasure, joy) : that of haschisch and similar drugs, certain stages of general paralysis of the insane, the sense of well-being experienced by the consumptive and the dying ; many people who have escaped a death which they considered certain have felt themselves overwhelmed on its approach by a feeling of beatitude, without further definition, which is perhaps only the absence of all suffering.[1]

2. Painful state (sadness, annoyance): the incubation period of most diseases, the melancholy of menstrual periods.

3. State of fear : without reason, without apparent causes, without justification, without object ; fear of everything and of nothing : a fairly frequent state, which we shall examine in detail when we come to the *phobias*.

4. State of excitability : connected with anger, frequent in neurosis ; it is an unstable and explosive state of being which, at first vague and undetermined, ends by taking form, attaching itself to a representation, and discharging itself on an object.

Finally, there are mixed states, formed by the co-existence or alternation of simple states.

From all which goes before it results that there is a pure and autonomous life of feeling, independent of the intellectual life and having its cause below, in the variations of the cœnæsthesia, which is itself the resultant and concert of vital actions. In the psychology of feeling the part played by external sensations is very scanty compared to that played by internal sensations, and certainly one must be unable to see beyond the first to set up as a rule "that there is no emotional state unconnected with an intellectual state."

Having made this point clear, we may return to our general picture of the evolution.

1. Above organic sensibility we find the stage of needs— that is to say, of purely vital or physiological tendencies with consciousness added. In man this period only exists

[1] For observations relative to this point see *Revue Philosophique*, March 1896.

at the beginning of life, and is translated by internal sensations (hunger, thirst, need of sleep, fatigue, etc.). It is
constituted by a bundle of tendencies essentially physiological in character, and these tendencies have nothing
added or external; they are life in action. Each anatomical
element, each tissue, each organ has but one end, to exercise
its activity; and the physiological individual is nothing but
the convergent expression of all these tendencies. They
may present themselves under a double form. In the one
case they express a lack, a deficiency; the anatomical
element, the tissue, the organism has need of something.
In this form the tendency is imperious and irresistible;
such is the hunger of the carnivorous animal, which
swallows its prey alive. In the other case they translate
an excess, a superfluity: such are, a gland which
needs to secrete, a well-nourished animal which needs
to move: this is the embryonic form of the luxurious
emotions.

All these needs have a point of convergence—the
preservation of the individual; to use the current expression, we see in them the exercise of the *instinct
of preservation.* On the subject of this instinct there have
recently been discussions which seem to me sufficiently idle.
Is the instinct of preservation primitive? is it derived?
Some authors are for the first hypothesis; others (especially
James and Sergi) lean towards the second. According to
the point of view each of these two solutions is admissible
and true. From the synthetic point of view the instinct of
preservation is primordial, since it is nothing else but the
resultant and sum of all the particular tendencies of each
essential organ; it is only a collective formula. From the
analytic point of view, it is secondary, since it presupposes
all the particular tendencies into which it is dissolved, since
each of its elements is simple, and since it adds nothing and
is nothing but their translation into consciousness. One
might ask in the same way if a sensation of sound is simple
or compound, and here also, according to the point of view,
the answer would vary. For consciousness the event is one,
simple and irreducible; for objective analysis the event is
compound, reducible to a definite number of vibrations.
In the various regions of psychology we might find many
problems of the same kind. The important point is to

understand that the instinct of preservation is not an entity, but an abbreviated expression indicating a group of tendencies.

2. Emerging from the period of needs, which are thus reducible to tendencies of physiological order accompanied by physical pleasures or pains, we now enter the period of *primitive emotions*.

We cannot at the present point determine rigorously and in detail what is meant by an emotion (see Part I., Chap. vii.) ; it is enough to give a rough but comprehensible definition. From our standpoint, *emotion is in the order of feeling the equivalent of perception in the intellectual order*, a complex synthetic state essentially made up of produced or arrested movements, of organic modifications (in circulation, respiration, etc.), of an agreeable or painful or mixed state of consciousness peculiar to each emotion. It is a phenomenon of sudden appearance and limited duration ; it is always related to the preservation of the individual or the species—directly as regards primitive emotions, indirectly as regards derived emotions.

Emotion then, even while we keep to its primitive forms, introduces us into a higher region of the affective life in which its manifestations become complex. But how can we determine these primitive forms—the simple irreducible emotions—for this is our principal aim ? Many neglect this determination, or leave it to arbitrary chance. The old authors seem at this point to have followed a method of abstraction and generalisation which could only lead them to entities. It was an accredited doctrine among them that all the " passions " can finally be reduced to love and hate ; we meet this thesis throughout. To reach this conclusion they seem to have brought together and compared the different passions, disengaged the resemblances, eliminated the differences, and by continued reductions abstracted from this multiplicity its most general characters.[1]

If by love and hate we are to understand the movements of attraction or repulsion which lie at the bottom of the emotions, there is nothing to be said ; but we are only given abstractions and theoretical concepts ; such a determination is illusory and without practical utility. If we understand

[1] Descartes is a brilliant exception to this method of procedure ; later on we shall have to consider his method (Part II., Chapter vii.).

love (what love? for nothing is vaguer than this word) and hate in a more concrete sense, and pretend to consider them as the primitive source from which to derive all the other emotions, that is a purely mental opinion, an assertion which nothing justifies.

The determination of the primitive emotions must be made not by abstraction and generalisation, but by *verification*. To attain this I can see but one method to follow—the method of observation, which teaches us the order and the date of appearance of the various emotions, and gives us their genealogical and chronological list. We may count as primitive all those which cannot be reduced to previous manifestations, all those which appear as a new manifestation, and those alone; all the others are secondary and derived.

The materials for this investigation can only be sought in the psychology of animals and in that of children. The first will give us but little help. No doubt special and authoritative treatises enumerate the emotions of animals, but without any distinction between the simple and the compound, and with no precise indication as to the order of their appearance. It is not the same with infantile psychology; the numerous studies published on this subject during the last thirty years have rendered possible an attempt which could not be made before.

The question is then to determine in accordance with facts the order in which the emotions appear, only taking into account those which seem primitive—that is to say, not reducible to other emotions. I limit myself to their simple enumeration, with an indication of their chief characters; each of them will be the object of a special study in the second part of this book.

1. Fear is the first in date, according to unanimous observations. Preyer finds that it is manifested from the second day. At the same time the fact which he records seems to me to agree with surprise rather than with fear properly so called. In any case, according to the same author, it is easy to note it after twenty-four hours. Darwin thought he could only observe it at the end of four months, Perez at two months. The last is inclined to believe that this emotion is first aroused by auditory sensations, and then by visual sensations. The precocity of its appearance

has been attributed to hereditary transmission, an assertion which we shall have to examine.

2. After the defensive emotion, the offensive emotion appears in the form of anger. Perez notes it between two and three months; Preyer and Darwin at ten months; they mean real anger, marked by the contraction of the eyebrows and other clear symptoms (to throw itself about, crying, etc.). Naturally the dates indicated for each emotion are not rigorously fixed; they must vary according to the child's temperament and circumstances.

3. Then comes affection. Some authors use the word sympathy, which seems to me too vague. It shows itself by its fundamental method of expression, the movement of attraction, the seeking for contact. Darwin, who has well described it, remarks that it probably appears very early in life, judging by the infant's smile, in the second month, but that he had no clear proof that the child recognised any one before the fourth month; at the fifth month he showed a wish to go towards his nurse, but only at twelve months did he show affection spontaneously and by plain gestures. Darwin adds that sympathy (?) was manifested exactly at ten months, eleven days, when the child's nurse pretended to cry.[1] According to Perez, it appears towards ten months.[2] It is from this source that complex forms of great import-ance must later on be derived—the social and moral emotions.

With fear, anger, and affection we remain in the region of the emotions which man shares with animals; for even affection is met with very low in the animal series, at all events in the form of maternal love. These three emotions

[1] Darwin, " Biographical Sketch of an Infant," *Mind*, ii. p. 285.

[2] It is probable that the dates assigned for the first appearance of emotional manifestations by Darwin, Preyer, Perez, etc., are mostly too late, as they were not the outcome of continuous observation. Mrs. Kathleen Carter Moore, in her recent elaborate monograph dealing with the early mental development of her own baby, whom she regards as an average infant, observed the tear secretion first on the tenth day, though it was not fully established until the sixteenth week; a smile when com-fortable was seen on the sixth day; the child smiled several times consecutively at his father on the seventh day with movements of excitement, and by the twentieth day smiling at persons had become more frequent and more intelligent. (See K. C. Moore, "The Mental Development of a Child," Monograph Supp'ement to the *Psychological Review*, 1896).—ED.

have therefore a very clear character of universality. We now make a step which introduces us into a purely human region.

.4. This stage is marked by the appearance of emotions connected with the personality, the ego. Hitherto we have had an individual, a living being with more or less vague consciousness of his life; but the child, usually towards the age of at least three years, becomes conscious of himself as a person. Then appear new emotional manifestations, of which the source may be called for lack of a better term the self-feeling or egoistic emotion (*selbstgefühl, amour propre*), and which may translate itself in two forms: in a negative form as a feeling of powerlessness and debility, and in a positive form as a feeling of strength and audacity. This feeling of plenitude and exuberance is the source from which later numerous emotional forms are derived (pride, vanity, ambition). Perhaps also we must connect with it all those which express a superfluity of life: the need of physical exercise, play in all its forms, curiosity or the desire for knowledge, the need of creation by imagination or action.

5. There remains the sexual emotion; it is the last in chronological order and the moment of its appearance is easy to fix, since it has objective physiological marks. It is an error to suppose that it can be derived from affection, or that affection can be derived from it, as has sometimes been maintained. The observation of facts completely condemns this thesis, and shows that they cannot be reduced one to the other. Later on we shall meet with evident proofs.

Now we meet with one of those embarrassing questions with which our subject is full. Must we here conclude our list of primitive emotions, or must we add two others: joy and grief? It is possible to incline to the latter view. Thus Lange has included joy and grief among the four or five simple "emotions" which he has chosen as types of his descriptions. The following reasons, in my opinion, are against this solution. No doubt joy and grief present all the characters which constitute an emotion: movements or arrest of movements, changes in the organic life, and a state of consciousness *sui generis*. But in that case physical pleasure and physical pain must also be included among the emotions, for they both present the characters above enumerated; moreover, there is an identity of nature between physical pleasure and joy on one side, physical pain and grief on the other side, as I hope to prove later on; the only difference is that the physical form is preceded by a state of the organism, the moral form (joy, grief) by a representation. In other words, we should have to class pleasure and pain (without qualification or restriction) among the primitive emotions. Now these two alleged emotions present, with reference to the five already named, an evident and capital difference: their character of generality. Fear is quite distinct from anger, affection from self-feeling, and sexual emotion from the other four by its specific mark. Each of them is a complex state, distinct and impenetrable; just as vision is in relation to hearing, or touch to smell. Each expresses a particular tendency (defensive, offensive, attraction to the like, etc.), and is adapted to a particular end. Pleasure and pain, on the contrary, express general conditions of being; they are diffused everywhere and penetrate everywhere. There is pain in fear, in certain moments of anger and of the self-feeling; there is pleasure in sexual emotion, in certain moments of anger and of the self-feeling. These two states have no domain of their own. Emotion, by its nature, particularises; pleasure and pain by their nature universalise; they are the general marks of the affective life, and if they coincide like the emotions with motor, vaso-motor, and other phenomena, that is because no form of feeling can exist without its physiological conditions.

Such are the reasons for which I refuse to class the agreeable and painful states among primitive emotions, and to consider them as of the same nature. As to the moment of their appearance, physical pain is held to co-exist with the very beginning of extra-uterine life; physical pleasure resulting from satisfied appetite, the sensation of warmth, etc., must begin almost at the same period. Joy and grief are later. According to Preyer, the smile and brightness of the eyes indicate joy; "from the second month an infant takes pleasure in hearing singing and the piano." I am not sure that this example is very decisive; I prefer to see here the pleasure that is mostly physical. Darwin observed it towards the fourth month, perhaps before, but very clearly towards twelve months on the return of an absent person.

Grief may manifest itself, according to Preyer, towards the fourth month (tears before the fourth week). Darwin, in the observation already quoted, makes the first appearance at six months. On the whole, the observations are few and wanting in harmony, because of the great difficulty at this moment of life in distinguishing with certainty between the two forms of pleasure and the two forms of pain.

At the root of each of the primitive emotions there is a tendency, an instinct; but I do not claim that this list exhausts the human instincts; later on we shall have to return to this point (Part II., Introduction). Let us admit as a provisional hypothesis that these five emotions alone are irreducible, and all the others derived from them. In the sequel I shall try to indicate how these secondary emotions are the result of a complete evolution, of an arrest of development, or of a mixture and combination (Part II., Chapter vii.).

III.

Above these emotions, which, though composed of several elements, are simple as emotions, and may be called innate since they are furnished by the organism itself, there are numerous forms of feeling manifested in the course of life, aroused by representations of the past or the future, by the construction of images, by concepts, by an ideal. As each primitive emotion will be studied in its total development, from its lower to its most highly intellectualised forms, it is useless now to attempt a sketch of this ascending march, which, when reduced to generalities, would be vague and confused. It reaches its last stage in the loftiest regions of science, art, religion, and morals.

One may assert without risk that these higher forms are unattainable by the great majority of men. Perhaps scarcely one person in a hundred thousand or a million reaches them; the others know them not, or only suspect them approximately and by hearsay. They are a promised land only entered by a few of the elect.

To reach the higher sentiments, in fact, two conditions are needed: (1) one must be capable of conceiving and understanding general ideas; (2) these ideas must not remain simple intellectual forms, but must be able to arouse certain

2

feelings, certain approximate tendencies. If one or other condition is wanting, the emotion is not produced.

The formula of the evolution during this period is very simple; the order of development of the emotions depends strictly on the order of development of general ideas; it is the evolution of ideas which rules that of feelings. Here we are in perfect agreement with the intellectualist theory.

. The faculty of abstraction and generalisation is very unequally apportioned. It depends on the race, the age, the individual. Some never pass the level of generic images which are only concrete images simplified and condensed. Some reach those medium forms of abstraction in which the word plays the part of substitute for the reality, but requires, in order to be understood, that the qualities of the thing which it represents should be figured by a vague scheme, the concomitant of the word. Some reach the stage of complete substitution, in which the word takes the place of the whole, and has need of no auxiliary to insure the mental operation. Each of these degrees (which include sub-divisions I do not indicate) has its possible echo in feeling. Thus every one, according to the range of his intelligence, may reach some or all these stages, and according to his temperament experience or not experience at each of them an emotional state. The emotions which are susceptible of a complete evolution will furnish the proofs. A very simple example may be found in the sexual impulse, which may in turn be physiological, psycho-physiological, chiefly psychological, and finally intellectual. At its lowest stage (in the micro-organisms and similar beings) we find facts of a purely vital and organic order, in my opinion unconscious; then consciousness appears, but the sexual emotion manifests itself in a purely specific shape without individual choice; it is simply an instinct, "the genius of the race making use of the individual to reach its own ends." Later on individuality becomes marked; we find choice; the tender emotions, not found in the early stage, are superadded. Then comes the moment of equilibrium between the organic elements and the psychic elements, as usually found in the normal average man. This state is very complex, resulting from the fusion or convergence of numerous tendencies, hence its power of attraction. Then comes a rupture of equilibrium, a period of interversion; the physiological element is slowly effaced, the psychic element gains in intensity; it is a repetition of the primitive period, but in the opposite direction. This is the intellectual phase of love; the idea appears first, the physiological phenomena come afterwards. At a more elevated stage of refinement the concrete personal image is replaced by a vague impersonal representation, an ideal, a concept; this is pure platonic mystical love, the organic accompaniment of which is so feeble that it is usually denied.

These subtle and refined forms which the intellectualists regard as superior are really only an impoverishment of feeling. They are besides rare, and except in a few cases ineffective; for it is a rule that every feeling loses its strength in the measure that it becomes intellectualised. The blind faith in " the power of ideas " is in practice an inexhaustible source of illusions and errors. An idea which is only an idea, a simple fact of knowledge, produces nothing and does nothing; it only acts if it is *felt*, if it is accompanied by an affective state, if it awakes tendencies, that is to say, motor elements. One may have thoroughly studied Kant's *Practical Reason*, have penetrated all its depths, covered it with glosses and luminous commentaries, without adding one iota to one's practical morality; that comes from another source, and it is one of the most unfortunate results of intellectualist influence in the psychology of the feelings that it has led us to ignore so evident a truth.

IV.

It may be remarked that in contemporary treatises the word *passion* has almost entirely disappeared, or is only met with incidentally.[1] Yet it has a long past which would be interesting to trace, if I had not forbidden myself all

[1] Höffding, *Psychologie*, pp. 392-394, second German edition. J. Sully, *The Human Mind*, vol. ii. p. 56, considers emotion as a genus of which affection and passion are the species: affection is a fixed emotional disposition; passion is the violent form of the emotion. Nothing can be vaguer and more uncertain than the terminology of our subject, and yet, as Wundt says in his *Essays*, it has made a very appreciable progress when compared to the confusion which existed at the beginning of the century.

historical digressions. At present the term emotion is preferred to designate the chief manifestations of the affective life; it is a generic expression; passion is only a mode of it. Ordinary language rightly preserves the word, since it answers to a reality; and passion is an event of too much practical importance for us to dispense with speaking of it, explaining how it differs from emotion, what its nature is, and under what conditions it appears.

There is a fairly general agreement as to its definition; and beneath different formulas, according as they emanate from a moralist, a theologian, a philosopher, or a biologist, we always find the same essential characters : " it is an intemperate want;" " it is an inclination or liking carried to excess;" it is a violent and sustained desire which dominates the whole cerebral being," etc.; the terminology alone varies.[1]

If we seek the special mark of passion and its characteristics among the phenomena of the affective life, we must distinguish it from emotion on one side and insanity on the other; for it is situated midway between the two.

It is difficult to express with clearness and precision the difference between emotion and passion. Is it a difference of nature? No, for emotion is the source whence passion flows. Is it a difference of degree? This distinction is precarious, for while there are calm emotions and violent passions, the contrary may also be met with. A third difference remains, duration. It is generally said that passion is an enduring state; emotion is the acute form, passion the chronic form. Violence and duration are the characters usually assigned to it; but we may further define its essential nature. *Passion is in the affective order what an imperative idea* (*idée fixe*) *is in the intellectual order ;* we might add what a contraction is in the motor order. It is the affective equivalent of the imperative idea. This needs some explanation.

The normal intellectual state is a plurality of states of consciousness determined by the mechanism of association. If at a given moment a perception or representation arises and occupies alone the chief field of consciousness, ruling as a sovereign, making a space around it, and only permitting associations which are in direct relation with itself, we

[1] Letourneau, *Physiologie des Passions*, liv. i. Chap. I.

have a state of attention. This "monoideïsm" is by its nature exceptional and transitory. If it does not change its object, persisting or repeating itself constantly, we have the fixed idea, which may be called permanent attention. It is not necessarily morbid, as Newton's celebrated phrase and other evidence show; but the latent or actual sovereignty of the fixed idea is absolute and tyrannical.

In the same way the normal state of feeling is the succession of pleasures, troubles, desires, whims, etc., which in their temperate form, and often dulled by repetition, constitute the prosaic round of ordinary life. At a given moment some circumstance causes a shock; that is emotion. Some tendency annihilates all the others, momentarily confiscating the whole activity to its profit; that is the equivalent of attention. Usually this passage of movements in a single direction is not enduring; but if, instead of disappearing, the emotion remains fixed, or repeats itself incessantly, always the same, with the slight modifications involved in passing from the acute to the chronic stage—that is passion, which is permanent emotion. In spite of apparent eclipses, it is always ready to appear, absolute and tyrannical.

Concerning the origin of passion, moralists and novelists have remarked that it comes into being in two different ways —by a thunderbolt or by "crystallisation," by sudden action or by slow actions. This double origin denotes predominance either of the affective life or of the intellectual life. When passion is born suddenly it issues directly from emotion itself and retains a certain violence of nature, so much at least as its metamorphosis into a permanent disposition admits. In the other case the initiative is taken by the intellectual states (images, ideas), and the passion is slowly constituted as the result of association which itself is only an *effect*, for it obeys a latent influence, a hidden factor, an unconscious activity only revealed by its work. Representations only attract each other and associate by reason of their affective similitude, of the emotional tone which is common to them, and by successive additions these little streams form a river. This form of passion, on account of its origin, has less ardour and more tenacity.

After distinguishing passion from emotion, it is still necessary to separate it from insanity, its other neighbour. Certain authors have at once classed all passions with insanity; I cannot accept this proposition. It may suit the moralist, by no means the psychologist. But the task of separation is very delicate, and cannot be attempted in this Introduction. The distinction between the normal and the morbid, always difficult, is especially so in the case of the psychology of the feelings. I shall endeavour elsewhere (Part I., Chap. iv.) to find the indications which enable us to establish this separation legitimately, and the task which we now put aside in its general form will come before us later on in the case of each particular emotion.

PART I.

GENERAL PSYCHOLOGY.

PART I

GENERAL BACTERIOLOGY

CHAPTER I.

PHYSICAL PAIN.

Its anatomical and physiological conditions; pain nerves, transmission to the centres—Modifications of the organism accompanying physical pain: circulation, respiration, nutrition, movements—Are they the effects of pain?— Pain is only a sign—The analgesias: unconsciousness of pain and intellectual consciousness—Retardation of pain after sensation—Hyperalgesia—Nature of pain: theory that it is a sensation; theory that it is a quality of sensation—Pain may result from the quality or the intensity of the stimulus—Hypotheses regarding its ultimate cause: it depends on a form of movement, a chemical modification.

MANY definitions of pain have, very unnecessarily, been offered. Some are even tautological, others imply a hypothesis as to its nature by relating it to strong stimulations.[1] Let us regard it as an internal state which every one knows by experience, and of which consciousness reveals innumerable modes, but which by its generality and its multiplicity of aspect escapes definition.

In its primitive form pain is always physical, that is to say, connected with external or internal sensations. Sufficiently precise as regards superficial parts of the body, especially the skin, its localisation is vaguer when it is seated in the deeper parts, the viscera, the instruments of organic life.

[1] "Pain is a powerful and prolonged vibration of the conscious nervous centres, resulting from a strong peripheral excitation, and consequently of a sudden change of condition in the nervous centres" (Richet). "It is the most violent stimulation of certain sensorial regions—a stimulation to which contribute the more extended stimulations of other regions" (Wundt).

In the last case, when the pain is of internal and non-peripheral origin, coming from the great sympathetic or the related vagus nerve, it is accompanied by a state of anxiety, of depression, or of anguish, which we shall often encounter, and which frequently causes it to be said that "it seems to the patient that the workings of nature within him are suspended." For the present, without distinguishing between these two origins, external and internal, we will study the *objective* characters of physical pain taken in general : first its anatomical and physiological conditions, then the bodily modifications which accompany it and in popular language are called its effects.

I.

The transmission of painful impressions from the periphery to the cortical centres is far from being determined in all the stages of its course.

The nerve terminations, from their outpost position, receive the first shock ; but what part do they play ? It is known that the nerves of the deep organs and the filaments of the great sympathetic have no specially constructed terminations. The nerves of special sense, on the contrary,—vision, hearing, smell, and taste,—possess special peripheral apparatus (retina, organ of Corti, etc.) of very complex anatomy ; it is known that their *rôle* is specially sensorial ; they are above all instruments of knowledge, seldom directly of pain or pleasure. So that the question of nerve terminations in relation to pain may chiefly be confined to the nerves of the tactile apparatus, taking the word in its largest sense. The extreme difficulty of isolating the purely peripheral impression from that which reaches the nerve itself renders almost insoluble the question as to the part played by these peripheral apparatus. Beaunis,[1] relying on the cases of localised anæsthesia in which the patient no longer feels pain but still perceives contact, thinks that analgesia would reach the nerves before acting on their terminations, shut up in more or less resistant capsules.

Are there special nerves for the transmission of pain?

[1] *Sensations internes*, Chap. xx , may be read for details on this point.

Goldscheider, well known for his researches on cold and heat points on the skin, at first maintained that there are.[1] According to him, the pain-bearing nerve filaments are interlaced with the sensorial nerves, more numerously with the nerves of general sensation (touch, heat, cold), less numerously with those of special sense. If the existence of these special pain nerves were well established, it would have as great an importance for our subject as the discoveries of Sachs and others, on the nervous filaments peculiar to the muscles, have had for the study of the kinæsthetic sense. But this physiologist has since repudiated his first assertion, and maintained that it was misunderstood; he admits pain points (points sensible to pain), but not a specific organ for pain nor special nerves to transmit it.[2] Frey, on the other hand, professes to have proved experimentally both pain nerves and appropriate terminal organs. His observations have been rejected as inaccurate. At the present time there is nothing to establish the existence of pain nerves, and most authors have given strong reasons against the probability of such a discovery. Rejecting this hypothesis, we may admit that an impression of pain, like any other impression, is transmitted by the nerves of general or special sensibility. When it has entered the spinal cord at the posterior roots, the road it follows to reach the higher centres has given rise to much investigation and discussion. According to Schiff, transmission takes place through the grey substance, tactile impressions passing by the posterior fibres; there would thus be two distinct paths, one for the feeling, the other for the sensation properly so-called. Brown-Séquard also admits distinct paths, but through the grey substance alone; the anterior region is devoted to touch, the median to temperature, the posterior to pain. According to Wundt, impressions of touch and temperature have a primary path through the white substance when stimulation is moderate, a secondary path through the grey substance acting as a surplus channel when stimulation is violent. The hypothesis of separate paths, whatever they may be, has the advantage of harmonising with the well-known fact, to which we shall return, that the transmission of pain is slower than sensorial transmission.

---

[1] *Archiv für Anatomie und Physiol.*, 1885.
[2] Goldscheider, *Ueber den Schmerz*, Berlin, 1894.

Lehmann, who takes up a rigidly intellectualist position, cannot admit that the element of feeling has a certain independence in relation to the element of sensation, existing by itself. He believes that the delay is explained by the fact that "pain requires a stronger excitation in the sensorial region than sensation without pain, and that consequently pain is only produced after sensation, as the excitation increases in intensity."[1] This explanation may be accepted, but it assumes that pain always depends on intensity of stimulus, which is not proved.

From the spinal cord we reach the medulla, to which some authors assign the chief part. The latest, Sergi, in his book *Dolore e Piacere* (Milan, 1894), makes it the seat of the affective phenomena in general (pains, pleasures, emotions). What in his opinion testifies to the importance of the medulla in the affective life is the number and nature of the nervous centres situated between the protuberance and the floor of the small ventricle, centres which act on the heart, the vessels, the lungs, the secretions, the intestinal movements. "The vital knot of Flourens is the vital centre and must also be the centre of pleasure and pain, which are merely alterations in the functions of organic life."[2] In his opinion (which is mine also) the part played by the brain in the genesis of states of feeling has been exaggerated; it only acts in two ways—by rendering the disturbances of organic life, the physical basis of the feelings, apparent to consciousness, and as a cause of stimulation by means of ideas.

However disposed we may be to restrict the part played by the brain—that is to say the cortical layer—it remains a predominant factor and the final terminus in the process of transmission. Here we plunge into darkness. Researches into cerebral localisation teach us on this subject nothing which is generally admitted. During the first period of such studies, which may be called that of circumscribed localisation *à outrance*, Ferrier placed the seat of the emotions in

---

[1] Lehmann, *Die Hauptgesetze des menschlichen Gefühlslebens*, pp. 46 et seq.

[2] In his preface Sergi briefly indicates the "antecedents of his theory." He finds it in the English anatomist Todd, in Hack Tuke, Laycock, Herbert Spencer, Brown-Séquard, etc. I may point out that Vulpian, relying on experiments of doubtful interpretation, localised the emotions exclusively in the medulla, *Leçons sur l'Anatomie du système nerveux*, xxiv.

the occipital lobes, because, in his opinion, that region of the cortex receives the visceral sensations, because the sexual instinct is dependent upon them, and finally, because these lobes are more developed in women than in men. It is needless to bring forward the numerous criticisms of this thesis. During the second and present period of localisation, which may be called that of disseminated localisation, functional rather than anatomical, authors are little inclined to admit a particular centre for the affective life in general, and still less for pain. All the sensory centres, and even all the motor centres (perhaps there are fundamentally only sensori-motor centres with preponderance of one or the other element), may under certain conditions of activity produce in consciousness a feeling of pleasure or pain.

The hypothesis of a cortical centre is not, therefore, probable; I shall return to this point in discussing the emotions.

II.

The modifications of the organism which accompany physical pain have been so often described that it is enough to trace a slight outline of them. They may be reduced to a single formula: pain is associated with diminution and disorganisation of the vital functions.

1. It acts on the movements of the heart, generally decreasing its frequency; in extreme cases the slackening may go so far as to produce syncope. In animals submitted for experiment in the laboratory, even after removal of the encephalon, painful impressions diminish the cardiac contractions. In man, though the frequency of the pulse is sometimes increased in one form or another, there is always a modification of the rhythm appreciable by the sphygmograph. Bichat was right when he said: "If you wish to know whether pain is real, examine the pulse."

2. The influence on respiration is more irregular and more unstable; the rhythm becomes abnormal, sometimes rapid, sometimes slow; the inspirations are successively short and deep. But the final result is a notable diminution in the carbonic acid exhaled—that is to say a real slackening of combustion. The temperature is lowered. "I had imagined," says Mantegazza, "that pain would be accompanied by an increase of heat, muscular action being very

intense under the influence of great suffering. Experiment on animals and on myself proved the contrary." [1] Heidenhain and Mantegazza have in fact noted an average diminution of two degrees centigrade, which, according to the latter, may last an hour and a half or more; it would be due to the contraction of the peripheral blood-vessels.

3. The action of pain on digestion is well known, and shows itself by retardation or disturbance: loss of appetite, arrest of secretions, indigestion, vomiting, diarrhœa, etc. If permanent it acts on the general nutrition, and shows itself in modifications of the urinary secretion, and lasting discoloration of the skin or hair. It is not infrequent to find blanching of the hair, the beard or eyebrows in a few days under the influence of great pain. [2]

4. The motor functions translate pain in two opposite ways: the passive form of depression, arrest, or total suppression of movements, in which the patient seems overcome; the active form, marked by agitation, contortions, convulsions, and cries. The latter case seems to contradict the general formula connecting pain with diminished activity, and seems to me to have been misinterpreted by some authors. This violent excitement, indeed, is an expenditure which quickly makes itself felt and soon leaves the individual enfeebled. It does not flow, as in joy or play, from a surplus of activity; it is weakening, irregular and spasmodic. It seems to me to originate in the instinctive expression of the emotions. The wounded animal shakes the painful part of his body, his paw or his head, as if trying to expel the suffering. All these disorderly and violent motor reactions are a defence of the organism, a useless and often hurtful defence, but resulting from acts which, formerly or under other circumstances, were adapted to their end.

Lehmann experimented on five persons, submitting them in turn to agreeable and disagreeable impressions, in both cases registering the changes in respiration and in the volume of the arm with the help of Mosso's plethysmograph. [3] His experiments led him to the following conclusions :—

---

[1] Mantegazza, *Fisiologia del Dolore*, chap. iii.
[2] For historical and other cases, see Hack Tuke, *Influence of the Mind upon the Body*, chap. iii.
[3] For details of the experiments see *Hauptgesetze* etc., pp. 77 *et seq.*, with the accompanying graphic traces.

Every agreeable impression produces an increase in the volume of the arm and in the height of the pulse, with increased depth of the respiratory cavity.

A disagreeable impression, when weak, immediately produces a diminution in the volume of the arm and the height of the pulse; but almost at once the volume begins to increase, notwithstanding the diminished pulse, and usually passes beyond its normal state, even when the pulse has returned to its first condition. If the impression is strong but not painful these changes are accentuated, and from the first are accompanied by deep inspirations. Finally, if the impression is painful, not only considerable changes of volume, but powerful respiratory movements and disturbance of the voluntary muscles are produced.

Disagreeable stimulation produces at first a spasm of the superficial vessels, relaxation of the deep vessels, and decreased fulness of the heart's contractions. The first two factors together produce a sudden and strong diminution in the volume of the limbs. The last two factors together produce a diminished height of pulse, and in consequence of the enfeebled cardiac contractions there is a stasis of the venous blood showing itself in the increased volume of the limb.

These bodily modifications, of which I have summarised the chief features, are commonly regarded as the effects of pain, and this opinion seems even to be accepted in many works on psychology. The opinion cannot, however, be accepted. Pain considered as a psychic event, an internal fact, a pure state of consciousness, is not a cause but a symptom. The cause is the stimulation (of whatever nature) which, coming from the exterior environment, acts on the external senses, or coming from the interior environment, acts on the organic life. It is shown in two ways : on the one hand in the state of consciousness which we call pain, on the other by the physical phenomena above enumerated. The consciousness expresses in one way what the organism expresses in another way. This is not a mere opinion, for experiment shows that circulatory, respiratory, and motor modifications are produced when consciousness is probably defective. Mantegazza has shown that if an intact animal is subjected to pricks, cuts, and burns, cardiac troubles follow; but that the same phenomena are produced after the removal of the encephalon. François-Franck, investigating the effects of painful stimulation on the heart, found that the anæsthesia of chloroform suppresses troubles of the heart, while, on the contrary, removal of the cerebral hemispheres fails to abolish them. Formerly, Longet and Vulpian maintained that in animals reduced to the medulla and lower parts of the cerebro-spinal axis the cries and movements that occur when they are pinched are purely reflex; this interpretation has been contested by Brown-Séquard. In human anencephalic (or headless) monsters, cries, movements of suction and the like have been observed during the few days they are able to live. We must then admit either that the state of consciousness we call pain can be produced in the absence of the brain, or else that the physical phenomena can exist alone without their psychic concomitant.

Pain (as a state of consciousness) is only a sign, an index, an internal event revealing to the individual his own disorganisation. The only case in which pain is a cause is when, being firmly fixed in consciousness and completely filling it, it becomes an agent of destruction, but then it is only a secondary cause. That is one of those cases, so frequent in the sciences of life, in which what is primarily an effect becomes in turn a cause. It is therefore an error, though common to most psychologists, to consider pain and pleasure as fundamental elements of the affective life; they are only marks, the foundation is elsewhere. What would be said of a doctor who confused the symptoms of a disease with its essential nature?

We touch here a point so important that it needs emphasis. The thesis that pain is only a symptom, and altogether, in spite of the sovereign part it plays in human life, a superficial phenomenon in relation to the tendencies which lie at the basis of the affective life, finds support in the facts of *analgesia*, the disappearance of capacity to feel pain. This insensibility presents itself under two forms: spontaneous and artificial.

Spontaneous analgesia is the rule in hysteria; it may vary in degree, position, and extent. The demonologists of the Middle Ages and the Renaissance knew these migrations of insensibility to various parts of the body, and they sought with care for the *stigmata diaboli*, that is, the regions insensible to pain. Some authors assign to it a purely psychic cause : painful impressions cannot be felt because they are outside the field of consciousness, which in these patients is in an almost permanently disassociated, scattered, and destroyed state.[1] It is, on the contrary, certain that an intense fixed idea, profound concentration of attention, fanatical exaltation, can produce temporary or permanent analgesia. Many soldiers, in the heat of battle, have not felt their wounds. Pascal, plunged in his problems, escaped his neuralgias. The Aïssaouas, the fakirs, certain Lamas of Thibet tear and cut themselves, secured against pain by delirium, and one may well believe that many martyrs, in the midst of their torture, have only experienced a sense of rapture. In certain forms of insanity (maniacal excitement, melancholia, idiocy, etc.) this spontaneous analgesia is frequent, and takes on extraordinary forms. Numerous examples may be found in special treatises.[2] One crushes glass in his mouth for half-an-hour without feeling any pain. Another breaks his leg in a struggle, and a fragment of the tibia projects through the torn skin, yet he continues to pursue the object of his rage, and then sits down to eat without the least sign of pain on his face. There are many who, intentionally or by accident, plunge their arms into boiling water or place them on a red-hot stove, until the skin falls off in shreds, without appearing to be disturbed. An endless series of such facts might be narrated.[3]

[1] Pierre Janet, *État Mental des Hystériques.*

[2] See especially Morel, *Traité des Maladies Mentales* (pp. 324 *et seq.*), for a summary of many curious facts.

[3] Weir Mitchell (*Medical Record*, 24th December 1892, quoted by Strong, *Psychological Review*, 1895, vol. ii. p. 332) reports the following extraordinary case of natural analgesia : Man who died at age of fifty-six, cheerful and corpulent, weighing some 250 pounds; intelligent, and vigorous both in body and mind, with a considerable reputation as a lawyer and politician. Having a finger wounded in a crush during a political campaign, he removed it himself by biting it off and spitting it on to the ground. He had an ulcer on the toe which resisted treatment for three years without ever causing him the slightest pain. He also had an abscess in the hand which spread to the fore-arm and arm, causing enormous swelling and endangering his life ; the lancet was used without precaution, and throughout he felt no pain. It was the same with an operation for cataract on both eyes ; he remained motionless as a statue. It was only during his last illness that he complained of some pain, but that quickly passed away, and he had returned to his state of natural insensibility before he died.

The artificial analgesias, produced by chloroform and the various anæsthetics employed in surgical operations, are more instructive. It has been asked if the movements, objurgations, and cries of some patients do not prove that the analgesia is not complete, even when it seems so. Richet has expressed the opinion that it is not consciousness but recollection which is defective; he regards the pain as so rapid that it is only a mathematical movement and leaves no echo behind it, there being a series of evanescent states of consciousness. It is quite possible to maintain this hypothesis; but the most important fact recorded by this author seems to me to be that, when pain has disappeared, a certain degree of knowledge of it remains. In other words, there is a process of scission: the feeling man has disappeared, the *intellectual* man remains. In many simple operations the contact of the instrument is often felt, but not the pain. But there are more complex cases. "In an operation for fissure of the anus with fistula, the patient felt the contact of the scissors and easily distinguished four incisions; she could not speak, but felt no suffering. In the course of a similar operation I asked the patient, 'How old are you?' She replied that she was forty-one, but when restored to consciousness she could recall no sensation of wound or burn and complained that the operation had not taken place. I asked another during the operation, 'How are you getting on?' the reply was, 'Not badly.' At the same moment I pricked her vigorously; she felt nothing. Again, in another case when I introduced a forceps into the mouth to hold the tongue the patient said, 'Take away that cigarette.' On awaking he could remember nothing. Another when a quill was passed beneath his nose said, 'Do not tickle me' at the moment when the large arteries were being tied, the most painful part of the operation. Finally, a man under chloroform, while his spermatic cord was being tied, heard the clock strike and tranquilly remarked, 'Half-past eleven,' recalling nothing when he awoke."[1]

I have quoted these facts to show the extent to which pain, as a state of consciousness, is *separable*, how it can be added or cast off, and to what extent it presents the character of an epiphenomenon.

[1] Richet, *Recherches expérimentales et cliniques sur la Sensibilité*, pp. 258, 259.

This relative independence of the pain-phenomenon, against which the intellectualists have always rebelled,[1] seems to me corroborated by the retardation which I have already noted in passing. If we strike a corn while walking, we feel the shock before the pain; the cold of the knife is felt before the pain of the incision. Beau estimates that pain is delayed seven-tenths of a second behind the tactile impression. Burckhardt, by precise investigation, fixes the rapidity of transmission in the cord at 12 m. 9 per second for painful impressions, and 43 m. 3 for the others. In certain diseases like tabes dorsalis the pain may be separated from the needle-prick which causes it by from one to two seconds. Many other facts may be quoted. If a fold of the skin is seized in a pressure forceps, stopping at the moment when the pressure is sufficient, pain, not felt at first, gradually appears, coming in waves, and being at last unbearable. A man whose thumb was seized in a machine only knew of his injury by feeling his arm drawn, and only began to suffer a quarter of an hour afterwards. It has also been remarked that the syncope produced by violent shocks and traumatism does not appear at once; between the accident and the fainting several minutes may elapse.[2]

Pain is the result of a sum of impulses. Naunyn has shown that, in tabes, a mechanical stimulus (like a hair on the cutaneous surface of the foot), which is below the threshold of consciousness both as contact and as pain, if repeated from 60 to 600 times a second, is perceived at the end of from six to twenty seconds, and soon becomes an intolerable pain to the patient.

Although excessive sensibility to pain (hyperalgesia) belongs to the pathology of our subject, which will be dealt with in a later chapter, it is necessary to say a few words about it in contrasting it with analgesia, especially in view of the conclusions here reached. This condition is more difficult to observe than insensibility, because here there is only a difference of degree, not the difference between being and not being. But in some cases there is so great a disproportion between the stimulus and the subject's

---

[1] See on this point Lehmann's embarrassed explanation, *Hauptgesetze*, etc., pp 51 *et seq*.

[2] Richet (*op. cit.*, pp. 289, 290 and 315, 316) gives many illustrations.

reaction that we may say without hesitation that sensibility is no longer normal.

It has been observed, in a general manner, that the lower races are not very sensitive to pain. Thus Negroes in Egypt endure, almost without suffering, the most extensive surgical operations (Pruner Bey), and Mantegazza (*op. cit.*, chap. xxvi.) reports a large number of examples. In the peasant sensibility is usually less keen than in the town-dweller, and it may be admitted without hesitation that susceptibility to pain increases with civilisation; what is called stoicism should often be called a feeble degree of sensibility. Hyperalgesia is best seen in cases of extreme nervous overexcitement. In some it is generalised, constituting the "supplicium neuricum," and the patient says that he is the prey of unspeakable torments. It is less frequent in the case of the special nerves, but is sometimes met. One suffers from the slightest noise, and cannot tolerate the least smell. Pitres quotes the case of a person who shut herself up in a dark room, only coming out at night with a thick shade against the rays of the stars. Those who entered her dark room during the day had to wear sombre clothes, completely concealing the shirt-collar, of which the white reflection was horribly disagreeable to her.[1] Cutaneous hyperalgesia is very common, sometimes extending over the whole body, sometimes disseminated in patches. Weir Mitchell, in his book on injuries of the nerves, reports numerous examples; among others, a wounded soldier to whom the mere crumpling of paper caused atrocious pain. Opium-smokers, when they interrupt their habits, feel the least breath of air as icy cold, and complain of intolerable pains in all parts of the body. Hyperalgesia of the deep tissues is also frequent among the hysterical and hypochondriacal.

It must be remarked in passing that just as insensibility to pain (analgesia) is independent of incapacity to receive sensorial impressions (anæsthesia), so hyperalgesia is distinct from hyperæsthesia. The latter is a power of perception much surpassing the average; it is known that certain races and individuals possess extraordinary visual, auditory, or olfactive acuteness; the tactile hyperæsthesia of the blind is also known, and in hypnotised subjects the delicacy of

[1] Pitres, *Leçons Cliniques sur l'Hystérie*, i. p. 182.

the senses has sometimes seemed miraculous. Hyperalgesia then, like analgesia, shows that pain is relatively independent of the sensations which arouse it.

III.

We may conclude, from what goes before, that though physical pain (of which alone I am speaking at present) is always bound to an internal or external sensation, and forms part of a psychic complexus, it may be separated and disjoined. It has then its own conditions of existence, and we may, in advance, say as much for pleasure.

What are these conditions of existence? or, more simply, what is pain in its nature? At the present time there are two distinct doctrines on this point: one, which counts few adherents, regards physical pain as properly a *sensation;* the other, more generally admitted, regards it as a *quality* of sensation, or more correctly, as an accompaniment, a concomitant.[1]

The first, though recent in its complete form, is not without antecedents. It found a momentary support in the supposed discovery of pain-bearing nerves. Nichols, one of the promoters of this hypothesis, has developed it in this direction; but the attempt has proved futile. Strong, one of its warmest partisans, supported himself on other grounds. In his opinion the difficulty arises from the ambiguity of the word pain, which may mean two things— displeasure (*Unlust*), or physical pain in the positive sense. He reduces the latter to cuts, pricks, burns—in short, to those pains that affect the skin. It is, in his opinion, strictly a sensation like blue or red—not an attribute, but a substantive. The pain of a burn, for instance, is a mixture of two sensations, heat and pain. General sensibility is composed of four kinds of sensibility: touch, heat, cold, and pain. Each can be abolished separately. Cocaine and chloroform suppress pain, not touch; saponine suppresses

[1] The debates on this subject have chiefly been carried on by American psychologists. See Rutgers Marshall, *Pain, Pleasure, and Æsthetics* (1895); Nichols, " Origin of Pleasure and of Pain " (*Philosophical Review*, i. pp. 403 and 518); Strong, " Psychology of Pain " (*Psychological Review*, July 1895, and for criticisms and replies, Sept. and Nov. 1895, Jan. 1896); Luckey, " Some Recent Studies of Pain " (*Am. Journal of Psychology*, Oct. 1895).

touch, not pain; syringomyelia destroys sensibility to pain and heat, not touch; in some forms of neuritis there is suppression of touch without analgesia. These various facts are invoked as the chief arguments in favour of the hypothesis of pain-sensation, though they may all be explained also by the other doctrine.

This hypothesis is full of difficulties. First, there is the absence of anatomical basis, of special organs and nerves. It will be necessary to return to this important point when dealing with pleasure (Chap. iii.). Nichols tells us that there is nothing to prove that nerves of pain do not exist, though they have not been experimentally established— which is indeed something; that histological research could not determine in the peripheral apparatus what belongs to touch and what belongs to pain; and that proof must be deduced from cases of tactile sensation without pain and *vice versâ*—which fails to constitute any degree of proof. Moreover, the distinction set up between displeasure (moral pain?) and physical pain is arbitrary, factitious, wholly unjustified. There is, however, a still less admissible distinction. Strong expressly declares that he limits himself to pains localised on the cutaneous surface. Now by what right can we cut off the group of physical —strictly physical—pains, the states of torture originating in the internal organs, the multiple neuralgias as intolerable as any external pain, without speaking of discomfort, prostration, exhaustion? Are these also sensations, or something else? We are not told. Finally—and Strong himself has stated the objection—it must be acknowledged that we should here have a strange kind of sensations which do not externalise themselves. While other impressions, visual, auditory, tactile, gustatory, olfactive, are referred to causes which provoke them, the pains of a prick, a cut, a burn remain strictly subjective and are not located in the needle, the knife, the burning coal, as we locate a sound in the bell, a bitter taste in absinth. The only possible reply (which the partisans of pain-sensation have not made) would be that this phenomenon has a character of its own; it always remains a sensation, and never becomes a perception, whence the absence of externalisation. But then why assimilate it to blue or red? Moreover, pain-sensation, as it exists in the adult, approaches so closely to the affective state, that what is essential in the doctrine of pain-sensation vanishes. Whatever may be thought of the probability of some future discovery of terminal organs for physical pain, as Rutgers Marshall remarks, it must be agreed that there is no proof of the existence in the environment of a special stimulus to which physical pain specially corresponds, and for that reason also it would be a great mistake to place in the well-determined class "sensation," a mental state which lacks one of the most marked characteristics of sensation in general. That conclusion is mine also.

The opposite doctrine, which has of late been called the *quale*-theory, is often maintained in an unsatisfactory form, because in fact it reduces itself to an affirmation of *quantity*. The pain which accompanies sensation may depend either on its intensity or on its quality alone.

It is needless to insist on the first case, since many old authors never cease repeating that the painful impression is the result of a stimulation which is strong, intense, violent, prolonged.

On the contrary, it is necessary to remark that this exclusive affirmation cannot be applied everywhere and always. This evidently appears in the cases of hyperalgesia, which is the reason why I brought them forward. The very disagreeable sensation which is caused by a knife against the skin certainly comes from the nature rather than the intensity of the stimulus. Beaunis remarks that certain odours, tastes, and contacts are painful at once, and do not need to be intense. Did the contact of the quill which threw Weir Mitchell's patient into a state of anguish act by its intensity? No doubt we must recognise that hyperalgesias constitute a group apart, not strictly comparable with ordinary cases; they are pathological forms, variable in degree; but the pathological is merely an exaggeration of the normal. The error of those who refer pain solely to intensity of stimulation is in considering *objective* conditions only; they forget the part played by the sentient subjects. Pains which depend on the quality of the stimulus are especially of *subjective* origin, because the degree of excitability in the patient's nervous elements is the essential ruling factor.

If we admit that these two conditions—intensity and quality—act one upon the other, what afterwards happens?

What is the intimate nature of the pain-producing process? The hypothesis which is most natural and simple, and in agreement with the mechanical conceptions predominant in the biological sciences, would be founded on the admission that pain corresponds to a particular form of movement. On this supposition, the affective nervous road, from the periphery to the centres, would be traversed by three different kinds of movement or of molecular disturbance: the first giving birth to pure sensation, that is to say a state of knowledge, an intellectual state; the second, which may or may not be present, giving birth to pain; the third, also either present or absent, giving birth to pleasure.

There is another possible hypothesis, quite different from the others, which I should be willing to accept, but which cannot be presented as more than a theory. It would consist in attributing the genesis of pain to *chemical modifications* in the tissues and nerves, especially the production of local or general toxins in the organism. Pain would thus be one of the forms of auto-intoxication. Oppenheimer alone seems to me to have worked in this direction.[1] In his opinion, as regards the origin of pain, "the real cause, in any sensorial or other organ, resides in a change in the tissues, especially a chemical change, by which either the products of destruction rise above the normal average, or else modifications result from the presence of a foreign body in the organism." The connection between the peripheral tissues and the centres would be by the vaso-motor nerves (constrictor or dilator). The tissues would be the terminal organs of pain, the vaso-motors the paths of conduction. In organs which only undergo slight changes when active (tendons, ligaments, bones, etc.) conscious sensibility is almost absent. "Pain is not, as many believe, the highest degree of sensation produced in the organs of special sense; it is the most intense sensation produced in the vaso-motor nerves under the influence of violent stimulation."

This hypothesis will perhaps be justified by the future. I shall return to it when studying the emotions. We shall then see that these are accompanied by deep and well-established chemical modifications in the organism.

[1] *Schmerz- und Temperaturempfindung*, Berlin, 1893.

Physical pain is a large subject, which, as may be seen, has not been neglected of late, and concerning which there is still much to say. It is not possible, however, to deal further with it here, since it only occupies a limited area in the psychology of the emotions.

CHAPTER II.

MORAL PAIN.

*Identity of all the forms of pain—Evolution of moral pain:
(1) the pure result of memory; (2) connected with
representations; positive form, negative form; (3) connected with concepts—Its external study; physical
signs— Therapeutics— Conclusions—A typical case of
hypochondriasis.*

IN passing from physical pain to moral pain we by
no means change our subject, or enter another world.
Languages with their special terms—"tristesse," "chagrin,"
"sorrow," "Kummer," etc.—create an illusion by which
psychologists for the most part seem to have been duped—
the illusion that between these two forms of pain there is
a difference of nature. In any case they do not explain
themselves clearly on the point, and seem to share the
common opinion.[1] It is the object of this chapter to
establish that, on the contrary, there is a fundamental
identity between physical and moral pain, and that they
only differ from each other in the point of departure, the
first being connected with a sensation, the second with
some form of representation, an image or an idea.

I.

At first sight it seems paradoxical, and to many even
revolting, to maintain that the pain caused by a corn or a

[1] Hartmann alone, so far as I am aware, has dealt with this point,
incidentally but very clearly: "When I have pain in my teeth or
my finger or my stomach; when I lose my wife, my friend, or my
situation, if in all these cases we distinguish what is pain and pain
alone, and not to be confounded with perception, idea, or thought,
we shall recognise that this special element is identical in all the
cases."—*Philosophie des Unbewussten*, vol. i., Part II., chap. iii.

boil, that expressed by Michelangelo in his sonnets concerning his inability to reach his ideal, or that felt by a delicate conscience at the sight of crime, are identical in their nature. I purposely bring together these extreme cases. Yet there is no call for indignation if we remember that we are concerned with the pain alone, not with the events which provoke it, these latter being extra-affective phenomena. The best method of justifying our thesis, however, is to follow the evolution of moral pain in its ascending march from its lowest to its highest point. It will suffice to note the chief stages.

First Period.—Moral pain is at first connected with an extremely simple representation, a concrete image—that is to say, the immediate copy of a perception. It may be defined as the ideal reproduction of physical pain. It only presupposes a single condition, memory. The child who has had to swallow an unpleasant remedy, or who has had a tooth extracted, experiences when the next occasion approaches a pain which may be called physical, since it is connected with a simple image, of which it is the weakened copy and echo. It may be said in the language of mathematicians, that in this case the moral pain is to the physical pain as the image is to the perception. This form is so simple as to be found in many animals not reckoned among the highest. It is not yet moral pain—grief or sorrow—in the complete and rigorous sense, but it must be noted, because it corresponds to what naturalists call a transitional form.

Second Period.—It is connected with complex representations and forms a very large class, the manifestations of which are the only ones met with in average human beings. At this stage moral pain presupposes reflection, or, more explicitly, first the faculty of reasoning (deductive or inductive), and secondly constructive imagination. It would be possible to quote a crowd of examples, taken at random : the news of a death, of an illness, of ruin, of frustrated ambition, etc. The point of departure is a dry and simple fact, but the pain attaches itself to all the *perceived* results which flow from it. Thus ruin means a series of privations, wretchednesses, labours begun over again, fatigues, and exhaustions. It is in this detailed transla-tion, varying according to individuals and cases, that moral

pain lies.   It is clear, and is proved by observation, that the
man endowed with an ardent and constructive imagination
will feel intense pain when another, with a poor and cold
imagination, remains indifferent, seeing nothing in his misfortune but the present actual fact—that is to say, a very
little thing; the sum of pains evoked is proportional to
the sum of representations evoked.   The child remains
insensible at the news of death or ruin; if he is moved
it is through imitation; there is nothing in his experience
enabling him to deduce what these fatal words contain,
and to represent the future.

Moral pain presents itself under various forms—positive,
negative, or mixed.

In the positive form it is an expenditure of movement, the
representation of an exhaustive labour, of an incessant effort
to begin again what is already felt in consciousness by
anticipation.   Such is the case of the candidate who fails at
an examination to which he must go up again.

In the negative form it is an arrest of movement, a
lessening, the consciousness of a deficit, a privation,
cravings ceaselessly arising and ceaselessly disappointed.
The death of a beloved person is the most perfect example.

In the mixed form we may see it in the ruined millionaire,
the dethroned king, who set to work again to reconstruct the
past.   On the one hand the representation of the long
labour of a new conquest; on the other, tendencies of all
sorts which were formerly satisfied, and are now inexorably
brought to a stop.

A complete study of the second group of moral pains
would include two moments: the egoistic form, the first in
date, and the sympathetic or altruistic form.   The latter
seems to appear early, since Darwin noted it at the age of
six months and eleven days in one of his children, who was
much affected when his nurse pretended to be unhappy and
cry.   Preyer even alleges, as we have seen, that grief appears
at the age of four months.   This sympathetic form of pain
is found in certain animals, especially those living in society.
In certain monogamous couples the death of one of the
partners may cause the other to perish.   I will not pause
here at present to describe these two great forms of the
affective life which will occupy us so often in the course of
this study.

Third Period.—Grief in this case is connected with pure concepts or with ideal representations. This is intellectual pain, which is much rarer, and produces little effect, at all events for any length of time, on the ordinary man. Such is the pain of the religious person who feels he is not sufficiently devout, of the metaphysician tormented by doubt, of the poet and the artist, conscious of an abortive creation, of the man of science who unsuccessfully pursues the solution of a problem.

These forms of pain are chiefly negative and secondarily positive. They consist, first, in unsatisfied needs, privations, lacunæ in existence; afterwards in effort, expenditure of force, fatigue, achieving nothing.

II.

Having shown that the pain-phenomenon, in the course of evolution, attaches itself to representations more and more elevated and finally to superior conceptions, we will examine moral pain objectively, *from without*, to show afresh its identity with physical pain, or, more exactly, to prove that pain is invariable in its nature, under whatever form it manifests itself.

1. Grief is accompanied by the same modifications in the organism as physical pain. It is needless to repeat the description: circulatory disturbance, constriction of the vaso-motors, syncope; decrease of respiration or constant changes in its rhythm, sudden or prolonged reverberation on nutrition, loss of appetite, indigestion, arrest or diminution of secretions, vomiting. I may remark that rapid change of colour in the hair, already noted, is specially met with in violent moral shocks (Marie-Antoinette, Ludovico Sforza, etc.). The voluntary muscles of the larynx, the face, the whole body, undergo the same influences and express them in the same ways. For moral as for physical pain, there are silent forms and agitated forms.

2. If we admit the old maxim: " Naturam morborum medicationes ostendunt," as we see every day the same general therapeutics applied to both forms of pain, we have here evidence in favour of their identity: no doubt there are curative methods proper to each; for moral pain, con-

solations, distractions, travel; but are not opium, sedatives, and tonics employed to relieve both?

3. I brought together at the beginning of this chapter the grossest forms of physical pain and the most refined forms of moral pain; but there are composite forms in which sensations and representations seem to form an equilibrium, so that such painful states might be entered under either head. This is the case with certain melancholics of whom I shall have to speak later, but we may take as a type the hypochondriacal person in whom we find the point of junction of the two pains. The physical troubles of hypochondriasis have often been described. There are localised pains, but in addition a large number of simply represented pains, enlarged as by a lens, and referred to the lungs, the heart, the liver, the spleen, the kidneys, the stomach, the intestines. The joints are cracking; there are conjectures concerning the appearance of the face, the tongue, the urine, and above all what perpetual anxiety! One of them said: " I feel better to-day, and that makes me anxious; it is not natural." Is this physical pain or moral pain? Sometimes one, sometimes the other predominates, according to the individual and the moment. Clouston has observed that in melancholics sadness often diminishes when physical pain increases. They are so intimately inter-twined that no point of departure can be established between them. This morbid state is worthy of mention because it also is a transitional form. We need have no hesitation in generalising, and saying that there is no physical (that is to say, localised) pain, however slight, unaccompanied by some fugitive mental irritation, and no mental irritation unaccompanied by some slight physical troubles.

The foregoing does not imply that grief is a very refined physical pain, or that it arises therefrom, as—according to the well-known formula: *Nihil est in intellectu quod non prius fuerit in sensu*—it is supposed that the superior forms of knowledge arise from sensation alone. That would be a misconstruction. Physical pain is not a genus of which moral pain is a species. The thesis which I maintain is that pain is always identical with itself, that it has its own conditions of existence, that the innumerable modes which it presents to us in the physical order and in the moral order are related to the sensorial or intellectual elements which excite and envelop it.[1]

The question still remains why certain representations have the unfortunate privilege of arousing pain. This is a question which I can only touch on, because it belongs to another part of the subject. For the moment I simply reply that it is because they are the beginning of mental disorganisation, just as physical pain is the beginning of physical disorganisation. The sentient being, man or animal, is a bundle of needs, of appetites, of physical or psychic tendencies; everything that suppresses or impedes them is translated into pain. Physical suffering is the blind and unconscious reaction of the organism to every hurtful action. Grief is the conscious reaction to every decrease of psychic life. The man shut in by narrow and commonplace surroundings would certainly feel no æsthetic pain, because having no need of æsthetic satisfaction he could not be impoverished or impeded by its absence.

In short, pain under all its forms reveals an identical nature. The distinction between physical pain and moral pain is practical, not scientific.

[1] Hahnemann distinguished 73 kinds of physical pain, Georget 38, Renaudin 12, etc. I give these numbers as curiosities. More recently Goldscheider (*Ueber den Schmerz*) establishes three stages in physical pain : (1) true, real (*echte*) pains ; they depend on the nerves of special sensibility, and are caused by mechanical, thermal, or chemical stimulations, by inflammation and poisons ; (2) indirect pains, pseudo-pains, which consist especially in a state of discomfort (*Schmerzweh*) ; in the case of the head, stomach, etc., they may be as oppressive and cause as much torture as "real" pains; (3) psychic or ideal (*ideel*) pains, which are a hyperæsthesia of the sensitive activity; they are met with in neuroses (neurasthenia, hysteria, hypochondria), in hallucinations, the hypnotic state, etc. This classification is perhaps acceptable in physiology. For psychology, every pain, in virtue of being a fact of consciousness, is "true" and "real."

CHAPTER III.

PLEASURE.

*Subject little studied—Is Pleasure a sensation or a quality?
—Its physical concomitants: circulation, respiration,
movements—Pleasure, like pain, is separable: physical
and moral anhedonia—Identity of the different forms
of pleasure—The alleged transformation of pleasure into
pain—Common ground of the two states—Hypothesis
of a difference in kind and in degree—Simultaneity of
two opposite processes: what falls under consciousness is
the result of a difference—Physiological facts in support
of the above.*

In treating of grief, one is apt to be embarrassed by the
abundance of documents, and the difficulty of being brief;
in dealing with pleasure the contrary is the case. Are
we to conclude that this is because, for centuries past,
physicians have been collecting observations on pain,
while there exists no profession having for its object the
observation of pleasure? Or is it because humanity is so
constituted as to suffer more from pain than it can enjoy
from pleasure, and therefore studies everything relating to
pain in order to find deliverance therefrom, while accepting
everything agreeable naturally and without reflection? We
cannot, however, accuse psychologists of having neglected
this study, although the bibliography of Pleasure is very
scanty compared with that of Pain. In general, they have
considered these two subjects as complementary to one
another, pleasure and pain being opposed to each other as
contraries, so that the knowledge of the one implies the
knowledge of the other. But this is only a hypothesis—
perhaps true, perhaps false—resting in great part only on

the testimony of consciousness, which is always open to question and never above suspicion. "It may be," says Beaunis, very justly, "that pleasure and pain, which seem to us two opposite and mutually contradictory phenomena, may in the end be nothing but phenomena of the same nature, only differing in degree. It is possible that they may be phenomena of different orders, but incapable of such comparison with one another as would enable us to declare one contrary to the other. It is possible that they may depend simply on a difference of excitability in the nervous centres. Again, it is possible that they may be included, sometimes in one category, sometimes in the other."[1]

I.

The formulas universally made use of in characterising pleasure indicate this vague position of the problem : "Agreeable states are the correlatives of actions which conduce to the well-being or preservation of the individual." "Generally speaking, pleasures are the concomitants of medium activities, where the activities are of kinds liable to be in excess or in defect" (Herbert Spencer). "Experience attests that, in all the sensory regions, sensations of moderate energy are specially accompanied by a feeling of pleasure. Thus this feeling connects itself with the sensations of tickling due to cutaneous excitations of slight energy" (Wundt). According to this writer, the gamut of pleasure is less rich and extensive than that of pain, and he finds the proof of this assertion in the language expressive of universal experience. "Language," he says, "has created numerous expressions for disagreeable feelings, emotions, and inclinations, while the joyful moods of the mind are dismissed with a brief general designation. This phenomenon arises less from the fact that man observes with especial care and minuteness his disagreeable or troublesome states, than from the greater uniformity which pleasurable feelings in reality possess. This is particularly evident in the case of the sensory feelings [those connected with the sensations]. Pain has not only numerous degrees of energy, but numberless gradations according to its seat."

[1] Beaunis, *Sensations internes*, chap. xxiii.

Mantegazza, when determining the synonyms of pleasure, appears to uphold the contrary view.[1] For my own part, I am of Wundt's opinion.

The anatomical and physiological conditions of the genesis and transmission of pleasure are a *terra incognita.* In cases of physical pleasure, what takes place at the peripheral terminations, in the nerves, in the cerebro-spinal axis? Most authors do not even propound 'these questions. The physiology of pain, in spite of its uncertainties, is rich and instructive compared with that of pleasure.

In recent times it has been maintained that pleasure, as well as grief, ought to be regarded as a *sensation,* not as the concomitant of various psychic states; that both are fundamental senses having their own proper nervous energies distinct from other sensations. In other words, the expression, "sensations of pleasure and pain," ought to be taken in the strict sense borne by the word sensation. I have already touched on this point in treating of pain, but it may not be out of place to return to it here; for, apart from its hypothetical character, I cannot think this assertion a happy one. In fact, if there is any psychological state clearly delimited and differentiated from all others, it is sensation.

Sensation is determined and circumscribed by a special organ serving for this purpose only, as in the case of sight, hearing, etc., or at least by special nerves and special peripheral terminations, as in the case of touch and temperature. Internal sensations, in spite of the nervous apparatus proper to them, have a vaguer character; hence some psychologists call them indifferently sensations or feelings. The kinæsthetic sensations, or those of movement, long included under the designation of muscular sense (an improper term, gradually falling out of use), have, though diffused through the organism, nerves peculiar to themselves; those of the muscular tissue, the articulations (the periosteum, the ligaments, the synovial

---

[1] *Fisiologia del piacere*, Part II., chap. ii. He enumerates the following expressions:— *Gusto, diletto, compiacenza, soddisfazione, conforto, contentezza, allegria, buon umore, gioia, giubilo, tripudio, delizia, voluttà, felicità, solletico, rapimento, trasporto, ebbrezza, delirio.* Perhaps the Italian language is in this point richer than the German.

membranes, the tendons). But pleasure and pain have neither special nerves nor special organs. We have seen the opinion admitted with regard to the pain-bringing nerves; as for the nerves of pleasure, I know no author who has hazarded such a hypothesis, however tentatively. It is true that one of those who admit the existence of nerves of pain (Frey) gets out of the difficulty very easily by saying that pleasure, consisting only in the absence of pain, requires no special nerves. May we not say, then, that it is a complete falsification of the meaning of words to class among sensations psychical phenomena answering to none of the required anatomical or physiological conditions? [1]

The manifestations taking place within the organism are better known when we are in a condition of pleasure. Let us take as typical the constant pleasures, putting aside those which, by their exuberance, as we shall see later on, border on pathological forms. Whether the point of departure is a physical excitation, a representation, or a concept, two distinct events take place, as in the case of grief: on the one hand an internal state of consciousness, which we describe as agreeable; on the other a bodily external condition, of which the following are the principal characteristics.

Taken as a whole, they may be opposed, almost point for point, to the description already given of the physical manifestations of grief, and betray a heightening of the vital functions. This contrast is not without importance in

---

[1] This thesis has been principally maintained in America by H. Nichols (*Philosophical Review*, July 1892), and in France by Bourdon (*Revue Philosophique*, September 1893). The former applies it to pleasure and pain, considering them fundamental sensations as distinct from one another as they are from other sensations. This article contains some ingenious considerations on the part played by the association of ideas. Bourdon applies it only to pleasure, and considers pain irreducible. He regards pleasure as a special sensation, not a common one or an attribute of all sensations; it is "of the same nature as the special sensation of tickling." By adducing the pleasure of tickling (in which he follows Descartes and others), Bourdon partially escapes the criticism already advanced. It must be remarked, however, that tickling is itself a sensation of which the organic conditions are very vaguely determined. Besides the cutaneous impression, there are certainly also diffused reflex actions which connect it quite as much with internal sensibility as with the sense of touch.

favour of the common thesis which regards pleasure and
pain as a pair of opposites.

1. The circulation increases, especially in the brain, as
shown by various symptoms, in particular the increased
lustre of the eyes. The experiments of Lehmann, already
quoted (Chapter I.), prove that physical, as well as æsthetic
pleasure, is accompanied by dilatation of the vessels and an
increase of the heart's contractions.[1]

2. The same thing is to be observed with regard to the
respiration, which becomes more active; in consequence,
the temperature of the body rises, and the nutritive
exchanges, becoming more rapid, result in a rich ali-
mentation of the organs and tissues. "In joy, all parts
of the body receive advantage, and are likely to last longer;
the cheerful and contented man is well nourished and
remains young. It is a truism that people in good health
are contented" (Lange). Joy also tends to make the
secretions (lacteal, spermatic, etc.) more abundant.

3. The innervation of the voluntary muscles expresses
itself by exuberance of movements, by joyful exclamations,
laughter, and singing. Certain cases of extreme and sudden
joy have been known to produce all the effects of alcoholic
intoxication. Sir H. Davy danced in his laboratory after
making the discovery of potassium. At the London International Congress of Psychology (1892), Münsterberg
communicated the following experiments under the title
of "The Psychological Foundation of the Feelings." A
line ten centimetres in length is drawn with the right
hand. When this movement has been thoroughly practised,
it should be repeated with closed eyes, passing the hand
first from right to left, with a movement of centripetal
flexion, then from left to right, with a movement of centrifugal extension. In such a case mistakes will be made,
sometimes in the one direction, sometimes in the other.
Let us repeat the same experiments under the influence of

[1] Dr. G. Dumas has made experiments on the condition of the
circulation in states of joy and of sadness. He has attempted an
experimental verification of Lange's theory by showing that a definite
condition of the circulation always accompanies various agreeable and
painful emotions, and that "joy and sadness may thus be regarded as
the mental reverberation of these circulatory conditions and their
organic consequences." See "Recherches expérimentales sur la Joie
et la Tristesse," *Revue Philosophique*, June-August 1896.—ED.

certain affective states (sadness, gaiety, anger, etc.), noting all errors and their direction. Münsterberg has discovered them to be determined by a very exact law. In vexation, the extensor movements (centrifugal) are too short (average error, 10 mm.), and the flexor movements (centripetal) too long, the average excess being 12 mm. In joy, on the other hand, the centrifugal movements are in excess by (on an average) 10 mm., and the centripetal movements too short by an average of 20 mm. From this he concludes that, in pleasure, motion tends to increase ; in pain, to diminish.

The manifestations of joy may be summed up in a single word—dynamogeny. Joy produces energy.

It is superfluous to say that we consider pleasure, for the same reasons as pain, to be an additional phenomenon, a symptom, a sign, a mark, denoting the satisfaction of certain tendencies ; and that it cannot be regarded as a fundamental element of the life of the feelings. Like pain, pleasure is separable from the complex of which it forms part, and under certain abnormal conditions may totally disappear. *Anhedonia* (if I may coin a counter-designation to analgesia) has been very little studied, but it exists. I need not say that the employment of anæsthetics suppresses at the same time pain and its contrary ; but there are cases of an insensibility relating to pleasure alone. "The sensation of sexual pleasure is, in very rare cases, subject to lesions affecting no other part of the organism. Brown-Séquard saw two cases of special sexual anæsthesia, all other kinds of sensibility, those of the urethral mucous membrane and the skin, still persisting. Althaus quotes another case. It would no doubt be possible to find such cases in larger numbers were it not for the false modesty which prevents patients from speaking of the subject. Fonssagrives cites a very remarkable example observed in a woman." [1] This insensibility exists not only for physical but also for moral pleasure (joy, high spirits, etc.). Apart from the cases of profound melancholy, which will occupy us later on, where the individual is untouched by the slightest impulse of joy, there are cases of anhedonia which seem simpler and clearer. "Antoine Cros mentions the case of a patient, a young girl, suffering from congested liver and spleen,

[1] Richet, *Recherches*, etc., p. 212.

which of course altered the state of her blood, and thus, for a time, modified her constitution. Her moral character was greatly altered by it. She ceased to feel any affection for father or mother; would play with her doll, but could not be brought to show any delight in it; could not be drawn out of her apathetic sadness. Things which previously had made her shriek with laughter now left her uninterested. Her temper changed, became capricious and violent."[1] Esquirol has recorded the case of a magistrate, a very intelligent man, suffering from a liver complaint. "Every affection seemed to be dead in him. He showed neither perversion nor violence, but there was complete absence of emotive reaction. If he went to the theatre (as he continued to do from force of habit) he could find no pleasure there. Thoughts of his house, his home, his wife, his absent children, affected him no more, he said, than a theorem of Euclid." We have here a specimen of what we may call a purely intellectual existence—that of the Wise Man of the Stoics.

These facts—and we shall find analogous ones in other chapters, under other headings—show that, as we have seen in the case of pain, pleasure does not depend simply on the *quantity* of excitement. To attribute all pleasures to excitements of medium energy is equivalent to the formula: "Pain is due to an intense and prolonged excitement." In both cases intensity alone is emphasised; but there are pleasures irreducible to medium energy and depending on the *quality* of the excitement and the nature of the sentient subject. Will it be said that sexual pleasures are the concomitants of a medium activity? The pleasure produced by harmonious chords is, for a musical ear, a matter of quality, not of intensity. We find it impossible, therefore, to reduce the objective conditions of pleasure to a single formula.

Although general opinion has established a distinction between sensory and spiritual pleasures, this distinction is purely theoretical. Pleasure, as an affective state, always remains identical with itself; its numerous varieties are determined only by the intellectual condition originating it—sensation, image, concept. It would be tedious to repeat in detail the analysis already given of pain in order

[1] Lewes, *Physical Basis of Mind*, p. 327.

to apply it to pleasure; it will be sufficient to indicate the principal points.

All forms of pleasure are accompanied by the organic modifications previously enumerated. Primarily, it can only be physical—*i.e.*, combined with a sensation, such as the pleasure of a soft, warm contact, the satisfaction of hunger and thirst in children and animals. Then pleasure becomes an anticipation, as in the case of a dog when his food is being brought to him; to employ the term used by Herbert Spencer, it is a presentative-representative state. Then, in this ascending evolution, pleasure appears attached to pure representations. This—as in the case of pain—is the main group, that of the varied and numerous joys which console humanity for its sufferings; these, too, are divided into egoistic and sympathetic pleasures. There remain the highest and rarest manifestations attached to pure concepts—the pleasures of æsthetic creation, those of the metaphysician or the man of science. We might further show how the transition from pleasure, considered as strictly physical (that of the thirsty man drinking a cool beverage in long draughts), to the subtlest, most ethereal intellectual pleasures, may in fact be gradually traced step by step; that the two elements—sensory and representative—are always coexistent, and that we qualify any given pleasure solely according to the preponderance of one or the other. Finally, if we have found in hypochondriasis a composite form, which might be classed with equal justice as a physical or moral pain, in the domain of pleasure it is not difficult to discover analogous forms. The æsthetic pleasure called forth by forms, by colours, and especially by sounds, affords us an example. It is incontestable that these three kinds of sensation can, unassisted, in and by themselves, produce a sensory pleasure. Certain colours, certain qualities of sound, certain chords, produce at once an agreeable impression. Then the representations evoked by memory excite, in their turn, a degree of pleasure quite distinct from the original sensations. Fechner, in his *Vorschule der Æsthetik*, distinguishes, in his analysis of the elements of the Beautiful, the direct factor, *i.e.* sensation, and the indirect or associative factor, that is to say, the associated ideas evoked. These two coexistent factors are only separable by psychological analysis, and the position established by Fechner for the intellectual elements has its equivalent for the emotional states.[1]

II.

The generally accepted formula connecting pleasure with medium activities is supported by a commonly observed fact—viz., that pleasure carried to excess or continued too long often transforms itself into its opposite. The pleasures of eating may lead to nausea, tickling soon becomes a torture, as well as heat and cold, and one cannot endure even a favourite melody when played for two consecutive hours. In a word, a sensation or representation at first agreeable may, either gradually or suddenly, be found to have its opposite associated with it. While the sensory or intellectual element remains the same—at least in appearance—the affective state is changed.

So familiar an occurrence, well known from the remotest antiquity, from which various consequences have been deduced by philosophers, would not in itself possess sufficient importance to arrest our attention, did it not, for all its insignificant appearance, afford us the opportunity of penetrating the depths of our subject.

We may remark that the same transformation takes place inversely—a state in itself disagreeable may become agreeable. This transmutation is to be found at the root of nearly all the pleasures which we call *acquired:* a taste or smell at first repugnant may become delightful.

The same thing happens with regard to certain physical exercises connected with touch and the muscular sense. The use of alcoholic drinks, of tobacco, of all sorts of narcotics, would furnish us with abundance of examples. Pleasure is found in certain forms of literature which were at first found revolting; the same thing may be said of painting; and the history of music is one long piece of evidence in favour of this transformation of tastes.

In the first place, we have to note that the hackneyed expression, " transformation " of pleasure into pain, and *vice versâ*, is inaccurate. Pain cannot be changed into pleasure or pleasure into pain, any more than black can be changed

[1] For further details on this point see Chapter VII.

into white. What is meant is that the conditions of existence of the one disappear to give place to the conditions of existence of the other. There is succession, but not transformation; a symptom does not transform itself into its opposite.

This succession, abrupt or gradual, leads us to ask whether there might not be a common basis, a certain identity of nature, between the two antagonistic phenomena. The question thus put may be answered by one of two alternative hypotheses.

1. The admission that the difference is fundamental and irreducible, that pain is as clearly to be distinguished from pleasure as the visual sensation is from the auditory sensation: that these feelings constitute an antinomy—an irreconcilable antagonism. The clearest affirmation of this thesis is found in those writers who make pleasure and pain "sensations" comparable to other sensations, and having their own specific character.

2. The admission that the difference is one of degree, not of nature; that the two contrary manifestations are only two *moments* of the same process; that they differ from each other only as sound differs from noise, or a very acute sound from a very deep one, both resulting from the same cause—the number of vibrations in any given space of time. I am myself inclined to maintain this second hypothesis.

Let us take as an example a simple case where the process is manifested in its totality. We have a person in a so-called indifferent, neutral, or medium state, that is to say, one which cannot be described as agreeable or painful; the individual is simply alive, that is all. He is sensitive to the perfume of flowers; some are placed in his room—pleasure is the result. At the end of an hour all is changed; the subject is incommoded by the smell of the flowers, and avoids them. Hence we have three successive moments: indifference, pleasure, pain.

But these three moments in consciousness have their correlatives in the modifications of the organism: circulation, respiration, motion, the various phases of nutrition. The first answers to the average vital formula of the individual; the second to an increase in the vital functions, and, according to the usual formula (which we shall examine later on), to an augmentation of energy; the third to a lowering of the vital functions and a diminution of energy. Such are the data of observation and experience. Féré's researches on the olfactory sensations (to mention no others) have shown that the feelings accompanying them, pleasant or otherwise, show themselves in an augmented or diminished pressure on the dynamometer. In a subject whose dynamometric force is normally 50–55, a disagreeable odour lowers the index to 45, an agreeable one raises it to 65. In another (a hysterical patient) the odour of musk, at first very pleasant, raises the dynamometer from 23 to 46; in three minutes it becomes disagreeable, and the pressure sinks to 19.[1] We find, therefore, that the organism is subject to perpetual fluctuations, indicated in the consciousness by agreeable or disagreeable feelings: the two opposites are connected with one and the same cause, the vital functions forming their common basis; and I should be inclined to propound the following hypothesis :—

In most cases, if not in all, two contrary processes are going on simultaneously—one of increase, the other of diminution; *what comes into the consciousness is only the result of a difference.*

A difference between what? Between receipt and expenditure. Let us, in order to show this clearly, take a point at which the destructive and constructive activities exactly balance one another, a condition corresponding to the neutral or indifferent state of psychologists, and let us represent the same by the numerical formula $50 = 50$. At a subsequent point of time the destructive activities predominate; let us suppose them equal to 60, while the value of the constructive falls to 40. On comparing the second moment with the first, we find a negative difference of -20, whose psychic equivalent is a painful state of consciousness. Let us then suppose a third moment, when the constructive activities are in the ascendent and equal 60, while the destructive fall to 40; there will be a positive difference of $+20$, whose psychic equivalent is a pleasant state of consciousness. I must beg the reader to take all this only by way of illustration.

Thus understood, the "transformation" of pleasure into pain, and pain into pleasure, is only the translation into the order of affective psychology of the fundamental

[1] Féré, *Sensation et Mouvement*, pp. 62, 63.

rhythm of life. The latter reduces itself to the ultimate fact of nutrition, consisting of two mutually interdependent processes, one of which implies the other, assimilation and dissimilation. Except in extreme cases, such as inanition and exhaustion on the one hand, and plethora on the other, in which one of the two processes prevails almost without counterpoise, they usually oscillate on either side of a medium, as pleasure and pain do on either side of an alleged neutral state. In physiology it happens that a very clear and easily verified phenomenon covers and hides a contrary phenomenon, so that the principal part of the occurrence is erroneously taken for the whole. Thus one knows that a muscle is heated by exercise, which seems to contravene the law of the transformation of energy, as the mechanical work done ought to consume a part of that mode of motion which we call heat. Béclard and several others after him have shown that there is a real lowering of temperature at the beginning of positive work, and that two opposite phenomena appear in the muscle when in action : one physical, absorbing heat and determining a cooling of the active muscle; the other chemical, producing a heating of the muscle. The latter masks the former. In the same way, the well-known experiments of Schiff have shown that the brain is heated when it receives impressions and elaborates them; it ought to grow cold, since it is doing work ; but Tanzi's experiments seem to establish the existence of alternating oscillations of cold and heat while the brain is at work. We recall these facts, though not in direct relation to our subject, to show that the coexistence of two opposite processes, the most apparent of which conceals the other, is not a chimera. There are frequently two simultaneous phenomena, of which the one is seen and not the other.

According to this hypothesis, then, the conditions of existence of pleasure and pain are implied the one by the other, and always coexistent. What is expressed by consciousness is a *surplus*, and what is called their transformation is only a difference in favour of one or the other.[1]

---

[1] This also seems to be the view adopted by Rutgers Marshall (*op. cit.*). In the first place, he always considers "pleasure-pains" as connected states, pleasure being experienced "whenever the physical activity coincident with the psychic state to which the pleasure is

I add some final remarks on the so-called transformation of pain into pleasure. Being rarer than its opposite, it presents some peculiarities to be noted.

Very acute pleasures exhaust quickly—a condition very favourable to the rapid appearance of pain; I do not see that acute pain ever changes into pleasure, except perhaps in a few cases to be examined in the following chapter.

The "transformation" does not take place abruptly, but always by a gradual transition.

Some have attempted to explain it by habit; but this is so general a term as to require fresh definition in each individual case. It has also been said that the painful sensation, being accompanied by disorganisation and lowering of the vital power, produces, *ipso facto*, an organic repair, a vital increase, which is the essential condition of pleasure. But this does not prove that the period of reintegration coexists with the first impression and imparts to it a contrary affective sign. The novice in the use of tobacco is at first incommoded by headache, nausea, etc.; then there follows a period of repair, but it is not directly connected with the act of smoking.

It seems to me preferable to admit, with Beaunis, that the agreeable states we speak of are not simple but complex, consisting of a certain number of elements. "It may happen that, among the elements which compose sensation, some are agreeable and some painful; with habit and exercise the painful element gradually disappears from the consciousness, and only the agreeable elements of the sensation remain. In this case there would not really be a transformation of the pain into pleasure, but an extinction, a disappearance of the disagreeable elements of the sensation, and a predominance of the agreeable ones."[1]

The cause of this change seems to me to lie in the biological function called adaptation, of whose true nature very little is known, and which appears to reduce itself to nutritive modifications. Experiment shows that its efficacy cannot be depended on: it succeeds in some persons, but fails in others.

---

attached involves the use of surplus stored force—the resolution of surplus potential into actual energy; or, in other words, whenever the energy involved in the reaction to a stimulus is greater in amount than the energy which the stimulus habitually calls forth."—P. 204.

[1] Beaunis, *Sensations internes*, pp. 246, 247.

CHAPTER IV.

MORBID PLEASURES AND PAINS.

Utility of the pathological method—Search for a criterion of the morbid state; abnormal reaction through excess or defect; apparent disproportion between cause and effect; chronicity—I. Morbid pleasures, not peculiar to advanced civilisation—Different attempts at explanation— This state cannot be explained by normal psychology: it is the rudimentary form of the suicidal tendency— Classification—Semi-pathological pleasures: those destructive of the individual, those destructive of the social order —II. Abnormal pains—Melancholic type—Whence does the painful state arise in its permanent form? from an organic disposition? or from a fixed idea?—Examples of the two cases.

THE title of this chapter may seem paradoxical, pleasure being as a rule the expression of health, and even of exuberant life, and pain, by its very definition, a diseased state. It must be admitted that, for the latter, the expression *abnormal* would be preferable. However, the facts we are about to study are not rare, and deserve separate examination, because the deviations and anomalies of pleasure and pain serve to make the nature of each better understood.

Taking our subject, for the first time, on the pathological side, a proceeding to be applied later on to each of the simple or complex emotions in turn, certain preliminary remarks are indispensable.

The application of the pathological method to psychology needs no justification; its efficacy has been proved. The results obtained are too numerous and too well known to need enumeration. This method, in fact, has two principal advantages—(1) it is a magnifying instrument, amplifying the normal phenomenon; hallucination explains the part played by the image, and hypnotic suggestion throws light on the suggestion met with in ordinary life; (2) it is a valuable instrument of analysis. Pathology, it has justly been remarked, is only physiology out of order, and nothing leads better to the understanding of a machine than the elimination or the deviation of one of its wheels. Aphasia produces a decomposition of memory and its different signs, which the subtlest psychological analysis could not attempt or even suspect.

The principal difficulty of this method lies in determining the precise moment when it can be applied. The distinction between the healthy and the morbid is often extremely difficult to establish. No doubt there are cases where no hesitation is possible; but there are also debatable zones lying between the territories of health and disease. Claude Bernard ventured to write, "What is called the normal state is purely a conception of the mind, a typical ideal form entirely disengaged from the thousand divergences among which the organism is incessantly floating, amid its alternating and intermittent functions." If this is the case with regard to bodily health, we may expect to find it still more so with regard to mental. The dilemma: Either this man is mad or he is not, is, in many cases, says Griesinger, meaningless. The psychical organism, being more complex and less stable than the physical, makes it still more difficult to fix a norm. Finally, this difficulty attains its maximum in our subject, because the emotional—the most mobile among all the forms of psychic life—oscillates incessantly around one point of equilibrium, always ready to sink too low or rise too high.

As, however, it is necessary to adopt some definite characteristics which may serve as pathological signs, as criteria for distinguishing the healthy from the morbid in the emotional order, we shall accept those proposed by Féré. According to him, an emotion may be considered as morbid—

1. When its physiological concomitants present themselves with extraordinary intensity (I think we should add, or an extraordinary depression).

2. When it takes place without sufficient determining cause.

3. When its effects are unreasonably prolonged.[1]

These three signs, which I shall call respectively abnormal reaction by excess or defect, disproportion (apparent) between cause and effect, and chronicity, will frequently be of service to us in the study of the emotions. For the moment we are only treating of pleasure and pain.

I.

Beginning with pleasure, I shall first examine a typical case studied by several physiologists, who have not furnished any, to me, satisfactory explanation. I mean the special state which has been called "the luxury of pity" (Spencer), pleasure in pain (Bouillier), and which it would be more accurate to call "the pleasure of pain." It consists in being pleased with one's own suffering and tasting it like a pleasure.

This disposition of the mind is not, as one might think, peculiar to *blasé* persons and to epochs of refined civilisation ; it seems inherent in humanity the moment it emerges from barbarism. Bouillier[2] has quoted from the ancient writers passages referring to it, not only in Lucretius, Seneca, and other moralists, but in the Homeric poems, which reflect a very primitive civilisation, yet in which a man "rejoices in his tears." Parallel passages might have been found in the Bible, and also, I suppose, in the epics of ancient India. We have not, therefore, to deal with a rare phenomenon, though it becomes more frequent as we advance in civilisation.

A few examples will be of greater value than any opinions I could cite. They may be found of all sorts—pleasure in physical pain, and pleasure in moral pain. Certain patients find intense enjoyment in irritating their sores. Mantegazza[3] says : "I knew an old man who acknowledged to me that he found an extraordinary pleasure, and one which seemed to him equal to any other, in scratching the inflamed surfaces surrounding a senile sore in his leg from which he had suffered for some years."

[1] Féré, *Pathologie des Émotions*, p. 223.
[2] Bouillier, *Du plaisir et de la douleur*, chap. vii.
[3] Mantegazza, *Fisiologia del piacere*, p. 26.

A celebrated man of the Renaissance, Cardan, says in his autobiography that "he could not do without suffering, and when this happened to him, he felt such an impulse arise in him, that every other pain seemed a relief." When in this state, he was in the habit of torturing his own body till forced to shed tears by the pain.[1] I might enumerate a long series of these pleasures of physical pain. Of the pleasures of moral pain I will give but one example: melancholy in the ordinary, non-medical sense—the melancholy of lovers, poets, artists, etc. This state may be considered as typical of the deliberate enjoyment of sadness. Any one may be sad, but melancholy is not to be attained by every one. I may mention also, in passing, the pleasures of ugliness in æsthetics, and the taste for sanguinary spectacles and tortures which we shall have to consider in another place.

If we leave the facts and come to the explanations proposed, we shall find that they are not numerous. Bouillier (*op. cit.*) seems to adopt the opinion of a Cartesian, who said, "If the soul, in all movements of the passions, even the most painful, is in some measure tickled by a secret feeling of pleasure, if it takes pleasure in pain, and does not wish to be consoled, it is because of a consciousness that the state in which it finds itself is the state of heart and mind best suited to its situation." I fail to understand this pretended explanation. I prefer that of Hamilton, who places the principal cause in the increased activity imparted to our whole being by the sense of our own sufferings. This, at least, is logical, since pleasure is connected with its habitual correlative—an increase of activity. Spencer has examined the problem at greater length.[2] "Here I will draw attention only to another egoistic sentiment, and I do this because of its mysterious nature. It is a pleasurably painful sentiment, of which it is difficult to identify the nature, and still more difficult to trace the genesis. I refer to what is sometimes called 'the luxury of grief.' . . . It seems possible that this sentiment, which makes a sufferer wish to be alone with his grief, and makes him resist all distraction from it, may

---

[1] A curious study of pathological psychology might be founded on the *De Vita Propria* of Cardan, who was evidently what would now be called a neuropath and a *déséquilibré*.

[2] *Principles of Psychology*, ii., § 518.

arise from dwelling on the contrast between his own worth, as he estimates it, and the treatment he has received—either from his fellow-beings or from a power which he is prone to think of anthropomorphically. If he feels that he has deserved much while he has received little, and still more if instead of good there has come evil, the conscious-ness of this evil is qualified by the consciousness of worth, made pleasurably dominant by the contrast. . . . There is an idea of much withheld, and a feeling of implied superiority to those who withhold it. . . That this explanation is the true one I feel by no means clear. I throw it out simply as a suggestion, confessing that this peculiar emotion is one which neither analysis nor synthesis enables me clearly to understand."

This explanation seems to me only a partial one, and not applicable to all cases. In my opinion, no efforts of this kind can be successful, because the authors remain on the ground of normal psychology. This class of facts ought to be treated by the pathological method. It may be said that this is only the substitution of one word for another. By no means, as we shall see by the result.

The mistake lies in attacking, in the first instance, phenomena of too delicate a nature, and considering them as isolated facts. We must proceed, not by synthesis or analysis, but by the cumulative method—i.e., we must establish a chain of facts, of which the last links, being of overwhelming importance, shall throw light on the first. I indicate the principal stages of this gradation thus—Æsthetic melancholy (transitory and intermittent); spleen, melancholia (in the medical sense);[1] then, advancing a step further, suicidal tendencies, and finally, suicide. This last term makes all the others comprehensible. The first stages are only embryonic, abortive, or modified forms of the tendency to self-destruction, of the desire which makes it seem agreeable. The weaker forms—checked in an immense majority of cases—approximate more or less to

[1] Krafft-Ebing remarks: "An abnormal mode of feeling on the part of melancholic patients is found in the enjoyment of pain (Leidseligkeit). In these individuals, ideas which, in a healthy state, would be provocative of pain, awaken in the diseased consciousness a faint feeling of satisfaction which represents the corresponding affective tone."

destruction, and can only be explained if compared with the extreme case.

The evolutionists have stated the hypothesis that there must have existed certain animals so constituted that, in them, pleasure was connected with destructive acts, pain with useful ones, and that, as every animal seeks pleasure and shuns pain, they must have perished in virtue of their very constitution, since they sought the destructive and shunned the preservative influences. There is nothing chimerical in this supposition, for we see men find pleasure in acts which, as they very well know, will speedily result in their deaths. A being thus constituted is abnormal, illogical; he contains within himself a contradiction of which he will perish.

But, one may say, if pain and hurtful acts on the one hand, pleasure and serviceable acts on the other, form indissoluble pairs, of such a kind that the painful state in consciousness is the equivalent of destructive acts in the organism, and inversely, we should here have an interversion—pleasure would express disorganisation; pain, reorganisation. This hypothesis is not a very probable one, and scarcely seems necessary. If we admit, as has been said in the preceding chapter, that there always exist two simultaneous and opposite processes whose difference is all that is perceptible to the consciousness, it is sufficient for one of the processes to be accelerated or the other retarded, in an abnormal manner, in order to change the difference in favour of one or the other. No doubt the final result contradicts the rule, since in the above cases the surplus which ought to be negative (pain) is positive (pleasure). But this is a new proof that we are confronted with a deviation, an anomaly, a pathological case to be treated as such.

I have taken by itself and studied a typical case; it now remains, not to enumerate, but to classify pathological pleasures in order to show their frequency. Taking as a guide the excellent definition of Mantegazza, "Morbid pleasure is that which is either the cause or the effect of an evil," I divide them into three classes.

1. Semi-pathological pleasures, which form the transition from the healthy to the frankly morbid. These require an excessive or prolonged expenditure of vital energy. We

know that the pleasures of taste, smell, sight, hearing, touch, muscular exercise, the sexual relations, produce fatigue and exhaustion, or even suddenly become painful. The pleasures of affection, of self-love, of possession, when they become passions—that is to say, when they increase in intensity and stability—cease to be pure pleasures; a painful element is added to them. This phenomenon is natural and logical, since every increase in activity entails losses, and consequently conditions of pain. This class is scarcely morbid, since pain here *succeeds* pleasure. This is not the case with the other two, in which pleasure rises from the midst of destruction, and dominates the consciousness.

2. Pleasures destructive of the individual. I do not stop to discuss certain anomalies of taste and smell which will be described elsewhere; but the pleasures due to intoxication and narcotics are so widespread that they seem inherent in humanity. At all times, in all places, even in the savage state, man has found artificial means of living— if only for a moment—in an enchanted world. He has himself created this pleasure for his own destruction. But there are still clearer cases—of tendencies not acquired or invented—when pleasure makes and dominates the process of disorganisation. Thus, during a certain period of the general paralysis of the insane, the patient believes himself to possess the supreme degree of strength, health, riches, and power; satisfaction and happiness are expressed in his whole bearing. Thus in certain forms of acute mania, on one side (which we shall pass over for the present) it shows itself in anger; on another, in exuberant spirits, abounding joy—a feeling of energy and vigour. Some patients say, after their recovery, that they never felt so happy as during their illness (Krafft-Ebing). We may also mention the case of consumptive patients, many of whom are never so rich in hopes or so fertile in projects as when at the point of death. Finally, we have the sense of well-being ("euphoria") of the dying. It has been attempted to explain this by analgesia, as if the suppression of pain were identical with the appearance of joy. Féré, who has examined the question in his *Pathologie des Emotions*,[1] concludes that this exaltation is due to momentary but positive conditions of the cerebral circulation.

[1] Pp. 170 *et seq.*

Must we admit that, in these cases, by an inconceivable derogation from natural determinism, pleasure becomes the translation into consciousness of a deep and incurable disorganisation? There is no need of this. It is more rational to admit that this pleasure is here, as elsewhere, connected with its natural cause, a superabundance of vital activity. Every pathological pleasure is accompanied by excitability; but the latter is not a normal activity, or the fever-patient and the neuropath would enjoy an excess of health. In reality, we are confronted with a complex case; on the one hand, a perpetual and enormous loss, which goes on rapidly, without becoming perceptible to the consciousness; on the other, a superficial excitement, which is momentary and conscious. The anomaly is in this psychic disproportion, or rather in the short-sighted consciousness, which cannot pass its narrow limits and penetrate into the region of the unconscious.

3. Destructive pleasures of a social character, which are connected, not with the suffering of the individual himself, but with that of others. Such is the pleasure felt in killing and seeing killed—in sanguinary spectacles, bull-fights, fights between animals, and, in a much feebler degree, in hearing or reading tales of bloodshed. These pleasures can be explained; they denote the satisfaction of tendencies to violence and destruction, which, strong or weak, conscious or unconscious, exist in all men. They may be studied under the heading of the pathology of tendencies, which I shall treat later on; let me only remark in passing that these tendencies involve a certain display of energy, which is one of the conditions of active pleasure.

One question in conclusion. Can pleasure, and joy in particular, be the cause of a grave catastrophe, such as madness or death? Some alienists—Bucknill, Tuke, Guislain, etc.—quote cases of madness which they attribute to sudden joy, such as an unforeseen inheritance, or success in obtaining a long-wished-for situation. The same thesis has been maintained in the case of death[1] occurring suddenly, or after syncope. Griesinger maintains that it is extremely rare—if it ever happens—for excessive joy *by itself* to produce

---

[1] For some facts, which may or may not be well authenticated, see Féré, *op. cit.*, p. 234.

madness. Others absolutely deny the fact.[1] It is certain that joy is seldom seen figuring in any enumeration of the causes of madness. Joy, as a state of consciousness, could not have such effects. The catastrophe can only be explained by sudden and violent organic troubles, which cannot have this effect unless there already exists a predisposition. It is not joy which maddens or kills, but the shock received by a being in an abnormal state. It would be more correct to say that an event which, in the generality of men, *ought* to cause joy, here produces a peculiar pathological state ending in madness or death.

II.

The other side of the subject may be briefly disposed of. We occasionally, though rarely, meet with people who grieve over good fortune when it comes to them; these have the pain of pleasure. I do not think that any psychologist has dwelt on them, and it seems to me useless to make a study of these cases. Though in form the reverse of the pleasure of pain, it fundamentally resembles it. This disposition of mind, found in certain pessimists, is rightly called eccentric or bizarre—*i.e.*, general opinion instinctively looks on it as a deviation, an anomaly. This, moreover, is only a special instance of a general state of mind—morbid or pathologic sadness—which we are about to study. I have remarked above that, as pain and sadness always involve a morbid element, the expression *abnormal* would be more accurate and less open to criticism.

In order to affirm that a physical or moral pain is outside the usual law, and may be described as abnormal, we shall have recourse to the three distinctive marks given at the opening of this chapter, and we can take, as our one type, that of melancholia in the medical sense. It presents the required characteristics: the long duration, disproportion between the cause and effect experienced, and excessive or insufficient reaction.

It is needless to give a description of the melancholic state; it may be found in all treatises on mental disease. This affection assumes many clinical forms, varying from *melancholia attonita*, which simulates a stupid apathy, to the

[1] Féré, *Pathologie des Emotions*, pp. 293, 294.

agitated form accompanied by incessant groans, from the slight to the profound and incurable forms. It will be sufficient to enumerate the most general features. In comparing melancholy with ordinary sadness, we may follow the cumulative method, because the morbid state is nothing but the normal condition thrown into high relief.

1. We know that the physiological characteristics of normal sadness are reducible to a single formula : lowering of the vital functions. The same is the case with melancholia, where, however, the organic depression is much more accentuated. Constriction of the vaso-motor nerves, resulting in a diminished calibre of the arteries, anæmia, and lowered temperature of the extremities; lowering of the cardiac pressure, which may descend from an average of 800 grammes to 650 and even 600 grammes ; a progressive slackening of nutrition, with various resultant manifestations, such as digestive troubles, checked secretions, etc. ; slow and rare movements ; a dislike of all muscular effort, all work, all physical exercise, unless there are (as sometimes happens in cases of agitated melancholia) moments of disordered reflex movements and attacks of fury. Such is the general condition. It is obvious that this represents pain carried to an extreme degree, and that we find, here too, as well as in normal melancholy, passive and active pains.

2. The psychic characteristics consist, in the first place, of an emotional state varying from apathetic resignation to despair; some patients are so crushed as to think themselves dead. It has been noted that, in general, persons of a gloomy disposition are inclined to melancholia, while those of a cheerful one rather tend towards mania. In both cases there is an exaggeration of the normal condition. The intellectual disposition consists in the slackening of the association of ideas, in indolence of the mind. Ordinarily, a fixed idea predominates, excluding from the consciousness all that has no relation to it; thus the hypochondriac thinks only of his health ; the nostalgic, of his country ; the religious melancholiac, of his salvation. Voluntary activity is almost *nil;* aboulia, "the consciousness of not willing, is the very essence of this disease" (Schüle). Sometimes there are violent and unexpected reflex

impulses, which are a new proof of the annihilation of the will. To sum up : while normal sadness has its moments of intermission, the melancholiac is shut up in his grief as if by an impenetrable wall, without the slightest fissure through which a ray of joy might reach him.

Here arises a question we cannot neglect, because it is connected with one of the principal theses of this work, the fundamental part played by the feelings. Passive melancholia, being taken as the type of the painful state under its extreme and permanent form, what is its origin? There are two possible answers. We may admit that a physical pain, or a certain representation, engenders a melancholic disposition, and poisons the affective life. Or we may admit that a vague and general state of depression and disorganisation becomes concrete and fixes itself in an idea. On the first supposition the intellectual state is primary, and the affective state resultant. On the second the affective state is the first moment, and the intellectual state results from it.

This problem, rather psychical than practical, has only occupied a very small number of alienists. Schüle admits the twofold origin.[1] Sometimes the patient, suffering from a painful and causeless depression, which he cannot shake off, inquires no further; but, most frequently, he connects the painful feeling with some incident in his previous or present life. Sometimes, *much more rarely*, the haunting idea is the first to appear, and forms the pivot of the melancholic state and its consequences. Dr. Dumas,[2] who has devoted a special work to this question, founded on his own observation, comes to the same conclusions as Schüle. One of his patients attributed her incurable sadness, in turn, and without sufficient reason, to her husband, to her son, to expected loss of work. In others, the melancholy is of intellectual origin : the loss of fortune, the idea of irrevocable damnation, etc. He is thus led to admit that a melancholia of organic origin is the most frequent, one of intellectual origin the rarest.

Can we trace back these two modes of manifestation to

[1] Schüle, *Traité clinique des maladies mentales*, Art. "Mélancolie" (French edition), pp. 21, 28.

[2] G. Dumas, *Les états intellectuels dans la mélancolie*, where may be found several detailed observations.

a common and deeper cause? This is Krafft-Ebing's [1] solution: "We must consider psychic pain and the arrest of ideas as co-ordinate phenomena; and there is reason to think of a common cause, of a nutritive trouble of the brain (anæmia?), leading to a diminished expenditure of nervous activity. Taken comprehensively, melancholia may be considered as a morbid condition of the psychic organism founded on nutritive troubles, and characterised on the one hand by the feeling of pain and a particular mode of reaction on the part of the whole consciousness (psychic neuralgia), on the other by the difficulty of psychic movements (instinct, ideas), and finally, by their arrest."

I am unwilling to incur the reproach of inferring more from facts than they contain, and of insisting on unity at any price; but it follows from the preceding that if the element of feeling is not everywhere and always primary, at least it is so in the majority of cases. Besides, it is closely connected with fundamental trophic troubles, so that we arrive at the same conclusion by another road. Dumas (*op. cit.*, pp. 133 *et seq.*) has insisted on the depressing influences of marshy soil, on the stagnation, the physical and moral apathy of the inhabitants of Sologne, the Dombes, the Maremma, and other regions infested by *malaria*, a condition which may be summed up in two words, sadness and resignation. These facts are quite in favour of the organic origin of melancholia.

The special study of the anomalies of pleasure and pain is not important for itself alone. The formula generally admitted since Aristotle, which couples pleasure with utility, pain with what is injurious, admits of many exceptions in practice. Perhaps the constitution of a pathological group in the study of pleasure and pain may permit us to solve some difficulties, to prevent the rule and the exceptions being placed on the same plane, and unduly assimilated to one another. We shall see that this is so in one of the following chapters.

---

[1] Krafft-Ebing, *op. cit.*, vol. ii., sec. 1, chap. i.

CHAPTER V.

THE NEUTRAL STATES.

*Two methods of study—Affirmative thesis founded on obser-
vation, deduction, and psycho-physics—Negative thesis:
the psychological trinity; confusion between consciousness
and introspection—Diversity of temperaments.*

UP to the present, pleasure and pain have been studied
first separately, as two perfectly distinct states, pure, by
hypothesis, from every admixture. We then examined those
singular cases where pain becomes the material or occasion
of pleasure, and *vice versâ.* We have still to speak of those
cases where the agreeable and the painful *coexist* in varying
proportions in the consciousness—*e.g.,* in the mountain-
climber who feels at the same time fatigue, the fear of the
precipices, the beauty of the landscape, and the pleasure of
difficulty vanquished. Nothing is more frequent than these
mixed forms; they would even be the rule if one could
admit, with certain authors, that there are no unmixed
pleasures or pains; but by their complex and composite
nature they are, in fact, emotions, and we shall come to
them again later on.

The subject of this chapter is quite different. It is the
much-discussed, still unsolved, and perhaps insoluble
problem of neutral states, states of indifference, free from
any accompaniment, either pleasurable or painful. Do such
exist? Both the affirmative and negative are maintained by
good authorities; there is even a psychologist who seems to
me to have adopted each thesis in turn.[1]

---

[1] For a short historical summary of the question up to the middle of
the nineteenth century, see Bouillier, *Du plaisir et de la douleur*,
chap. xi.

The question can only be entered on in two ways—by observation and by argument. Let us examine the results of these two methods.

1. Does the state of indifference exist as an *observable fact?* Bain is, among contemporary writers, the principal champion of this thesis, which has excited a lengthy discussion.[1] He does not pretend to affirm that there is a single state of feeling free from every agreeable or disagreeable element; but if these elements only exist as infinitesimal quantities, psychology need take no account of them. Pleasure and pain are clearly defined generic states; yet there is a practical interest in knowing whether any neutral conditions exist. Bain finds the type of these in cases of simple excitement, which may be accompanied either by pleasure or by pain, but remain distinct from either. The sensation of burning, the smell of asafœtida, the taste of aloes, these are modes of excitement which we call pain, because in them pain predominates. The noise of a mill, the confused murmur of a great city, are modes of excitement which may be called agreeable or disagreeable; but the excitement is the essential fact, the pleasure and pain are accidental.

Bain does not appear to me happy in most of the examples he has chosen. I quote some of them. The shock produced by surprise—but surprise is only a mitigated form of fear, and in nearly all cases instantaneously assumes a painful or pleasurable character. The state of expectation: "The intense objectivity of one's looks when following a race, or a great surgical operation, is not, strictly speaking, unconsciousness, but a maximum of energy with a minimum of consciousness. It is rather a mode of indifference—more of an excitement than an affective state." Here we may make the same comment; moreover, there is in expectation a feeling of effort which soon becomes fatigue, and, in most instances, expectation involves the anticipation of some event either desired or dreaded.

Those who do not attempt to prove the existence of neutral states by direct observation deduce them from general principles. Thus Sergi considers them as the necessary effect of determinate biological conditions. Pleasure and pain being the two fundamental forms—the two poles

[1] See *Mind*, Oct. 1887, Jan. and April 1888, Jan. 1889; and J. Sully, *The Human Mind*, vol. ii. pp. 4, 5.

of the life of feeling, there must exist between them a neutral zone corresponding to a state of perfect adaptation. Pain is a state of consciousness revealing a conflict of the organism with exterior forces—a want of adaptation of one to the other; whence a loss of energy. Pleasure is a state of consciousness which makes it evident that the reaction of the organism is connected with external excitations, whence arises, by synergy, a heightening of vital activity. Indifference is the neutral state of consciousness showing a perfect adaptation of the organism to constant and variable intensities—in other words, excitations which neither increase nor diminish vital activity, but preserve it, produce a state of equilibrium and appeal to the consciousness neither as pleasure nor pain.[1] This hypothesis—viz., that at certain moments the sentient being neither loses nor gains, and that such is the substratum of the psychic state called neutral, seems to me extremely probable, but remains no more than a hypothesis.

Now let us question the psycho-physicists who have treated this subject according to their own special method, while coming to different conclusions. It is difficult to adopt a procedure more theoretical than theirs, or one better adapted to show the insufficiency of the intellectualist method in this domain of psychology. In truth, the subject treated by them is a special aspect of the problem, not its totality; they are inquiring whether, in the "transformation" of pleasure into pain, and *vice versâ*, there is, in the passage from one contrary to the other, a point of neutrality or indifference. Wundt graphically represents the phenomenon by a curve: the portion of this curve above the line of the abscissa has a positive value, and corresponds to the development of pleasure; the portion below corresponds to the development of pain, and has a negative value; the precise point where the curve cuts the line of the abscissa (to rise in the direction of pleasure or descend in that of pain) corresponds to neutrality or indifference. Lehmann, who, however, admits that weak sensations are neutral states, gives a curve rather different from that of Wundt. From an observation first made by Horwicz, and experiments conducted by Lehmann himself, it appears that, if one dips

[1] *Psychologie physiologique*, iv., ch. i., pp. 309 *et seq*. (French edition.)

one's finger into water whose temperature gradually rises from 35° to 50° Centigrade during a space of 2 minutes and 20 seconds, one feels first an agreeable warmth, then some slight, unpleasant prickings, then oscillations of intense prickings with moments of rest, and lastly, pain. His conclusion is contrary to Wundt's, for he finds that the passage from pleasure to pain does not take place in a neutral state.[1]

Experiments are not to be despised; but as for the figure supposed to illustrate the phenomenon, it is merely mis-leading; this mathematical conception explains nothing. The assimilation of pleasure to a positive, and pain to a negative value, is quite arbitrary. Moreover, the passage from *plus* to *minus* quantities through zero is an operation which has its base in our faculty of abstraction, and for its materials abstract and homogeneous quantities. The different degrees of pleasure and pain are nothing of this sort. We do not even know if these two phenomena have a common foundation, if there is a common measure between the two, if they are not both irreducible, and we have no right to place, theoretically, a *Nullpunkt* at the point of transition from one to the other. The problem is one of a concrete order; it is a question of fact, whether soluble or not, which is put before us.

2. Let us now listen to those who refuse to admit states of indifference.

Every state of consciousness is a trinity in the theological sense: it is the knowledge of some exterior or interior event; it includes motor elements; it has a certain tone of feeling. We describe it as intellectual, motor, or emotional, according to the preponderance of one of these elements, not its exclusive existence. It is a well-known fact that the clearer a perception, the weaker is its tone of feeling, and the more intense an emotion, the more attenuated the intellectual element which has evoked it; but diminution is not equivalent to disappearance. If neutral states existed,

[1] Wundt, *Grundzüge der physiol. Psychologie* (4th German ed.), vol. i. pp. 557 *et seq.*; Lehmann, *Hauptgesetze*, etc., §§ 236-241. One of Wundt's most distinguished pupils, Külpe, in his *Umriss der Psychologie* (1895), considers the existence of a state of indifference "can hardly be doubted in the face of a long series of observations which support it." (English edition, p. 242.)

one of the fundamental elements of psychic life would exist only in an intermittent form, and at some moments even cease to be.

Besides this, let us observe ourselves and interrogate our own consciousness. "Let us consider ourselves at one of those moments of calm and apparent indifference, when it seems as if nothing could move us, and our numbed sensibility remains, as it were, suspended between pleasure and pain. This deceptive appearance of insensibility and aridity always masks some more or less feeble sensations of ease or uneasiness, some more or less slight and confused sentiments of joy or grief which are none the less real for being in nowise vivid or exciting. Moreover, how could our sensibility fail to be, constantly, more or less impressed by so many general causes which, independent of particular causes, so constantly act upon us, at every instant of our life, and which, so to speak, ceaselessly besiege us, from within and from without?" Bouillier, the author of this passage (*op. cit.*, chap. xi.), supports his assertions by citing the innumerable impressions which come from the internal organs, from the state of the air and sky, from light, from the most trivial incidents of common life.

It is certain that the domain of the indifferent states, if existent at all, is very scanty. Yet, however skilfully Bouillier may support his thesis, there is one irrefragable objection to be urged against it : the testimony of the consciousness, always doubtful, is here more so than elsewhere. What he proposes to us is, in fact, to *observe* ourselves. From the moment when we begin to do this, we no longer have to deal with the natural consciousness, in its raw state, but with that somewhat artificial consciousness which is created by attention. We look, not with our eyes, but through a microscope; we amplify, we enlarge the phenomenon; and here the method of enlargement is not to be trusted. It causes certain subconscious states to cross the threshold of the consciousness; it makes them pass out of the penumbra into full light, and disposes us to believe that such is their normal condition. We know that some individuals, by fixing the attention firmly on some particular part of the body, can bring about in it a sensation of weight, of irritation, of arterial pulsation, etc. Do these modifications always exist, unperceived only so long as the attention is not directed to them? or does attention produce them by means of an increased vascular activity, increasing, but not creating? The latter supposition is the more probable. The hypochondriac who obstinately and patiently watches the details of his organic life feels within himself the motion of the vital mechanism which escapes most men. It would be easy to give other examples, proving that we must distinguish between consciousness pure and simple and internal observation, and that it is the less allowable to argue from one to the other, since in practice the problem is reduced to a difference of intensity.

This question well deserves to be called, as it has been by J. Sully, " one of the *cruces* of psychology." Those who wish to take sides in it can only guide their decision by probabilities and preferences. I am inclined to favour the thesis of indifferent states. I find it difficult to admit that certain perceptions or representations, incessantly repeated, imply anything more than the fact of knowledge. The sight of my furniture, arranged in its usual order, causes me no appreciable degree of pleasure or displeasure; or if these exist as infinitesimal quantities, psychology, as Bain justly says, has no concern with them. Fouillée also points out that the feeling of indifference is not primary, but due to an effacement.[1]

The repugnance of certain psychologists to admit indifferent states arises from the fact that this thesis appears to them to introduce discontinuity into the affective life. The mobile and incessantly alternating series of pleasurable or painful modifications would, in that case, have moments of interruption, gaps, and vacant spaces. I yield to no one in asserting the continuity of the affective life; but it must be sought elsewhere. It is in the appetites, the tendencies —conscious or unconscious—the desires and aversions, which, for their part, are always at work, permanent and indestructible. Here, again, we find the mistake of considering pleasure and pain, which are only symptoms, as essential and fundamental elements.

I find it strange, moreover, that, in a subject so much studied and discussed, no one should have contributed an observation which seems to me of some importance. Each author supposes the formula adopted by himself to be

[1] Fouillée, *Psychologie des idées-forces*, i. 68.

applicable to all men. This is to state the question in a philosophical, not in a psychological form—*i.e.*, without taking into account individual variations of temperament and character, an element by no means to be neglected. It is to suppose, without the least proof, that all cases are reducible to unity. On the contrary, there are presumptions that the solution adopted, whatever it is, may be true for some men and false for others. A nervous, excitable temperament, in a perpetual state of vibration, constantly kept on the alert by the workings of passion or thought, may, by its very constitution, leave no moment accessible to an intermission of the incessantly renewed states of pain and pleasure. A lymphatic temperament, on the other hand, a cold disposition, a limited intelligence, poor in ideas, constitute a soil perfectly suited to the frequent appearance and long continuance of indifferent states.[1]

These differences, which are matter of common observation, show the necessity of distrusting an over-simple solution.

[1] I give an instance of a similar character, narrated by a historian, from Arabic sources. "The Emir Mohammed (at Granada, in 1408), finding himself dying, and anxious to secure the throne to his son, sent orders for his brother Yussuf, whom he was keeping in captivity at Salobreña, to be put to death. The alcalde, when he received this order, was playing at chess with his prisoner, whose gentleness had gained the heart of his gaolers. On reading the fatal despatch he was troubled, and did not dare to communicate its contents to the prince. But Yussuf guessed from his confusion what was the matter, and said to the alcalde, 'Is it my head that is asked of thee?' The latter, for all answer, handed to him his brother's letter. Yussuf asked only for a few hours' delay, in order to take leave of his wife; but the messenger of death declared that the execution must take place at once, the hour of his return being fixed beforehand. 'Well,' replied Yussuf, 'let us at least finish the game.' But the alcalde was so distressed that he advanced his pawns at random, and Yussuf was obliged to inform him of his mistakes. However, the game was never finished. Some knights, riding from Granada at full gallop, saluted Yussuf as Emir, and announced to him the death of his brother. When thus passing from the scaffold to the throne the Mussulman prince remained master of himself, as he had been in the face of death. Still doubting his good fortune, he set out for Granada, where he was received by the people with cries of joy." (Rosseuw St.-Hilaire, *Histoire d'Espagne*, vol. v., p. 227.) Analogous traits are recorded of various historic personages.

CHAPTER VI.

CONCLUSIONS ON PLEASURE AND PAIN.

The beginning of life—I. Conditions of existence of pleasure and pain; lowering and heightening of vital energy— Féré's experiments—Meynert's theory—II. Finality of pleasure and pain—Exceptions: explicable cases; irreducible cases.

I SHALL not delay long over the question, as much debated as the one we have just quitted and still less accessible : Which first makes its appearance in consciousness, pleasure or pain ? In our own day, especially, optimists and pessimists have contested this point at great length, although, in my opinion, they have no concern with it. Their doctrines are two antithetical conceptions of the world, depending solely on temperament and character, which could neither be confirmed nor invalidated by the solution of this problem. It is clear that it is a question of origin, of psychogenesis, foreign to experimental psychology, and admitting only of probable solutions.

Descartes expressed the singular opinion that " joy was the first passion of the soul, since it is not credible that the soul should have been placed in the body, except when the latter was well disposed ; hence the natural result would be joy." Others, following theoretic views less strange in character, maintain that, pleasure having for its cause the free play of our activity, pain is connected with the arrest of pleasure, and hence is posterior to it.[1] The majority of writers appear to me to favour the contrary hypothesis; the impressions of cold, of contact, the beginning of pulmonary

---

[1] For the historical summary, see Bouillier, *op. cit.*, chap. xii.

respiration, etc., are cited as proving the priority of pain;
still more so, the cries of infants and of the new-born young
of animals. Yet Preyer, in two passages which have not
excited much remark, refuses all significance to the cry, and
sees in it nothing but a reflex action.[1] It does not seem
doubtful that psychic life, in its first or intra-uterine and
earlier extra-uterine phases may almost be reduced to a
series of pleasurable and painful impressions. Do they
resemble those of the adult? It is probable that they do;
but it must not be forgotten that to assimilate the plastic
forms of the primitive epoch to the fixed and rigid ones of
adult life is a mode of reasoning conducive to numerous
errors.

Leaving aside this question of origin, it is impossible to
close the study of pleasure and pain without a summary
recapitulation of the general theories forming the philosophy of our subject. These may be classified under two
heads : the *how* and the *why;* what are the conditions of
existence of pleasure and pain? and what is their utility?

[1] " The first cry of the new-born infant was formerly considered anything rather than a reflex action. It is, however, very probable that
this first vocal manifestation, accompanying an expiration, is a reflex
pure and simple. Kant wrote (without, indeed, having himself
observed new-born children or animals) : ' The cry uttered by the child
just after birth has not the intonation of fear, but that of irritation or
anger. It is not because it is suffering, but because something displeases it. No doubt it would like to move and feels its impotence, as
it might feel a chain restricting its liberty. What could have been the
object of Nature in making the infant born into the world utter cries
which are in the highest degree dangerous? Yet no animal save man
announces its existence, at the time of birth, by similar cries.'

" This remarkable conception has been much commented on, and
widely adopted. At the present time many people still think that the
crying of new-born infants has considerable psychic significance. But all
comments of this kind are met by the objection that a totally anen-
cephalous infant cries at birth, and that many healthy infants do not cry,
but sneeze, on their entry into the world, as noted by Darwin. . . .

" The reflexes of pains which, in later life, show themselves in the
acutest manner, are those best developed in early life. Gunzmer's observations on about sixty infants showed him that, during the first few days,
they are almost insensible, and during the first week, very slightly
sensitive, to the pricking of a needle.

" New-born infants have been, in the course of their first day,
pricked with fine needles, on the nose, the upper lip, and the hand,
deeply enough to draw a drop of blood; yet the child manifested no
symptom of consciousness, and did not start once."—Preyer, *Seele des
Kindes*, pp. 177, 193.

I.

On the first point there has been, from antiquity to the present day, an almost universal and very rare agreement between different schools : pleasure has, as its condition, an increased, pain a diminished activity. I employ this vague formula designedly, because it covers all special formulas. Of these it would be idle to enumerate even the chief.   At bottom, in language varying according to the era and the doctrine, all authors say the same thing, employing, according to their cast of intellect, a metaphysical, physical (Léon Dumont), physiological, or psychological formula. The intellectualists themselves agree with the others; considering sensibility as a confused form of intelligence, they say that pleasure is a confused judgment of perfection, and pain a confused judgment of imperfection.   In short, if each formula is stripped of the variations adapting it to the particular philosophy of each author, there is a common residue, which, in all alike, is the essential.

The history of these variations on the same theme would be monotonous and unprofitable; it is as well, however, to note that, as our own century advances, the theoretic conception of the ancients tends to grow more precise, to rely more on the support of experience and be justified thereby. We have already seen the two formulas—augmentation, diminution—taking definite shape, showing themselves in the objective and observable changes of nutrition, of the secretions, the movements, the circulation, and the breathing.

Féré's experiments, he says, "agree perfectly, in showing that pleasurable sensations are accompanied by an increase of energy, and disagreeable ones by a diminution.   The sensation of pleasure resolves itself, therefore, into a feeling of power, that of displeasure into a feeling of impotence.   We have thus reached the material demonstration of the theoretic ideas propounded by Bain, Darwin, Spencer, Dumont, and others." [1]   I may remind the reader that Féré has applied his dynamometric researches to all kinds of sensations : to smell, to taste, to

[1] Féré, *Sensation et Mouvement*, p. 64.   This work is to be consulted for the details of the experiments about to be summarised.

vision modified by glasses of the principal colours of the spectrum, red giving a dynamometric pressure of 42, which progressively descends to 20–17 for violet. For auditory sensations, he finds that the dynamic equivalent is in proportion to the amplitude and number of the vibrations. The same results are found to follow motion, the movements of the upper or lower limb exercising a dynamogenic influence on the corresponding member. Still further: an excitation *imperceptible to the consciousness*, a latent perception, determines a dynamic effect just as much as a conscious impression. Suggested hallucinations, agreeable or the reverse, are equally accompanied by an increase or diminution of pressure on the dynamometer.

If the formula, "diminution of vital energy," of which we have found that melancholia is an extreme instance, can give rise to no ambiguity, this is not the case with the opposite formula; and certain authors have, for this reason, thought—and rightly so—that it ought to be stated in precise terms. Pleasure corresponds to an increase of activity; but if we understand by this expression a large quantity of work done, the pleasure would result from a *diminution* of the potential energy of the organism, as Léon Dumont has pointed out—*i.e.*, from an impoverishment, which is contradicted by experience. We must therefore understand this increase of activity in the sense that the work done does not expend more energy than the nutritive actions; or, to employ Grant Allen's formula, "Pleasure is the concomitant of the healthy action of any or all of the organs or members supplied with afferent cerebro-spinal nerves, to an extent not exceeding the ordinary powers of reparation possessed by the system."[1]

Finally, we must remark that, if every external or internal sensation, whatever its nature, is a transmission of movements coming from without, a new acquisition for the nervous system and the brain, *every* sensation ought at first to produce at least a momentary increase of energy. Féré, who has foreseen the possibility of this objection, admits in all cases a primary excitement. "If there appear to be cases in which phenomena of depression arise

[1] *Physiological Æsthetics*, p. 21. This point has been well discussed by Lehmann (*op. cit.*, pp. 205-208).

suddenly and subsist by themselves, it is only because they have been insufficiently observed."[1] There would then be a very short phase of increase, immediately masked, according to him, by the phase of diminution. The physiologists, as we have seen, are always inclined to explain pain by intensity of sensation; but, if we take into account its nature, its quality, and the susceptibility of the nervous system to certain modes of motion received, nothing prevents the loss being immediate.

Meynert, in his *Psychiatrie*, is the only writer who has attempted to advance any nearer to an explanation, and to determine the *mechanism* which produces pleasure and pain. His hypothesis, in its principal points, is as follows:—

As far as pain is concerned, his theory may be summed up as an arrestive action of two categories of reflex movements, motor and vascular. The painful state is the translation into consciousness of this physiological mechanism.

1. *Motor reflexes.*—Let us suppose the head of a sleeping child to be slightly tickled. As the child's sleep is sound, and there is no pain, nothing takes place but a slight withdrawal of the hand. If we suppose a slight prick, there will be few movements, and these limited to a small part of the body. But if we suppose some severe pain, such as the extraction of a tooth, or a burn extending over a large portion of the skin, the result will be prolonged and terrible reflex movements in *all* parts of the body, which (in our opinion) may be considered as defensive. So much for external facts; what is taking place internally?

We know that vibrations are conducted slowly in the grey matter (twelve times as slowly, according to Helmholtz, as in the white). When an excitation increases, as we have seen, the number of muscular groups set in motion, resistance to transmission increases in the same proportion. "The sensation of pain presupposes a reflex movement and an arrest of nervous conduction in the grey substance of the spinal marrow." It is this process of inhibition, in varying degrees, which is felt by the consciousness as pain.

2. *Vascular reflexes.*—Peripheral excitation also has reflex effects on the vaso-motor system; it produces contraction of the spinal arteries, of the carotids, and of the cerebral

[1] *Pathologie des émotions*, p. 226.

arteries. Hence the syncope which frequently accompanies acute pain, and the sleep (the result of anæmia) which has more than once been recorded in the case of prisoners undergoing torture. This constriction of the arteries produces a chemical change, a deficit of oxygen and nutritive elements in the cells of the cortex; the respiration of the tissues is interfered with, and the distressed state of the organism is psychologically rendered by pain.

Conversely, the excitations contributing to the well-being of the individual are accompanied by a free transmission of nervous force, by vaso-motor dilatation, by hyperæmia of the nervous centres, and, in the motor series, by "aggressive movements," such as the singing of birds, the joyous barking of dogs, and other analogous manifestations in the human subject.

Meynert—vaguely enough, and relying for support on the association of ideas—has applied his explanation to the case of moral pain. It would not be difficult to adapt this hypothesis to the different forms of vexation and sadness; but with a more complicated mechanism. The point of departure is no longer a perception, but a representation. The phenomenon is no longer of peripheral, but of central origin; so that it starts from the brain and returns to it, or, in psychological terms, begins in a purely intellectual state of consciousness and ends in a state that is primarily one of feeling. If, reading by chance a list of deaths in a newspaper, I find, with no possible opening for doubt, the name of a friend, what takes place in me is this : the other unknown names pass through my consciousness like empty words, or a simple visual percept; suddenly everything is changed; the reflex and vascular movements above described are produced, then the arrest of the medullary and cerebral centres, whose expression in consciousness will be grief. But these reflex actions are only possible if the word read suggests the recollection of former deaths, that is to say, of a sum of privations, negations, and checked desires, the result of a mass of accumulated experiences rising up together and acting, whether consciously, subconsciously, or unconsciously.

An English alienist, Clouston, who has published a critical analysis of this hypothesis of Meynert's, considers it as the best in the present state of the science of nervous physiology, although full of lacunæ, and, after all, rather theoretical than experimental. It is not in accordance with several facts; e.g., in anger, which is a painful state, there is an afflux of blood, combined with aggressive movements.[1] On the other hand, it harmonises with a great number of manifestations observed in mental disease; thus, at the third stage of general paralysis, a puncture causes a painless reflex action, because the grey substance, being disorganised, no longer has any inhibitive power. In the evolution of melancholia, the patients sometimes at first suffer from purely physical pains (neuralgia, headache, etc.), which disappear to make way for the melancholic state, which, in its turn, disappears with the return of the physical pain. Everyday experience shows that physical and moral pain cannot coexist in any degree of intensity; a burn may for a time arrest the progress of melancholy, and we all know what happens to many persons as soon as they arrive at the dentist's. It seems as though the organism had but a limited capacity for either pleasure or pain, and that neither feeling can exist at the same time in its double (physical and moral) form.

II.

Much has been written on the finality of pleasure and pain, though two entirely distinct methods of procedure have been adopted.

The first, that of theologians and moralists, is an extrinsic explanation; pleasure is an attraction, the charm of life; pain is a vigilant monitor warning us of our disorganisation. They exist in us by the beneficent grace of Providence or Nature; they have a transcendental cause.

The second, which has only found complete expression in the evolutionist school, is an intrinsic explanation. It keeps to the analysis of facts, and shows that pleasure and pain have their *why* in the animal's conditions of existence, and that consequently their causality is immanent. Thus understood, the problem of *why* is pretty nearly identical with that of *how*, mechanism and finality being very nearly confounded.

---

[1] *British Medical Journal*, August 14, 1886, pp. 319 *et seq.* We shall see, later on, that the mechanism of anger is not so simple as Clouston seems to admit.

Herbert Spencer (followed by Grant Allen, Schneider, and others) has clearly shown that the connection between pleasure and utility, pain and injury, is an almost necessary relation, having its root in the nature of things, and that it has been an important factor in the survival of the fittest. Every animal as a rule persists in actions which cause it pleasure—that is, in a mode of activity which tends to its preservation; while it usually avoids what causes it pain, that being the correlative of injurious actions. The animal has thus two useful guides in the course of its life, to enable it to survive and perpetuate its species.

If this rule were without exception,—if pleasure universally accompanied utility, and *vice versâ*,—it would be sufficient to state the law of the conditions of existence and nothing more. But the exceptions to the rule are numerous, and require critical study. Some can be explained, others seem to me irreducible to any law.

1. Herbert Spencer relieves us of a large number of exceptions, which are, in fact, only the result of civilisation. Prehistoric man, according to this author, was well adapted to his environment and to a predatory life; but when, under pressure of want, the transition to a sedentary and civilised existence took place, the human being found itself ill-adapted to its surroundings. The conditions of social existence have been superposed on those of natural existence, constituting a new *milieu*, and requiring other forms of activity. In consequence of this, frequent discordances have arisen which he has enumerated at great length: the survival of predatory tendencies difficult to satisfy, the necessity of repugnant and monotonous labour, excess of labour compensated for by excess of pleasure, as so frequently happens in great cities, etc.[1] All these interversions are the work of man, the result of his irrational struggle against nature, of his will, of his artificial activities. "In the case of mankind, there has arisen, and must long continue, a deep and involved derangement of the natural connections between pleasures and beneficial actions, and between pains and detrimental actions—a derangement which so obscures their natural connections that even the reverse connections are supposed to obtain." Spencer thinks that a readjustment will take place in the long

[1] *Principles of Psychology*, vol. i., §§ 125, 126.

run; I leave this consolation—without sharing it—to the optimists.

2. Besides these exceptions, due to the intercurrence of social causes, there are others of an individual character, which also can be explained. Certain poisons are agreeable to the taste, and cause death; a surgical operation is painful, but beneficial; many persons intensely enjoy a *far niente* which leads them to ruin; it is pleasant to live in the world of pure fancy, but the reaction leaves one enervated and unable to fulfil one's daily task. Many other cases of this kind may be met with in ordinary life. All these exceptions to the rule are only apparent ones. Consciousness reveals only the *momentary* phenomenon, and, within these limits, its verdict is accurate; it expresses the processes actually going on in the organism at the moment, as we have seen in the euphoria of the dying; it cannot tell us what will follow. The explanation reduces itself to Grant Allen's saying, "Neither pleasure nor pain is prophetic."[1]

3. There are other facts which the partisans of final causes prudently pass over in silence, and which certain evolutionists have attempted to explain.

Spencer remarks (*loc. cit.*, § 127) that, "while the individual is young and not yet fertile, its welfare and the welfare of the race go together; but when the reproductive age is reached, the welfare of the individual and of the race cease to be the same, and may be diametrically opposed. . . . Very frequently, among invertebrate animals, the death of the parents is a normal result of propagation. In the great class Insects, the species of which outnumber all other animal species, the rule is that the male lives only until a new generation has been begotten, and that the female dies as soon as the eggs are deposited." There is, therefore, says the English author, a qualification to be made.

Schneider, in his interesting work *Freud und Leid*, inspired by the transformist hypothesis and the ideas of Spencer, gets rid of the difficulty by connecting pleasure and pain with the conditions of existence, not of the *individual*, but of the *species:* pleasure corresponding to specific utility and pain to specific injury. This state-

[1] See Lehmann, *op. cit.*, § 201; Höffding, *Psychologie in Umrissen* (2nd ed.), p. 380.

ment of the problem is ingenious, but arbitrary. Pleasure and pain are essentially subjective, individual states. They can only assume a specific character by means of generalisation—*i.e.*, as a conception of our minds, which has no reality or value, except so far as abstracted from particular cases.

Restricting our attention to man, and not occupying ourselves with the antagonism between the individual and the race, we shall find that there are cases very difficult to bring under the law. A grain of sand in the eye, an attack of dental neuralgia cause a degree of pain enormously out of proportion with the amount of organic injury sustained. On the other hand, the dissolution of certain organs essential to life is frequently almost painless. The brain may be cut and cauterised almost without suffering; a cavity may be formed in the lung, a cancer in the liver, without the slightest warning of danger. Pain, that "vigilant sentinel" of the advocates of final causes, remains dumb, or only warns us when the evil is already of long standing and irremediable. Nay, more, it often misleads us as to the actual seat of the disease. Examples of false localisation abound; an irritation in the nose is due to intestinal worms, a headache to a morbid condition of the stomach, a pain in the right shoulder to liver complaint. Many other instances of this kind have been studied by physicians under the names of painful synæsthesia, or synalgia.

Schneider is, I believe, the only one who has attempted to explain these deviations from the generally admitted formula,[1] by reducing the problem to the two following questions :—First, whether the development of an acute sensibility of the internal organs—*i.e.*, a relation of causality between their lesions and the feeling of pain—is, in general, possible ; secondly, whether, such development having taken place, this faculty of feeling, as pain, any lesion of the internal organs could be a means of protection, as it is found to be in the case of the skin. The internal organs are only in contact with an interior surface, which is tolerably uniform; if an opposite state of things arises, *i.e.*, if they are laid bare by some profound lesion, death ordinarily ensues, at least in animals and in primitive man. Only the slow progress of surgery has made it possible to remedy such

---

[1] *Freud und Leid des Menschengeschlechts* (1883), pp. 35 *et seq.*

accidents. If, through spontaneous variation, a case of sensibility of the internal organs had ever occurred, it would be useless; it could neither become permanent nor be transmitted to descendants, since the lesion, resulting in death, would render the further evolution of this quality impossible. Besides, had this sensitive faculty of the internal organs existed, it must have remained useless, since it could only become efficacious when combined with protective and retractile movements of the organs, which, by the very constitution of the animal, cannot take place. In fact, the whole of the sensibility has been concentrated in the exterior parts of the body, which, by protecting themselves, also protect, in the degree to which this is possible, the internal organs.

I have insisted on the exceptions (certainly they are not without a cause, whether we accept that alleged by Schneider, or prefer those of other authorities), because they are only too readily forgotten. The connection of pleasure and utility, pain and injury, is a formula which originated with the philosophers—that is, with intellects which always, and before all things, demand unity. Psychology must proceed otherwise, must incessantly confront the formula with facts, check it by experience, note the exceptions; it is content with empirical laws, embracing the generality, but never the totality of cases.

CHAPTER VII.

THE NATURE OF EMOTION.

Analogy between perception and emotion—Constituent elements of emotion—Summary of the theory of James and Lange —Application of this theory to the higher emotions (religious, moral, æsthetic, intellectual)—Illegitimate confusion between the quality and intensity of emotion— Examination of a typical case: musical emotion—The most emotional of all the arts is the most dependent on physiological conditions—Proofs: its action on animals, on primitive man, on civilised man; its therapeutic action —Why certain sensations, images, and ideas awaken organic and motor states, and, consequently, emotion— They are connected either with natural or social conditions of existence—Differences and resemblances between the two cases—Antecedents of the physiological theory of emotion—Dualist position, or that of the relation between cause and effect—Unitary position; its advantages.

I.

IN entering on the subject indicated by the title of this chapter, we pass from the general manifestations of feeling (pleasures and pains) to its special manifestations; we descend from the surface to the deeper strata, in order to arrive at the fundamental and irreducible fact at the root of all emotion: attraction or repulsion, desire or aversion, in short, motion, or arrest of motion.

Already, in the Introduction, we have marked the place of emotion in the development of the life of the feelings, and, later on, in the second part of this book, we shall examine separately each of the primitive emotions, with its special determining characters. For the moment, we have only to do with the general characters common to all emotions.

This term, in the language of contemporary psychology, has replaced the words "passions," "affections of the soul" (*passiones, affectus animi*), in use during the seventeenth century. Besides being consecrated by use, it has the advantage of emphasising the motor element included in every emotion (*motus, Gemütsbewegung*). Maudsley says that this word is an induction, summing up the experience of the human race, and the term "commotion," formerly used to designate the same phenomena, expresses the fact still more clearly.

At first sight, and without entering into any analysis, every emotion, even of slight intensity, appears to us as affecting the entire individual, and expressing, in its complete form, what Bain has called the law of diffusion. Its external symptoms are movements of the face, the trunk, and the limbs; its internal, numerous organic modifications caused and dominated by the circulation—the organic function *par excellence*. The experiments of Lombard, Broca, Bert, Gley, Mosso, Tanzi, etc., have shown that any and every form of mental activity is connected with an increase in the circulation; but the latter is always above the average when an emotion is manifested. Emotional activity of a given kind, says Lombard, produces an increase of temperature in all parts of the body; it is, in general, more rapid and stronger than that which comes from intellectual activity. Mosso, who, by some well-known experiments, has been enabled to study even the slightest modifications of the circulation, concludes that "the action of the emotions on the cerebral circulation is much more evident than that of intellectual work, whatever its energy." Emotion not only presents these vague and different characteristics, but every separate emotion is a complexus. Let us take the simplest and commonest—fear, anger, tenderness, sexual love; each one of them is a complete state in itself, a psycho-physiological fascicule constituted by a grouping of simple elements, differing with each emotion, but always comprising a particular state of consciousness, particular modifications of the functions of organic life, movements or tendencies to movement, arrest or tendencies to the arrest of particular movements. Every primary emotion is an innate complexus expressing directly the constitution of the individual; the emotions are *organised* manifestations of the life of the feelings; they are the reactions of the individual on everything which touches the course of his life, or his amelioration, his being, or his better being. In a certain manner, the primary emotions are analogous to the perceptions, which require a psycho-physiological organism adapted to a special function in relation to the external world; with this difference, that sight, hearing, smell, etc., have their own special and inalienable organs, while fear, anger, etc., have a diffused organism, the elements of which, combined in another manner, become the organism of another emotion.

It follows that the study of the emotions, from the point of view of pure psychology, can come to no definite conclusion. Internal observation, however subtle, can only describe the internal fact and note its gradations; regarding the conditions and the genesis of emotion, it can give no answer; it can only seize a bodiless emotion, an abstraction. There is no manifestation of psychic life, not excepting the perceptions, which depends more immediately on biological conditions. The great merit of James and Lange is that both of them, simultaneously and independently, have demonstrated the capital importance of physiological factors in emotion.

It is not my intention to explain at length the thesis of these two authors, though it is the most important contribution made to the psychology of the emotions for some time. It is becoming very well known, and, in any case, is easily accessible.[1] Reduced to its essence, it may be summed up in two principal propositions:—

1. Emotion is only the consciousness of all the organic phenomena (external and internal) which accompany it, and are usually considered as its effects; in other words, that which common sense treats as the effect of emotion is its cause.

[1] Lange's book *On the Emotions* first appeared in Danish, and has been translated into German (1887) by Dr. Kurella, and into French (1895) by Dr. G. Dumas. W. James first explained his theory in an article in *Mind* (1884), and subsequently in his *Principles of Psychology* (1890), vol. ii. chap. xxv.

2. One emotion differs from another according to the quantity and quality of these organic states and their various combinations, being only the subjective expression of these different modes of grouping.

In order to treat a subject scientifically, says Lange, we must fix our attention on objective marks; the study of colours only became scientific on the day when Newton discovered an objective character—the difference of refrangibility in coloured rays. Let us do the same with the emotions, for we shall find it possible. Each one of them shows itself by gestures, attitudes, organic phenomena, which are often, though very erroneously, considered secondary, accessory, consecutive. Let us study them, and so substitute for introspection an objective process of research. As it is best to begin with simple things, the author has confined himself " to some of the most definite and best characterised emotions: joy, fear, sorrow, anger, timidity, expectation," and abstained from considering "those in which the physical facts were not very marked, and not easily accessible."

This is followed by a minute description of the emotions already enumerated, and their physical symptoms, for which I refer the reader to the work itself. If we generalise, we shall see that the phenomena described can be classed in two groups—(1) modifications of muscular innervation: it diminishes in fear or sorrow, but increases in joy, anger, impatience; (2) vaso-motor modifications: constriction in fear and sadness, dilatation in joy and anger. Are these two groups of equal importance?—are they both primary? or is one subordinated to the other? As far as the actual state of our knowledge permits us to answer the question, says Lange, the vascular changes must be assumed as primary, since the slightest circulatory variations profoundly modify the functions of the brain and spinal marrow.

What is the significance of all this as regards the emotions? According to the current psychology, an emotional state subjected to analysis yields the following result:—(1) an intellectual state, perception, or idea, as a starting-point (e.g., a piece of bad news, a terrifying apparition, an injury received); (2) a state of feeling—the emotion: sorrow, anger, fear; (3) the organic states and movements resulting from this emotion. But the second point—the emotion conceived as such—is only an abstract entity, a mere hypothesis. Now, to be admissible, a hypothesis ought to explain all the facts and be necessary to their explanation. This is not the case here. We find, both in normal and in pathological life, emotions which are derived from no ideas, but, on the contrary, engender them: wine gives rise to joy, alcohol to courage; ipecacuanha causes a depression akin to fear, haschisch produces exaltation, and shower-baths calm it. Asylums are full of patients whose irritability, melancholy, and anguish are "causeless"—*i.e.*, result from no perception or image. Here, we seize the true cause at its source; it lies in the physical influences. Let us therefore get rid of the useless hypothesis of a psychic entity called emotion, supposed to be intercalated between the perception or idea, and the physiological occurrences. Reversing the order admitted by common sense, we say: First an intellectual state, then organic and motor disturbances, and then the consciousness of these disturbances, which is the psychic state we call emotion.

W. James, in another way, and with other arguments, maintains the same thesis: "The bodily changes follow directly the *perception* of the exciting fact, and our feeling of the same changes as they occur *is* the emotion." Reversing what is usually accepted as common sense, we must say that it is because we weep that we are sad, because we strike that we feel anger, because we tremble that we are afraid. In fear, suppress the palpitation of the heart, the hurrying breath, the trembling of the limbs, the widening of the muscles, the peculiar state of the viscera; in anger, the heaving of the chest, the congestion of the face, the dilatation of the nostrils, the clenching of the teeth, the *staccato* voice, the impulsive tendencies; in sorrow, get rid of tears, sighs, sobs, suffocation, anguish—what will remain?—a purely intellectual state, pale, colourless, cold. A disembodied emotion is a non-existent one.

This, no doubt, is a hypothesis without decisive proof. The *crucial* experiment could only be furnished by a man affected by total anæsthesia, external and internal, but without paralysis. Could such an one still experience any emotion? The case is absolutely unrealisable; James has only been able to find three individuals at all approaching it—one of whom (Strümpell's case) is well known : the subjects are apathetic, but the emotional life is not entirely absent; Strümpell had on several occasions noted surprise, fear, and anger.[1]

We shall have to give up all hope of a positive and decisive experiment. The thesis in itself has so paradoxical a character that many objections may be raised against it.

1. Are there any real proofs that certain perceptions produce, by immediate physical influence, corporeal effects preceding the appearance of emotion? Assuredly. The reading of a poem—the recital of heroic deeds—music—may instantaneously cause a shudder of the whole body, cardiac palpitations, tears. If you scrape one piece of steel against another the whole nervous system is exasperated. Is it not well known that the mere sight of blood will cause syncope in certain persons? Finally, James alleges the pathological cases mentioned above by Lange, where "emotion is without object"—i.e., evidently dependent on a purely physical cause.

2. If the theory is true, we ought to be able to awaken the emotion itself, by voluntarily producing the manifestations of a special emotion. In the majority of cases, this criterion is inapplicable, for the majority of the organic phenomena manifesting emotion cannot be produced at will; the experiment therefore remains a partial one. However, so far as it is possible, it rather corroborates than invalidates the hypothesis. If you remain seated for a long time in a melancholy attitude, you will be overcome by sadness. If you are sad assume a cheerful attitude, join a merry company, and you will gradually leave your sadness behind. It is objected that many actors, while playing their parts, present the perfect appearance of an emotion which they do not feel. James gives the results of a remark-

---

[1] Since the publication of James's book, Dr. Berkeley has reported, in *Brain* (iv. 1892), two cases of general anæsthesia, cutaneous and sensory: the subjects are apathetic, but the presence of shame, sorrow, surprise, fear, and repulsion (the last-named as a substitute for anger) has been observed. Dr. Sollier, in an article in the *Revue Philosophique* (March, 1894), has reported some experiments made on subjects in a profoundly hypnotic state, in whom the peripheral and visceral sensibility had been abolished by suggestion. He comes to the same conclusions as James and Lange.

able census taken in America on this point; the answers do not all agree, some saying that they act with the brain, others with the heart; some feel the emotions of the character, others do not. I think that James might have mentioned what takes place with certain hypnotised subjects; if their limbs are placed in the attitude of prayer, anger, menace, or affection (which amounts to a suggestion conveyed by the muscular sense), the corresponding emotion is produced.

3. The manifestation of an emotion, instead of increasing, causes it to disappear; thus, a violent burst of tears relieves sorrow. This objection does not discriminate between the feelings *during* the manifestation and those *after* it. Emotion is always experienced while the manifestation persists; but, when the nervous centres are exhausted, calm naturally follows. Is it not said of certain men that they would feel more if they were less "demonstrative"? This is because the exuberance of their mode of expression rapidly exhausts them, and does not permit the emotion to be a lasting one, while a bilious temperament, which does not spend itself, remains like a quiescent volcano.

I have only quoted from James and Lange what was strictly necessary in order to understand their theory. I declare my acceptance of it in the main, but without admitting the dualist position which they seem to have adopted. I shall explain myself on this point in subsequent parts of this chapter; for the moment, we have to show that the physiological theory applies to the whole region of the emotions.

II.

We have seen, in fact, that Lange expressly confines himself to some simple emotions, and refuses to venture further. W. James concentrates his efforts on the "coarse emotions," the others ("the subtler emotions") he only refers to in passing, limiting himself to some remarks on æsthetic emotion. However, I think it necessary to treat this subject otherwise than by merely passing it by. Indeed, the very numerous advocates of the opposite view have maintained that the physiological theory, while it may be accepted, for want of a better, for the inferior forms of emotion, becomes insufficient as we rise to the higher, and that every attempt to apply it to the superior forms would result in failure.

We must first come to a clear understanding of the value of the terms inferior and superior, coarse and subtle; they can only denote degrees in evolution. The inferior or coarse emotions have also been called "animal," because common to man and the greater number of animals. The superior or subtle emotions are properly "human," though their germs are to be found in the higher animals.

The first are connected with sensations and perceptions, or with their immediate representations; they are in close and direct relation with the preservation of the individual or the species. The second are connected with images of a less and less concrete character, or with concepts; they are related in a more vague and indirect manner to the conditions of existence of the individual or the species.

We may also say that "inferior" is synonymous with "primary, simple"; "superior" with "derivative, complex." How is the transition from inferior to superior forms produced? For the moment, it is of no importance to know—it is sufficient to observe that it has taken place.[1]

Thus, just as, in the intellectual order, there is an ascending scale, leading from the concrete, successively, to the lower, medium, and higher forms of abstraction, so in the affective order there is a scale ascending from fear or anger to the most ideal emotions. And in the same way as the highest conception retains the characteristics of the concrete whence it sprang, on pain of being merely an empty word, so the most ethereal sentiments cannot entirely lose the characters which constitute them emotions, on pain of disappearing as such.

I shall not insist on these theoretic remarks; the direct observation of facts is preferable, and gives a clearer answer.

The superior and truly human forms of emotion are reducible to four principal groups : the religious, moral, æsthetic, and intellectual sentiments. Although the somatic characters accompanying each of these will be noted with the greatest care in the second part of this work, it will be necessary, even at present, to enumerate the principal in advance. We must more especially be on our guard against the common error which insists in seeking emotion

[1] *Vide infra*, part ii. chap. vii.

where nothing remains of it save a mere survival and shadow. If, *e.g.*, we take the most intellectualised forms of the religious or the æsthetic sentiment, we shall have much trouble in recovering the physiological conditions of its existence. There is nothing surprising in this, all we have in this case being an abstract or extract of emotion, a simple mark, an emotional scheme, an affective substitute equivalent to those intellectual substitutes which take the place of the concrete. What we must study is true emotion, felt and expressed, not inadequately recalled to memory, a pale remnant of what once was an emotion.

1. The religious sentiment is attached—perhaps more than any other—to physiological conditions, because closely connected with the instinct of self-preservation, with the saving of the soul, under whatever form the believer may conceive it. The *intensity* of the emotion alone is what concerns us; its quality is a matter for critical appreciation. We take the observable fact in the rough, whether legitimate or not. Now, does not the believer, whatever his degree of culture, whatever his religion, at the moment when he feels the emotion, tremble, turn pale, exhibit the *sacer horror*, the overwhelming awe which may end in unconsciousness, the prostrate attitude? Have not the mystics over and over again described the violent disturbances which agitate them, the internal tempest which ravages them, till, calm being re-established, they express themselves in language frequently recalling that of sexual love? The designation "hysterical," bestowed, rightly or wrongly, on many of them, is based on the physical symptoms described by themselves. And have not the methods employed to excite, revive, or strengthen religious emotion, from the wine of the ancient Bacchanals to the noisy concerts of the Salvation Army, a direct physiological influence on the organs? What of the action of the rites which are only the fixed expression of a particular form of belief? and the miracles which happen in all religions to those who have "the faith which saves"—do they not take place in the organism? We might fill many pages with the mere enumeration of the material conditions surrounding, sustaining, evoking the religious sentiment, as we find it *in fact* in contemporary life, or in history. Nothing is more chimerical than to conceive religious emotion as an unmixed

act, a psychological entity existing in and by itself, independently of its physiological concomitants. Suppress all these, and what remains?—a pure idea, cold and colourless. It is very evident that the physiological factors which show themselves so vividly in intense emotion, are attenuated by the effect of temperament, of repetition, and of custom; but in the same measure also, emotion is enfeebled and attenuated; a lofty religious *conception* and a profound religious *emotion* are two exceedingly different psychical phenomena. We shall come back to this point later on.

2. Moral emotion, also, must not be confounded with the moral idea. The abstract notion of justice, duty, categoric imperative, acts on some, and is without influence on others. Moral emotion, not factitious and conventional, but really felt and experienced, is a shock and an impulse that carries one away; it always shows itself by internal and external movements; it acts like an instinct. Sympathy, which places us in unison with others, making us feel their happiness and misery, is (as we shall see later) a property of animal life which imperatively requires physiological conditions, and cannot exist without them; now the part played by sympathy in the genesis of the moral emotions is quite clear. Is not the man who runs to arrest a thief or a murderer, being merely a witness, and not himself robbed or assaulted, subjected to a disturbance which is really physiological? In explosions of maternal love, in acts of sudden self-devotion, is there not a *raptus* which shakes the whole individual from head to foot? If these facts, among so many others, are not sufficient, let us consider what takes place in masses of people under strong excitement, in certain cases of the psychology of crowds. "If into the term morality we import the momentary appearance of certain qualities, such as abnegation, devotion, disinterestedness, self-sacrifice, the sense of justice, we may say that crowds are sometimes accessible to a very lofty morality . . . a much loftier one, indeed, than that of which the isolated individual is capable. Only collectively is humanity capable of great acts of disinterestedness and devotion."[1] But in this state of enormously magnified moral emotion, is it conceivable that the physiological factors are negligible?

[1] G. Le Bon, *Psychologie des foules*, pp. 46 *et seq.*

Are they not the natural and necessary vehicles of moral contagion ?

3. I shall be very brief in treating of intellectual emotion, since it is rare, and usually temperate in character; however, when it springs up with the true characteristics of intense emotion, it does not deviate from the rule.   Most human beings are not passionately eager for the search after or the discovery of pure truth, any more than they are afflicted by privation of it; but those possessed by this demon are given up to him, body and soul.   Their emotion is no more independent of physiological conditions than any other. The biographies of learned men furnish us with innumerable examples : the perpetual physical sufferings of Pascal, Malebranche nearly suffocated by the palpitations of his heart when reading Descartes, Humphrey Davy dancing in his laboratory after having made the discovery of potassium, Hamilton suddenly feeling something "like the closing of a galvanic circuit" at the moment of discovering the method of quaternions, etc.   There is no need to extend our search so far; everyday life provides us moment by moment with examples which, though prosaic, are none the less valuable as proofs.   The instinct of curiosity is at the root of all intellectual emotion, whether lofty or commonplace.   Does not the man who perpetually watches his neighbour's conduct and the thousand petty details of his life, feel when his puerile curiosity is baffled, all the physical anguish of unsatisfied desire ?

4. If we are to believe certain over-subtle critics, æsthetic emotion would have the privilege of moving in the region of pure contemplation.   This assertion is founded on the error pointed out above, which consists in taking into account only the *quality* of the emotion, not its intensity. They put a critical emotion, purified, sublimated, stripped as far as possible of its somatic resonance, in the place of the true, primitive emotion, whence all the others have issued, and which they, like the rest of men, have begun by experiencing ; for even the most refined cannot begin at the end.   It is an abstract mode of feeling substituted for the concrete.   W. James makes, on this point, some excellent remarks, to which we refer the reader (*op. cit.*, pp. 428 *et seq.*).   Complete æsthetic emotion, without regard to its quality, does not always require advanced culture.

The savage who, along with his companions, excites himself over his dance and song, becomes intoxicated with sound and motion; the naïve spectator quite carried away by the interest of a crude melodrama; the Spanish peasant, contemplating his church crammed with *rococo* ornaments and strangely-dressed saints : all these experience the concrete emotion which shakes the frame, makes the heart beat, produces tears, laughter, or gestures.

Besides, it is enough to recall the researches inaugurated by Fechner in his *Vorschule der Æsthetik*, and since continued, especially in Germany, under the name of elementary æsthetics,[1] which so greatly emphasise the part played by the sensory element in the genesis of æsthetic pleasure and pain. We may thus briefly summarise them : There are two constituent factors in the æsthetic sentiment—one direct, connected with sensations and perceptions; the other indirect, connected with representations (images and associations of ideas). One or the other predominates, according to the particular art : the direct factor in music and the plastic arts, the indirect in poetry. The direct factor, by its very definition, depends on the organism. The colours are not simple sensations, they have an affective tone proper to themselves. According to Wundt, white suggests gaiety; green, a quiet joy; while red corresponds to energy, strength, etc. We may or may not admit these correspondences; Scripture gives others, and they probably vary from one individual to another; but the principle is unassailable. Féré's previously quoted experiments, on exciting and depressing colours, tend in the same direction. It is the same with sounds :—according as they are high, deep, or medium, they induce a special mood. If from simple sensation we pass to perceptions, direct physical action is not doubtful; we find it in the arrangement of colours, in the phenomena of contrasts, in the outlines and forms of certain lines, in the innate pleasure of symmetry and regularity, in rhythm, measure, cadence, in the perception of harmony and dissonance, etc. In truth, the authors cited, have insisted rather on the sensory action than on the

---

[1] Wundt, *Physiologische Psychologie*, 4th (German) ed., chap. xx.; Külpe, *Grundriss der Psychologie*, p. 250 (English edition), § 38; Sully, *Sensation and Intuition*, Part II.; Grant Allen, *Mind*, July 1879 ("The Origin of the Sense of Symmetry").

organic and motor modifications accompanying it. But it always remains indisputable that the æsthetic sentiment is necessarily connected with physiological conditions.

Since we are maintaining the proposition that the intensity of even the superior emotions is in direct ratio to the quantity of the physiological occurrences accompanying them, I propose in the following paragraphs to examine a single one separately, and in some detail.

Which is the most emotional of all arts? Music. There is no possible doubt as to the answer—eliminating, of course, those persons on whom it has no effect, and who must be rejected for the purposes of this argument. No art has a deeper power of penetration, no other can render shades of feeling so delicate as to escape every other medium of expression. So much is unanimously admitted.

Is the most emotional art also—as required by our thesis—the most dependent on physiological conditions? Yes, and if we wish to demonstrate this, facts are so numerous that the only difficulty is to choose between them. Let us leave aside every intellectual element, all representations, either vague or distinct, evoked by music; let us, further, avoid all metaphysical dissertations on its nature and its revelation of the Infinite, or its origin in the human species, in order to confine ourselves to its physical and affective aspect, and to grasp the connection.

In the first place, we shall find that music has an effect on many animals. Although on this point many nursery tales and marvellous anecdotes have been handed down from antiquity, yet—having made deduction of all apocryphal stories—we find a large number of observations and experiments which must be considered accurate. They are to be found in the writings of various musicians or historians of music (Grétry, Fétis, etc.). Dogs, cats, horses, lizards, serpents, spiders, not to mention many birds, are the examples most frequently quoted. Experiments made at the Jardin des Plantes, Paris, particularly on the elephants, at the beginning of this century, have been many times referred to, and are both varied and conclusive.[1] Are we to conclude from them that these animals are melomaniacs? Some authors appear to have no doubt on this point, having a natural inclination to neglect the physical side of the

[1] They will be found in Beauquier, *Philosophie de la musique*, p. 65.

nomenon, and to interpret it in a quasi-human sense. is much more probable that the sensations of sound and movement (animals being very sensitive to rhythm) act directly on the organism, and indirectly on the vital functions, and produce a physical state of pleasure or pain; perhaps in the highest, such as the elephant, a certain affective state approximating to emotion. In short, music acts like a burn, like heat, cold, or a caressing contact. I have on this point consulted writers of recognised competence in musical psychology. M. Dauriac writes to me : " Relative consonances and dissonances, composed of major or minor thirds, produce pleasurable or painful effects on the organism, independently of any impression or æsthetic judgment." M. Stumpf has been kind enough to reply by a long letter, amply furnished with quotations from original authorities, whence he concludes that "der Grund hiervon dürfte ein rein physiologischer sein."

Let us turn to primitive man. The question becomes less simple; but the physical element still preponderates. Music consists only of rhythm, marked by clumsy and noisy instruments, whose principal effect is to increase the vibration of the nervous system. The aborigines of America are able, during four consecutive hours, to intoxicate themselves with rhythmic sounds having no melodic significance. Among certain tribes, diviners and sorcerers employ the drum in order to produce in themselves a sort of ecstasy;[1] it is a true intoxication through sound, and especially through motion—i.e., an affective state excited directly by external and internal sensations. We have here before us the genesis of emotion.

Civilised man, exceptions apart, is sensitive to music in different degrees, from the peasant or artisan, who, like the savage, prefers tunes with a well-marked rhythm, to the most cultivated amateur. But for all states the primary effect is a physical one. "Musical vibration is only one particular mode of perceiving that universal vibration— that music of life which animates all beings and all bodies, from the lowest to the highest. From this point of view, musical art may be called the art of sensibility *par excellence*, since it regulates the great phenomenon of vibration,

[1] For details on this point, Wallaschek's interesting work on *Primitive Music* should be consulted.

into which all external perceptions resolve themselves, and transfers it from the region of the unconscious, in which it was hidden, to that of consciousness."[1] Music acts on the muscular system, on the circulation, the respiration, and the parts dependent on them. Intense sounds (the big drum, kettledrum, etc.) give the whole body a shock, over-acute sounds cause muscular contractions. I know a musician who is thrown into convulsions by too marked a discord. Let us add to these the well-known effects of horripilation, of thrills passing down the back or over the scalp, of sudden sweats, of tickling, of epigastric constriction. Grétry had already noted that the pulse is sensitive to rhythm; and he has recorded several observations made on himself, showing that the pulsations are accelerated or retarded according to the rhythm of a chant heard internally. It would be an interminable task to enumerate the purely physical effects of the musical impression. The conclusion to be drawn is, that while certain arts at once awaken ideas which give a determination to the feelings, this of music acts inversely. It creates dispositions depending on the organic state and on nervous activity, which we translate by the vague terms—joy, sadness, tenderness, serenity, tranquillity, uneasiness. On this canvas the intellect embroiders its designs at pleasure, varying according to individual peculiarities.

We might go further, and pass from the general to the particular. If music, by its effect on the organism, creates dispositions, momentary affective situations, the differences in voice, instrument, *timbre*, must produce different and special dispositions, which is indisputable. The tonality of a piece must act in the same way, which is also admitted by many composers. It is true that they are not agreed on the definition and the significance of every tone, and that many amusing discrepancies might be selected from their writings. (So the key of E flat minor, which, for Gevaert, is powerful and majestic, indicates, according to Grétry, an imminent catastrophe.) Here, more than elsewhere, over-precise definition is injurious.

Let me add a remark on the therapeutic action of music. We have abundant evidence that this was known in the most ancient times. From the Greek physicians to Leuret,

[1] Beauquier, *op. cit.*, p. 56.

who employed it in his moral treatment of insanity, a long series of cures have been attributed to it. A well-known Russian physiologist, Tarchanoff, has recently lauded and recommended its rational employment in disorders of the nervous system; but it does not act through occult, mysterious, spiritual influences; it acts physically, as a kind of vibratory medicine. The reseaches of Boudet de Paris, Mortimer Granville, Buccola, Morselli, Vigouroux, furnish proofs of this.

Although we might say much more on this subject, the above will be sufficient to show that the most emotional of the arts is also that most intimately dependent on the modifications of the organism. This has seemed to me an argument not to be neglected in favour of the physiological theory of emotion.[1]

III.

We have just shown that the so-called higher forms of emotion do not escape from the necessity of physiological conditions; but there is yet another question, still in obscurity and suspense, which, by reason of its importance, ought to be elucidated. It is this: Why have certain internal or external states, certain images, certain ideas, the privilege of exciting certain organic and motor states, and, in consequence, emotion? How is this connection, this *nexus*, established? for experience teaches us that it is not necessary: in the same individual the same perception or idea may awaken an emotion, whereas in another case it may produce nothing. In other words, there are perceptions, images, and concepts which remain purely intellectual states without affective accompaniment, at least with none accessible to consciousness. There are others which are immediately enveloped and, as it were, sub-

---

[1] Gurney, in a criticism of James's hypothesis (*Mind*, ix. 425), says: "There is plenty of music from which I have received as much emotion in silent representation" [*i.e.*, by purely internal audition, or merely reading the notes] "as when presented by the finest orchestra; but it is with the latter condition that I almost exclusively associate the cutaneous tingling and hair-stirring." Professor James has, in my opinion, answered this objection (*Psychology*, ii. pp. 469, 470), which I should be inclined to refer to the problem of the "revivability of impressions," to be examined later on.

merged in the emotion which they produce. Let us note that the question comes before us, whatever opinion we may adopt as to the genesis of emotion. As usually accepted, the order is this : intellectual state, affective state, organic states. According to the physiological hypothesis, the order is as follows : intellectual state, organic states, affective state. Passing from one thesis to the other, the problem is subject to but one variation : Why is a certain intellectual state sometimes coupled with an intellectual state, and sometimes not? This is on the first hypothesis. Why is a certain intellectual state sometimes accompanied by organic and motor modifications, sometimes not? This is on the second hypothesis.

The answer is the same in both cases : the intellectual state is accompanied by an affective state whenever there is a direct relation with the conditions of existence, natural or social, of the individual. In order to justify this proposition we must examine in succession these two forms of the conditions of existence.

1st Period.—*Sensations or images connected with the natural conditions of existence.*

We have here to do with a question of genesis; we must therefore begin with the humblest phenomena. The primordial sense, the only one in certain animals, is touch combined with internal sensations. Let us remark that, in its origin, the "knowledge" which we take in its lowest degree has only a *practical* value; sensation is a monitor, an aid, an instrument, a weapon with only one aim— the preservation of the individual,—and completely subordinated to that end ; otherwise, it is nothing but a useless manifestation, a luxury. The *nexus* between the sensations and the organic and motor reactions is therefore innate—*i.e.,* it results from the very constitution of the animal. If it fails, the conditions of existence are at fault. The primordial tissue, says Spencer, must be differently affected, according as it is in contact with nutritive matter (ordinarily soluble) or with innutritive matter (ordinarily insoluble). The contraction by which the tactual surface of a rhizopod absorbs a fragment of assimilable matter is caused by a commencing absorption of this matter, *i.e.,* contact and absorption are the same thing. The action of certain agents is followed by a retractile movement, or, on the contrary, by movements of a character to assure the continuance of the impression. These two kinds of movement are, in this writer's view, respectively the phenomena and the signs of pleasure and pain. The tissue, therefore, acts in such a manner as to assure pleasure and avoid pain, by a law as physical and natural as that by which a magnet turns towards the pole, or a tree to the light. Without inquiring whether pleasure and pain exist in this case—a purely hypothetical assumption—there are, at least, objective phenomena denoting a *nexus* of utility between the sensation and the expansive or retractile movements.

Passing from these inferior organisms to those provided with several senses, we find no change. Each order of sensation acts in the same way. The animal is better informed, and consequently better protected and armed—that is all. Finally, when certain images (*i.e.*, recollections of pleasures and pains experienced) excite an emotional state, the mechanism remains the same, and tends towards the same end. It is therefore not without reason that we have above assimilated every form of primary emotion to a psycho-physiological organism adapted to a particular end.

It is needless to review the primary emotions and to show that the sensation, the perception, or the image only produces organic or motor troubles when the preservation of the individual or the species is at stake. The intellectual state (sensation, perception, or image) can instinctively— *i.e.*, through an innate mechanism—produce immobility, oppression, withdrawing into one's self, flight (fear) ; or, on the contrary, aggressive movements, attack (anger), or movements of attraction, accompanied by phenomena peculiar to each species (sexual love).

To sum up, every event of this kind, reduced to its simplest expression, consists in (1) an intellectual fact, analogous to a spring moving the whole machine, (2) an unconscious, half-conscious, or conscious reaction of the instinct of self-preservation ; this being by no means an entity, as we have already said, but the organism itself under its dynamic aspect.

2nd Period.—*Perceptions, images, or ideas connected with social conditions of existence.*

Up to the present, we have only considered emotional reaction in its relations with nature—*i.e.*, with the physical environment. Its domain is much more extensive ; in man, and in many animals, it is adapted to the social environment. At bottom, the mechanism remains the same. A perception, an image, or an idea excites an emotion, because related, directly or indirectly (in the latter case the relation is conceived, inductively or deductively), to the social conditions of the individual. The natural *ego* has its needs and tendencies ; the same is true of the social *ego*, grafted on the other, or rather, one with it ; consequently, the mechanism comes very frequently into play ; the circumference is extended, but the centre remains the same.

Let us note the differences between the two periods. In the latter we have (1) a preponderance of representations and concepts—*i.e.*, the superior forms of knowledge ; (2) instead of a natural, innate association between certain perceptions and certain emotional reactions—associations which may be called anatomical, because fixed in the individual organism—there are secondary, acquired associations, less solidly fixed, sometimes entirely artificial, which result from experience, from education, from habit, from imitation. I give some examples, by way of elucidation, and in order to avoid repetition.

The feeling of property is derived from a natural condition of existence—nutrition. It is first manifested—in the form of a prevision—in some animals who store up a reserve of food for the future. In primitive man this instinct extends to clothes, weapons, the cave or hut which he inhabits ; later on, with the nomadic life, to herds and flocks ; then to agricultural products, silver, gold, paper money ; finally to that impalpable thing called credit, which has merely an imaginary existence. Thus it gradually takes on a social character. The knowledge of any loss or any gain, actual or possible, produces an emotion in the individual, because it shows him that his adaptation to social conditions is diminished or augmented.

The sentiment of "self-feeling" is innate, primary. Let us imagine ourselves in a society where the questions of rank, precedence, etiquette, are of capital importance—in an aristocratic monarchy like that of Louis XIV.—and we shall see what a ferment of emotions may be raised by an occurrence which, to our eyes, seems futile and irrelevant. If we read Saint-Simon's *Mémoires*, we see him boiling over with indignation when a courtier is unduly accorded the privileges of a duke and peer, and his wife is granted a stool in the Queen's presence. He spends his time in incessant visits, forms coalitions, does all in his power to move the ministers or the Parliament, and finally exults in his victory. However factitious and puerile this agitation may seem, it results from the same physiological mechanism as the simplest emotions: from the instinct of personal preservation—not of his natural *ego*, but of his *ego qua* courtier of the Grand Monarque. If he fails, he is injured, depreciated, lessened in his conditions of social existence.

The case already cited, of Malebranche, to whom Descartes' *Traité de l'homme* "caused such violent palpitations of the heart that he was obliged continually to leave his book in order to breathe," called forth Fontenelle's remark that "Truth, which is invisible and of no practical utility, is not wont to find so much sensibility among men." No doubt; but to the true man of science the pursuit of truth is one of the necessary conditions of existence. For others it is a mere luxury, to the loss of which they are quite indifferent.

I think we have thus replied to the question previously put—why certain sensations, images, ideas, have the privilege of producing organic and motor changes which, translated into the language of consciousness, constitute the emotional state—and justified our answer. The sensation, the image, the idea, are only occasional causes, incapable by themselves of producing any emotion: it springs from the inmost personality of the individual—from his *organisation*—expresses it directly, and participates in its stability and its instability.

IV.

The hypothesis of James and Lange—considered, at first, as a paradox—has suggested so many remarks, criticisms, objections, answers, and arguments for and against, that I find it impossible to give a summary of them.[1] Yet it is not without precedent. Lange, in his *Addenda*, mentions as his precursors, Malebranche, Spinoza, and some other less celebrated authors. The legitimate claims of Descartes, in his treatise *Sur les Passions de l'Âme*, have also since been vindicated.[2] The physiologists, too, ought not to be forgotten: Maudsley indicated the same view, without insisting on it.[3] The superiority of James and Lange consists in having put it clearly and endeavoured to support it by experimental proofs. I have already said that it seems to me the most probable explanation for those who do not represent the emotions to themselves as psychological entities. The only point in which I differ from these authors relates to their way of putting the proposition, not to its substance.

It is evident that our two authors, whether consciously or not, share the dualist point of view with the common opinion which they are combating; the only difference being in the interversion of cause and effect. Emotion is a

---

[1] I may indicate, somewhat at random, the principal documents for this controversy: Wundt, *Philosophische Studien*, vi. 3, p. 349 (he criticises Lange only); Gurney, *Mind*, July 1884; Marshall, *ib.*, October 1884; Stanley, *ib.*, January 1886; Worcester, *Monist*, January 1893; *Psychological Review*, September and November 1894, January 1895, etc.

[2] "Though written in the earliest days of modern science, this work will bear comparison with anything that has been produced in recent years. It will be difficult, indeed, to find any treatment of the emotions much superior to it in originality, thoroughness, and suggestiveness. The position maintained is similar to that now held by Professor James, but Descartes does not content himself with defending in a general way the assertion that emotion is caused by physical change. After coming to the conclusion that there are six passions from which all the others are derived, he attempts to show that a special set of organic effects is concerned in the production of each of these primary states."—D. Irons in *Philosophical Review*, May 1895, p. 291.

[3] "When any great passion causes all the physical and moral troubles which it will cause, what I conceive to happen is that a physical impression made on the sense of sight or of hearing is propagated along a physical path to the brain, and arouses a physical commotion in its molecules; that from this centre of commotion the liberated energy is propagated by physical paths to other parts of the brain; and that it is finally discharged outwardly through proper physical paths, either in movements or in modifications of secretion and nutrition. The passion that is felt is the subjective side of the cerebral commotion—its *motion* out from the physical basis, as it were (*e-motion*), into consciousness."—*Pathology of Mind*, 1879, p. 222.

cause of which the physical manifestations are the effect, says one party; the physical manifestations are the cause of which emotion is the effect, says the other. In my view, there would be a great advantage in eliminating from the question every notion of cause and effect, every relation of causality, and in substituting for the dualistic position a unitary or monistic one. The Aristotelian formula of matter and form seems to me to meet the case better, if we understand by "matter" the corporeal facts, and by "form" the corresponding psychical state: the two terms, by-the-bye, only existing in connection with each other and being inseparable except as abstract conceptions. It was traditional in ancient psychology to study the relations of "the soul and the body"—the new psychology does not speak of them. In fact, if the question takes a metaphysical form, it is no longer psychology; if it takes an experimental form, there is no reason to treat it separately, because it is treated in connection with everything. No state of consciousness can be dissociated from its physical conditions: they constitute a natural whole, which must be studied as such. Every kind of emotion ought to be considered in this way: all that is objectively expressed by movements of the face and body, by vaso-motor, respiratory, and secretory disturbances, is expressed subjectively by correlative states of consciousness, classed by external observation according to their qualities. It is a single occurrence expressed in two languages. We have previously assimilated the emotions to psycho-physiological organisms; this unitary point of view, being more conformable to the nature of things and to the present tendencies of psychology, seems to me, in practice, to eliminate many objections and difficulties.

Whether we adopt this theory or not, we have in any case acquired the certainty that the organic and motor manifestations are not accessories, that the study of them is part of the study of emotion. We shall therefore have to speak of them in some detail.

CHAPTER VIII.

THE INTERNAL CONDITIONS OF EMOTION.

Confused state of this question—Popular versus Medical Psychology—Part played by the brain, the centre of psychic life—Hypotheses on the "seat" of the emotions—Part played by the heart, the centre of vegetative life—Popular metaphors and their physiological interpretation—Are the internal sensations reducible to a single process?—Part played by chemical action in the genesis of emotion—Cases of the introduction of toxic substances—Auto-intoxication—Modifications in the course of mental maladies.

As the physiological substratum of emotion, or its material (the reader may use which expression he prefers), comprises the organic or internal functions, and the motor functions showing themselves outwardly, we shall follow this division. Although it may seem artificial, it is not altogether so ; the internal manifestations are, for the most part, outside the action of the will; the external manifestations are, in many cases, subject to that action. In any case, this somewhat arbitrary distinction is desirable for the sake of clearness in exposition.

I.

The relation of different emotions to the internal functions is a subject yet in its infancy. Our knowledge of it is still in a vague and confused state. It is at the same point where the problem of the expression of the emotions was before Charles Bell and Darwin; *i.e.*, we have before us a purely empiric set of observed facts without sug-

8

gested explanation. No doubt it is well known that vaso-motor and respiratory disturbances vary according to the emotions, but the reasons for the differences between one case and another are often unknown and even unexplored. Although Lange has done much in this direction, we cannot congratulate ourselves on having a complete presentation of all the organic and functional manifestations which accompany the simple emotions, not to speak of the complex forms. Still less do we know, clearly and positively, why these and not other manifestations are produced. Thus Hack Tuke asserts it to be a matter of common observation that while the blush of shame begins in the cheeks and the ears, that of anger begins with the eyes, and that of love with the forehead. Supposing this fact to be firmly established, we should still have to find out why, in each case, that particular vascular region should be affected by preference. In short, the study of the external conditions of emotion remains at the present time fragmentary and descriptive.

The part played by the viscera in the emotions and passions is so evident that in all ages it has arrested the attention of mankind. On this point, for a period of several centuries, we find, on the one hand, a popular psychology, — which in all languages has become fixed in the form of metaphors, — full of errors and prejudices, but also of very sound observations; on the other hand, scientific attempts at explanation, varying with the physiology of the period, and expressed in terms of the current medical doctrine. During this long period we can distinguish two principal directions of thought: one tending to localise the passions exclusively in the viscera, especially the heart, the other to place them in the brain. Without distorting facts, we might find in these two tendencies the incomplete and unconscious form of the two reigning theories in affective psychology, the organic and the intellectualist.

It would be of no interest to retrace this long history, to remind the reader that Plato placed courage in the breast and the sensual appetites in the abdomen, that the School of Salerno attributed anger to the gall, joy to the spleen, love to the liver. The organic or visceral theory long had an overwhelming preponderance, and Bichat, at the beginning of the century (1800), did not hesitate to write, "The brain is not affected by the passions which have for their *exclusive* seat the organs of internal life—the liver, lungs, heart, spleen, etc." From the seventeenth century downwards, the cerebral theory becomes more accentuated; with Gall and Charles Bell the heart is quite dispossessed, and, by way of reaction, the part played by the viscera was almost forgotten.

At the present day no one maintains that the heart or any other organ is the seat of an emotion in the sense of feeling it; the consciousness of the affective life only exists through the brain, in which the internal sensations coming from the viscera are represented as external sensations; it is an echo. The brain, says Hunter, knows perfectly well that the body has a liver and a stomach, or, as Carus expressed it, each organ has its *psychische Signatur*. The ideal would be to determine, by means of a complete and well-conducted elementary analysis, the part contributed by each internal organ and function to the constitution of a particular emotion. Nothing of this sort can be attempted: there exist, on this point, only scattered materials and con- jectures supported chiefly by the phenomena of morbid states. We shall return to this later on. (See Part II.) Let us at this moment confine our attention to the two predominant organs—the brain, the centre of psychic life ; the heart, the centre of vegetative life.

1. The brain is not merely the echo of internal sensa- tions; it receives and reacts according to its disposition; it centralises, but while taking its own part in the concert; it puts its mark on the impressions it receives. Already (Chap. I., § 1) we have seen the theories propounded as to the "seat" or "centre" of pain or pleasure: bulb, protuberance, temporal lobe, occipital lobe, etc. Natur- ally, each author has extended his hypothesis to the emotions properly so called. However, the search for "emotional centres" appears still more chimerical. A particular emotion has no determinate centre, is not local- ised in a restricted area of the encephalon. Not only does neither observation nor experience indicate anything of the sort, but if we consider the complexity of any emotion whatever, we shall understand that it requires the activity of several cerebral and infra-cerebral centres: (1) the sensory

centres of sight, hearing, smell, etc.; (2) the centres scattered through the motor zone and regulating the movements of different parts of the body; (3) and lastly, the centres corresponding to the phenomena of organic life. These constitute several stages: in the spinal cord, the respiratory centre, that which accelerates the movements of the heart, the genito-spinal, the vesico-spinal (it is well known that the bladder is as good an æsthesiometer as the iris), etc.; in the bulb, the respiratory and vaso-motor centres, and those of cardiac and thermic inhibition. As regards the cortical layer, there are many open questions as to the position of the vascular, thermic, trophic, glandular centres, of the organic movements which determine the contraction of the intestines, the bladder, the spleen, etc. This very incomplete and confused enumeration is sufficient for our purpose—viz., to show that we must speak, not of a centre, but of the synergic action of several centres, differently grouped according to the cases.[1]

It is well known that the vaso-motor nerves of the head, the upper limbs, the lower limbs, the viscera, are furnished in part by the nerve-reticulations of the sympathetic system, in part by the rachidian nerves issuing from different parts of the spinal cord. Now, an experiment of Claude Bernard's, made as far back as 1852, shows that the section of the great sympathetic in the neck produces on the same side an expansion of the vessels, and an increase in the temperature, nutrition, muscular tonicity, and sensibility. On the contrary, galvanism applied to the same nerve produces constriction of the vessels and the contrary phenomena to the preceding. Féré points out that the manifestations of the first case are, in general, those of the sthenic emotions, as those of the second are of the asthenic emotions.[2]

---

[1] In his lectures on Hysteria (Vol. i., Lecture 21), Pitres incidentally inquires into the existence of encephalic centres of the affective states, and concludes that "the molecular changes corresponding to the activity of the cellular elements shaken by the passions, radiate in every direction, stimulate or depress the excitability of adjacent elements, rebound on the motor and sensitive centres, and on the originatory nuclei of the visceral nerves, and finally determine the state of emotion, i.e., the psycho-physiological state which is the special expression of the reaction of the nervous centres to psychic excitations."

[2] Op. cit., pp. 490, 491.

Whatever we may think of this comparison, the incontest-able and so often recorded characteristic of emotion—diffusion—shows us that it is everywhere· that, if we could see with our eyes the cerebral mechanism supporting it, we should be spectators of the co-ordinated work of the multiple centres; that, consequently, the hypothesis of a localisation, of a seat in the limited sense, is in no way justified.

2. It is needless to remind the reader that the majority of idioms make the heart the incarnation of affective life, and that the antithesis of reason and passion is, in current speech, that of the brain and the heart. This opinion is not entirely a prejudice, as contemporary physiologists have shown.

Why is the heart, an unconscious muscle, promoted to the position of an essential and central organ of the emotions and the passions? It is so in accordance with the well-known physiological law which makes us transfer our psychic states to the peripheral organ which communicates them to our consciousness. It feels the rebound of all the impulses which strike us; it reflects the most fugitive impressions; in the order of the sentiments, no manifestation takes place outside it, nothing escapes it; it vibrates incessantly, though in different manners.

Claude Bernard, and after him, Cyon, have undertaken to justify the popular expressions regarding the heart, to show that they are not mere metaphors, but the result of accurate observation, and that they can be translated into physio-logical language. I here summarise their principal remarks. The heart, the centre of organic life, and the brain, the centre of animal life, the two culminating organs of the living machine, are in an incessant relation of action and reaction which shows itself in two principal states,—syn-cope and emotion; the first due to the momentary cessation of the cerebral functions through intermission in the arrival of the arterial blood; the second due to the transmission to the heart of a circulatory modification. There is always an initial impression which slightly arrests this organ (accord-to Claude Bernard), whence a passing paleness, then a reaction which the heart, by reason of its extreme sensi-bility, is the first to feel; for, as the brain is the most delicate of the organs of the animal life, the heart is the most sensitive of the vegetative vital organs.

When it is said that the heart is *broken* by grief, this expression corresponds to actual phenomena. The heart has been arrested by a sudden impression, whence, sometimes, syncope and nervous attacks. The heart's being "big," answers to a prolongation of the diastole, which causes a feeling of fulness and oppression in the præcordial region. The "palpitation" of the heart is not merely a poetic formula, but a physiological reality; the beats being rapid and without intensity. The facility with which the heart is emptied, the regularity of the circulation being kept up by slight pressure, corresponds to the "light" heart. Two hearts beat "in unison," under the influence of the same impressions. In the "cold heart" the beats are slow and quiet, as if under the influence of cold; in the "warm" heart, the contrary is the case. When we tell a person that we love him "with all our heart," this expression signifies, physiologically speaking, that his presence, or the recollection of him, awakens in us a nervous impression, which, transmitted to the heart by the pneumogastric nerve, causes in our heart a reaction of such a kind as to produce in the brain a sentiment or an emotion. In man, the brain, in order to express its feelings, is obliged to take the heart into its service.[1]

Let us further recall the well-known observations of Mosso, who was able directly to study the circulation of the blood in the brain in three patients, in whom the cranium had been destroyed by various accidents. He ascertained that the mere fact of looking attentively at one of his patients, the entrance of a stranger, or any other occurrence of slight importance, immediately quickened the cerebral pulse. In one, a woman, the height of the pulsations suddenly increased, without apparent cause; she had just perceived in the room a death's-head, which somewhat frightened her. The same thing took place with another patient when he heard the clock strike twelve; this was because he did not feel able to say his noon prayers. I do

[1] For further details see Claude Bernard, *La science expérimentale*, *Étude sur la physiologie du cœur*, 1865, and Cyon's Address to the Academy of St. Petersburg, "The Heart and the Brain," translated in the *Revue Scientifique*, November 22nd, 1873. Also, Mosso, *Sulla circolazione del sangue nel cervello* (1880), and *La Paura* (*Fear*, English translation, 1896).

not dwell on his researches by means of the plethysmograph, which have special relation to intellectual work.

It will therefore be understood how popular opinion has come to look upon the heart as the seat, or the generator, of emotions. This is the instinctive expression of a quite correct view : the supreme importance to the affective life of the visceral action summed up in a fundamental organ.

II.

Since, for the moment, we are eliminating movements in order to confine our attention to the *internal* conditions of emotion, it is easy to see that these conditions reduce themselves to that which we designate by the name of internal, organic, vital sensations. This is not the place to enumerate the modifications of each in the case of each special emotion (for which the reader is referred to Part II.) ; the question, taken for the present in its generality, is put thus : Are the internal sensations reducible to a single and fundamental process ? If the answer is in the affirmative, the internal conditions of emotion would find themselves simultaneously determined under their most general form. We can, at any rate, try.

The first difficulty consists in our not having a complete enumeration, on which all authors are agreed, of the internal sensations, as we have in the case of the special sensations. Beaunis gives a very detailed classification in eight groups ; Kröner adopts a somewhat different one ; both include pleasure, pain, and the emotions. Let us eliminate this last group (the affective manifestations) and confine ourselves to the vital sensations properly so called, connected with purely physiological needs, with the organs and functions indispensable to life : the different sensations of the alimentary canal (hunger, thirst, *malaise*, nausea, etc.) ; those of the respiratory apparatus (the need of fresh air, dyspnœa, asphyxia), of the circulatory apparatus, of the excretions and secretions ; of the sexual organs in the normal state or in transitory phases (puberty, menstruation, pregnancy, menopause) ; the need of muscular movement, of rest, of sleep ; the sensation of fatigue ;—we have nearly all, if not all, the elements of cœnæsthesia, *i.e.*, the consciousness of the body as living and acting.

Have these multiplied sensations a common cause ? Are

they different modes of one and the same process? Do
they imply, at their origin, the same stimulus, the same
kind of excitement, as all the varieties of visual sensations
suppose luminous vibrations, and the varieties of auditive
sensations, sonorous vibrations? Kröner maintains that,
for all internal sensations, the initial excitation is of a
chemical nature. "Every organic sensation is based on a
chemical process, and arises according to the laws of
diffusion and osmosis."[1] The author justifies his assertion
by the enumeration of a large number of facts, for which I
refer the reader to his book. Chemical action, according
to him, either takes place under the gaseous form (a person
passes from the open air into a room full of deleterious
miasma) or under the liquid (alcohol, toxic substances in
solution in the fluids of the organism and introduced into
the circulatory current).

It is not very certain, *pace* Kröner, that *all* internal
sensations are caused by chemical action, under one or
other of the forms we have mentioned, and that their vague
localisation is due to this cause alone, and not, as generally
admitted, by their arising in organs incapable of movement.
Thus tickling, giddiness, the muscular sensations (which
Kröner and Beaunis include in this group) appear to
depend on mechanical excitations rather than on chemical
causes.   At any rate, one cannot deny that the internal
fundamental sensations—connected with nutrition and its
immediate conditions, with fatigue and sleep, both of which
result from a poisoning of the muscles and the nervous
centres, with sexual life—are due to chemically caused
excitations.   This granted, we may go one step further
in the track of James and Lange, and say that the emotions
depend not only on physiological conditions, but still more
intimately on the chemical action going on in the tissues
and fluids of the organism.

In support of this extreme condition of the genesis of the
emotions, we can only offer some fragmentary remarks,
which, however, show how closely they depend on the
variations of the intra-organic environment.

1. We have, in the first place, the group of exciting,
tonic, depressing, toxic substances : wine and the various
alcoholic beverages, haschisch, opium, coca, the aphro-

[1] Kröner, *Das körperliche Gefühl* (Breslau, 1887), pp. 102-112.

disiacs, etc. Although they are artificial products, introduced from without, not engendered in and by the organism, we know how far they modify the interior environment, and consequently the temper, character, intensity, and direction of the passions.

2. But there are also the substances which the living body compounds or modifies for itself. It has been said that the organism is the receptacle and laboratory of poisons; in the state of emotion, the only one with which we are concerned at present, the function of this chemical process is manifested at every instant. We are always speaking of the weakening or the increase of the circulation of the blood; yet the emotional dispositions or modifications are connected, not only with variations of quantity, but also with those of *quality* in the blood (anæmia, aglobulia, malarial poisoning, etc.). The popular expression regarding the emotions which "curdle the blood" is not so ridiculous as it might seem. Anger, fear, fatigue are often accompanied by changes in the intimate constitution of the sanguinary fluid. We may incidentally note the ascertained relations between certain cardiac affections and affective dispositions: in aortic affections, anæmia, excitement, irritability; in cases of mitral insufficiency, congestion, and a taciturn and melancholy humour. We shall elsewhere have occasion to enumerate the facts which show the correlation of certain emotions with toxic changes in the saliva and the lacteal secretion. Perspiration may, in certain affective states, be coloured red, yellow, green, or blue, not to mention the varieties of odour, which are assuredly of chemical origin. Even apart from mental disease, the urinary secretion could furnish a long list of chemical changes (azoturia, oxaluria, phosphaturia) coinciding with variations of the affective order, such as apprehension, melancholy, irritability. In gouty and rheumatic patients, the modifications of temper, depending much more on general nutrition than on active suffering, have often been pointed out. We know the relations between the secretion of the gastric juice and pleasurable or painful states; dyspeptics have a well-established reputation for being neither cheerful nor comfortable to live with. Beaumont ascertained, in the case of his famous Canadian, that under the influence of anger or

other very strong emotions, the lining of the stomach was irritated, became red, dry, and very sensitive, and an attack of indigestion was the result. The rutting time (that of sexual excitement) is, in many animals, accompanied by deep-seated chemical changes, showing themselves externally by modifications of colour and odour, and, internally, not limited to the sexual organs, but extending to the whole of the body. It is known that the flesh of game is uneatable during this period, and that many fish, at spawning-time, become poisonous. It should not be forgotten that, during the same period, the animal becomes vicious, violent, aggressive, and dangerous. It would be easy to develop this point further, even as regards man (puberty, gestation, lactation, menstruation).

3. It has long been observed that, in the great majority of cases, mental disease begins by affective disturbances and that the intellectual aberrations only make their appearance later. Much more recently, a doctrine has been propounded which tends to seek the primary cause of these affective disturbances in a self-intoxication—*i.e.*, in "the disorders produced in the interior of the organism by the excessive formation or the morbid retention of normal poisons; in particular, by those originating in the digestive canal and the urine." Nutritive troubles through acceleration, retardation, or perversion, are assigned as the most general cause. In support of this, we are referred to the relations between melancholia, hypochondria, a pessimistic disposition, with hyperchlorhydria of the stomach, and the good results of purgative medicines; the numerous mental modifications coinciding with organic chemical modifications—*e.g.*, certain attacks of mania in arthritic subjects. "One characteristic of the mental state of diabetic patients is the way in which the fluctuations of the mental state correspond with those of the sugar, and the barometric (if one may so call it) influence of the composition of the urine on the moral disposition." This liquid, in mania, loses, to a great extent, its toxic character, in consequence of the morbid retention of normal poisons which are no longer eliminated.[1]

[1] Bouchard, *Leçons sur les auto-intoxications; Leçons sur les maladies par ralentissement de nutrition.* Régis, *Traité des maladies mentales*, pp. 112, 415, 423, etc. Féré, *Pathologie des émotions*, pp. 264, 495 *et seq.*

A long enumeration of facts bearing on this as yet insufficiently studied question would be here out of place. Besides, it could only be of real value if systematic—*i.e.*, if under the heading of each emotion were grouped the physiological facts invariably accompanying it, and all the chemical modifications exclusively peculiar to it.   We have only included the chemical conditions in our study, in order to penetrate as far as possible into the most general conditions of affective life, and show once more why it betrays the inmost constitution of the individual.

When treating of pleasure and pain, we remarked that they were too exclusively attributed to intensity of excitation (excessive, it was said, for pain ; moderate, for pleasure), and that its *quality* was forgotten.   Since we have to do with hypotheses as to the part played by chemical conditions in affective life, since they are the most general, and since pleasure and pain also have this character of generality, it may be permitted to hazard a conjecture. This would consist in admitting that pleasure arises either when excitement increases chemical activity in the organism, without producing toxines, or when this augmentation of activity brings about the disintegration of the normal poisons; and that pain arises either when excitement creates an environment appropriate to the formation of toxines, or when, directly and at once, it promotes their formation, either generally or locally.   But I would not insist on a simple *obiter dictum*, for which I can offer no proof, thrown out merely as a suggestion with regard to a question not as yet fully examined.

We have spoken throughout of the chemical modifications as coinciding with emotional changes.   Are they effects or causes, or both, according to circumstances?   It is clear that this question is not new to us.   It is the antithesis between the psychological and physiological theories of emotion, presenting itself under another aspect; there is no occasion for discussing it a second time.

CHAPTER IX.

THE EXTERNAL CONDITIONS OF EMOTION

Empiric period—Pre-Darwinian period of scientific research —Examination of Darwin's three principles—Wundt and his explanatory formulas: Innervation directly modified, Association of analogous sensations, Relations of motion with sensory representations.

THE movements of the eyes, mouth, face, the upper and lower limbs and trunk, and the modifications of the voice constitute the external expression of emotion which is principally reducible to muscular action. For the last half-century this subject has been studied in works so well known that it behoves us to be very brief. I shall confine myself to indicating the actual state of the question.

For some thousands of years this question remained in the stage of pure empiricism, or of so-called scientific speculations which had scarcely a better reputation than alchemy, astrology, or chiromancy. J. Müller, in the name of physiology, declared the expression of the emotions completely inexplicable. However, the researches were already beginning which were to prove him mistaken—those of Lavater with his rare talent of personal observation, and those of Charles Bell by a more objective method. After this, Duchenne, of Boulogne, went still further, substituting experiment for mere observation. It is well known that, in the case of an old man suffering from facial anæsthesia, he caused the contraction of an isolated muscle, by the aid of electricity, and thus produced certain modes of expression in the countenance. He concluded from this that the contraction of a single muscle often suffices to express a passion; and that every emotion has, so to speak, its accurate, precise, and unique note, produced by a unique local modification.   Thus, the frontal is for him the muscle of attention, the upper orbicular of the lips the muscle of reflection, the pyramidal (inter-superciliary) expresses threats; the great zygomatic, laughter; the lesser zygomatic, weeping; the triangular muscle of the lips, disdain, etc. In spite of the somewhat artificial nature of the experiments, and the too sweeping character of the conclusions, this was a great step in advance.[1]

At last appeared Darwin's epoch-making work.   Supported by the results of a long series of experiments on adults, children, lunatics, animals, members of the different human races, Darwin was the first to put, and to attempt to answer, the fundamental and only question—Why and how is such and such an emotion connected with such and such a movement and not with another?   He stated the problem under its scientific form.[2]

In Darwin's works we find two elements : a detailed and complete description of each individual emotion or affective state—by which we shall profit later on—and the exposition of the general laws of expression, as reduced to three well-known principles.   What remains of these three principles after the criticism to which they have been subjected?

[1] Lavater (1741-1801), *Essai sur la physionomie destiné à faire connaître l'homme et à le faire aimer;* Charles Bell (1806), *Anatomy and Philosophy of Expression;* Duchenne (1862), *Mécanisme de la physionomie humaine, ou analyse électro-physiologique de l'expression des passions.*   For ancient works on physiognomy, consult Mantegazza's book on *Physiognomy and Expression* (Contemporary Science Series).

[2] Duchenne has the following curious passage :—" The Creator, not being obliged to study mechanical requirements, was able, according to His wisdom or (if I may be pardoned for using this form of expression) by a Divine fantasy, to put in action this or that muscle—a single one, or several at once, when it was His will that the signs of the passions, even the most evanescent, should be temporarily inscribed on the human countenance.   This physiognomic language once created, it was sufficient, in order to render it universal and immutable, to give to every human being the instinctive faculty of always expressing his feelings by the contraction of the same muscles."   Thus, for this writer, the question remains within the region of first causes.   He has ascertained a relation of coexistence between a determinate emotion and certain movements of the muscles, but without seeking the reason and the natural explanation of this *nexus.*   We know that certain philosophers hold the theory of the Divine institution of language ; this is its equivalent, being a theory of a divinely instituted gesture-language.

This is the only point we have, for the moment, to examine.

1. The principle of the association of serviceable habits remains the most firmly established. It consists in admitting that movements which are of service in satisfying a desire, or getting rid of a disagreeable sensation, become habitual, and continue to take place, even when their utility becomes *nil*, or at any rate doubtful. In other words, there are attitudes, gestures, movements, which can be directly explained, because they are nothing but emotions actualised, objectivised, or embodied, such as the movements of contact in tenderness, of aggression in anger, of erection and swelling in pride. But there are others, of which the explanation is less direct and obvious. How are the contraction of the eyebrows in perplexity, tears in sorrow, the showing of the teeth in anger, to be explained as serviceable to us? According to Darwin, these acts, formerly serviceable, have continued to exist as survivals. Here Darwin's successors have rightly reproached him with not being enough of a psychologist, and have found a better explanation : the important fact is not the survival of serviceable movements, but the transference of a primitive mode of expression to an analogous emotion.

2. The principle of antithesis has been definitively abandoned ; it is purely hypothetical, and explains nothing. According to Darwin, there is a primitive and general tendency to associate with feelings the contrary gestures to those expressing the opposite feeling. Léon Dumont has subjected this assertion to a very close and cogent criticism. Taking, one by one, the facts quoted by Darwin, which, besides, are not very numerous, he has shown that they may be quite otherwise explained.[1]

3. The principle of the direct action of the nervous system cannot be placed in line with the other two, because it far surpasses them in generality, and, in relation to it, they are subordinate and not co-ordinate. Before Darwin, Spencer (*Principles of Psychology*, ii. §§ 495, 502) had stated an analogous principle, to which he reduced the expression of the emotions. He calls it the

---

[1] L. Dumont, *Théorie scientifique de la sensibilité*, chap. vi. p. 236. Fouillée, *Psychologie des idées-forces*, i. 467, admits Darwin's principle, but interprets it in another way.

Law of Nervous Discharge. It may show itself in two forms—the diffused and the restricted. The former depends on the quantity or intensity of the emotion, and serves as its measure. It follows, in its propagation, an invariable course: it affects the muscles in an inverse ratio to their mass and to the weight of the parts they have to move. In man, it acts first on the delicate muscles of the voice and the small facial muscles; then it invades, in succession, the arms, the legs, the trunk. The movements of the tail in dogs and cats, of the ear in horses, and many analogous ones in other animals, are illustrations of this law. The restricted discharge depends on the quality or the nature of the emotion; it is due "to the relations established in the course of evolution between particular feelings and particular sets of muscles habitually brought into play for the satisfaction of them."[1] This scarcely seems to me to differ from Darwin's principle of "useful habits."

The *Expression of the Emotions* gave rise to other publications of the same kind, those of Piderit, Mantegazza, and Warner, who, in his *Physical Expression* (1885), has attempted a purely objective, and consequently extra-psychological study of the subject. But among all the attempts to trace back expression to its fundamental principles, and find a substitute for Darwin's (already greatly shaken) theory, that of Wundt seems to me the best.[2] Like his predecessor, he admits three principles (though different from Darwin's) which can act simultaneously and concur in the production of an isolated movement.

1. The principle of direct modification of innervation—that is to say, that the intensity of the muscular and vaso-motor movements depends on the intensity of the emotions; the movements which most escape the control of the will more especially depend on this principle. This is the equivalent to Darwin's third principle, placed first, which is, in fact, its right position.

2. The principle of the association of analogous sensations consists in those dispositions of the mind which are analogous to certain sensory impressions, manifesting them-

[1] *Principles of Psychology*, vol. ii. p. 545.
[2] *Physiologische Psychologie*, vol. ii chap. xxii. He has also treated the question in a special collection of articles entitled *Essays*.

selves in the same manner. At the outset, we have only pleasures, pains, and needs of the physical order, whose mode of expression is innate, and, so to speak, anatomical. Later on come the pleasures, pains, and desires of the moral order, which make use of the pre-existent modes of expression in order to show themselves outwardly. It is a language turned aside from its primary signification, which in the order of gestures is the equivalent of a metaphor. This principle explains much more easily than Darwin's a number of apparently very perplexing modes of expression. If a man, when puzzled, scratches his head, coughs, rubs his eyes, it is because a slight *malaise* of physical origin and a slight embarrassment of psychical origin have a deep-seated analogy, betraying themselves by the same expressive movements. Wundt has well described the mimicry of the mouth in the tasting of sweet, acid, or bitter substances; as soon as an emotion arises which has some affinity with these gustatory sensations (sweet joy, bitter grief, sharp reproaches), the expression of the mouth, the nose, the face reappears. This is because, in both cases, the state of the feelings, the emotional tone are the same, the expressive movements identical. As Mantegazza has rightly said, there are such things as mimic synonyms.

3. The principle of the relation between movements and sensory representations lies in the fact that the muscular movements of expression relate to imaginary objects. Wundt considers as chiefly amenable to this principle the mimicry of the eyes, the arms, and the hands. We represent something large by raising the hand, a small object by lowering it; the future by a forward movement, the past by a backward one. It might be objected that these gestures indicate intellectual rather than affective states; but it is certain that many emotions have a mimicry addressed to absent objects. Gratiolet (1857) collected a tolerably large number. The indignant man, even if alone, clenches his fist against an absent adversary. We shut our eyes, or turn aside our face, to escape the sight of a disagreeable object; we do the same when disapproving of an opinion. When we approve, we incline the head forward, as if in contemplation. In negation, we turn the head to right and left, exactly as is done by children and animals, when an unattractive object is placed in front of the mouth.

The expression of disdain, contempt, disgust, reproduces the physiognomy of a man rejecting nauseating food.

I am not quite sure that Wundt's third principle is of the same importance as the other two, or that it cannot be reduced to a still simpler form. But the theory I have just summarised, with a few examples borrowed elsewhere, presents itself as the one most calculated to bring out the importance of the physiological factors, unduly neglected by the pioneers of the science.

All the work relating to this question, whatever may be its *lacunæ* at present, has demonstrated that the expression of the emotions is not an adventitious, purely external, extra-physiological fact, whose study is only incumbent, as science, on the physiologist, and, as art, on the physiognomist, but emotion itself objectivised, its inseparable embodiment. In my opinion, we have to distinguish two strata in the very numerous modes of muscular movement which express the emotions. One is primary, depending on the anatomical and physiological constitution; the other, secondary, depending on the psychological constitution. The relation between them is that which in every developed language exists between the primary and the derived sense of words. Analogy is the great artisan of intellectual language; its action is more restricted as regards emotional language. But when, to the emotion of the first hour, having already its fixed mode of expression, there succeeds a new emotion, which the consciousness, rightly or wrongly, has felt as analogous, the pre-established expressive mechanism has served a new purpose, like an old word whose meaning is extended and modified. In both cases the mind proceeds in the same way, obeying the guidance of one and the same unconscious law.

CHAPTER X.

CLASSIFICATIONS.

Their discrepancies—Reduced to three types: (1) Classification of pleasures and pains—(2) Classification of emotions: two forms, empiric and analytico-comparative—(3) Classification of representations, intellectualist form—Critical remarks—Impossibility of any classification.

THE confusion of that department of psychology which deals with the feelings and the vagueness of its terminology appear in all their fulness with the problem of classification. Although, for reasons which will be given at the end of the chapter, a complete and satisfactory classification seems to me impossible, there has been no lack of attempts, and it must be admitted that they are not illegitimate, at any rate as approximative efforts towards a provisional order.

Within the last fifty years, in spite of the very moderate amount of zeal with which psychologists have studied the feelings, we find about twenty treatises signed by well-known names, not to mention minor variants.[1] They are far from being in agreement, except on some few points, and when they are compared, in order, if possible, to reconcile them, the first impression is one of inextricable confusion and hopeless divergence. If we examine them a little more carefully, we begin to see light. We see that the differences are only in the objects classed and the methods followed; in one word, it is possible

[1] For a historical summary of these classifications, consult especially Sully, *The Human Mind*, vol. ii., Appendix F, p. 357, and Bain, *Emotions*, Appendix B.

to attempt a classification of these classifications; and when this is done, we find, if I am not mistaken, that they can all be reduced to three types. (1) Some writers, virtually, classify only pleasures and pains, tracing back the whole of affective life to their modalities. (2) Others classify the emotions properly so called; and here we must distinguish two groups, according as the method employed is purely empiric, and founded on current observation, or has recourse to analysis and genetic research, after the manner of the so-called natural classifications. (3) Lastly, others classify intellectual states pure and simple, and, conversely, the affective states which accompany them: this is the intellectualist method.

In order to justify our distinction, we shall successively examine these three types. This excursion on an ungrateful soil will not be altogether without, at least, a negative utility.

I.

As many writers show a common tendency to reduce the whole of the affective life to pleasures and pains, considered as essential and fundamental phenomena, it is natural that one category of classifications should have been based upon these.

"In the science of pleasure and pain," says Léon Dumont, "we no longer find ourselves, as in other sciences, in presence of separate organs and functions; for pleasure, like pain, belongs to all organs and all functions. Thus, we think that to recapitulate in this science the classification of the perceptive and intelligent faculties, and of the will, is to give way to a psychological tautology, which, though it causes no serious inconvenience, in any case throws little light on the analysis" (*op. cit.*, Pt. II., p. 1). No more could be said than this. Yet, to classify, we require a directing principle, and where shall we find it? "This basis is supplied to us by our own definition of pleasure and pain: pleasure being the augmentation of force in the whole of the conscious individuality, pain its diminution." Thence, Dumont deduces the divisions found in many authors: pain is positive when it results from an increased expenditure, negative when it depends on absence of excitement; pleasure is positive when there is increased excitement, negative when the expenditure is diminished. In other terms, if we compare the total "force" to a continually renewed capital, we have, in the one case, either more expenditure or less receipts, in the other either more receipts or less expenditure.

But Dumont does not stop there; he passes on to details; he insists on classifying the species under those four generic headings, and thus we have—Positive pains: effort, fatigue, the ugly, the hideous, the immoral, the false. Negative pains: weakness, exhaustion, inanition, physical pain properly so called, *ennui*, perplexity, doubt, impatience, expectation, sorrow, fear, sadness, pity. Negative pleasures: rest, cheerfulness. Positive pleasures: those of the senses, those of activity, such as games, dreaming, amusements, æsthetic and intellectual pleasures, sublimity, admiration, beauty, and their varieties.

I have transcribed this classification as Dumont gives it. I shall raise no objection, either to a division so arbitrary as to include physical pains among the negative pains, or to the abuse of a vague word, "force," which he shows a marked inclination to take in a transcendental sense. I will only consider one point, the transition which is *surreptitiously* made from a classification of pleasures and pains to a classification of the emotions or something analogous. The writer does not keep his promise of not classing "the perceptive and intelligent faculties, and the will;" and it is not in his power to keep it. In fact, what he has followed is the old classic division (pleasures and pains of the senses, the heart, the mind), which may possibly serve for a didactic exposition, but for no other purpose.

Beaunis has proposed a classification of pleasures and pains which also has as its basis a single principle: the various modes of motion. He discriminates three classes of pains: the nervous centres may be inactive through insufficiency of motion; their activity may be in excess through exaggerated motion; or their activity may be suddenly checked by arrest of motion. The same classification is adopted for pleasures: inaction, activity, arrest. I am inclined to think this division preferable to the other. He has also attempted a detailed classification of physical

(p. 176) and moral (p. 235) pains; but he gives none for pleasures.[1]

For my part, I am inclined to believe that a classification (in the exact sense of the word) of pleasures and pains is an impossible task. As these characters are very general, one can only establish exceedingly general divisions. As soon as we go beyond this, we are, in reality, classing internal or external sensations, percepts, images, concepts, modes of action, accompanied by a pleasurable or painful state, positive or negative, due to activity, overactivity, or arrest; but the modalities of the pleasurable and painful, which, besides, are infinite, are not classed in and for themselves. The varieties of physical pain, the simplest, commonest, and best studied kind, the easiest to isolate, and the most free from concomitant representation, have never yet been subject to a fixed classification, from Hahnemann, who reckoned them as 73 in number, to Beaunis, who enumerates 83.

In short, the "science of pleasure and pain," as L. Dumont somewhat emphatically calls it, belongs to the category of sciences which do not proceed by way of classification, since they do not as yet possess the material. We can only lay down extremely general divisions, and then proceed by *incomplete enumeration.*

II.

The emotions, at least the simplest and best defined, present themselves as psychic states having their own specific characteristics. They differ among themselves, not as one mode of pleasure or pain differs from another mode, but as one thing differs from another thing; in this way, they appear as *objects* susceptible to classification. We have already said that two methods have been adopted.

(1) The first strongly resembles the so-called artificial classifications, which might also be called concrete or synthetic. It takes the emotions as realities and places itself before them as the zoologist and the botanist place themselves before the varieties of animals and plants. It is empirical—*i.e.*, it has no guiding principle; it classifies

---

[1] Beaunis, *Sensations internes,* chap. xxi.

according to observation only, following external resemblances and differences.

Bain may be cited as one of the principal representatives of this method. I will not insist on a piece of work unworthy of such a psychologist; yet he has done it twice over, without arriving at an agreement with himself.

His earlier classification gives as fundamental the emotion of relativity (surprise, astonishment), terror, tenderness, self-esteem, anger, the sense of power, of activity, of mental exercise, æsthetic emotion, moral emotion.

The later includes eleven groups: love, anger, fear, the sentiment of property, the pleasure of power and its correlative pain of subjection, pride, vanity, activity ("plot-interest"), knowledge (the intellectual feeling), æsthetic emotion (beauty), moral sentiment. Three of these are "simple"—anger, love, and fear; but we find, a little later on, that love and anger are called "the giants of the group, the commanding and indispensable members of the emotional scheme;" so that fear would seem to be eliminated.

The incoherence and inconsistency of this attempt are sufficiently obvious, and I need not insist on them. (It should be noted that, in both cases, the religious sentiment is omitted.) I can find only one valuable remark—viz., that "pleasures and pains are contained in every one of the classes to be described, just as the natural orders of plants may each contain food and poison, sweet aromas and nauseating stinks." [1] I have only referred to this classification in order to show how, by its very nature, it is condemned to failure. Floating at haphazard, without fixed principle, when not contradictory, it can only be arbitrary.

Herbert Spencer has criticised it in a well-known passage, which I will briefly recapitulate, since it serves as a transition to the second form of classification, and throws some light on the latter. [2] Bain has overlooked the fact that in confining his attention to the most obvious characteristics of the emotions, he is following the method of the ancient naturalists, who classed the cetacea among fishes. Every

---

[1] Bain, *The Emotions and the Will*, p. 76.
[2] H. Spencer, *Essays*, vol. i. (Library Ed., 1891), pp. 241-264.

classification should be preceded by a rigorous analysis. For this purpose it would be necessary, as a preliminary, to study the ascending evolution of the emotions through the animal kingdom, to find out which of them are the first to appear, coexisting with the lowest forms of organisation and intelligence, and to note the existing differences, as regards emotion, between the higher and lower human races. Those common to all may be considered as simple, and those peculiar to the civilised races as ulterior and derivative.

2. Inspired by the above observations, Dr. Mercier has worked out a classification which I shall give as an example of the analytic and comparative method. It is in any case the most recent and the most detailed.[1] Proceeding after the manner of zoologists and botanists, he divides into classes, sub-classes, genera, and species, forming seventeen tables. We gather from these that there are 6 classes and 23 genera, under which may be ranged (after deducting all repetitions and duplicate entries) 128 manifestations of feeling, such as are to be found in common experience and rendered in current language. It is not possible, nor would it serve any useful purpose, to present this classification here in detail; I shall only indicate the 6 great classes with some sub-divisions, which will enable us to understand their nature.

The first class includes the feelings primarily affecting the conservation of the physical or mental organism. It comprises 2 sub-classes (according as the primary excitation is initiated by the environment, or within the organism itself), 2 orders, and 9 genera.

The second is that of the feelings primarily affecting the perpetuation of the race, considered as simple wants. Two sub-classes : primary (sexual emotion and its varieties) and secondary (paternal, maternal, filial, etc., feelings).

With the third class we leave behind the region of the primitive and fundamental feelings. It includes those which relate to the common welfare (community, family, etc.). It comprises 2 orders, each of which is further divided into several genera—viz., the patriotic and the ethical emotions.

[1] *The Nervous System and the Mind* (1888), pp. 279-364.

The fourth class (only vaguely differentiated from the preceding) is that of the feelings relating to the welfare of others: sympathy, benevolence, pity, and their opposites.

The fifth class comprises the feelings which are neither conservative nor destructive, so that here we pass beyond the region of pure utility, whether individual or social. It is divided into 2 orders and 5 genera—viz., admiration, surprise, the æsthetic feeling, the religious feeling, and the "feeling of recreation."

The sixth and last class is that of the feelings which correspond to abstract relations (in ordinary nomenclature designated as intellectual feelings)—conviction, belief, doubt, perplexity, scepticism. It has no sub-divisions.

Even when all details are omitted, the general drift of this work must be sufficiently apparent to the reader. Although conducted according to a fixed method, it does not escape the difficulties inherent in *every* classification of the emotions. In the first place, the order of filiation is not always very well marked. The author himself recognises that an arrangement in series is not possible, but this difficulty has also presented itself in zoology and botany. We meet with repetitions, *i.e.*, forms of sentiment figuring several times over in different categories. This, too, is inevitable. The complex emotions (or some of them, at least) are formed by anastomoses: they are rivers formed by converging streams coming from various sources lying in different directions. One may legitimately refer them to one or other of these origins; but the attribution will be partial and arbitrary. The religious sentiment, for instance, is included in the class of intellectual emotions. But its social character is undeniable (a point we shall return to in the proper place); let us recall, in passing, the worship of ancestors and deified heroes, and the strictly national religions of antiquity, the communities, orders, confraternities, corporations, the missionary work carried on in modern times, and, above all, the contagious character of religious emotion in general. It is false, moreover, to say that this emotion "tends neither to the preservation nor the destruction of the individual." It might therefore be just as well—or just as ill—placed in the third class. As soon as we pass from simple to complex emotions, it is of more importance to determine their composition than their filiation. Now, this procedure belongs rather to chemical than to zoological classification.

III.

A third type of classification, peculiar to the intellectualists, consists in classing according to the intellectual states, in so far as these are accompanied by affective elements. This system sprang from the psychology of Herbart, is based on it, and is met with in the works of the principal representatives of his school, Waitz, Drobisch, and especially Nahlowsky in *Das Gefühlsleben* (pp. 44 *et seq.*). This method is peculiar to Germany, and its influence is still perceptible even in Wundt, and more recently in Lehmann's book (*op. cit.*, pp. 338 *et seq.*). In England, Shadworth Hodgson approaches this type.

Apart from the procedure common to all, these classifications agree still less in detail than those of the first two types. Taken broadly, they have an academic aspect; they are frittered away in divisions, sub-divisions, distinctions, whence there arises more darkness than light. There is, however, a dichotomy peculiar to them corresponding to a reality which is not met with in the two previously-mentioned types, and, on this account, deserves notice.

This kind of classification, in the first place, establishes two great categories of emotions—those depending on the *contents* of the representations, and those depending on the *course* of the representations. Let us compare the flux of the states of consciousness to that of a river, which, according to the nature of the soil and the state of the sky, runs, sometimes clear, sometimes muddy, sometimes blue or green, sometimes greyish. Besides these various aspects, there is yet another kind, depending on the movement of the water, sometimes slow, sometimes rapid, here stagnant, there broken by the abrupt windings of the banks. One of these corresponds to the course, the other to the contents of the representations on which the affective states are based.

The first class (the contents) comprises the qualitative emotions, which are generally divided into inferior or sensory, and superior, which are intellectual, æsthetic, moral, or religious, according as the ideas exciting their feelings are those of the true, the beautiful, the good, or the absolute.

The second class (the course of the representations) comprises the *formal* emotions—*i.e.*, those depending on the different forms of the course of ideas, on the relations existing between them. Nahlowsky distinguishes four species—(1) the feeling of expectation and impatience; (2) that of hope, anxiety, surprise, doubt; (3) of *ennui;* (4) of refreshment and work.

The only merit of this classification is its showing that there are affective manifestations depending only on relations—transitions from one intellectual state to another. This merit, however, depends on the essential defect of the system, which consists in dealing with perceptions, representations, and ideas only—not with affective states taken in themselves, and directly. As this method of procedure is, definitively, an intellectual classification, it ought not to omit any form of knowledge, not even those blurred and evanescent states—the relations—which unite, disjoin, exclude, draw together, eliminate, subordinate, in short, indicate the *movements* of thought, and which students have often made the mistake of forgetting. It remains to be known whether many relations are not states of an affective rather than an intellectual nature; this is a point which I shall examine later on.

We may console ourselves for this multiplicity and divergence of classifications by saying that the naturalists have not been more successful. It will be granted without difficulty that it is easier to classify animals than affective states; yet, to take our own century only, how many systems! — from Lamarck, Cuvier, Oken, to Blanville, Geoffroy St. Hilaire, Siebold, Ehrenberg, Richard Owen, Von Baer, Vogt, Agassiz, and finally to Häckel—if we cite only the principal names !

I have indicated in passing why a true classification of the emotions—*i.e.*, a distribution into orders, genera, species, according to the dominant and subordinate characters—is impossible. Every classification, if not purely empirical, expresses a general theory of affective life, a "system," and, consequently, a hypothesis. More than this, it can never congratulate itself on having exhausted its matter, for every emotion, simple or compound,

admits of innumerable varieties determined by the individual, the race, the epoch, and the course of civilisation;
some are extinct, others, again, of recent origin. Lastly,
the existence of mixed emotions—which are numerous—is a
fatal objection to every attempt at distribution into a linear
series. The only track to follow is that of genetic filiation
—viz., to state first the simple, primary emotions, then
to find out by what mental processes, conscious or unconscious, the composite and derived emotions have
arisen from them. We shall attempt to define these in
a future chapter.[1] But this work is no longer a classification.

[1] See Part II., chap. vii.

CHAPTER XI.

THE MEMORY OF FEELINGS.

*Can emotional images be revived, spontaneously or volun-
tarily ?—Summary of scattered facts relating to this
subject—Inquiry into this question, and method followed
—Emotional and gustative images—Internal sensations
(hunger, thirst, fatigue, disgust, etc.)—Pleasures and
pains ; observat.ons—Emotions: three distinct forms of
revivability according to observations—Reduction of the
images to three groups: revivability direct and easy,
indirect and comparatively easy, difficult and sometimes
direct, sometimes indirect.—The revivability of a representation is in proportion to its complexity and the motor
elements included in it.—Reservations to be made on
this last point—Is there such a thing as a real emotional
memory ?—Two cases: false or abstract, and true or
concrete memory—Peculiar characters and differences of
each case—Change of the emotional into an intellectual
recollection — Emotional amnesia: its practical consequences—There exists a general emotional type and
partial emotional types—Confirmatory observations—
Comparative revivability of agreeable and disagreeable
states—To feel acutely and to recall an acute impression of the feeling are two different operations.*

I.

AFTER the numerous researches made, during the last
twenty years, into the nature and the revivability of
visual, auditory, tactile-motor, and verbal images, it seems
paradoxical to maintain that there is still an unexplored
region in the domain of memory. As a matter of fact,
however, we find at most a few scattered remarks on the

images derived from smell, taste, internal sensations, pleasure, pain, and emotion in general. The question of the emotional memory remains nearly, if not quite, untouched.[1] The object of this chapter is to begin its study.

The impressions of smell and taste, our visceral sensations, our pleasant or painful states, our emotions and passions, like the perceptions of sight and hearing, can leave memories behind them. This is a matter of common experience on which it is needless to insist. These residua, fixed in an organisation, may return into the consciousness ; and it is known that images may be revived in two ways—by provocation, or spontaneously.

Revivability on provocation is the simplest of all. It consists in an actual occurrence awakening the images of similar occurrences at some former time, and takes place, beyond possibility of doubt, in the class of images which occupies us just now. The actual sensation of fatigue, of the smell of a lily, of the taste of pepper, of pain in a certain tooth, appear to me as the repetition of sensations formerly experienced, similar to the present one, or at least apparently identical, so that, consequently, it revives them.

But can the images of olfactory and gustatory sensations, of internal sensations, of past pains and pleasures, of emotions formerly experienced, be revived in the consciousness spontaneously, or at will, independently of any actual occurrence which might provoke them ? We know that, in some painters, the inner vision is so clear that they can draw a portrait from memory; that, in some musicians, the inner hearing is so perfect that they can, like Habeneck, ideally hear a symphony just played, recalling all the details of the execution, and the slightest variations in the time. Are there in the order of emotional representations any cases analogous to these ? Such is, in its precise form, the question which we shall examine in detail. We shall subsequently see that it has a practical bearing, and is not a mere psychological curiosity.

Before entering on the subject, I will summarise the

---

[1] I see no reason for mentioning any authorities except H. Spencer, *Principles of Psychology*, i., §§ 69 and 96 ; Bain, *Emotions*, ch. v. ; W. James, *Psychology*, ii. pp. 474, 475 ; Fouillée, *Psychologie des Idées-forces;* Höffding, *Psychologie* (3rd German edition), vi., B. 3; Lehmann, *Hauptgesetze*, pp. 261-263.

principal facts relating to this question to be found scattered through the works of various authors. I divide them into four groups:—

1. We may take taste and smell together. This last sense is much more extensive, much richer and more varied than the other; common speech often confounds them, enriching taste at the expense of smell. Although unscientific, this confusion does not greatly concern us.

Every one knows that professional tasters, cooks, certain chemists and perfumers, can distinguish the most delicate gradations and correctly identify them with previous sensations; but this is a provoked recollection. Does a spontaneous or voluntary relation exist between these two groups of images? Examining the fullest monographs drawn up by physiologists[1] we find scarcely any information on this point. Cloquet, Müller, Valentin have reported cases of subjective sensations attributed by them to internal causes; but other physiologists, such as Ludwig, without denying these, are of opinion that sapid particles in the mouth, and odoriferous molecules on the mucous membrane of the nose, may act in a similar manner; so that the alleged images would, in fact, be sensations.

Dreams may afford us a better starting-point. Among the numerous writers who have treated of this subject, some resolutely deny the existence of representations of taste and smell. It is impossible to accept this opinion. Though they are comparatively rare, examples may be found which are proof against all criticism. A person who, for hygienic reasons, has abstained from wine for several years, assures us that he has had a very clear impression of its taste in the course of a dream. We may recall the hypnagogic hallucinations so well described by A. Maury, who was subject to them; he mentions the taste of rancid oil, and the smell of burning as occurring apart from its objective cause.

Among hallucinations properly so called, it is known that those of smell are of very frequent occurrence. Many authorities hesitate to admit those of taste, which they reduce to the status of mere illusions; but we know that

---

[1] See Von Vintschgau, art. "Geruch" and "Geschmack" in Hermann's *Handbuch der Physiologie*, vol. iii.; Gley, art. "Gustation"; François-Franck, art. "Olfaction" in the *Dictionnaire encyclopédique des sciences médicales*.

the distinction formerly maintained between these two pathological manifestations has been, in our day, much disputed.

2. Internal sensations play a prominent part in the emotional life. Are these susceptible, in the normal condition, of spontaneous or voluntary revival? I have not been able to find any precise information on this point. In the pathological condition we can find numerous examples in hypochondriacs, hysterics, and neuropaths, in insane patients who complain of the suppression of some of their organs, of inversion of the stomach. In any case it would be necessary to determine the part played by the organ itself, and its actual state in the majority of these cases of revival, which is extremely difficult.

3. As for pleasures and pains, under their double (physical and mental) form, there is no doubt. The recollection of a blinding light, of a discord or a strident sound, of the extraction of a tooth, or some more serious operation; the prospect of a good dinner to an epicure, of the approaching holidays to a schoolboy — all the states of psychic life generally included under the designation of imaginary pleasures and pains, show how frequent is the revival of impressions on the feelings. And, in fact, the difficulty is not to establish their existence, but to determine their nature.

We may also recall the facility with which, in hypnotised subjects, pleasant or painful conditions of all sorts may be induced by suggestion.

Finally, in certain cases, the impression may even become completely hallucinatory—*i.e.*, equal in intensity to the reality itself. "A student," says Gratiolet, "playfully struck his companion's out-stretched finger with the handle of a scalpel. The latter felt a pain so acute that he thought the instrument had pierced his finger to the bone." During a popular tumult in the reign of Louis-Philippe, a combatant received a slight contusion from a spent bullet on his shoulder. The skin was not even scratched, but "he felt a torrent of blood flowing from the wound over his breast." Bennett relates that a butcher remained hanging by one arm from a hook. He was taken down by the terrified bystanders, uttered frightful cries, and complained that he was suffering cruelly, while all the time the hook had only penetrated his clothes, and the arm was uninjured.[1] This condition might be termed a *hallucination of the feelings.*

4. The supply of observations and documents relating to the revivability of the emotions and passions is a very scanty one. In fact, we may admit that what has already been said as to pleasures and pains is also applicable to this last group. But it is not on the question of fact that the attention of psychologists has been concentrated. They are occupied entirely with theory, and in determining the nature of emotional memory. The majority consider the recollection to be merely that of the accompanying circumstances of emotion. Others hold it to be a recollection of the emotion itself, as such. As this is the principal point of my subject, and will have subsequently to be discussed in detail, I must limit myself, for the moment, to the mere indication of the two opinions.

In short,—confining ourselves to the normal, and setting aside the pathological states,—the facts collected seem to me utterly inadequate for answering the question stated above.

II.

It was for this reason that I proposed to myself the task of collecting fresh documents, and of inquiring whether there are not great differences between one individual and another as regards the memory of impressions. This would explain the want of harmony among authorities on this point.

Having eliminated all vague and doubtful answers, and those which are not to the point, I have collected about sixty *dossiers.* Each person (all being adults, of both sexes, and various stages of culture) was directly questioned by myself, and the answers immediately noted. Besides these, I have received several long written communications, which I reckon among my best material. The nature of the questions asked will be sufficiently evident from the following summary, which contains the principal results of my inquiry. I shall confine myself to a bare statement of the facts; the interpretation will come later.

[1] Hack Tuke, *Influence of Mind upon the Body*, p. 181, where other facts of the same kind may be found.

1. *Images of taste and smell.*—I was disposed to admit that they are not subject to any spontaneous revivability, and still less to a voluntary one, being, for my own part, quite incapable of recalling a single one, even in the faintest degree. The answers have put me completely in the wrong—the negatives being 40 per cent., the positives 60 per cent. More accurately, 40 per cent. persons revive no image, 48 per cent. revive some, 12 per cent. declare themselves capable of reviving all, or nearly all, at pleasure.

The majority of cases, therefore, allows of the spontaneous revival of some odours only. Those most frequently mentioned are pinks, musk, violets, heliotrope, carbolic acid, the smell of the country, of grass, etc. The conditions under which the image appears are various. For some persons this is unaccompanied by any visual, tactile, or other representation. With the majority, the imaginary odour ultimately excites the corresponding visual image (that of a flower, a bottle of scent, etc.). Many have first to evoke the visual image, and, in time, succeed in exciting the olfactory one. Two individuals affirm that, on reading the description of a landscape, they immediately perceive the characteristic odours. Here the sign is sufficient. One of them, a novelist, is sometimes conscious of thirst under the same conditions.

In the two following cases the "olfactory image" only exists in a single instance, and appears to be produced by the combined operation of concomitant circumstances.

Case 1. " I had been to the hospital, to see my friend B., who was suffering from a cancer in the face. . . . When he spoke it was necessary to come quite close in order to hear what he said, and thus, in spite of the antiseptic dressings, an acrid, fetid odour forced itself on one's nostrils. . . . I was to go again to see him—I had promised to do so ; but this prospect was .intensely repugnant to me. While walking in a part of Paris, where neither space nor fresh air was wanting, I reproached myself silently for not having gone to see the poor patient. . . . At this very moment I perceived, as though I had been close to him, the same acrid odour, recognisable as that of a cancerous tumour—so suddenly that I instinctively held my sleeve to my nose in order to see whether I had not brought away the smell in my clothes. This, however, was immediately succeeded by the reflection that I had not been to the hospital for five days, and that, moreover, I was not wearing the same overcoat as on the occasion of my visit."

Case 2. "I can only recall two odours: one inextricably connected with the memory of a sick-room—a stale smell of drugs and vitiated air, truly disagreeable when it recurs, as at the present moment. . . .

"It has happened to me to discover a very peculiar and indefinable odour in the presence of a hypnotiser (M. R——) when he was putting me to sleep, and I had not quite reached the lethargic state. I have since noticed that very often (not always) the memory of this curious odour accompanies the recollection of the hypnotiser. This seems to me all the more convincing, because, the odour being very subtle when M. R—— is near me, the revival must be absolute to allow of the return of the sensation, in however slight a degree."

I should hesitate to admit the spontaneous or voluntary revival of almost all odours, if this fact had not been affirmed to me, in perfect good faith, by educated and competent witnesses. I give some extracts from these declarations: "I can perceive nearly all characteristic odours, and can call them up at will; at this moment I am thinking of the country of the Rhine, and am fully conscious of its odour." "I can recall the greater number of odours (but not all) either spontaneously or voluntarily. (In the latter case time is required.)—Can you perceive, *here* and *now*, the scent of roses, and, if so, of what kind?— I perceive it *in genere;* but, on further persevering, I find it to be the scent of withered roses. The visual representation occurs afterwards." The only person who has told me that he finds all odours perceptible at will always finds a preliminary visual representation necessary.[1]

As to the recollections of tastes, by themselves, the answers are very vague. One remembers "easily, and at will, the taste of salt, with a very clear visual impression," but less easily the other three fundamental tastes. Another,

---

[1] Galton, in a note entitled "Arithmetic by Smell," has described an arrangement by means of which he convinced himself that some arithmetical operations can be carried out by the help of olfactory images, as is done by means of visual and auditory representations. He trains himself to regard two whiffs of peppermint as equivalent to one of camphor, and three of peppermint with one of carbolic acid; he performs small additions, and, later on, operates with images only (visual and auditory representations being excluded). For details, see *Psychological Review*, January 1894.

who uses for his throat three different kinds of lozenges, "feels the taste of them beforehand, as soon as he needs them, on either seeing or touching them." In general, the revivability of tastes appears to me especially connected with that of ordinary food, and with the state of the alimentary canal (hunger).

2. *Internal sensations.*—My inquiry does not include the whole of these, but only the commonest and most easily observed.[1]

As regards hunger, I have received 51 definite answers, 24 persons saying they can distinctly recall it, 27 that they cannot. (The question has always been put at an hour when the real sensation did not exist, and some have told me that in their normal condition they never feel either hunger or thirst.) It is usually described as a tactile sensation in the œsophagus, or a twitching pain in the stomach, etc. One person only affirms that he can, "at will, feel hunger and thirst, even after having eaten and drunk."

Thirst is imagined much more frequently than hunger, and, as it seems, more clearly (36 affirmative to 15 negative answers). It is described as dryness in the throat, heat, etc.

As regards the representation of fatigue, the answers have without exception been affirmative. The modes of representation are various. Some feel it (ideally) in the muscles; others under a cerebral form. Here are some examples: "muscular twitchings in the calves of the legs, the back, and the shoulders; the eyes feeling swollen, but no heaviness in the head;" "a feeling of relaxation, of a weight, localised in the shoulders, because, in a normal state, I find stooping very difficult;" "slowness of movement, with a feeling of weight in the head;" general lassitude, of a diffused kind, especially a feeling of weight in the head, and mental weariness;" "pains in the joints, and a heavy feeling in the brain." Although all my correspondents can revive the feeling of fatigue, three or four can only succeed in doing so "with difficulty and to a slight extent."

We find the same results with regard to the representation of

[1] The memory of internal sensations, though distinct from that of states of feeling properly so called, approximates so closely to it that the two subjects appear to me inseparable.

disgust. I find only three negative answers, all accompanied by the remark, "I have a good digestion." One of these cases is the more singular because the subject has suffered from sea-sickness. In its acute form the representation is described as "like the beginning of nausea." For others, it is "a pain in the stomach, with a retractile movement, connected with the idea of cod-liver oil, or of tainted meat." Among those who have experienced the sensation of sea-sickness, I have not met with one who cannot easily revive it (giddiness, feelings of a rocking motion, which disinclines them to persist in reviving the impression). M. X—— (a very competent observer in psychological questions) says: "I have a pretty good visual memory, but no auditive, either musical or linguistic; I cannot spell a foreign language. Except for muscular memory, which in me is *nil* (so that I have never succeeded in acquiring any physical exercise, or playing on any instrument), I can revive all internal sensations: hunger, thirst, disgust, fatigue, giddiness, difficulty in breathing; I prefer not to insist upon this last state, as were I to think of it any longer I should actually bring it on." [1]

3. *Pains and Pleasures.*—To the question, "Can you revive in yourself the memory of a given physical pain, a sorrow, a pleasure, or a pity?" the answer is nearly always in the affirmative. But, put in this bald way, it teaches us nothing. We require more detailed information. We here return to the main point of our subject, and I am obliged slightly to anticipate my conclusions. The observations, carefully taken, show that there are two distinct forms of emotional memory, one *abstract*, the other *concrete*. Later on, I shall insist on their differences; for the moment, I shall confine myself to the enumeration of facts.

Painful States.—Toothache, being very common, has supplied me with many answers. I note in nearly all of these the predominance of the motor elements: shooting and throbbing pains, contortions of the jaw, etc. When the extraction of a tooth is recalled there is a jarring of the whole head, a feeling of twisting, snapping, noises, etc. In many cases the painful element seems to be scarcely revived,

---

[1] A great swimmer has had feelings of suffocation which he can recall with much vividness.

or not at all; in many others it reappears with the utmost clearness.

Case 3. "I send you a personal observation made during the last few days. I had suffered from toothache, which was very acute, and certainly intenser than the unpleasant feeling experienced when the dentist operates on your teeth with his revolving machine. Yet when I think of it now, and try to recall, on the one hand the pain, on the other the rubbing of the teeth by the machine, it is the latter which seems to me, in my recollection, the most disagreeable. I explain this by the fact that this rubbing is accompanied by a noise which I can recall most vividly, and this auditive representation is by itself sufficient to evoke a disagreeable feeling. The pain in the teeth is also connected with different accessories : inclination of the head, closing of the eye on the side affected, movement of the hand to the corresponding cheek, etc., but these accessories have no great influence on me ; they are not so characteristic of toothache as the peculiar noise of the machine. This last representation is very vivid; when I think of it I feel a chill run down my back and a slight trembling in the arms. The representation of the actual pain is, in my case, much more vague ; it is diffused, I have to eke it out with verbal descriptions, and it does not act on me so disagreeably as the first."

Cuts, burns, etc., are remembered tolerably well. "In my youth I was wounded by a pistol-shot; I have a perfect recollection of the shock, which first produced a tactile sensation radiating from a centre, and afterwards pain, but I have a difficulty in recalling the painful element in the sensation." Another can well remember the vesical contractions of a cystitis; but not without the help of the motor elements, as in the case of toothache. M. B———, who appears to belong to the affective type (I shall explain later on what I mean by this), feels the beginnings of a lancinating neuralgia in the eye, a cramp in the stomach, a smarting of the anus, a bite on the tongue. Another (same type) says, "If I were to try, I could recall the feeling of neuralgia, but I cannot represent to myself the pain of a boil." Another : "There are some pains which I can feel at will ; I either feel nothing at all, or the representation is so vivid that it almost amounts to actual pain. This is true especially of cardiac pains."

It was my intention to question those who had undergone important operations; but, from the very general use of anæsthetics, there was little to be hoped for from such an experiment. There remains a case of frequent occurrence —the pains of childbirth. The answers are contradictory. One woman, who has had five confinements, declares that "as soon as it is over, there is nothing more." This is a woman of vigorous health and unshaken optimism. Another says, "As soon as the pain is over, I can forget it at once." The physician of a lying-in hospital told me that "nearly all, during their confinement, say that nothing would induce them to undergo such suffering again; yet nearly all return to the hospital." Others say that they have, afterwards, a very clear and precise recollection of the labour-pains. Though these answers are so contradictory, we shall see, further on, how they are to be reconciled with one another.

Case 4. No revivability of the impression of labour-pains. Nervous subject. Good visual memory; no auditive memory; cannot recall either a taste or a smell; has made observations on herself in view of the subject in hand, and has sent me the following notes :—

"The first acute pains appeared about every fifteen or twenty minutes; during these intervals of repose they vanished, leaving no trace. During the intervals between the crises, the patient tried to represent to herself the pain she had just passed through, and found it absolutely impossible to do so. She could describe the pain in words,—pains in the back, the side, etc.,—and it was this verbal description which came back to her whenever she tried to recall her feelings at the time. Afterwards the pains became more and more frequent, and she could make no more observations. When they were extremely acute, she screamed and talked the whole time. It is curious to note that she did not pronounce her words as usual, but uttered each syllable several times, as thus: '*ça, ça, ça, ça, fait, fait, fait, fait, très, très, maaaaal.*' She entreated her husband to kill her, to cut her into small pieces, to tear her asunder, if only there might be an end of it. After five hours of suffering, the doctor declared that all these pains had in nowise advanced the situation—that everything was as at the beginning. This declaration produced an acute feeling of despair, added to the pain. Five hours later all was over. Next day, when she tried to represent the pain to herself, there came into her mind only the verbal description, and afterwards the sum of her utterances during labour; she remembered that she had been unable to contain herself, that she understood the absurdity of what she had been saying to her husband, but thought, at the same time, 'People sometimes do absurd things—why should he not do what I ask him?' She remembered clearly that, after the doctor's declaration, she had a feeling of despair; but she recalled it in words, not as a feeling."

In conclusion, I will quote from Fouillée, in connection with physical pain, an interesting observation made on himself:—

"If I want to recall any given attack of toothache, I must form a mental image of the teeth where the pain was localised, and then of the word *pain* which serves as a sign; but how am I to form an image of the pain *in itself*? Some philosophers declare the thing impossible, and allege that we only reproduce perceptions, intellectual states, and words. This is, in fact, what usually happens; but one can also, in my opinion, reproduce in the consciousness (though incompletely) the *painful* element of toothache. To this end we must employ an indirect method. This procedure consists in directly calling up the images and motor reactions which accompany or follow toothache. I make the experiment, localising my thoughts in one of the molars on the right side; then I wait. The first thing to revive is a vague and general state, common to all painful sensations. Then this reaction grows more precise, as I concentrate my attention more and more on the tooth. At last I feel a greater afflux of blood into the gum, and even throbbings. Then I represent to myself a certain movement passing from one point of the tooth or gum to another; this is the passage of the pain. Thus I also revive the motor reaction caused by the pain, the convulsion of the jaw, etc. Finally, by thinking fixedly of all these circumstances, I end by feeling in a more or less dull way the rudiments of shooting pains. In an experiment just made, I have brought on real toothache in a molar, which, however, is subject to it. . . . The experiment leaves behind it a general irritability of the teeth, and an inclination to pass the tongue over the gums."[1]

Except for a few exceedingly clear observations, which I shall give later on, I have only vague replies regarding the revivability of sorrow, or moral pain, after the elimination of the conditions in which it had its origin. One person represents to himself "a general inertia and a febrile condition." Another, who, during his time of military service, underwent periods of depression and *ennui*, "a year later, when the recollection comes back to him, sees everything of a grey hue." We shall see presently that in some

[1] Fouillée, *op. cit.*, vol. i. pp. 200, 201.

individuals the revival of moral pain is as acute as the initial state.

Pleasant States.—The same results are obtained, *mutatis mutandis*, as with the preceding group. I note a very marked predominance of the motor elements. The pleasures most frequently mentioned are those of skating, swimming, the trot or gallop of a horse, and various physical exercises. Those who *really* revive agreeable recollections, describe a general state of excitement, a dilatation of the chest, a lighting up of the countenance, a tendency towards childish gestures. One, in thinking of his rides, feels the pleasure of rapid motion, the wind playing over his cheeks, etc. Musicians can easily revive their pleasure by means of inner hearing alone. We find one who cannot think of the *Walkürenritt* without feeling himself lifted as if by motor impulses.

4. *Emotions.*—The phenomena of this group, though more complex, are, in fact, only a prolongation of our third group. But, in order to obtain a correct notion of their revivability, we must not proceed by way of generalities. To ask any given individual whether he is capable of reviving past emotions would be a useless question. I have always asked persons to try and recall a *particular* case of a particular emotion (fear, anger, love, etc.). The answers are reducible to three categories, which I shall enumerate in the order of their frequency.

In the greater number of cases, only the conditions, circumstances, and accessories of the emotion can be recalled; there is only an *intellectual* memory. The past event comes back to them with a certain emotional colouring (and sometimes even this is absent), a vague affective trace of what has once been but cannot be recalled. In the affective order these subjects are analogous to those of moderately good visual and auditory memory in the intellectual order. C——, who, when standing on a rock, narrowly escaped being surrounded by the tide, sees the waves rising, and recalls his desperate rush for the shore, which he reached in safety; but the emotion as such does not return to him. At Constantine, some years ago, I nearly fell into the gorge of the Rummel. When I think of the incident I can see before me quite clearly the landscape, the state of the sky, all the details of the spot; but the only return of feeling is a slight shiver in the back and legs.

Others (far less numerous) recall the circumstances *plus* the revived condition of feeling. It is these who have the true "affective memory"; they correspond to those who have good visual or good auditory memories. This is the case with the majority of emotional temperaments. As we here touch on the most obscure and disputed part of our subject, it will be convenient to give some examples.

Irascible subjects, on hearing the name of their enemy, at the mere thought can revive the rising feelings of anger. The timid person shudders and turns pale when recalling the danger once incurred. The lover, thinking of his mistress, completely revives the state of love. If we compare the recollection of an extinct passion with the occurrence to the mind of a passion still existing, we shall clearly perceive the difference between intellectual and affective memory, between the mere recollection of the circumstances and the recollection of the emotion as such. It is a serious error to assert that only the conditions of the emotion can be revived, not the emotional state itself. I now only touch on this question, to which I shall return.

Several of my correspondents affirm that the memory of an emotion affects them as strongly as the emotion itself, which I have no difficulty in believing. Does not the recollection of a foolish action make one blush? One asserts that "her representation of emotions is more acute than the emotions themselves, and that she can recall them much better than visual, auditive, and other sensations." But a few detailed observations will make the nature of true affective memory clearer.

Littré relates that, at the age of ten, he lost a young sister under very painful circumstances. He felt acute grief at the time; "but a boy's sorrow does not last long." At an advanced age this grief suddenly returned, without apparent cause. "Suddenly, without wish or effort on my part, by some phenomenon of affective autumnesia, this same event reproduced itself with feelings no less painful, certainly, than those I had experienced at the moment of its occurrence, and which went so far as to bring tears into my eyes." It was several times repeated in the course of the following days; then it ceased and gave place to the habitual recollection, *i.e.*, to the purely intellectual form of memory.[1]

It is natural to suppose that emotional revival must be of frequent occurrence in poets and artists. M. Sully-Prudhomme, whose philosophical aptitudes are well known, has favoured me with a written communication on this subject, from which I extract some passages, with his permission.

" . . . It is my habit to separate myself from the verses I have written before finishing them, and to leave them for some time in the drawers of my writing-table. I even forget them sometimes, when the piece has seemed to me a failure, and it may happen to me to find them again several years after. I then re-write them; and I have the power of calling up again, with great clearness, the feeling which had suggested them. This feeling I pose, so to speak, in my inner consciousness, like a model which I am copying by means of the palette and brush of language. This is the exact opposite of improvisation. It seems to me that at such times I am working on the recollection of an affective state.

"When I remember the emotions aroused in me by the entry of the Germans into Paris after our last defeats, I find it impossible not to *experience this same emotion afresh*, simultaneously and indivisibly; while the mnemonic image of the Paris of that day remains in my memory very distinct from any actual perception. When I remember the kind of affection which, in my childhood, I felt for my mother, I find it impossible not to become, in some sort, a child again, at the very moment when I call up this memory—not to allow my heart of to-day to participate in the former tenderness due to recollection. I am almost inclined to ask myself if every *recollection of feeling does not take on the character of a hallucination.*

"When a student, I formed a connection in which I was grossly deceived; so everyday an occurrence that the correctness of my observations can probably be tested by most men from their own recollections. There was nothing very deep in my love, imagination being the principal factor, and I have long ago forgiven the injury, which, after all, chiefly concerned my vanity. Both rancour and affection vanished long ago. Under these circumstances, if I call up the recollection, I recognise at the outset that I am now a stranger to the feelings which I can remember; but I soon notice that I only remain a stranger to them so long as the memories are vague and confused. As

---

[1] *Revue positive*, 1877, p. 660.

soon as, by an effort of recollection, I make them more precise, they cease *ipso facto* to be memories only, and *I am quite surprised to feel the movements of youthful passion and angry jealousy renewed in me*. It is indeed only this revival which could enable me to retouch the verses which this little adventure of long-past years induced me to perpetrate, and to allow the expression of my former feelings to benefit by the experience acquired in my art."

Case 5. H—— (20 years). On the *memory* of the feeling of *ennui* experienced on the first day in barracks.—" In order to *represent* to myself thoroughly this feeling of *ennui*, which was very intense, and lasted a whole afternoon, I shut my eyes and abstract my thoughts. I feel, first, a slight shiver down my back, a certain *malaise*, a feeling of something unpleasant which I should prefer not to feel over again. After this first moment comes a certain uncomfortable state, a slight oppression of the throat; this feeling is connected with vague representations which do not fix themselves. In the experiment here described, I first picture to myself the barrack-yard, where I used to walk; then this picture of the yard is replaced by that of the dormitory on the third floor. I see myself seated at a window, looking at the view, of which I can see all the details. This, however, does not last; the picture soon disappears; there remains only a vague idea of being seated at a window, and then a feeling of oppression, weariness, dejection, and a certain heaviness in the shoulders. At this point I break off the experiment and open my eyes, still experiencing a general sense of uneasiness, which soon passes off."

The whole experiment lasts a little more than ten minutes. To sum up, we have, first, a feeling of weight and oppression, a shudder in the back, but no clear representation of surrounding objects; then a feeling of discomfort becoming more and more intense, visual representations varying either in their nature or their intensity; and finally, the total disappearance of these visual representations, the feeling of *ennui* being persistent throughout.

Case 6. A woman, aged 28. "Three years ago, I used to go and see a relative who was undergoing treatment at an establishment in the neighbourhood of P——. My visits were very frequent, and always began with a long wait in a room overlooking the garden. If I wish to repeat the impressions of this time of waiting, which was always disagreeable to me, all I have to do is to sit down in a chair, as I was then seated, to close my eyes and put myself in the same frame of mind, which I can do quite easily. Not half a minute passes between the evocation and the clear and absolute reconstruction of the scene. First, I feel the carpet under my feet, then I *see* its pattern of red and brown roses; then the table with the books lying on it, their colour and style of binding; then the windows, and through them the branches of the trees, of which I hear the sound as they beat against the glass; lastly, the peculiar atmosphere of the room, its unmistakable smell. After this, I feel over again all the weariness of waiting, complicated by an intense dread of the doctor's arrival, a state of apprehension ending in a violent palpitation of the heart, which I find it impossible to escape. When once I have entered on this train of thought, I have to follow it out to the end, passing through the whole series of states which I passed through at the time. If I wished to eliminate any of them I am sure that I could not do so, as when, in a dream, one tries, without ever succeeding, to avoid an unpleasant fall which one foresees."

Here nothing is wanting, either the circumstances, or the repetition of the emotion itself; and this case shows that the complete revival of an emotion is the beginning of the emotion itself.

Lastly, there remains a third category of answers, of which I have only four cases. I mention these merely as a curiosity, and in order to omit nothing. These persons represent the emotion *objectively* to themselves, by localising it in another. One can only represent anger to himself under the force of some particular angry man. Another incarnates fear and hatred in a certain person whose countenance or attitude expresses fear or hatred. The emotional state is, for these, only represented under its bodily form.

Is this because they have, personally, little experience of these different emotions?

III.

This series of facts, with their multiform and often contradictory manifestations, may perhaps leave the reader in perplexity, which would be still greater were I to enumerate all. Let us try to bring them into some sort of order, and understand their significance.

If—placing ourselves at the point of view of the question stated above, the possibility of a revival not produced by an actual occurrence—we propose to ourselves to classify all images whatsoever, we shall see that they fall into these groups, viz.:—

Those of direct and easy revivability (visual, auditory, tactile-motor, with some reservations for the last named).

Those of indirect and comparatively easy revivability: pleasures and pains, emotions. They are indirect, because the emotional state is only induced through the intermediary of the intellectual states with which it is associated.[1]

Those of difficult revivability, either direct or indirect. This heterogeneous and difficult group includes tastes, odours, and internal sensations.

What are the reasons for these differences? I reduce them to two principal ones, which I may briefly state thus—

The revivability of an impression is in direct ratio to its complexity, and consequently in inverse ratio to its simplicity.

The revivability of an impression (with certain exceptions to be mentioned afterwards) is in direct ratio to the motor elements included in it.

1. It is an incontestable fact that an isolated state of consciousness, with no relation to what precedes, accompanies, or follows it, has small chance of fixing itself in the memory. I hear a word of an unknown language, it immediately vanishes; but if I read and write it, if I associate it with some object or with various circumstances, it is fixed. It is easier to remember a group or a series than an isolated and unrelated term. Now, by their very nature, the visual images arrange themselves in complex aggregates, and the auditive in sequences (or even, in the case of harmony, in simultaneities), while the motor images are associated in series, every term of which awakens and brings with it the last. They accordingly fulfil the conditions of

---

[1] A characteristic peculiar to emotional affective revivability is the slowness with which it develops and the time required. While the visual or auditory image may be called up instantaneously and at command, the emotional representation arises slowly. This is because it passes through two stages. The first (intellectual) consists in the evocation of conditions and circumstances—a toothache, a burn, a passion. Many do not get beyond this stage, and the concomitant emotional tone, accordingly, is faint, or even *nil*. The second or emotional stage adds to this the rise of states of excitement and exultation, or of dejection and lowered vitality. The latter requires organic conditions, a difference in the organism, an excitement of the motor, vascular, respiratory, secretory, and other centres.

immediate and easy revivability. It is the same with pleasures, pains, emotions. Always connected with intellectual states (perceptions, representations, or ideas), they form part of an aggregate, and are involved in its resurgent movement.

The case is different with the images of our third group. They are not associated with one another; they have an isolated and individual character; they contract no relations, either of space or time, among themselves.

Let us take the case of odours. One excludes another; they are not associated in the imagination as visual images are in the recollection of a beautiful landscape. One of my correspondents is able to recall at will the scent of pinks; she tried to do so while walking in a wood full of decaying leaves and their smell, but without success; one odour excluded the other. Neither can they be arranged in sequences. I am aware that an English chemist, Piesse, has claimed the ability to class scents in a continuous series, like notes, patchouli corresponding to lower c in the key of F, and civet to the upper f in the key of G—the whole in tones and semitones; but no one, so far as I know, has taken this fancy seriously.

In the same way, tastes may be associated with other images, as of hunger (I have collected several cases of this), which makes their revival more difficult. Among themselves they do not form associations, but combinations. If associations ever occur they are extremely rare and limited in character.

Hunger and thirst are special, indecomposable states. Disgust and fatigue are revived easily enough, and, as we have seen, by almost every one; but it must be remembered that these states are composed of somewhat heterogeneous —sensory and motor—elements, and that they approach the character of aggregates.

This antithesis between the first two groups and that of odours, tastes, and internal sensations, depends, no doubt, on certain physiological conditions. As we can do nothing but hazard conjectures on this point, it is better to abstain.

2. The second theory stated above—viz., that the revivability is in direct ratio to the motor elements included in the image—is more open to question. I only give it as a *partial*, secondary, subsidiary explanation, applicable to

many cases but not to all, and allowing of numerous exceptions. Since we have to do with an empirical law—a pure generalisation from experience—we must test it by facts, in order to fix its bearing and value. This rapid examination will justify my restrictions and reservations.

Among all our impressions, those of sight and hearing are those most easily revived. Now, though the visual faculty has at its disposal a very rich, varied, and delicate motor apparatus, this is not the case with the auditory. Considering the superior position of the latter among the senses, it is very poor in motor elements; movements of the head, accommodatory movements of the tympanal membrane, in extreme cases movements of the vocal organs, and, according to the latest hypotheses, a certain function of the semi-circular canals. The difference between the two senses in respect of motor elements is very striking.

The sense of smell is much more varied and of greater extent than that of taste. It is far superior as a means of information, yet inferior as regards the sum of the movements at its disposal for exercising itself.

Pleasures, pains, and pleasurable or painful emotions, all include motor elements. So much is evident, yet let us remark what follows : if we divide the affective states— roughly, yet sufficiently for our purpose—into two groups, on one side pains and painful emotions, on the other pleasures and pleasurable emotions, a difficulty presents itself. The first group, that of the "asthenic" states, manifests itself by a diminution of movements, circulation, respiration, etc. The second group, that of the "sthenic" states, manifests itself by the reverse phenomena, increased movement, circulation, etc. Shall we say that the second group, which contains more motor elements, is revived more easily and more frequently than the first ? The conclusion would be logical, but contrary to experience. We should even find, I believe, that the contrary opinion has more supporters.[1]

Organic sensations appear to depend principally on the chemical action taking place in the organism; it is thus with hunger, thirst, suffocation, disgust, fatigue, etc. Here the part played by the motor element is but trifling. As

---

[1] This opinion will be discussed later on.

this revival is vague, this group seems to conform to the law stated above.

To sum up: when examined in detail our formula is only a partial explanation, a generalisation of limited application.

IV.

We have now arrived at the principal question, for which all that has hitherto been said was only a preparation : Is there such a thing as a real revival of impressions? Although most psychologists do not put this question at all, or only treat it in a cursory manner, the majority of answers are certainly in the negative. It is maintained that we remember the conditions and circumstances of an emotional occurrence, but not the emotional state itself.

I feel obliged completely to reject this theory, which would never have been maintained if the subject had not been treated *a priori,* in an offhand manner, without sufficient observations. A closer study, supported by the facts which I have adduced, and others which will follow, shows that there are two quite distinct cases. Some people have a *false* or *abstract* memory for feelings, others a *true* or *concrete* one. In the former the image is scarcely revived, or not at all; in others it is revived in great part, or totally. In order the better to explain the difference between these two forms of memory, let us examine the constituent elements and the mechanism of each separately.

1. The *false* or *abstract* memory of feeling consists in the representation of an occurrence, *plus* an affective characteristic—I do not say an affective state. This is certainly the most frequent form. What remains of the small incidents of a long journey but the recollection of the places where they happened, the details, and the fact that they *were once* disagreeable. What remains of a vanished love-affair but the impression of a person, of attentions paid to her, of adventures, and, besides, the recollection that this *was once* happiness? How much does the adult retain of the memory of his childish games? How much of his former religious or political belief remains to a person who has become totally indifferent? In all cases of this kind, and there are thousands, the remembered emotional char-

acteristic is *known*, not felt or experienced; this is only an additional intellectual character. It is added to the rest as an accessory; pretty much as, in picturing to ourselves a town, a monument, a landscape visited long ago, we add the recollection of a bright or cloudy sky, of rain or fog which surrounded it.

I call an emotional memory "abstract," and I justify this term. Emotional states are just as susceptible of abstraction and generalisation as intellectual states. One who has seen many men, who has heard many dogs bark or frogs croak, forms to himself a generic image of the human figure, of the barking of dogs, or the croaking of frogs. This is a schematic, half-abstract, half-concrete representation, formed through the accumulation of rough resemblances and the elimination of differences. In the same way, a person who has several times suffered from toothache, colic, or headache, who has had paroxysms of anger or fear, hate or love, forms to himself a generic impression of these different states by means of the same procedure. This is the first step. It would be beside the point to follow here in detail the ascending progress of the mind to higher and ever higher generalisations. In their highest degree, concepts like force, movement, quantity, etc., suppose two things: a word which fixes and represents them, and a potential or latent knowledge, hidden under the word and preventing it from being a mere *flatus vocis*. He who does not possess this potential knowledge, who is incapable of resolving the superior abstractions, first into medium, then into inferior ones, then into concrete *data*, possesses only an empty concept. So for the affective states the terms emotion, passion, sensibility, etc., are nothing but abstractions, and in order to verify these terms and give them a real significance, we must have experiences in the region of feeling, concrete data. People who speak of a state of feeling which they have never experienced, which they know only by hearsay, have an empty concept. States of feeling are a material susceptible of all degrees of abstraction, like sensory material.

The false or abstract memory of feeling is only a sign, a simulacrum, a substitute for the real occurrence, an intellectualised state added to the purely intellectual elements of the impression, and nothing more.

2. The true or concrete memory of impressions consists in the *actual* reproduction of a former state of feeling, with all its characteristics. This is necessary—at least in theory —if it is to be complete. The nearer it approaches to totality, the more accurate it is. Here the recollection does not consist merely in the representation of conditions and circumstances, in short, of intellectual states, but in the revival of the state of feeling itself as such, *i.e.*, as *felt*. I have already given instances of this : Fouillée's experiment, the cases of Littré and Sully-Prudhomme ; those numbered III. and IV., so clear and precise, show that a true memory of impressions, independent of its intellectual accompaniment, is no chimera.

Bain says that the emotions, "in their strict character of emotions proper, have the minimum of revivability; but being always incorporated with the sensations of the higher senses, they share in the superior revivability of sights and sounds." On which Professor W. James makes the following comment: "But he fails to point out that the revival of sights and sounds may be *ideal* without ceasing to be distinct; whilst the emotion, to be distinct, must become real again. Professor Bain seems to forget that an 'ideal emotion,' and a real emotion prompted by an ideal object, are two very different things."[1]

I maintain, on the contrary, that we have here only two different stages of the same thing; the first ineffectual and abortive, the second complete; and the subject which now occupies us must either have been in a very confused state, or very negligently treated, for a clear mind like that of W. James not to have seen that affective memories, like others, aim at becoming actual states of feeling. We ought not, however, to forget the indisputable fact that our consciousness only exists in the present. For a recollection, however distant, to exist, as far as I am concerned, it must re-enter the narrow area of *present* consciousness; otherwise it is buried in the depths of the unconscious and equivalent to the non-existent. We have thus (not to speak of the present-future) a present-present and a present-past—viz., that of memory; and this is only distinguished from the other by certain additional marks which it is needless to enumerate, but which consist principally in its appearing

[1] *Psychology*, ii. 474.

like an initial state, though, in general, less intense. Now these indispensable conditions of memory are the same for both intellectual and emotional states. If, with my eyes shut, I can call up the vision of St. Peter's at Rome (if I were an architect, with a good visual memory, I should see it in all its details), my impression is an *actual* one, and only becomes a memory by the addition of secondary character-istics, such as repetition and a lower degree of intensity. The two cases are similar; in both, the revived impression, according to the law formulated by Dugald Stewart and Taine, is accompanied by a momentary belief which places it in the position of an actual reality. But the recollection of a feeling, it will be said, has this special property, that it is associated with organic and physiological states which make of it a real emotion. I reply that it *must* be so, for an emotion which does not vibrate through the whole body is nothing but a purely intellectual state. To expect that we should actually revive a state of feeling without reviving also its organic conditions, is to expect the impossible, to state the problem in contradictory terms. We should, in that case, simply have its substitute, its abstraction, *i.e.*, the false affective memory which is a variety of intellectual memory; the emotion will be *re*cognised, not *re*vived.

Finally, the ideal of every recollection is that, while keeping its character of being already experienced, it should be adequate in such measure as was possible for the original impression. The revival of impressions is an internal operation, whose extreme form is hallucination. For the two forms of memory, intellectual and emotional, the ideal is the same, only each has its special mechanism for realising it.

There are all possible degrees of transition from the simple bald representation of the words pleasure or pain, love or fear, to the acute, fully and entirely felt representa-tion of these states. In a crowd of people taken at random, one might, with the help of adequate information, determine all the intermediate degrees, from the abstract to the concrete. Still more, these may be met with in the same individual. When the poet says that "Sadness departs upon the wings of Time," his meaning, in psychological language, is that the affective memory is gradually trans-formed into an intellectual memory. We know that certain artists, in order to get rid of the memory of a sorrow or a passion, have fixed it in a work of art. This was Goethe's method; every one knows the story of *Werther*, to quote but one example. One of my correspondents employs the same procedure with success; *i.e.*, in the case we are dealing with, the question is how to transfer emotion to the region of the imagination, and, consequently, intellectualise it.

I have said that in certain persons the revival of emotional states seems to be complete. Is it so in fact? I believe that it is impossible to give a precise answer to this question; and here we have a point where the emotional memory differs from the intellectual memory.

A given recollection is considered accurate; but in the majority of cases this is only an illusion. Nearly always, in revived impressions, there are deductions and losses, sometimes additions; sometimes they include *plus*, sometimes *minus* factors. At any rate, in the intellectual order, there are certain cases where one can say that the recollection is perfect, without the least gap or error; and this affirmation is legitimate because verifiable. It is quite sufficient to compare the copy with the original. If I enter a hall of the Alhambra with my eyes closed, I can ascertain whether the inner vision which I have retained from a former visit is adequate to the reality. I can check my recollection of a passage of music by the actual hearing of the same. The painter mentioned by Wigan who executed his portraits from memory, Mozart reconstructing Allegri's *Miserere*, are the classic examples of perfect cases where the impression is revived with irreproachable exactitude.

But in the region of the feelings this comparison is impossible, because two subjective states, of which one is the original and one the copy, cannot co-exist in the same individual, and because the primary impression cannot be objectivised. I see but one way of getting over the difficulty so as to arrive at an approximately correct answer. This would consist in comparing the revived emotional state with a written document dating from the moment of the first impression; and even this impression is open to doubt. J. J. Rousseau, speaking of the enthusiasm aroused by the love-letters of the *Nouvelle Héloïse*, tells us that they were inspired by his own love for Madame d'Houdetot, and adds, "What would they have said could they have read the originals!" It is possible that Rousseau was more or less mistaken; but this is a comparison of the kind I am suggesting. A correspondent, well equipped for psychological observations, and accustomed to note down the day's impressions, had promised me to attempt such a comparison between the actual recollection and the written document; but various causes have prevented the accomplishment of this purpose. One might possibly, without much trouble, chance to recover a letter written under the impression of the moment, and compare it with the present emotional recollection which, rightly or wrongly, we consider most correct. For my part, I am inclined to doubt whether, in the case of feelings, there is ever a complete correspondence between the original and the copy; but this is merely a hypothetical view.

It still remains to say a few words on forgetfulness in the region of the emotions. Affective amnesia is found in two forms—one pathological, the other normal.

I pass over in silence the morbid manifestations, whose study would be both extensive and curious, but would lead me away from my principal aim, which is a practical one. We find numerous examples of the loss of altruistic, moral, or religious feelings, of partial or total indifference to the past, of complete insensibility—the *Gemütslosigkeit* of the German alienists.

I confine myself to the consideration of affective amnesia under its simplest and most widely-known form. Nothing is more frequently met with. In the first place, the single fact that most psychologists either neglect or deny the phenomenon of emotional memory, constitutes a presumption that its function is not a very obvious one. Moreover, that emotional memory which I have designated the false or abstract one, may, without prejudice, be considered as a mitigated form of forgetfulness. Finally, eliminating the non-emotional temperaments as irrelevant to our subject, we may find, even among the emotional, many who feel acutely, but do not retain their emotions. Every one knows people whose whole nature is shaken by sorrow, joy, love, indignation; they seem for a long time as if possessed; a few weeks later, not a trace remains. Emotions glide off their minds as a thunder-shower does off the roofs. Now this affective amnesia has a great influence on conduct.

Here, in fact, are two general truths derived from experience, and in my opinion incontestable :—

On the one hand, pleasant and painful sensations are the most powerful, if not the only motive forces of human activity.

On the other, there are people in whom emotions are revived strongly, weakly, or not at all.

The conclusion is that the portion of individual experience resulting from the pleasures and pains experienced, will show itself, as to its efficacy, strongly, feebly, or not at all, according to the individual. The prodigal who has ruined himself and is restored to opulence by an unexpected chance, if he has not preserved a lively recollection of his privations, will begin his extravagant career over again; if his painful recollections are of a stable character, they will act on his natural tendencies as a restraining or inhibitory force. The drunkard and the glutton will not repeat their excesses as long as the impression of the after-effects remains vivid. The educator, as every one knows, has no hold over a child on whom the recollection of rewards and punishments has no effect. I have already mentioned the state of mind which frequently succeeds dangerous confinements; this, again, is a case of affective amnesia. The absence of sympathy, in many men, is only an incapacity for reviving the recollection of the ills they have suffered themselves, and consequently for feeling them in others. These are well-known facts, of which it is needless to lengthen the list; but however well known they may be, their psychological reason is, in my opinion, not always apprehended, because the importance of the emotional memory has not been recognised.

Affective amnesia, therefore, plays a much more important part in human life than we are apt to think. It often lets us into the secret of strange modes of action, though I would not assert that it *alone* is sufficient to explain these everywhere and always.

V.

The study just made seems to me to lead to the following conclusions :—

1. There exists an AFFECTIVE TYPE as clear and well-

defined as the visual, the auditory, and the motor types. It consists in the easy, complete, and preponderant revival of affective impressions

I have simply applied to an almost unexplored region of memory the methods of research inaugurated for objective sensations by Taine and Galton, continued by many others, and successful in their hands. It will, perhaps, be objected that the complete emotional type is rarely found; but neither is it certain that the visual, auditory, and motor types are of very frequent occurrence in a pure state. This, however, is of little consequence, the essential point being to determine its existence. Those who belong to this type will easily recognise it. I foresee that those whose memories are of the opposite type will refuse to admit it; but the members of the Royal Society and the Académie des Sciences,— being for the most part possessed of non-visual memories,— when questioned by Galton, failed to understand his queries, and would probably have rejected his conclusions. Many men have an incurable tendency to wish that every one were constituted like themselves, and to refuse to admit the existence of any departures from their type. Yet in psychology, even more than elsewhere, we must be distrustful of too extensive generalisations.

2. There exists not only a general emotional type; it admits of varieties, and it is even probable that *partial* types are the most frequent. Here I note a resemblance between my researches and those made with regard to impressions of objective origin. It is known that some persons have an excellent memory for faces, figures, concrete objects, but not for colours or visual signs, such as printing and writing. Others have an excellent memory for languages but none for music, or inversely. Moreover, have not numerous pathological phenomena demonstrated the fact that, in a determinate category of images, a whole group may disappear, without appreciable injury to the rest?

I have not at present a sufficient supply of documents to enter on the study of the varieties of the affective type; but it is certain that they exist; that, for some, a clear and frequent revival only takes place in the case of pleasurable impressions; in others, of gloomy or of erotic images. I have obtained conclusive affirmative answers on this point, but will only transcribe a case which deals with fear.

Case 7. "I am not what would be called a general emotional type, but I have a special emotional memory—that of fear, which in me is very pronounced. . . . I have had in my life, like every one else, many joyful moments ; I will frankly say that, when I remember those incidents in my life which have caused me great joy, I feel no joy whatever. Besides, it is very difficult to recall the moments in which I felt joyful, or even the incidents which produced my joy—probably because the representative memory has not been reinforced by the emotional memory. I do not know how this may be, and do not attempt to draw any inferences from my own case. I am only speaking of myself.

"I have tried to recall one of the moments in my life when I had the acutest sense of joy—it was in April 1888. [Here follows a long description of honours obtained by the author at the age of twenty, and the applause—unexpected at his age—of a numerous public assembly.] I have a clear and very accurate recollection of the incidents I have just been describing; I can remember the cause to which, rightly or wrongly, I attributed my success; I could repeat nearly every word I said on that occasion; I could remember (though not so easily) the hall and the faces of the audience; but I find, to-day, no joy whatever in thinking of all this.

"As regards my capacity for reviving sad recollections the same may be said as in the case of joyfulness.

"To return to fear. I have two very conclusive examples of special emotional memory. When a boarder at the S—— *lycée* at Bucharest, I dreaded all the staff of the institution on account of a punishment they were in the habit of inflicting on me —that of confinement to the schoolroom on holidays. I remember having such a fear of this imprisonment that, once I had left the building, it was with great difficulty I could bring myself to pass the gateway, for fear of being stopped. In later years, having finished my studies, and kept up friendly relations with all persons concerned, I used sometimes to return on a visit to the Lycée, but never without feeling a kind of terrified shudder on my entrance.

"More than this: having remained three years at Paris, without visiting my own country, I returned to Bucharest, and went to see a new director, with whom I was on friendly terms. Even then, when approaching the door of the institution, I felt a sort of uneasiness which was nothing else but my old dread in an attenuated form.

"In the first year of my stay at Paris I entered my name for the more advanced lectures of the Lycée L——. I only attended them for a week. In the class-room I was conscious of an uneasy feeling; I feared something without knowing what it was; I felt a horror of all the staff, though they were full of consideration for me, and at my age (twenty-two) I was no longer on the footing of a schoolboy. What could I have been afraid of? for I might have left whenever I wished it. Though accustomed to work for many hours together in libraries, I could do nothing in this class-room. I believe this state to have been a reminiscence of my old fear—that of the Bucharest *lycée*. . . . Long afterwards, when a student attending the lectures of the Faculté de Droit, I had every day to pass the Lycée L——. I would hurry past it as quickly as I could, feeling the same dread as at the time when I used to pass the gateway of the Bucharest *lycée*.

"I have a good motor, no visual, and a very slight auditory memory."

It might be said that in this case the revival is often artificially produced, and associated with special circumstances; but it seemed to me of too clear and definite a character to be omitted.

I need not point out that these individual differences in the revivability of emotional states certainly play a great part in the constitution of different types of character. Moreover, the existence of variations of the emotional type cuts short the question, acrimoniously debated by some writers, whether pains can be more easily remembered than pleasures. Optimists and pessimists have fought fiercely over this phantasmal problem; but it is a vain and factitious question so long as we suppose that it admits of but one solution. There is not, and cannot be, a general answer.

Certain individuals revive joyful images with astonishing facility; sad memories, when they arise, are immediately and easily trodden down. I know an inveterate optimist, successful in all his undertakings, who has much difficulty in picturing to himself the few reverses that he has experienced. "I remember joys much more easily than painful states" is an answer I frequently meet with in my notes.

On the other hand, there are many who say, "I remember sorrows much more easily than pleasurable states." In the course of my inquiries I have found that the latter are the most numerous; but I do not see my way to draw any conclusion from this fact. One says, "I find it much easier to revive unpleasant feelings, whence my tendency to pessimism. Joyous impressions are evanescent. A painful recollection makes me sad at a joyful moment; a joyful recollection does not cheer me at a sad one."

These are straightforward cases. Outside them the question above stated can only be solved at haphazard, and by a merely mental view.

3. Revivability depends on cerebral and internal conditions (whatever these may be, known or unknown) rather than on the primary impression itself. To feel emotions acutely and revive them acutely are two widely different operations; one does not imply the other. We have seen that, in many cases, revivability even seems to be in inverse ratio to the intensity of the initial phenomenon. This brings us back to the question of characters. It does not matter whether the impression is a vivid one; what is wanted is that it should be fixed. Often it is heightened by a process of latent incubation depending on individual temperament. Chateaubriand, speaking of a gamekeeper to whom he was much attached, and who was killed by a poacher, says, "My imagination (at sixteen) pictured to me Raulx holding his entrails in his hands, and dragging himself to the hut where he died. I conceived the idea of revenge; I wished to fight the murderer. In this respect I am singularly constituted; at the moment of a blow I scarcely feel it, but it engraves itself on my memory; *the recollection, instead of being weakened, grows stronger with time;* it sleeps in my heart for years together, then the most trivial circumstance awakens it with renewed force, and my wound becomes more painful than on the first day."[1] Here we have another analogy with what takes place in the order of objective impressions. It is not sufficient to have good eyes in order to have a good visual memory, and I know short-sighted persons whose inner vision is excellent.[2]

I may terminate this inquiry, which is a sketch rather than a study of the subject, by reminding the reader that

---

[1] *Mémoires*, vol. i. p. 77. The italics are not in the original.

[2] This has recently been experimentally demonstrated; the observations made by Dr. Toulouse (with the assistance of specialists) on M. Zola may be specially mentioned. In this case the coincidence of a somewhat low degree of sensory acuteness with a very high degree of delicacy and precision in revived sensory impression was found not only in the case of vision, but especially in that of smell. (Toulouse, *Emile Zola: Enquête Medico-psychologique*, 1896, pp. 164, 173, 179, 206.)—ED.

the facts ascertained for the other, the intellectual part
of memory, have not been the work of one man or of one
day.[1]

[1] This chapter was first published in the *Revue Philosophique* for
October 1894. It called forth some new communications, two only of
which have been added to the original text. The affirmation of a type
of affective memory has, as I expected, provoked both criticism and
denial. My principal opponent, Prof. Titchener, has published on
this subject a somewhat extensive article in the *Philosophical Review*
(November 1895), in which he reproaches me with not having cited a
single case of pure emotional memory—*i.e.*, memory from which all
sensory and ideational elements are absent, and where there is a revival
of feeling *as such*. An example of this kind, which should be quite
conclusive, seems to me almost impossible to produce. A pleasure, a
pain, an emotion, are always associated with a sensation, a representation, or an act; revival necessarily bringing back the intellectual state
which forms part of the complexus and supports it. But the real
question is elsewhere : Is revival, in certain persons at least, a dry
record, or a *felt* state? In this last case—and it does occur—there is
the recollection of the emotional state as such.

There is another objection : Can it be said that an emotion is the
reproduction of an antecedent emotion, and not a new emotion? The
reproduction of an emotion can itself be nothing other than an emotion,
but it bears the marks of repetition. Without returning to what has
been said above, I remark that those contemporary psychologists, who
study with admirable patience the mechanism of memory, neglect that
of its most general conditions. Now the chief of these is that every
recollection must be a *reversion*, by virtue of which, the past once more
becoming a present, we live at present in the past. The recollection
of an emotion as such does not escape the action of this law; it must
become actual once more—must *be* a real emotion, whether acute or
obtuse.

Taking account of the criticisms, and of the new material supplied to
me, I may once again sum up my inquiry thus—

1. The emotional memory is *nil* in the majority of people.

2. In others there is a half intellectual, half emotional memory, *i.e.*,
the emotional elements are only revived partially and with difficulty, by
the help of the intellectual states associated with them.

3. Others, and these the least numerous, have a true—*i.e.*, complete—emotional memory; the intellectual element being only a means
of revival which is rapidly effaced.

CHAPTER XII.

THE FEELINGS AND THE ASSOCIATION OF IDEAS.

The function of the feelings, as the cause of association—The law of affective association, conceived as general, and as local—I. Function of unconscious feeling: ancestral or hereditary unconsciousness; personal unconsciousness arising from cœnæsthesia; personal unconsciousness arising from the events of our life—Law of transference by contiguity, by resemblance: wide or narrow—II. Function of the conscious feelings: accidental cases, permanent cases, exceptional or rare cases.

IN this chapter we have still to deal with the relation between the feelings and the memory, but under quite another form, seeing that we have to study the feelings as a *cause.* Instead of establishing, as we have hitherto done, that there is such a thing as a real memory of the feelings, our present aim is to determine the function of states of feeling in the recalling of recollections and the association of ideas. Their importance as a hidden factor of revivability has been recognised by several contemporary writers,[1] some even having a tendency to exaggerate it.

We know that the theory of the association of ideas has been reduced to two fundamental laws—that of contiguity and that of resemblance. I may remark, without insisting on the fact, that they are not of the same nature; the first, being purely mechanical, the result of experience, while the

---

[1] I may specially mention Horwicz, *Psychologische Analysen,* vol. i. pp. 160 *et seq.,* 265-331, 369 *et seq.*; Fouillée, *Psychologie des idées-forces,* vol. i. pp. 221 *et seq.*; J. Sully, *The Human Mind,* vol. ii. pp. 76-80; Shadworth Hodgson, *Time and Space,* p. 266; W. James, *Psychology,* i. 571; Höffding, *Psychologie* (2nd ed.), p. 331.

second supposes, in addition to this, a certain degree of mental labour, for a complete correspondence between two states is rarely met with, and can only be grasped in consequence of a dissociation or abstraction operating on the raw materials. These two laws are purely intellectual; they are regulative principles deduced from facts, nothing more. They are rather descriptive than explanatory. They reveal the mechanism, but not the motive force. They suppose something beyond, unless we admit that ideas are psychic atoms endowed with some mysterious attraction or affinity. With regard to the determining reasons, they are dumb. Now it cannot be doubted that in many cases (not all) the cause of the association is to be found in a permanent or momentary state of the feelings.

The writers who have pointed out this influence (often efficacious though latent) have conceived this superior law, which might be called the Law of Feeling, in two different ways, some as absolute and universal, others as partial and local. I take my stand among the latter.

1. Fouillée (as also, it seems, Horwicz) has maintained the former thesis. "The association of ideas presupposes that of the emotions, and, with the latter, that of the impulses. The dominant impulse awakens, by association, the secondary impulses tending in the same direction. The tie which unites them is the unity of an aim in relation to which the impulses are medium, the unity of an effect in relation to which they are co-operating forces. . . . The laws of association and contrast are what dominate the association of the feelings" (*loc. cit.*, p. 221). I shall not be suspected of hostility to the essential spirit of this thesis, since the present work is only one long vindication of the primordial nature of tendencies. But unless we are led astray by the mirage of unity at any price, it is impossible to admit that *every* association supposes an emotional factor as a determining reason. Not to speak of the numerous cases resulting from contiguity, in which the part played by the feelings is very doubtful, I find an important category of purely intellectual associations, where the intervention of the feelings appears to me impossible to verify. Is it likely that the mathematician and the metaphysician who connect together a long series of abstractions have an emotional state as the support and vehicle of their thought,

whether the latter be discursive or constructive? I do not see, in theory or in fact, any reason for admitting this, unless we wish to involve the love of truth; and in any case this would only be a *primum movens*, not the direct and immediate cause of the associations.

2. The influence of emotional states must be stated as a principal, but not an exclusive cause. It is summed up in what Shadworth Hodgson has called the "Law of Interest." In a past event, everything is not equally interesting; in its revival, all the elements are not equally active, the most emotional bringing the others with them. "Two processes are constantly going on in redintegrations. The one a process of corrosion, melting, decay; the other a process of renewing, arising, becoming. . . . Those parts of the object, however, which possess an interest, resist this tendency to gradual decay of the whole object." [1] Coleridge rightly says that "The true practical general law of association is this: that whatever makes certain parts of a total impression more vivid or distinct than the rest will determine the mind to recall these, in preference to others equally linked together by the common condition of contemporaneity or continuity. But the will itself, by confining and intensifying the attention, may arbitrarily give vividness or distinctness to any object whatsoever." [2] The power attributed by Coleridge to the attention and the will finally resolves itself into an emotional state as ultimate cause, and from it alone can an increase of intensity be derived.

I shall insist no further on these generalities, as it will be more instructive to determine by means of a few details the influence of the emotional life on the memory. To this end I shall divide our study into two parts, the function of unconscious feeling, and that of the conscious feelings.

I.

It is not always easy to determine positively the degree in which unconscious feeling influences the memory in order to awaken it, or to connect ideas with one another. I have

[1] Shadworth Hodgson, *Time and Space*, p. 266; quoted by W. James, i. 572.

[2] *Biographia Litteraria*, chap. vii. p. 61 (Bohn's ed.); quoted by James, i. 572.

purposely employed the vague term "unconscious feeling" as prejudging nothing with regard to its nature. We may form any conception we like of it, either considering it as purely physiological or assigning to it a psychological character—that of a consciousness diminishing to infinity. Both these opinions have their partisans, but this does not matter as regards the following considerations. In this unconscious feeling I distinguish three strata, passing from the deepest upwards, from the more obscure to the less obscure.

1. Hereditary or ancestral unconsciousness. I mention this merely for the sake of completeness. It would consist in the influence of certain modes of feeling, inherited and fixed in a race, which might, without our knowing it, exercise some sway over our associations. Under this form, at least, it appears to me extremely hypothetical. Laycock[1] (1844), one of the founders of the physiology of the unconscious, attempts to explain by this means certain national and individual tastes ; the Hungarians are supposed to like plains because these appeal to the ancestral recollection of the Mongolian steppes, their primæval home. Herbert Spencer, who, however, has not occupied himself much with the influence of sentiments on the association of ideas, says incidentally that, in the impression produced by a landscape, "along with the immediate sensations, there are partially excited the myriads of sensations that have been in time past received from objects such as those presented ; further, there are also excited certain deeper, but now vague combinations of states which were organised in the race during barbarous times, when its pleasurable activities were chiefly among the woods and waters."[2] Schneider assumes this ancestral revivification in every æsthetic perception. We shall return to this subject in Part II. The predatory tastes of primitive man would explain certain agreeable associations (e.g., the pleasure of constructing a bloodthirsty drama) which contrast with the habits of civilised man.

These facts seem to me reducible to a single explanation. There are in every man latent tendencies, which may remain latent throughout his life, but may also be awakened and revealed by some accidental occurrence. They might be

---

[1] A Chapter on some Organic Laws of Personal and Ancestral Memory, 1875.
[2] Principles of Psychology, i., § 214.

called hereditary, since they are found in an inherited organism; but it would be quite as correct to call them innate. In any case, it is very difficult to prove that they are a survival, and above all a resurrection of once existing tendencies.

2. Personal unconsciousness arising from cœnæsthesia, *i.e.*, from the internal sensations collectively. This imperceptibly brings us down to consciousness, from the moment when the affective state can be verified without induction. A certain disposition, a certain manner of feeling, is the direct and immediate cause of association. It is permanent or transitory. If permanent, it answers to the temperament or disposition. As the subject is cheerful, melancholy, erotic, or ambitious, an unconscious selection is exercised on the ideas arising in consciousness; an artist and a practical man, in face of the same object, have two totally distinct modes of association. If transitory, it corresponds, in the same individual, to states of health and sickness, to changes of age; each one of these distinct states produces a distinct selection. The unity of certain dreams, in spite of the apparent difference of associations, has its easily discovered cause in an organic or affective disposition—fatigue, depression, oppression, circulatory or digestive troubles, sexual excitement. The simplicity and frequency of these facts will permit us to dispense with insisting upon them.

3. Personal unconsciousness, a residuum of affective states connected with anterior perceptions, or with events of our life. This emotional residuum, although latent, is no less active, and can be recovered by analysis. This case, one of the most important connected with our subject, has recently been studied by Lehmann [1] under the name of displacement (*Verschiebung*) of the sentiments, and by Sully under the name of *transference* of feelings; this second denomination seems to me the clearer and more accurate of the two.

Under its most general form—for its mechanism is not always the same—the law of transference consists in *directly* attributing a sentiment to an object which does not itself cause it. There is no transference in the sense that the

---

[1] *Hauptgesetze*, etc., pp. 268, 250-357; Sully, *The Human Mind*, ii. 78; cf. *Outlines of Psychology*, p. 349.

feeling is detached from the primary event in order to be connected with another; but there is a moment of general-isation or extension of the sentiment, which spreads like a drop of oil. This transference can be symbolically repre-sented. Let us represent an intellectual state by A, and by s the affective state which accompanies it; A by associa-tion excites B, C, D, E, etc., while s is successively transferred to B, C, D, E, etc. Thus we have, first, $\frac{A}{s}$, B, C, D, E, etc., then $\frac{A, B, C, D, E, \text{etc.}}{s}$, so that C, D, or E can directly produce s quite as A can, and even without the assistance of A. " The feeling is excited without the mediacy of the particular presentative element of which it was originally a concomitant" (Sully).[1] This law of transfer is of sufficient importance to delay us a little, because it plays a somewhat important part in the forma-tion of complex emotions, and we shall need to recall it more than once. Besides, it does not always operate in the same manner. I distinguish two principal cases, according as the transfer is the result of contiguity, or of resemblance.

Transference by Contiguity.—When intellectual states have co-existed and formed a complex by contiguity, and one of them has been accompanied by a special sentiment, any one of these states has a tendency to excite the same sentiment.

We can find numerous and simple examples in common life. The lover transfers the sentiment at first called forth by the person of his mistress to her clothes, her furniture, her house. For the same reason, hatred and jealousy vent their rage on inanimate objects belonging to the enemy. In absolute monarchies the reverence in which the king's person is held is transferred to the throne, to the emblems of his power, to everything directly or indirectly connected with his person. The following charming passage from Herbert Spencer relates to a less simple case of the same nature: "The cawing of rooks is not in itself an agreeable sound; musically considered, it is very much the contrary. Yet the cawing of rooks usually produces pleasurable feelings—feelings which many suppose to result from the

[1] *The Human Mind*, ii. 79.

quality of the sound itself. Only the few who are given to self-analysis are aware that the cawing of rooks is agreeable to them because it has been connected with countless of their greatest gratifications—with the gathering of wild flowers in childhood; with Saturday afternoon excursions in schoolboy days; with midsummer holidays in the country, when books were thrown aside and lessons were replaced by games and adventures in the field; with fresh, sunny mornings, in after years, when a walking excursion was an immense relief from toil. As it is, this sound, though not causally related to all these multitudinous and varied past delights, but only often associated with them, rouses a dim consciousness of these delights; just as the voice of an old friend, unexpectedly coming into the house, suddenly raises a wave of that feeling which has resulted from the pleasures of past companionship." We must remark that in the transfer by contiguity, which, by its very nature is automatic, the intellectual states act as *causes*, since the extension of the sentiment is subordinated to them.

Transference by Resemblance.—When an intellectual state has been accompanied by a vivid sentiment, every similar or analogous state tends to excite the same feeling.

In this psychological fact lies the secret of the emotion of love, tenderness, antipathy, respect, which we feel towards a person at first sight, without apparent reason, and which we are apt to put down to the account of instinct. But those who devote themselves to the analysis of their own consciousness will discover, in many cases, a more or less close resemblance to a person who inspires, or has inspired, us with love, tenderness, antipathy, or respect. A mother may feel a sudden sympathy for a young man who is like her dead son, or even merely of the same age. The explanation of many of these cases lies in an unconscious state which is not easy to seize, but which, if it returns to consciousness (a process in which the will is only very indistinctly concerned), elucidates everything. There are also so-called instinctive fears, without conscious motives, which, by going a little below the surface, can be referred to the same explanation.[1]

This transfer can take place in two ways, one narrow, the

[1] This point has been well treated by Lehmann, *op. cit.*, p. 244.

other broad. The narrow method rests on resemblance only: B resembles A, the perception or representation of whom is or was accompanied by a certain feeling; the transfer goes no further. The broader method rests on analogy, and has a much wider scope; it passes from one individual to several—to a class or classes. "A friend of mine," says Lehmann, "hated dogs; circumstances forced him to keep one; he attached himself to this animal, and gradually his feeling of sympathy spread to the whole canine race" (*loc. cit.*). This possibility of a limited transfer has been a social and moral factor of the first importance; it has allowed of the extension of the sympathetic sentiments from the small exclusive clan to more and more distant groups—the tribe, the nation, the human race. The wider transfer has been the great agent of the transition from particularism to universalism.[1]

II.

From the unconscious states to the affective states, of which the subject is fully conscious, the transition is made gradually and through doubtful forms; but whether obscure, semi-obscure, or clear, their influence remains the same. Among the numerous cases in which the association of ideas depends on a conscious affective disposition we may distinguish three groups :—

1. Individual, accidental, ephemeral cases. These can be reduced to a single formula: when two or more states of consciousness have been accompanied by the same emotional state, they tend to be associated with one another. Emotional resemblance unites and intertwines disparate impressions. It is a case of association by resemblance, *but not intellectual;* impressions are associated because they resemble one another in a common emotional colouring, not *qua* impressions. Examples of this are abundant. L. Ferri (in his *Psychologie de l'Association,* where, by-the bye, he does not note this emotional law) tells

---

[1] The mechanism of the suppression of the presentative intermediary between the initial state A and the distant states O, H, I, etc., has been studied by J. Sully (ii. 79). I do not insist on this point, which belongs rather to the psychology of association than to that of the emotions.

us that one day, being stung by a fly, he suddenly remembered a child seen by him, long ago, when himself very young, on its death-bed. Whence this sudden vision? "In the first place, I was lying on my bed, then I had been stung by a fly, and lastly, the sight of the corpse had caused in me a deep sadness, while, at this same moment, I also happened to be very sad." Association through emotional identity or resemblance is of frequent occurrence in dreams, as has been already said. I remember, among many others, a dream whose unity, in spite of the apparent incoherence of the association, was due to a general sense of fatigue. A road without milestones stretched before me, of which I was about to complete the last stage; steep mountains kept rising one behind another; my eyes were wearied with trying to catch sight of the longed-for town on the horizon; and every time I wished to inquire the way I had to speak a foreign language which I understand but imperfectly, and in which it is very difficult for me to express myself. I awoke, feeling a general aching and heaviness of all the limbs. Sully relates a dream whose unity consisted in a sense of anxiety and vexation. He was suddenly called upon to give a lecture on Herder; he began by stammering out some generalities; then he was addressed by one of his audience, who suggested difficulties to him; then the entire assembly broke up tumultuously. One of his children, who had seen, for the first time, the great clock at Strasburg, and, after an interval of two days, the Swiss glaciers, dreamed on the following night that the figures of the clock were walking about on the snow. In this case the groundwork of the dream is a feeling of admiration or surprise.

2. Permanent and stable cases; to be met with everywhere, because involved in the structure of the human mind. They are fixed in language. When dealing with the expression of the emotions (Chap. IX.) we met with "the principle of association of analogous sensations," formulated by Wundt. Adapting it to our present subject, we may say that sensations imbued with a similar emotional colouring are easily associated, and strengthen each other. Nothing can differ more in nature than our external sensations (except smell and taste), and the qualities which they make known to us; the data of

sight and hearing have no resemblance to one another as cognitions of the external world, yet we speak of sombre voices, clear voices, screaming colours, coloured music. We associate sight with thermal sensations, as when we speak of warm or cold colours. Taste also has its share— bitter reproaches, subacid criticism. Finally, touch, as Sully-Prudhomme has remarked, is perhaps the most abundant source of associations between the idea of the physical sensation and an emotional state; compare the terms touching, hard, tender, heavy, firm, solid, harsh, penetrating, poignant, piquant, etc. At the bottom of all these associations there is a common emotional colouring which both causes and supports them. Perhaps it would be more accurate to class them among the cases of semi-conscious emotional influence; but we have already said that our division into conscious and unconscious factors is superficial and of no great importance.

3. Exceptional and rare cases. Flournoy, in his important work on "coloured hearing," rightly explains this anomaly by "emotional association." We know that several hypo-theses on the origin and cause of this phenomenon have been constructed. On the embryological one, it would be the result of an incomplete differentiation between the sense of sight and that of hearing; a survival, we are told, from a primitive epoch when this state was the rule. On the anatomical theory, we suppose anastomoses between the cerebral centres of the visual and auditory sensations. Be-sides these we have the physiological theory, or that of nervous irradiation, and the psychological, or that of associ-ation. I do not inquire if all cases may be reduced to a single explanation; certainly most seem reducible to association. We are not, however, dealing with any and every form of association—it must be a psychological one, as Flournoy was the first to remark. "By emotional association, I mean that which establishes itself between two impressions, not on account of a qualitative resemblance (for the two may be as disparate as sound and colour), nor in virtue of their regular and frequent concurrence in the consciousness, but in consequence of the analogy between their emotional characteristics. Each sensation or perception possesses, in fact, along with its objective quality or its intellectual con-tent, a sort of subjective coefficient, springing from the

roots which it sends down into our being, and from the peculiar way in which it impresses, pleases or displeases, excites or subdues us, in a word, makes our whole nature vibrate. We can conceive how two absolutely heterogeneous sensations, incommensurable as far as their objective content is concerned, such as a colour and the sound *i*, may be comparable with one another and resemble each other more or less, by virtue of vibrations produced by them in the organism; and by the same process of thought it is conceivable that this emotional factor might become a link between the two, an associative bond by means of which one awakens the other."[1]

Let us add that we meet, though much more rarely, with cases of coloured smell and taste, and even, it appears, of coloured pain.[2] This abnormal association between determinate colours and determinate tastes, odours, pains, may be explained in the same manner.

Shall we attribute to the same cause a fact, ascertained (exceptionally, however) in the case of certain hysterical subjects in the hypnotic state, which may be described as follows? The excitation of certain circumscribed regions of the body immediately causes to arise in the mind either ideas or feelings which are imperiously imposed on the consciousness and last as long as the excitement which provoked them. Pitres, who has made an extended study of these "*zones idéogènes*,"[3] has discovered about twenty scattered over various parts of the body in the same subject. The effect of excitation (by friction or compression) is always the same in the same individual, but varies from one individual to another, which excludes the hypothesis of a previously existing mechanism. Among the feelings aroused by this procedure I note sadness, cheerfulness, anger, fear, eroticism, piety, ecstasy.

Most writers have limited themselves to the statement of the fact, without attempting to explain it. Pitres alone proposes the hypothesis of auto-suggestion, which is not far from an association of ideas. Must we admit an original

---

[1] Th. Flournoy, *Des phénomènes de Synopsie* (1893), p. 20.

[2] Suarez de Mendoza, *L'audition colorée* (1890), pp. 58, 59.

[3] *Leçons cliniques sur l'hystérie et l'hypnotisme,* vol. ii., lecture 39. Here will be found the historical part of the subject (Braid, Chambard, Féré) and the personal observations of the author.

fortuitous coincidence between a local bodily modification and a certain emotional state (or idea), whence an association through contiguity fixed and strengthened by repetition, so as to become indissoluble? Or can it be that friction and compression produce in certain subjects peculiar organic reactions, capable of exciting a special emotional state? We can only hazard conjectures.

In conclusion : the influence of emotiônal dispositions on the memory is great, and continually active; it contributes to the revival and association of ideas. Now, the emotional states are not entities, but modes of consciousness, the psychical equivalents of certain organic reactions—visual, vaso-motor, or muscular; so that the emotional influence reduces itself to all this. And is all this to be reduced to movements? A marked tendency towards this opinion is visible in several of our contemporaries. Fouillée, as we saw a little while ago, refers all association to that of impulses; Horwicz does the same under another form (*loc. cit.*). He places in the feelings the basis of all conservative memory, and the basis of all feelings in motion. "We recall our emotional state in proportion as we can reproduce the movements implied in it." By a different road—that of experiment—Münsterberg has attempted to show that so-called successive association is reducible to a rapid simultaneity, and that, if we suppress all movements during the reception of impressions, memory is much diminished and reproduction difficult.[1] It is true that his experiments were limited to articulatory movements.

I merely indicate in passing this general hypothesis. Whether admitted or not, the relation between the feelings and the association of ideas, though often misunderstood, has been indubitably proved by a mass of facts which, in spite of their heterogeneous character, all point to the same conclusion.

---

[1] Sommer (*Zeitschrift für Psychologie*, vol. ii.) reports an observation on an aphasic patient, which admits of an analogous interpretation.

PART II.

SPECIAL PSYCHOLOGY.

INTRODUCTION.

Importance of the study of special feelings—Utility of historical documents—Causes of the evolution of the feelings: (1) intellectual development; (2) hereditary influence, perhaps reducible to influences of environment—Cases in which the evolution of ideas precedes that of feelings—Inverse cases—The intellect swayed by the principle of contradiction; feeling by that of finality—Classification of primitive tendencies—Method to be followed—Group I.: physiological (reception, transformation, restitution)—Group II.: psycho-physiological—Group III.: psychological—Their enumeration.

I.

THE special study of the various manifestations of the emotional life enables us to penetrate much further into psychology than do the preceding generalities. This study is not a merely supplementary or elucidatory one to be abbreviated, treated cursorily, or even omitted altogether, as is done by some representatives of the intellectualist theory. As long as we have not considered, *seriatim* and in detail, every feeling, whether simple or compound, we have no idea of their rich multiplicity of aspects, of which general formulas are only meagre abridgments.

Some say or imply, contemptuously, that this is a purely descriptive study. But so long as we have found no other method of treating the question, it will always be better than silence. Hitherto, experimentation applied to the feelings has been kept within very narrow limits, and has done scarcely anything beyond corroborating the data furnished by observation. We must therefore modify our

point of view and seek elsewhere; anthropology, the history
of customs, of arts, religions and sciences, will often be
more useful to us than the contributions of physiology.
The experiments of the laboratory inspire some with a
faith not to be shaken; but the evolution of the feelings in
time and space, through centuries and races, is a laboratory, operating, for thousands of years, on millions of
men; and its documentary value is a high one. It would
be a great loss to psychology if these documents were
neglected. Having been long confined to introspective
observation, it has deliberately cut itself off from the
biological sciences, considering them alien or useless to
its work. It would not be desirable to fall into a similar
error with regard to the concrete development of human
life, and, after mutilating the study from below, to do
so from above. If the intellectual life has its roots in
biology, it is only in social facts that it can find its
full development. A science never gains by excessive
restriction of its scope; it is better to err in the opposite
direction.[1]

Since, therefore, we have to pass in review all the forms
of feeling, lower and higher, primary and derived, to
note the successive moments of their development, and to
follow them in their transformations, one question dominates
our whole subject: what causes determine the evolution of
the feelings?

In order to give to this question a clear and concrete
form, let us take primitive man, as reconstructed by the
anthropologists, not without much hypothesis and con-

---

[1] Among the causes which have given some impulse to the psychology
of the feelings during the last half of this century, Ladd (*Psychology,
Descriptive and Explanatory*, pp. 163, 164) mentions: (1) the theory
of evolution, because the affective phenomena are fundamental and
permanent, and men differ from one another far less in their appetites,
emotions, and passions than in their ideas and thoughts; and because
this doctrine affirms that, underlying the highest forms of feeling, there
is always some instinctive tendency; and (2) the literary and artistic
movement which began with J. J. Rousseau, and asserts itself more
and more in the Wagnerian music and the modern novel, and which
should invite psychologists to attempt its analysis. It would be well to
add the contemporary sociological studies which have shown the important part played by emotional elements, simple or complex, deliberately eliminated by the economists from their theories of social
organisation.

jecture. Whether he were the ferocious wild beast described by some, or a puny, feeble, naked being, chipping his first weapons among the rolled flints of a river-bed, keeping up with difficulty his famished life from day to day, and finding a precarious shelter from incessant dangers in the hollows of the rocks, it is in any case certain that he made originally but a poor figure on the surface of the globe. How has he progressed from primitive cannibalism to his present moral and social culture? from the bestial sexual act to chivalrous love? from coarse fetichism to religious metaphysics or mysticism? from the rude drawings of the Neolithic age to the refinements of the æsthetic sentiment? from a narrow and limited curiosity to a disinterested enthusiasm for science? How has the passage been accomplished from one extreme to the other? It is clear that a new form of feeling cannot arise by spontaneous generation; it can only be the work of a transformation, of a physiological development. How has this happened? What causes have brought about this metamorphosis?

The principal, essential, fundamental cause is intellectual development.

Another cause, adduced by many writers, but more doubtful and more limited in its action, is transmission by heredity.

1. In spite of its importance, the first cause need not detain us long, since it can only be presented, for the moment, under the form of vague generalities. Its action consists in the ascending progression which rises from the inferior forms of knowledge (sensations and perceptions) to concrete representations, then to abstract representations (generic images), then to the medium and superior forms of abstraction, and involves in its movement concomitant modifications of affective life produced by reaction. Primitive man, like the child and the animal, is at first only a bundle of wants, tendencies, instincts which, when not simply unconscious, are connected with external or internal tendencies. The instinct of self-preservation, a synthetic formula expressing a group of subordinate and convergent instincts, adjusts itself differently according to circumstances—sometimes defensive, sometimes offensive. It is only determined by the successive ends which it has to

attain, just as the muscular force of my arm may be equally
well employed in raising a weight, in firing a gun, in striking
a blow, or in caressing. The intellectual element, whatever
it may be, is always the determining principle; never, alone
and by itself, the spring of action. The process always
follows the same course, and remains identical from start
to finish; it passes from the simple into the complex, as we
shall see in discussing each separate emotion. The child
who feels acutely the possession of a toy, or the deprivation
of it, is not affected by the beauty of a landscape, by reason
of his limited intellectual power. We know that (in spite of
common opinion) a savage, even a barbarian, is not moved
by the splendours of civilised life, but only by its petty and
puerile sides. Its greater aspects inspire him neither with
desire, admiration, nor jealousy, because he does not understand them. Bougainville, in the last century, had already
remarked this fact, which has frequently been confirmed
since. Speaking of the profound indifference of the Pacific
Islanders to the skilled construction of his ships and
the instruments belonging to them, he says, "They treat
the masterpieces of human industry as laws and phenomena of nature."

2. Must we admit heredity as a special and independent cause of emotional evolution? This problem has
been hotly debated. Darwin, Spencer, and many others
following them, admit that certain acquired variations or
modifications in the range of the feelings may be heredi-
tarily transmitted, then fixed and organised in a race. They
give as examples, fear, the benevolent feelings, the love of
nature, the musical sense, etc.; the sudden return of so-
called civilised individuals to savage or nomad life, for
want of a hereditary tendency fixed by the habit of several
generations; while the co-existence of predatory tendencies
with the highest culture is for them a case of atavism or
reversion.[1] On the other hand, the dominant opinion for
the last twenty years (I think it shows symptoms of
declining) is radically opposed to the inheritance of
acquired modifications. Weismann and Wallace, who, more

[1] For further details, see my *Hérédité psychologique*, Bk. I. chap. v.
and Bk. III. chap. iii. Bain has discussed the question at great length
from the strictly psychological point of view (*The Emotions*, chap. ii.).
He inclines to a " probability " of transmission in certain cases.

than others, have touched on the psychological parts of this subject, are decidedly for the negative. The question is therefore an open one, and I accept it as such, in order to escape the accusation of a bias in favour of heredity. But even while admitting that there is no fact strictly conclusive in favour of the transmission of psychic peculiarities, it nevertheless remains true that some occurrences of this sort are probable enough, especially in the pathological order. These belong to the category of appetites, tendencies, and passions, much more than to the group of intellectual states. This might have been foreseen, physiological heredity being more stable than psychological, and physiological conditions affecting the emotional life much more immediately than the intellectual.

If then, by a reserve which is perhaps superfluous, we eliminate heredity as a factor in the evolution of the feelings, the functions of conservation and consolidation ordinarily attributed to it ought to be assigned to other causes—the influences of environment, imitation, tradition, education, with its multitudinous influences. It is clear that a new mode of emotion, arising in an isolated human consciousness, cannot last, increase, or become contagious, in totally different and uncongenial surroundings. Religious mysticism was irreconcilable with the bloodthirsty cult of the Aztecs; and what could a native St. Vincent de Paul have done among a tribe of cannibals, or a Mozart among the Fuegians?

But these influences of environment bring us back, indirectly, to our original cause; for manners, customs, traditions, institutions, all these are *ideas* which, with their accompanying feelings, have fixed and incarnated themselves in certain acts serving as starting-points for a new stage in evolution.

Nevertheless, the preceding statements cannot be admitted without qualification. We have stated it as a law that the intellectual development involves the evolution of the feelings; but this rule is not absolute, and should be taken with important reservations. In the first place, these two forms of evolution rarely advance *pari passu*. Not to mention the cases in which ideas remain completely ineffectual and abortive, and produce no movement, their action, in general, is only felt in the long run, and emotional evolution is retarded. In the second place, there are certain cases where the evolution of feelings is *direct*, and precedes that of ideas.

The philosophical historian, Buckle, in his study of the factors of civilisation, points out two as essential—intellectual progress and moral progress; after which he puts to himself what he calls a very grave question: which of these two is the more important, and dominant over the other? He is decisive in choosing the first. Buckle's question is in great part ours; for, though not comprehending all the manifestations of the emotional life, the moral sentiments form at least a very important fraction of it. His answer seems to me a legitimate one; but he was too much imbued with the notion that it is sufficient for an idea to be true and clearly conceived to make it an incentive to action; and he seems never to suspect that an idea can only supplant a feeling on condition of becoming a feeling itself.[1]

The intellect is capable of instantaneously finding out a new truth, or recognising an idea as just and conformable to the nature of things; but all this remains in a theoretic condition—*i.e.*, without emotional colouring or tendency to realise itself. That which is discovered so rapidly by means of logic, takes years, or even centuries, to become a motive for action. "If the Greeks were unable to extend their feelings of humanity so as to include the barbarians, the cause lay, not in intellectual insufficiency, but in the arrestive power of their national feeling. Christianity overthrew these barriers, not by means of intellectual reflection, but by the effect of an acute and deeply-seated feeling. Afterwards, within the limits of Christianity, intolerance raised new barriers, and fettered the natural development of religion."[2] We might find in history numerous examples of this inertia of the feelings, as in the case of slavery, etc.

---

[1] The discussion is to be found in his *Civilisation in England* (vol. i., chap. iv.). It may be summed up in the very questionable sentence quoted by him from Cuvier, "Le bien qu'on fait aux hommes, quelque grand qu'il soit, est toujours passager; les vérités qu'on leur laisse sont éternelles." He thus counts for nothing the institutions which have arisen from an original effort, a new growth of moral sentiment. The saying is a purely academic aphorism.

[2] Höffding, *Psychologie* (4th edit., German translation, 1893), pp. 411-412, where this point is briefly but ably treated.

We imagine the emotions as in a state of perpetual
motion and instability, whilst a habitual manner of feeling, in fact, possesses a formidable arrestive power, only
gradually lost under the influence of time. It is a
common saying that an argument has never changed a
conviction; but this is only the case if we regard the
present; it can act by incubation and at a great distance of
time.

Another reason for disagreement between the two modes
of development, the intellectual and the emotional, may be
expressed under a form which, though rather pedantic, is
clear and precise. Intellectual evolution is subject to the
principle of contradiction, emotional evolution is not; it is,
indeed, subject to a logical principle to be determined later,
but the principle is another. Let us suppose a purely
intellectual being: affirmations and negations regarding
the same object cannot co-exist in his brain; one elimi-
nates the other. If we suppose a purely emotional being
it will be found that two opposite tendencies can
be simultaneously active in him, each working towards
its own end, provided that they do not bring about the
destruction of the individual. In every individual who
contradicts himself there is, at the moment when he
contradicts himself, an emotional element at work. We
shall see later on that this is the key to all contradictory
characters, which are quite natural from the emotional
point of view, though they are the stumbling-blocks of the
intellect.

Finally, in certain cases the emotional development is
completely detached from the other, and even in advance
of it; this is direct evolution. Feeling, as has been said,
is the pioneer of knowledge—*i.e.*, it sometimes involves a
confused knowledge; it is the anticipation of an ideal.
In this case it is not an idea which excites a feeling, but
the development of a feeling which ends by taking concrete
form in an idea; its source is in the temperament and the
character. The theory of evolution has familiarised us
with the notion of spontaneous variations in animals and
plants. This phenomenon is also found in psychology—
in the intellectual order, in the emotional order, in the
order of action. We are too much inclined to believe that
inventors, revealers, initiators, exist only in the region of

knowledge or activity; but in the region of feeling, too, there are spontaneous variations, both serviceable and injurious. If there are original ways of thinking, there are also original ways of feeling, which impose themselves on others, create a contagion. We shall find examples of this in abundance, for these "variations" have played a great part, especially in the evolution of the moral sentiment.

These remarks are of too general a character, but will be supplemented later on, when we come to study each form of emotion in its turn. Such is the object of our second part. It will consist of a series of monographs of varying length. Except for a general survey of the law which seems to govern the dissolution of the feelings, their pathology will not be treated in a special section, but will be distributed throughout the work, terminating the study of each normal form, but only in such measure as will serve to render their nature more comprehensible, in which case it partakes of the character of psychology.

II.

Before setting out on our journey we must map out our route. At the beginning of this work I presented the reader with a general survey of the emotional life; it will be necessary to return to this subject in a briefer, more precise, and more limited manner. Since complex emotions are derived from simple emotions, and the latter from needs and instincts, whether satisfied or thwarted, from tendencies which are the direct and immediate expression of our physical and mental constitution; since the irreducible element is a motor phenomenon, actual or virtual, realised or in a nascent condition, it is indispensable to draw up a list of those primitive tendencies or instincts which are the roots of emotion.

On this point we have very little clear knowledge. Some writers do not notice it at all; others content themselves with a haphazard enumeration. W. James, who has seriously occupied himself with the question, lays down the principle that man has as many instincts as the animals, and even more, which seems to me indisputable. But his list, which he closes by saying that some will find it too long and others too short, contains very heterogeneous elements: instincts which are certainly primitive, derived instincts (as the love of possession), instincts whose existence as such is disputed (as imitation), pathological instincts (as the phobias or pathological fears, kleptomania, etc.), which last can only be considered anomalous, and, therefore, very different from simple and indecomposable instincts.[1]

Although it is rash to engage in a campaign in which some have fled and others failed, we must nevertheless attempt to draw up a list of primitive instincts (or tendencies), since these are the sources of all pleasures, pains, emotions, and passions. I can see but one method of attaining this end—a method long employed in animal psychology: that of admitting to the list of human instincts only those which present the following characteristics:—(1) They are innate. This does not imply that they appear at the very hour of birth, but that they are anterior to experience, not acquired; that they appear ready made, as soon as the fitting conditions exist. Those which are called *deferred* instincts, which make their appearance late, such as the sexual instinct in man and many animals, are none the less innate. (2) They are specific. They exist in the entire race, except for some individuals, who by reason of their exemption are, on the point in question, abnormal; so various instincts are wanting in the idiot. (3) They are fixed, in a relative sense; for no one now maintains the theory of the absolute invariability of instinct; and in man its plasticity is extreme, because a superior power, that of intelligence, moulds and adapts it to its designs.

These characteristics being determined, it remains to apply them in chronological order, and, starting with the birth of the individual, to draw up the catalogue of actual, strictly innate instincts. We shall then follow the course of life, noting the appearance of every new and indecomposable instinct, and thus continue till we have exhausted the list.

I propose to divide the instincts into three groups: the earliest in date being essentially physiological in its nature, the second psycho-physiological, the third essentially psycho-

[1] James, *Psychology*, ii. pp. 403-440.

logical. We shall not need to study them all, because some are outside the domain of general psychology, and others unconnected with the psychology of the emotions. The enumeration will be made, for the moment, in a very bald form, like a table of contents.

Group I. These belong to the life which biologists call organic or vegetative, as opposed to the life of relation. All these converge towards a single end, the fundamental act of life—nutrition. To simplify the matter as much as possible, let us divide this act into three stages: reception, transformation, and restitution.

(1) The first only has any psychological interest, showing itself in consciousness by two very energetic needs —hunger and thirst. It is almost superfluous to say that these instincts pass beyond the bounds of psychology into the domain of sociology, where their function is a very important one, as is seen by the phenomena of dearth, famine, theft, crimes, cannibalism, deadly combats for the possession of a little water, etc. Their pathology is thus more instructive than one would think, because it states and resolves, as we shall see, in a simple form, the problem of whether the tendency is anterior to pleasure and pain.

(2) The stage of transformation is purely physiological. It, too, shows itself in needs, of which the most pressing is that of breathing, an indispensable condition of the combustion of matter and the consequent interstitial exchanges. If air had to be acquired and conquered, like food, this instinct would show itself in consciousness, as do hunger and thirst; but this rarely happens (dyspnœa, asphyxia). Its pathology is not instructive, and only comprises individual peculiarities, such as always breathing either hot or cold air, sleeping with open windows, etc.

(3) The stage of restitution outwards (secretions, ex-cretions, etc.), though showing itself by instinctive move-ments, is only very indirectly connected with our subject; and though, in fact, *nothing* which takes place in the organism is quite unconnected with psychology, we may pass this over in silence.

Group II. These instincts belong to the so called relative life, and correspond to two stages—those of recep-tion and restitution. The first stage is represented by all the forms of external perception, and comprises the tendencies connected with the exercise of each of our senses, the tendency of each sensory organ to fulfil its function: the eye tends to see, the hand to grasp and feel. These tendencies, if satisfied, are agreeable; if obstructed, unpleasant. Hence result pleasure and pain, but not emotions properly so called. The second stage is represented by all the forms of muscular movement, tendencies to action, to the production of noises, as in certain animals, to cries, vocalisation, gestures, and bodily attitudes. We have seen that all these things, in popular opinion, serve to express emotions, while, in our view, they are integral parts of them.

Group III. This group of tendencies no longer has for its end reception or restitution, but the conservation and development of the individual as a conscious being. They express not his physical, but his psychical constitution, his mental organisation under its different aspects; they embody his needs as a spiritual being; as breathing, hunger, thirst, etc. embody his needs as a living being. They all therefore have a psychological character, and are the source of that complexus of pleasant, painful, or mixed movements and states which we call emotions.

Let us recall the chronological order of their appearance already indicated elsewhere: (1) The instinct of conservation under its defensive form expressed by fear, with its varieties and morbid forms (*phobias*). (2) The instinct of conservation under its aggressive form—*i.e.*, anger and its derivatives, and (in a morbid form) the destructive impulses. (3) The sympathetic tendencies and the tender (non-sexual) emotions. It may, however, be questioned whether sympathy can be called a tendency in the strict sense; it seems to me to be rather a general property of sentient beings, a point which will be examined later. The same thing may be said of the imitative instinct or tendency to imitation, which does not appear to be indecomposable.

These three primitive tendencies and emotions, with their derivatives, form the first storey of the building. Fear and anger especially have an extremely general character; we can descend very low in the animal scale before we find them absent. The tender emotions, based on sympathy (the source of social and moral emotions), cover a much narrower area; they are, however, to be found among the lower animals under the form of temporary or permanent associations.

The other tendencies are slower in appearing, and their circle is more restricted: (4) The play-instinct, if we use this word to designate the tendency to expend superfluous activity. This is a stock which puts forth several branches: (*a*) the need of physical exercise; (*b*) the taste for a life of adventure; (*c*) the passion for gambling, which so soon becomes morbid; (*d*) æsthetic activity. (5) The tendency towards knowledge (curiosity) only appears with a certain degree of intelligence and attention; at first connected with the exercise of the senses (looking at an object, touching it, etc.), it is strictly practical, though at a later stage producing all the varieties of the intellectual sentiment. (6) At a later epoch, and perhaps in man alone, are manifested the egotistic tendencies (self-feeling, *Selbstgefühl, amor proprius*), which express the *ego*, the personality as conscious of itself, and show themselves in the emotion of pride, or its opposite, and their varieties. (7) There remains the latest in date (at least in man), the sex-instinct, of which the exceedingly general character is well known.

Such are the tendencies which, in my opinion, are the roots of all simple or compound emotions, present, past, or future. This assertion will be justified or invalidated by the following studies.

CHAPTER I

THE INSTINCT OF CONSERVATION IN ITS
PHYSIOLOGICAL FORM.

*Hypothesis regarding the relation between the nutritive organs
and the brain—Perversion of the instincts relating to
nutrition — Pathology of hunger and thirst — Proofs
furnished of the priority of these tendencies in relation
to pleasure and pain—Facts in support of this—Negative
tendency; disgust—Its biological value as a protective
instinct.*

THE above title may seem quite unconnected with psychology, or at least of a nature to throw little light on our
subject. This is not the case. This group of tendencies
—for we have seen that the conservative instinct is a sum,
a total—represents the principal factors in what is called
cœnæsthesia, the very soil on which emotional life grows
and bears fruit. Moreover, the nutritive instincts have
their pathology, which enables us to watch, not the genesis
(which would be impossible) of new tendencies, but a
radical transformation, a complete change of orientation,
whose effects are easily observable and instructive. In a
normal state the instincts are presented to us as ready made
and in action; we cannot, either in ourselves or in others,
go back to that distant and obscure period when the unconscious impulse, the blind tendency, showed itself for the
first time, without antecedent experience of the pleasant or
unpleasant consequences. So that our affirmation that
tendency is antecedent to pleasure and pain may be stigmatised as merely theoretical so long as we are unable to
cite indubitable facts in demonstration of it. These facts
we are about to furnish.

I.

The nutritive acts take place in the inmost recesses of the tissues and organs. By what channels are they connected with the cortex, either when undergoing its influence or transmitting the echoes of their slackening, accelerative, and other modifications? On this point physiologists know little. According to some (Schiff, Brown-Séquard), there are relations between the digestive tube and the optic layer, the striated body, the cerebral peduncles; the psychic actions which modify respiration being transmitted through the third ventricle and the anterior corpora quadrigemina. The experiments of Pitres and François-Franck on the sensori-motor zone of the cortex show that excitement, at any given point, results in: augmentation, retardation, or even arrest of breathing; acceleration of the cardiac rhythm, and, if powerful, inhibition or even syncope; vaso-motor effects, a contraction or relaxation of the bladder; an influence on uterine contractions; on the secretion of the saliva and the pancreatic juice, and on trophic action in general. According to Goltz, the destruction of the anterior lobes produces atrophy, that of the posterior the contrary effect. These discrepancies and uncertainties are to us of small importance; but it remains certain that the nutritive functions especially depend on the pneumogastric and the great sympathetic nerves, that they are in some manner represented in the cerebral cortex and form the principal contents of cœnæsthesia. Though in the adult they play only a latent and intermittent part by reason of the preponderance of external sensations, images, and ideas, it is probable that in animals, particularly in voracious ones, the functions are inverted, and that cœnæsthesia, as a synthesis of the organic functions, passes to the front rank. This has even been asserted to be the case in children and savages, the argument being based on the fact that they have, in proportion, larger stomachs and longer intestines, and on various other characteristics.[1] However this may be, when deep-seated disturbances take place in the organism, cœnæsthesia is modified; which involves modification of the tendencies, and, consequently, of the position of pleasure and pain.

[1] Brugia, *Patologia della cenestesia* (1893).

The facts I am about to enumerate relate to nutritive needs only; but we shall find their equivalents or analogies in the other manifestations of emotional life. We can, therefore, already generalise so far as to say that when abnormal or morbid tendencies, however absurd or violent, show themselves, their satisfaction involves pleasure, their non-satisfaction, pain. Where the normal man, with normal tendencies, places pleasure, the abnormal man, with abnormal tendencies, places pain. Conversely, that which the man with normal tendencies feels to be agreeable, the man with abnormal tendencies feels to be unpleasant. Pleasure and pain follow the changes of tendency, as the shadow follows the movements of the body.

Let us look at the facts. We have at this moment to do only with the perversion of instincts relative to nutrition.

Pregnancy produces during the first few months digestive, circulatory, secretory disturbances, incomplete nutrition, and at the same time those grotesque aberrations of appetite, those depraved tastes, which every one knows, and of which the catalogue would be endless. Not to digress from the subject of this chapter, I say nothing of those morbid tendencies of another kind which show themselves at the same time in some women—homicidal or suicidal tendencies, aversion to husband, kleptomania, etc.

In anæmic, chlorotic, hysteric, and other subjects, if badly nourished, we sometimes find an acute pleasure in earth, straw, tobacco, chalk, sand, charcoal, etc., and an aversion to the most savoury foods.[1]

---

[1] I must here repeat Briquet's remark on this point: "However strange these appetites may appear, their origin can frequently be discovered. Thus a young woman, who would greedily devour the embers of her foot-warmer, told me that she had, from the beginning, been fond of the crust of bread; from this she came to like the crust of toasted bread, then charred bread, and so gradually acquired the taste for small pieces of charcoal. I am inclined to think that, were we to inquire into the origin of many of these strange tastes, we should find it as simple as the above." Pierre Janet (*État mental des hystériques*, ii. p. 71) transcribes this passage, and adds, "I have often followed this advice and been in a position to appreciate its value." This psychological inquiry is very ingenious, but only removes the difficulty a stage further back. It shows us through what series of associations the final result is attained; but association alone is not sufficient to arrive at this result, still less to render it permanent. It is only the external mechanism which explains, at the utmost, why the deviation should

There are many instances of hypochondriacs searching for and devouring with enjoyment worms, toads, spiders, caterpillars, etc.; and the beginning of insanity is often marked by an eccentric and disordered dietary.

Again, at a still lower stage, we have coprophagy and scatophagy (the swallowing of excrements, urine, the contents of spittoons, etc.), which are rarely, if ever, found in any but idiots and those suffering from dementia, *i.e.*, in beings whose simplest instincts have been abolished or perverted. The voracity of certain idiots has been attributed to paralysis of the gastric branch of the vagus nerve.[1]

The same would apply to the sense of smell, so intimately associated with that of taste that it has justly been called "tasting at a distance." (We must not, moreover, forget its close connection with the sex-instinct.) Certain persons, who cannot endure the most delicate aromas, enjoy the odour of valerian, of asafœtida, and of still more repulsive substances.

To sum up, we may say that, in a given race, at a given moment of its development, there is a certain average of alimentary tastes, whose satisfaction is pleasurable; but on the appearance of deep-seated disturbances in the organism everything is changed, tendencies, desires, and aversions; the pleasurable and painful states, *which are merely effects*, vary with and in the same manner as their cause.

The physiological acts, which have for their aim the maintenance of nutrition, scarcely enter into the consciousness, except under the guise of hunger and thirst, whose psychology cannot be studied here, because it forms part of another department—that of the sensations. All the phenomena previously enumerated are reducible to anomalies or

---

have taken this particular direction. Many persons are fond of crust, even of burnt crust, who will never come to have the slightest appetite for charcoal. Many have eaten charcoal out of curiosity, or by accident, but without acquiring a taste for it. It is some deeper and more powerful cause than association which lies at the root of these feelings and renders them active.

[1] For details, see Campbell "On the Appetite in Insanity," in the *Journal of Mental Science*, July 1886, pp. 193 *et seq.*, and Belmondo, "Pervertimenti dell' istinto di nutrizione," in Tamburini's *Rivista*, 1888, pp. 1 *et seq.*, where is cited the case of an insane patient in whose stomach were found 1841 objects, such as nails, bits of lead, and the like, weighing in all eleven (English) pounds, ten ounces.

deviations of hunger. The pathology of thirst is simpler, for it may be summed up as dipsomania, a condition whose modalities and clinical varieties have no interest as regards the psychology of instinct; but so far as this need is concerned, the transformation of the normal and natural tendency into a morbid one does not differ in its mechanism and results from what we have already stated in the case of hunger.

There exist, in general and special treatises, many descriptions of dipsomania to which we may refer the reader. Leaving aside all hallucinations, motor disturbances, intellectual and moral decadence, we shall only consider the genesis, the development, and the consolidation of this morbid tendency.

" It is not every one who can be a dipsomaniac." To drink too much, whether voluntarily or by accident, is a thing which may happen to any one; but such an occurrence does not necessarily bear the fatal and inexorable character of an insatiable instinct. The period of incubation—*i.e.*, of gradual action tending towards complete metamorphosis—presents clearly-marked psychological characteristics, showing a disturbed state of cœnæsthesia and belonging to the region of the emotions: *malaise*, sadness, lack of energy and courage, apathy, moral insensibility, vague presentiments of danger. After this the eruption takes place in the form of an intense, devouring thirst. Many try to react on this and cheat themselves by the aid of water or mucilaginous substances, which shows, as several writers on the subject have remarked, that alcoholism properly so called is only a paroxysm: under the pressure of a progressively intensified craving the decisive step is taken. We shall find a great variety in the numerous observations published on this subject, a struggle at the beginning only, a struggle preceding every attack, indignation of the patient against himself, under the influence of which he calls himself names, and forces himself to swallow strange and repugnant beverages; all these phenomena are found in various cases. To sum up, the history of this psychological metamorphosis is briefly this : incubation, formation of a fixed idea, obsession, final fall.

It is scarcely necessary to point out once more that the primary fact is the transformation of a natural tendency,

in consequence of changes in the organism, and that satisfaction and appeasement only come *afterwards*.

II.

Nutrition—*i.e.*, the essential act of physiological life—
is safeguarded by two distinct kinds of tendencies. (I
am still speaking of those only which come within the
bounds of consciousness, and therefore have a psychological
character.) On the one hand, we have the positive tendencies, consisting in an attraction towards and attack on the
external world (in this case, food and drink)—viz., hunger
and thirst. On the other hand, the negative tendencies
consisting in aversion, refusal, flight, and summed up in the
state known as disgust.

Disgust is due to excitement of the pneumogastric nerve,
producing vomiting, nausea, or mere *malaise*. This repulsive instinct is connected (1) directly and immediately
with taste and smell, two senses which can scarcely be
isolated, and whose function is to watch over all substances
entering the organism ; (2) indirectly and through association of ideas with visual and tactile sensations (sticky,
slimy bodies, etc.), by analogy and metaphorically with
certain objects which have nothing in common with the
nutritive functions—the ugly, the immoral, etc. In virtue
of that law of transference or association of analogous
sensations, of which we have spoken, the tendency departs
more and more from its primary form ; but in all cases
there is a common groundwork of repulsion, refusal, desire
to escape, etc.

Disgust under its primary form (the only one now
occupying us) has not been much studied. Writers have
contented themselves with classing it among organic sensations, while neglecting its emotional side, *i.e.*, its function in
the conservation of the individual. The only work I know
on this subject is the excellent monograph of Ch. Richet,[1]
of which I here give a summary.

Disgust is connected with conservation ; it is "an instinctive feeling of protection." In order to justify this state-

[1] "On the Causes of Disgust," in *L'Homme et l'Intelligence*,
pp. 41-84.

ment, the author passes in review the various objects in nature, noting those which inspire us with disgust, and inquiring into the cause of this. The inorganic kingdom, in general, leaves us indifferent; yet sulphuretted hydrogen, ammonia, and various other gases cause a marked repulsion. This is the effect of an association of ideas; the smell recalls that of decomposition, of a corpse. As regards the vegetable kingdom, the herbivora, by reason of their diet, are the best subjects for observation; their instinct scarcely ever deceives them in the choice of food. We are reminded that, on their arrival in the New World, the Spaniards, hesitating before an unknown flora, whose properties were unknown to them, trusted the judgment of their horses. In man, Richet attributes the repellent influence exerted by bitter aromas to the fact that they frequently co-exist with toxic properties; he takes as types the vegetable alkaloids (quinine, nicotine, etc.), whose power as poisons is in some degree proportioned to their bitterness. So that we have always, at bottom, "the love of life and the horror of death." In the animal kingdom disgust is aroused by putrescent matter, which indicates or suggests cadaveric decomposition and toxic substances; by parasites, by animals really venomous, or so reputed; for instinct, which sees everything in mass, confounds in the same repugnance the toad and the frog, the venomous serpent and the harmless snake.

In its general bearing, the thesis of the finality of disgust is incontestable. There are, no doubt, many exceptions, many facts difficult to explain (some have been pointed out by Richet); but if we take into account the complexity of the question, all objections fall to the ground.

That tastes are not to be argued about is a platitude which has been worn threadbare for centuries past. Taken literally, it would reduce disgust to a purely intellectual manifestation, with no biological bearing; it would deprive it of all specific character, and utterly eliminate it as an instinct. This, however, is a merely superficial position. Contradictions in taste may be compared with contradictions in morality. Variations in manners and customs, according to race, epoch, country, and even caste, do not exclude the existence of a law which has this characteristic common to all cases—that it is derived from the conditions of existence of each group, and is by that right imposed on it. In the same way, disgust exists everywhere, under one form or another, as a protective instinct. The question is complicated, in man, by his intellectual development, and the consequent modification, transformation, or even suppression of this instinct. Between reasoned knowledge and instinctive tendency a battle has been fought, in which the victory inclined sometimes to one side, sometimes to the other. We know the repugnance of animals towards a change of food. The same thing is seen in children, and in the inferior races, when not pressed by necessity. Plasticity grows with civilisation.

We may add to this the necessity for new adaptations; thus, in a besieged town, people devour unclean food; the instinct of physiological conservation is a "divided house," where the positive form struggles against the negative with results, varying in different individuals. To this antagonism between primitive instinct and more complex rational motives let us add the influence of imitation and of fashion, and there will remain few or no unexplained exceptions.

As for the *origin* of this instinct, if we accept the hypothesis of acquired modifications, we may say that the animals and men best fitted for abstaining from hurtful substances, have *ipso facto* better chances of survival, and that they have been able to transmit to their descendants certain qualities which became fixed and organised as an innate tendency. Whether or not we admit this hypothesis does not matter, our only aim being to remind the reader that disgust is not a capricious and irrelevant phenomenon, but has its roots in the unconscious depths of our organisation.

CHAPTER II.

FEAR.

*Fear the conservative instinct under its defensive form—
Physiology—Psychology—First stage: Instinctive fear—
Hypothesis of heredity—Second stage: Fear founded on
experience—Pathology—Morbid or pathological fears—
Two periods in their study—Attempts at classification—
How are they derived from normal fear? Two groups,
connected respectively with fear and disgust—Inquiry
into the immediate causes: events in life of which a
recollection has been retained; of which no recollection
has been retained—Occasional transformation of a vague
state into a precise form.*

THE instinct of individual conservation, under its defensive
form, is the origin of the emotion called fear, and its
varieties. We have already said, more than once, that it
is the first in chronological order of appearance, showing
itself, according to Preyer, at twenty-three days; according
to Perez, at two months; while Darwin puts it as late as the
fourth month. It is the first manifestation in the consciousness of emotion properly so called, as a psycho-physiological complexus. Following the method which will be
invariably applied to every emotion, simple or composite,
we shall examine in turn its psychology and its pathology.

I.

It has been defined as "the particular emotive reaction
which takes place through a sufficiently vivid and persistent

representation of possible pain or evil."[1] This formula, though good in the majority of cases, does not seem applicable to the first stage of fear, as we shall see presently.

The physiology of fear has been worked out by Darwin, Mantegazza, Mosso, and Lange. I prefer the last writer's description, as being more systematic; it is not a collection of isolated facts, but a logically arranged synopsis. We know already the importance attached by him to the physiological conditions of each emotion. The characteristic marks of fear are :—

1. As regards the innervation of the voluntary muscles: a greater weakening than in the case of sorrow, a convulsive tremor; in extreme cases, suppression of all movement, one is fixed to the spot; voice hoarse and broken, or complete dumbness; in short, a more or less accentuated paralysis of the whole voluntary motor apparatus.

2. As regards the muscles of organic life : arrest of the lacteal secretion, of menstruation, of the salivary secretion; the mouth dry, the tongue adhering to the palate; cold sweats, "goose-flesh," bristling of the hair, arrest of respiration, oppression, constriction of the throat. Fear also, as is well known, influences the intestinal secretions.

3. As regards the vaso-motor apparatus : a spasmodic constriction of the vessels, shiverings, violent spasm of the heart ; and if the impression is of excessive violence, paralysis, which may end in death; pallor, and peripheral anæmia.

These manifestations collectively express a lowering of the vital tone which in no other emotion is so complete and so clearly marked. It has been maintained with reason that fear has a teleological character, that it is adapted to an end—that of withdrawing, escaping, exposing one's self as little as possible to attack, and remaining on the defensive in view of possible approaching evil. However, the case is not so simple as it appears. The slight or moderate forms of fear, through the feeling of weakness produced by them

---

[1] J. Sully, *The Human Mind*, vol. ii. p. 91. The reader should also consult Mosso's well-known monograph on *Fear* (English tr.), and Bain, *The Emotions*, ch. viii. Fear has been tolerably well studied. The absence of monographs concerned with the other emotions is another proof that emotional psychology is yet in its infancy, whereas for the memory, perceptions, images, etc., we find, on the contrary, a large number of special studies on special points.

in the consciousness, are a protection against hurtful actions by inducing withdrawal or flight. But the grave forms, such as terror and fright, accompanied by trembling and. motor annihilation, place us face to face with a great difficulty. When existence is menaced, at the most decisive moment, when attack, defence, or flight is urgently demanded, we see men and animals, paralysed with agitation, fall victims, unable to make any use of what strength they have. Darwin confines himself to remarking that the problem is very obscure (ch. xiii.). Mantegazza (*op. cit.*, ch. vii.) alleges that trembling is extremely useful, because it tends to produce heat and warm the blood, which, under the influence of terror, would soon grow cold. Mosso has very good reasons to oppose to his compatriot's thesis. He considers the "cataplexy" which accompanies the extreme forms of fear as a grave imperfection of the organism. "One would think that nature, in making the brain and spinal cord, was unable to devise a substance of extreme excitability which should at the same time, under the influence of exceptionally strong stimuli, be capable of never passing in its reactions beyond the limits needful for the preservation of the animal." In short, terror and fright appear to him in the light of morbid phenomena. From the naturalistic point of view this extra-teleological position is perfectly admissible. A finalist conception of the world admits of no exceptions, and has to explain everything according to its own principle; but if we content ourselves with saying that the conditions of existence of a living being are sometimes given, sometimes absent, we have no more to do but verify the cases in which they are wanting and the occurrences logically following therefrom.

The psychology of fear includes two stages, to be studied quite distinctly. There is a primary, instinctive, unreasoning fear preceding all individual experience, and a secondary, conscious, reasoned fear posterior to experience. They are generally confounded with one another, and as the second is by far the most frequent, it serves as the typical form in descriptions.

First Stage.—Numerous observations prove the existence of an innate fear, not attributable to any individual experience. In children, Preyer [1] maintains the existence of

---

[1] *Die Seele des Kindes*, chap. vii.

"a hereditary fear manifesting itself on occasion." Many are afraid of dogs and cats, though they have never been bitten or scratched; thunder makes them cry out— why? The fear of falling, says the same author, during first attempts at walking, is as strange as the fear shown towards animals. At fourteen months, this writer's son could not venture to take a step without support, and was full of terror if the person holding him let go; yet he had never experienced a fall. He concludes, very justly, that "it is quite erroneous to think that the child who has not been taught to fear things does not know fear. The courage or fearfulness of the mother certainly exercises a great influence; but there are in children so many cases of motiveless fear that we must admit some hereditary influence." The same fact has been observed in young animals: Spalding's experiments on newly-hatched chickens and their instinctive terror of the hawk are well known. Preyer repeated this experiment, with like results. Gratiolet, as I have already said, relates that a little dog, who had never seen a wolf, on smelling a piece of the skin of that animal, was seized with indescribable terror. Adult man, though his fears are in general based on experience, sometimes manifests (at least this is the case with ignorant and primitive people) vague, unconscious fears of the unknown, of darkness, of mysterious powers, witchcraft, sorcery, magic, etc. Ignorance is a great source of terror; and Bain has said, not without reason, that knowledge is the great remedy against fear.

How shall we explain the apprehension of an evil which has never been experienced? Even if we admit that fear may sometimes, and from the very beginning of life onward, start from analogies, resemblances, associations of ideas, there remain many cases which can be reduced to no simple form. We have seen that Preyer, following Darwin, Spencer, and other evolutionists, admits the influence of heredity. It is a well-known fact that birds on uninhabited islands show no fear when they see man for the first time; they are taught by hard experience to distrust him, and the acquired fear is, on this theory, transmitted to their descendants. According to this hypothesis, fear would be, always and everywhere, the result of experience, whether individual or ancestral, and what we have called the second stage would be the first, and indeed the only one.

This explanation is naturally rejected by those who refuse to believe in the inheritance of acquired qualities, though they have nothing satisfactory to propose in its place. Besides, this is a question of origin, on which experimental psychology may well recognise its incompetence. Not to remain on debatable ground, we must admit—since individual experience cannot be appealed to—that the bases of fear exist in the organism, form part of the constitution of animals and men, and help them to live by a defensive adaptation, which in most cases proves useful. As for the obscure mechanism of this instinctive fear, we may suppose that certain sensations produce a painful shock which excites the organic, motor, and vaso-motor relations constituting emotion, and that the conservative instinct, in order to escape *actual* pain, reacts blindly, with or without profit. This makes it impossible to explain certain innate fears by reason.

For my own part, I consider the hypothesis of a hereditary disposition to certain fears as extremely probable.[1]

Second Stage.—The definition given above may be unrestrictedly applied to conscious and reasoned fear posterior to experience. It is based, not on the intellectual, but on the emotional memory. The attempts of the earlier associationists to account for fear as a mere product of association, as in James Mill's doctrine that it is the idea of a painful sensation associated with the idea of its being future, were wholly inadequate through ignoring the essential factor, the emotional element, the organic disturbance.[2] If I am to be afraid of the extraction of a tooth, it is necessary that, in the memory of a former

---

[1] Since the above was written the same conclusion has been reached by Professor Stanley Hall in a report founded on a statistical inquiry into the fears (some 6500 in number) of 1700 children and young persons. He concludes that " we must assume the capacity to fear or to anticipate pain, and to associate it with certain objects and experiences, as an inherited *Anlage*, often of a far higher antiquity than we are wont to appeal to in psychology." He considers that such fears are analogous to rudimentary physical organs, though they still retain a certain use. (" A Study of Fears," *American Journal of Psychology*, vol. viii., No. 2, 1897.)—ED.

[2] J. Sully, *op. cit.*, ii. 91.

operation, its painful colouring should be revived, at any
rate in a modified form; if I have only a dry recollection,
with no physiological vibration, fear will not arise.   There
is no need to insist on a point already fully treated of in the
First Part.

It results from this that we are accessible to fear in
proportion as the representation of future evil is intense,
i.e., emotional and not intellectual, felt and not understood.
In many persons the absence of fear only amounts to the
absence of imagination.   This explains how it is that every
lowering of vitality, whether permanent or temporary, pre-
disposes to this emotion; the physiological conditions which
engender (or accompany it) are all ready; in a weakened
organism fear is always in a nascent condition.

The emotion which now occupies us exists in all degrees,
from such feeble forms as suspicion and apprehension to
the extreme ones of panic and terror.   These gradations,
fixed by language, cannot have a distinct psychological
description made of each of them.   Nevertheless, Bain has
attempted to enumerate the different kinds of fear, and some
experiments of Féré's indicate the different physiological
effects following each degree of fear.[1]   When an owl, a
serpent, or a spectre was caused to appear, by suggestion,
the muscular reaction, shown in graphic tracings, was
different in every case.

II.

To draw a distinction between the normal and morbid
forms of fear is a task which, at first sight, might appear
tolerably difficult.   We have, however, a criterion to guide
us.   Every form of fear which, instead of being useful,
becomes hurtful, which, ceasing to be a means of protection,
becomes a means of destruction, is pathological. We have
already (Part I., chap. iv.) indicated the marks which enable
us to discriminate between the healthy and the morbid ; I
recall them once more.

Morbid emotion presents one or more of the following
characteristics: it is apparently disproportionate to its cause;

---

[1] *Dégénérescence et Criminalité*, pp. 28 *sqq.*, with the illustrative
figures.

it is chronic; its physical accompaniments are of extra-ordinary intensity.

On the question of morbid fears, now known by the name of *phobias*, there exists a great mass of observations, notes, and papers, which is increasing day by day, and contains far more enumerations and descriptions than attempts at explanation. J. Falret and Westphal (in his essay on agoraphobia, 1872) seem to be the first who have entered on this path. To Westphal's fear of open spaces and Falret's fear of contact may be added many others; and we pass through a first period, where we find a veritable deluge of *phobias*, each having its special name; one person fears needles, another glass, one low places, another high places, one water, another fire, etc. Every morbid manifestation of fear is immediately fitted with a Greek designation, or one so reputed, and we have aïcmo-phobia, belenophobia, thalassophobia, potamophobia, etc., even siderodromophobia (the fear of railways) and tria-kaidekaphobia (fear of the number 13!). The list of these *phobias* would fill pages, and it is clear that there is no reason why it should ever stop; all the objects in creation might be included in it, if clothed in pseudo-Greek garb.

Accordingly, a reaction has taken place. Instead of, as was at first done, considering each phobia separately, naming it after its object, and so losing one's self in endless varieties, the tendency now is to regard them only as individual cases of a general morbid disposition, whose essential psychological characteristics are a fixed idea or obsession, and symptoms of fear sometimes reaching the dimensions of a paroxysm, and expressing themselves in convulsions and hysterical attacks.

Several classifications have been proposed, with a view to introducing some order into this multiplicity. Some proceed subjectively, classifying according to the sensations, per-ceptions, images, ideas, or feelings which form the basis of the fear. Thus the fear of contact is connected with touch, agoraphobia with sight, and so on. Others proceed ob-jectively; Régis proposes five groups: (1) the fear of inanimate objects; (2) of living beings (fear of crowds, solitude, inoffensive animals); (3) of spaces (agoraphobia, claustrophobia); (4) of meteorological phenomena; (5) of illness (nosophobia, with its very numerous varieties). To be accurate, these classifications, though they may be useful to the clinical lecturer, are of no great advantage to the psychology of fear; the interesting problem lies elsewhere.

Before reaching this, let us remark that, apart from any particular fears, there exist some observations on a vague but permanent state of anxiety or terror, which has been called panphobia, or pantophobia (Beard). This is a state in which the patient fears everything or nothing, where anxiety, instead of being riveted on one object, floats as in a dream, and only becomes fixed for an instant at a time, passing from one object to another, as circumstances may determine.

If, leaving aside the endless enumeration of the kinds of fear and their description, we seek—for this is the task incumbent on psychology—to determine their derivation from normal fear, and the causes which excite them, we enter an almost unexplored region and pass from riches to indigence.

As far as concerns their psychological origin, *i.e.*, the determination of the normal type from which they are deviations, I propose reducing them to two groups.

The first is directly connected with fear, and includes all manifestations implying in any degree whatever the fear of pain, from that of a fall or the prick of a needle to that of illness or death. The second is directly connected with disgust, and seems to me to include the forms which have sometimes been called *pseudophobia* (Gélineau). Such are the fear of contact, the horror of blood, and of innocuous animals, and many strange and causeless aversions.

Let us remark, furthermore, that fear and disgust have a common basis, being both instruments of protection or defence. The first is the defensive-conservative instinct of the relative life, the second the defensive-conservative instinct of the organic life. As both have a common basis of aversion, they show themselves in equivalent ways: fear by withdrawal, departure, flight; disgust by vomiting or nausea. The reflexes of disgust are the succedanea of flight; the organism cannot escape by movement in space from the repugnant body which it has taken into itself, and goes through a movement of expulsion instead.

After having traced back all morbid fears to two sources—

which may indeed be reduced to one—we have to seek for
their causes. One very general cause, with which most authors
content themselves, is degeneracy. I shall speak of this
elsewhere (see Conclusion); but as it is constantly brought
in to explain the most dissimilar manifestations, it assumes
such a general character that it becomes necessary to
supplement it. Let us then, if any importance is attached
to this, assume degeneracy as the soil on which morbid
fears spring up and multiply; then let us seek the complementary causes, which are less vague and nearer to the
facts. I would propose three such.

1. The cause is in some event of a man's previous life *of
which he retains the recollection.* For example : A man
walking on a terrace on the top of his house failed to
perceive that the balustrade was missing at one spot; he was
walking backwards, and would have fallen over the edge
had he not been stopped; he contracted permanent agoraphobia.[1] A morbid fear of railways is frequently found
in overworked engineers, and especially in men who have
narrowly escaped with their lives in a railway accident.
The well-known case of Pascal seeing an abyss at his left
side, which prevented him from walking forward unless
some one held him by the hand, or a chair was placed for
him to lean on, was a consequence of his accident at the
bridge of Neuilly. It is also said that Peter the Great,
having been nearly drowned when a child, felt, on passing
a bridge, a fear which he had some difficulty in over-
coming.

We can easily see that many *phobias* come under this
category. Now, the cause here is only the exaggeration of
a normal fact. Every serious accident leaves behind it a
recollection, which, for some, is merely a bald record of the
event and the circumstances (intellectual memory), for
others, a revival in some degree of the fear formerly
experienced (emotional memory); for "phobic" subjects
it is (at least potentially) a permanent state, ready to
arise when suggested by some association.[2]

2. Some morbid fears have their origin in occurrences of

[1] Gélineau, *Des peurs maladives*, p. 34; see also pp. 18, 109,
126, 169, etc.
[2] Many "phobias" seem to me fresh proofs in favour of the existence
of a true emotional memory.

childhood *of which no recollection has been retained*. When appealing to the unconscious memory, we place ourselves in a fatally unfavourable position; we enter the domain of the obscure and hypothetical, and lay ourselves open to criticism of all sorts, all the more so as some writers have made an excessive use of the explanation by the unconscious. A minute inquiry into each particular case would be needed. If, however, this hypothesis is difficult to justify by means of positive proof, the part played by the unconscious in psychic life, and particularly with regard to the memory, is so incontestable that we may legitimately admit its sure though secret action. Perhaps those who are seized by strange fears might, if they questioned themselves, discover the cause in some past occurrence. Here, at least, is a case which I give as typical of this group. Mosso asked a soldier, aged seventy, what he had been most afraid of in his life, and the man's reply was, "I have been face to face with death in many battles; but I am never so frightened as when I come across a lonely chapel in a remote part of the mountains; because, when quite a child, I once saw in such a place the corpse of a murdered man, and a maidservant wished to shut me up with it as a punishment."[1] Supposing the conscious recollection to be gradually effaced with years, the impression might well remain indelible, though latent, becoming active under given circumstances. Is it rash to say that there are many cases of this kind, with this difference, that the traces leading back to the original cause have vanished?

Cases of strange and insurmountable fear or antipathy have been noticed in some celebrated men: Scaliger was seized with nervous trembling at the sight of water-cress, Bacon fainted during eclipses, Bayle at the sound of running water, James I. at the sight of a naked sword (Morel). Among average human beings many like cases occur, but never become known, for lack of biographers to record them. I am inclined to think that there lies at the root of them some impression of early childhood, embedded in the constitution of the individual, and originating a repulsive tendency which acts as though it were natural.

[1] *Fear*, chap. xi.

3. The morbid fear may be the result of the *occasional* passage of a vague and indeterminate state into a precise form. Panphobia, mentioned above, might be a preparatory stage, an undifferentiated period, to which chance, a sudden shock, for instance, may give a direction and fix it, as in the fear of epidemics, of microbes, of hydrophobia, etc. This is the passage from a diffused emotional state to the intellectualised state, *i.e.*, one concentrated and embodied in a fixed idea: an analogous process to that of the "delusions of persecution," in which the suspicion, at first vague, attaches itself to an individual and will not be diverted from him. The cases, much less frequent than others, in which several distinct fears coexist, seem to me to be distinguished from this group. In short, the true cause is a general state (an emotive condition of fear), but chance plays a great part in it.

I do not pretend to explain everything by means of these three kinds of causes. When we come to examine the legion of morbid fears we are often greatly embarrassed by cases which refuse to come under any of the rules. Here is a well-known and very trite one : the sight of blood producing *malaise* or even syncope. This is inexplicable by reason, since the blood is the life; but reason has nothing to do with the matter. Let us seek elsewhere. It might be said that blood recalls violent pain, destruction, slaughter; but its sight affects children who can have no such recollections. Some have tried to explain it by constitutional weakness or nervousness, but syncope sometimes takes place in very vigorous subjects,[1] while neuropaths remain unaffected. Heredity has been called in, but I fail to see what it explains, for, going back from generation to generation, we must come at last to the primitive men, fighters who were not afraid of blood. Many other explanations might be proposed, which might be met by other criticisms.

I have cited this single fact in order to show that, so soon as we pass beyond the enumeration and description of morbid fears, and try to trace their origin, we enter on a part of the subject which is almost untouched.

---

[1] See a curious case in Gélineau, *op. cit.*, p. 99.

CHAPTER III.

Anger the conservative instinct in its offensive form—
Physiology—Psychology—Anger passes through two
stages, one simple, the other mixed—Its evolution—
Animal form, or that of actual aggression—Emotional
form, or that of simulated aggression—Appearance of a
pleasurable element—Intellectualised form, or that of
deferred aggression — Pathology: Epileptic insanity,
corresponding to the animal form; the maniacal state,
corresponding to the affective form—Disintegrated forms
of anger—Overpowering tendencies to destructiveness—
How do they arise and take a definite direction?—
Return to the reflex state—Essential cause: tempera-
ment—Accidental causes.

I.

THE instinct of individual conservation, under its offensive form, is the origin of anger—the type of violent and
destructive tendencies. This emotion is the second in
chronological order, appearing at two months, according to
Perez, and, definitely, at ten months, according to Darwin
and Preyer.

Bain defines it as "a conscious impulse which drives one
to inflict suffering and to draw a positive enjoyment from
the fact." This definition does not seem to me strictly
applicable to the inferior or animal forms of anger, as we
shall see presently.

Considered objectively, or from without, anger presents

itself with very clearly defined characters as regards its physiology and its mode of expression.[1]

1. Dilatation of the blood-vessels, augmentation of the cutaneous circulation, redness and swelling. This is also found in joy, but, remarks Lange, with less intensity. Besides, anger has a special manifestation of its own—*i.e.*, the distention of the greater veins, especially on the face and forehead. In its extreme form (rage) it may cause nasal or pulmonary hæmorrhage, the rupture of vessels, and death.

2. The innervation of the voluntary muscles is increased, but in an un-coordinated and spasmodic form; the voice is broken and harsh, the body leans forward in the attitude of aggression, the movements are violent and destructive ; "one strikes blindly," the breath comes in gasps with the well-known symptom of the dilated nostrils, the object of which, according to Piderit, is that of taking a full breath while the mouth is shut and the teeth clenched. According to Charles Bell, it is due to the habitual co-action of all the respiratory muscles, as the nostrils of an angry man may be seen to become dilated, although his mouth is open.

3. According to Lange, and in spite of popular opinion, there is no increase in the biliary secretion; but this is not the case with the saliva, as is proved by the phrase, "foaming with wrath." It is important to note that anger sometimes gives the secretions a toxic character. Van Swieten, Bichat, Trousseau, and others have verified this in the case of the saliva, when the quantity of ptomaine is augmented ; and it has long been known that the bite of furious animals is dangerous, while analogous facts have been ascertained in the case of one human being bitten by another in a fit of rage. The lacteal secretion may also become toxic, and produce on the nursling the effect of poison. These facts once more show the close relations between emotion and physiological or even chemical phenomena.

In short, the organism in general, and the active organs

---

[1] For detailed descriptions see Darwin, chap. x. ; Lange, *op. cit.* ; Mantegazza, *op. cit.*, chap. xiii. The latter transcribes the picture drawn by Seneca in his *De Ira*, and is of opinion—in which I agree with him—that it is traced by a master hand.

in particular, being excited, we may say with Spencer, "that what we call the natural language of anger is due to a partial constriction of the muscles which actual combat would call into full activity, all signs of irritation, beginning with the rapid shadow which passes over the brow when some slight cause of irritation occurs, being different degrees of the same contractions."

Anger and fear form an antithesis, but the former has, both physiologically and psychologically, a more complex character. In fact, fear, in all its degrees and throughout its whole duration, invariably remains within the category of painful emotions, while anger passes through two stages. The first, or asthenic, corresponds to the cause, the external occurrence, the immediate shock, and consists in a short depression, which is an entirely painful state; the second, or sthenic, corresponds to the offensive reaction, and, by its symptoms, approaches much more closely to pleasure than to pain. We need only remember the sardonic laughter which accompanies not merely the outbreak of anger, but some of its mitigated forms, and expresses the joy of seeing others suffer. Anger is therefore a mixed emotion; it does not belong altogether to the category of painful states of consciousness, though the painful side is predominant.

Considered as an internal and purely psychical pheno-menon, it eludes description, like every state which defies further analysis, and, in its acute forms, cannot be seized by internal observation. It scarcely admits of retrospective examination. Its psychology is the history of its evolution, comprising three principal periods :—

1. The *animal* form, or that of real aggression. It is primitive and general. In animals it is seen in a pure state, because there are no antagonistic, alterative, or restraining tendencies. Those which live by prey, the voracious carnivora, present the complete type. Besides the physiological phenomena already described there is the actual attack, each species using its natural weapons— teeth, claws, poisonous liquids. The feeling has the violence of a hurricane, of an unchained force of nature. This is because it is connected with extremely powerful instincts; that of nutrition, which requires its prey, the struggle for life under its most implacable form, that of attack—the necessity of destroying or being destroyed. At

this stage the element of pleasure is *nil*, or very slight, because the destruction has a blind and unconscious character. Bain thinks that monkeys are almost capable of enjoying the agonies of their victims, and perhaps elephants also. If this is correct, the fact is only met with in the case of the higher animals. It is needless to add that this animal form of anger is seen not merely in savage, but also in civilised man.

2. The emotional form properly so called, or that of simulated aggression. Much less general than the preceding, this is peculiarly human. Through the preponderance of the psychic element, or at least, the relative effacement of the destructive impulses, it appears to me the typical stage of anger as an emotion. It is frequently seen in the higher animals; the dog, meeting his enemy, stops, growls, erects his hair, and offers all the symptoms of aggression in the nascent stage. Man most usually confines himself to threats, with some degree of violence, unaccompanied by destructiveness. The affinity of this form with the first is evident, and evolutionists have drawn from it a psychological argument in favour of descent from animals; those beings nearest to nature—*i.e.*, the lowest in evolution— are continually exercising their anger: children on animals and weak people; savages, coarse-natured people, idiots and imbeciles on any one who does not resist them.

But the important point to note at this stage of evolution is the definite appearance of a new element—the pleasure of seeing suffering. With this, anger begins to grow refined. "There seems little doubt," says Bain, "that the primary fact in the pleasure of anger is the *fascination for the sight of bodily affliction and suffering*. Singular and horrible as the fact may appear, the evidence is incontestable" (*The Emotions*, p. 178). The author goes on to give instances which need not be repeated.

In my opinion, the fact is not so "singular" as the author supposes, it can be explained if we notice that, at this juncture, *another instinct* makes its appearance—one we have not yet studied, that of domination. We find here the first germ of a more slowly evolved emotion, that of triumphant power, of strength, superiority, pride. Henceforth, so far as psychological analysis is concerned, anger is no longer in a perfectly pure state. We have the destructive instinct *plus* a variable dose of the satisfied instinct of domination.

3. The intellectualised form, or that of deferred aggression. We may also say that this is the civilised form of anger. The principal representatives of this group are hatred, envy, resentment, rancour, etc. We have here two antagonistic forces confronting one another: on one side the aggressive instinct which urges forward, on the other, reason and calculation, which obstruct and restrain the tendency to attack. The result is an *arrest of development*. I do not wish to insist on a point which will be freely treated later on, in studying the transition from simple to composite emotions; a few brief remarks will suffice. In biology, the arrest of development modifies the organ in its function and structure, and often acts by rebound on other organs; in psychology the same thing happens, and, in addition, the arrested development of a tendency modifies its nature and its reaction on cognate phenomena. Mantegazza (*op. cit.*, chap. xiii.) has drawn up a good synoptic table of the mimicry of hatred. Those who will take the trouble to study it in detail, comparing it with the expression of outspoken anger, will understand, better than by means of any dissertation, what constitutes an arrest of development in the psychological order, and the modifications which it involves. I note, among others, one accurately observed point: the suffering which one inflicts on one's self, such as biting one's hands or gnawing one's nails; the destructive tendency when repressed, expends itself internally, at the cost of the envious man.

In this intellectualised form of anger, the feeling of the pleasure of destruction, realised, or merely imagined, becomes acute, as proved by the expressions, "tasting his hatred," "enjoying his revenge," etc.

Such are the three stages in this ascending evolution, and their identity of nature and common basis are clearly shown by the fact that hatred, if the power of arrest ceases, becomes outspoken anger; and the latter, if it increases, assumes the form of actual aggression, thus coming back to the primitive type.

II.

The ancients defined anger as a short madness, which would relegate it at once and entirely to the region of pathology. Without qualification, this formula cannot be accepted. So long as anger is not injurious either to the individual himself, or to others, it is normal, and even useful; for an animal or man devoid of any instinct for active defence and reprisals, would be very poorly provided. However, it must be recognised that the area of normal anger is exceedingly restricted, and that no emotion more quickly assumes a morbid character. Of the three tests which permit us to judge whether it does so or not, one —that of violent reaction on the organism—is of no use, because it gives too much scope to personal estimates and conjecture. There remain two others: the absence of rational motives, and chronicity, or excessive duration, normal anger being only a passing affection. Now, we find among mental diseases two derivatives of anger, two heightenings of this condition in paroxysmal form, and we have to establish between them a psychological difference which is the repetition of the normal state.

Epileptic madness corresponds to the blind, animal, often bestial form of anger, composed entirely of violent movements and painful feelings.

The maniacal state corresponds to the violent and conscious form of anger, mingled with a pleasurable element.

1. I have nothing to say of the numerous varieties of epilepsy, its concomitant hallucinations, and its intellectual and moral consequences; I confine myself to those aspects which assimilate it to anger.

Even in periods of calm, the universally noted psychological traits reveal a sombre, morose, irritable, but above all, irascible disposition—the "choleric" character *par excellence*. In the paroxysmal period, we find the symptoms of anger carried to extremity: "The patient" (I borrow Schüle's description) "throws himself on his surroundings with a blind rage, a bestial fury; he spits, strikes, bites, breaks everything he can reach, shouts and storms. His face is congested, his pupils are sometimes contracted, sometimes—and more frequently.—dilated, the conjunctivæ are much injected, the look is fixed; there is abundant salivation, pulsation of the carotid, acceleration of the pulse." Where is the starting-point of these discharges of fury, and by what mechanism are they produced? The authorities are not at one on this question, some attributing the principal share in this activity to the bulb, others to the brain. Recently an auto-intoxication of the nervous centres has been admitted. However, all this is only indirectly concerned with psychology. In the ensuing period of stupor, the acts of blind violence usually leave no trace in the memory; for it is a sort of psychological law that the intensity of consciousness should vary inversely as the intensity of the movements produced.

2. Mania presents many varieties. Let us take the typical form, acute mania, the nearest to anger. After a period of incubation, during which melancholia prevails, a violent reaction takes place, in sudden paroxysms. The maniacal state may pass through all degrees, from simple excitement to fury. Externally, it shows itself, in its milder form, by continual goings and comings, by an incessant craving for motion, a possibility of performing active exercise without feeling fatigue; in the intense form, we have the symptoms of rage already described: congestion of the vaso-motor system, redness of the face, violent palpitations of the heart, foaming at the mouth, furious and destructive impulses, etc. Internally the case is analogous; it is "chaos in motion" (Esquirol): and as the principal external symptom consists of motor disturbances, the principal internal symptom consists in an intellectual exuberance, a flux of ideas so disorderly and rapid that they succeed each other by no fixed rule, and the laws of association seem to be suspended, and speech, in its impetuous course, betrays the swiftness and discontinuity of thought. But there is besides, though not always, an expansive humour, a state of satisfaction, a feeling of pleasure scarcely in accordance with the rest. Many, after recovery, declare that they never felt so happy as during their illness.

The cause of this unexpected tendency to joy has been much discussed. Some attribute it to the superabundance of ideas, and consequently assign to it an intellectual origin. This is a fresh example of intellectualist prejudice which sees but a single effect in the modifications of the emotional life. Besides, as Krafft-Ebing remarks (vol. ii., sec. 1, chap. 2), in delirious fever-patients there is a flow of ideas without accompanying joyousness, and, inversely, alcohol may produce gaiety without accelerating the course of thought; and, accordingly, this author admits—and rightly, as it seems to me—that these two phenomena, viz., increased intellectual activity and pleasurable feeling, are subordinated to a deeper cause; they have their functional basis in an easier expenditure, and a deceptive sense of power and vigour, depending on pathological over-activity.

These two morbid forms, which have their psychological prototype in anger, suggest one remark. They are not evoked by any external excitement, such as the sight of an enemy, injury, or disobedience. Their cause, whatever it may be, is internal; it sets going a pre-established mechanism identical with that of anger (violent and disordered movements, vaso-motor phenomena, etc.), and the psychic state which follows is anger, or an analogous emotional form, with or without a concomitant state of pleasure. This seems to me a new argument in favour of James's and Lange's theory.

Epileptic and maniac rages are not the only ones to be entered under the heading of anger; there is besides these a group of irresistible impulses of a destructive character which ought, psychologically, to be included in the same class. With a difference, however: in the epileptic and maniac, the physical and psychical symptoms constitute a complexus similar or analogous to the normal form, and only to be reckoned as pathological on account of the want of adaptation and rational motives, while the irresistible impulses are only partial manifestations—*disaggregated forms of anger*.

Among overpowering tendencies we can only examine at present those which concern the offensive instinct. I therefore eliminate those grafted on another stem (dipsomania, erotomania, kleptomania, etc.) and those which, by their nature, are inoffensive, ridiculous, or puerile (the incessant craving for travelling, for counting, for discovering the names of men and things), and confine myself to those which have the violent and destructive character of anger, such as the impulses to wound, kill, destroy, or set on fire (pyromania). The fatal impulse to suicide will be studied under another heading (Chap. V.). It is needless to describe these violent impulses separately, or to recapitulate observations which may be found almost anywhere; a sketch of the characteristics common to all will be sufficient.

1. They pass through a physiological period of incubation, marked by palpitations and vaso-motor disturbances, rushes of heat to the head, headaches, præcordial anxiety, insomnia, agitation, fatigue, *malaise*, and undefined suffering. 2. The entrance into the psychological period is marked by the appearance of a fixed idea. Why one rather than another? This question will be examined later. The fixed idea, reigning as a tyrant in the consciousness, gives an aim to the tendency, determines its orientation. Some maintain that there are such things as purely intellectual fixed ideas, with no emotional accompaniment. Others think that the fixed idea always includes in some degree an emotional state. I share this second opinion, since every fixed idea is the beginning of an impulse. 3. The third period is that when it passes into action, sometimes sudden, more often preceded by a violent struggle between the overmastering impulse and the arrestive power of the will.[1] There are some cases where the fixed idea never passes beyond the second stage; these are abortive forms, of incomplete development. The passage into action is the rule, it being a psychological law that every intense representation of a movement or an act is the beginning of a movement. The act, whatever it may be, is accomplished, and there results a feeling of satisfaction, peace, and relief.

As regards those destructive tendencies which are to anger what phobias are to fear, a problem presents itself, the only psychological problem: that of their origin or cause. This question I divide into two: How do they arise? How do they take a determinate direction?

I. To explain the origin and appearance of irresistible impulses, most writers have recourse to the hypothesis of degeneration. As it is also called in to explain the converse phenomenon of phobias, it becomes necessary to be a little more precise. Without entering for the moment on the discussion of the different interpretations of this vague word, degeneration, let us take it as synonymous with dissolution or regression.

---

[1] Tamburini distinguishes three kinds of fixed ideas: simple, emotive, and impulsive, according as the obsession determines forced attention, a state of anguish, or an action.

The ideal of heredity, as a conservative principle, is to transmit under a healthy form a healthy organisation, *i.e.* (so far as our subject is concerned), one with harmonious and convergent tendencies. If dissolution is total, we have the idiot, or the dementia patient. If it is partial, we have a breach of equilibrium in favour of one or more tendencies. This disaggregation is not fortuitous; it has a retrogressive character, it is a return to the reflex movements. It approaches the character of the animal, the idiot, or the imbecile; it goes back to that stage of psychic life when the will under its higher form, the arrestive power, was not yet constituted.

II. In any case, there remains the principal question: Why was such a tendency predominant? What causes determined the particular direction taken by retrogression— homicide in one case, suicide or erotomania in another? Attempts have been made to explain this by alleging that every irresistible impulse results from the excessive irritation of an *isolated* group of brain-cells. Besides being purely hypothetical, this explanation is, in spite of its apparent precision, extremely vague. Is there an isolated group of homicidal, or one of kleptomaniac cells? This explanation is really too simple.

As far as we can penetrate the very obscure psychological genesis of the destructive impulses (and this may be held to apply to the whole group of irresistible tendencies), we find two sorts of causes at work, the essential and the accidental.

1. The essential, principal, fundamental cause which, after the period of physiological incubation, gives a deter- minate direction to the tendency is constitution, tempera- ment, character. It may be admitted, at least theoretically, that *all* tendencies exist, actually or potentially, in every one of us. In ordinary cases, one or more predominate. Contemporary research has familiarised us with the fact of the varieties of memory. Such and such a person has an excellent one for figures, or music, or colour, or form, but only moderate for everything else. This is a natural gift singularly capable of being developed by exercise. This fact has its equivalent in the motor order, or that of tendencies: there exist natural dispositions only wanting an opportunity to become preponderant, and morbid conditions are the culture-medium which favours their

development. The most violent tendency has its source in normal life. "There is," says Gall, "an inclination gradually rising from the pleasure of seeing anything killed to the most overpowering desire to kill." This is not put strongly enough; it is possible to pass, by imperceptible gradations, from the extreme case to the normal state in the following order: the pleasure of killing, the overpowering desire to kill, the pleasure of looking on at killing (the sight of a murder, gladiatorial combats, etc.), the pleasure of seeing the blood of animals shed (bull-fights, cock-fights, etc.), the pleasure due to the representation of violent and bloodthirsty melodramas (this is only in appearance, but the stage always presents a momentary illusion of reality); lastly, the pleasure of reading bloodthirsty novels, or hearing accounts of murders, which is purely an affair of the imagination. We thus pass from the act to the perception, the simulacrum, the mere image suggested by signs read or heard. I do not wish to assert, assuredly, that the spectators of the drama or readers of the novel are all potential murderers; but, as there are other men to whom such sights and such reading are abhorrent, we must recognise certain differences of natural disposition. Now the peculiarity of retrogression (or degeneration) is to act on the line of the strongest attraction or the least resistance, which is a characteristic of reflex action and the opposite of the inhibitive will, which acts on the lines of weakest attraction and strongest resistance.

2. The accidental causes which determine the direction of a tendency cannot be enumerated, because they vary for every individual case: we may note sex, social position, degree of culture, various maladies, etc. Tendencies to homicide and suicide are apt to spring up in a melancholic nature; alcoholism favours the incendiary impulse (pyromania); the epileptic and the general paralytic are more inclined to theft, and so on. Still more: the same impulse is variously modified, according to the soil in which it germinates; "the epileptic kills in a different way from the hypochondriac, the latter otherwise than the alcoholic or paralytic" (Schüle).

This shows the part played by accidental and consequently unassignable causes, and is still better shown in the abrupt substitution of one irresistible tendency for another in the same individual. Ordinarily, each shows his own special peculiarity; one constantly repeats his attempts at suicide, another at theft. But in cases of deep-seated dissolution, the direction is uncertain. The author of the theory of degeneration gives an excellent example of this: a hypochondriac possessed in turn by irresistible impulses to suicide, homicide, sexual excesses, dipsomania, and pyromania, and who finally gave himself up to justice, saying that he was "happy, because his sufferings were about to end." [1] We may say of all these overmastering impulses, *in radice conveniunt;* and thus the study of those which tend to destruction has led us, more than once, to speak of the other kinds.

[1] Morel, *Maladies mentales*, pp. 420 *et seq.*

CHAPTER IV.

SYMPATHY AND THE TENDER EMOTIONS.

Sympathy is not an instinct, but a highly generalised psycho-physiological property—Complete sense and restricted sense — Physiological phase: imitation — Psychological phase: first stage, psychological unison; second stage, addition of tender emotion — Tender emotion — Its physiological expression—Its relations with touch—The smile—Tears: hypotheses as to their causes—Tender emotion indecomposable.

SYMPATHY is not an instinct or a tendency, *i.e.*, a group of co-ordinated movements adapted to a particular end, and showing itself in consciousness as an emotion, such as fear, anger, sex-attraction; it is, on the contrary, a highly generalised psycho-physiological property. To the specialised character of each emotion, it opposes a character of almost unlimited plasticity. We have not to consider it under all its aspects, but as one of the most important manifestations of emotional life, as the basis of the tender emotions, and one of the foundations of social and moral existence.

I.

Sympathy, in the etymological sense (σύν, πάθος), which is also the complete one, consists in the existence of identical conditions in two or more individuals of the same or a different species; or, according to Bain, the tendency of an individual to enter into the active or emotional states of others, these states being revealed by certain media of expression. In its general and original form it is that and nothing else. We must therefore begin by getting rid of a prejudice, consecrated by usage in various languages, which identifies sympathy with pity, tenderness, benevolence, and the feelings which establish a tie of concord and a state of reciprocity between two beings. Thus understood, in its restricted sense, the term sympathy is neither accurate nor sufficient; for in all benevolent inclinations there are, besides the general fact of sympathy, other emotional elements, which will be determined in their proper place.

Before it becomes moral, before even it becomes psychological, it is biological. At bottom, it is a property of life, and its complete study would be a chapter of general psychology. If, limiting ourselves to what is strictly necessary, we try to follow the evolution of sympathy, from its most rudimentary to its highest forms, we distinguish three principal phases. The first, or physiological, consists in an agreement of motor tendencies, a *synergia;* the second, or psychological, consists in an agreement of the emotional states, a *synæsthesia;* the third, or intellectual, results from a community of representations or ideas, connected with feelings and movements.

First Phase.—In its primitive form sympathy is reflex, automatic, unconscious, or very slightly conscious; it is, according to Bain, the tendency to produce in ourselves an attitude, a state, a bodily movement which we perceive in another person. This is imitation in its most rudimentary form. Between sympathy and imitation, at any rate in this primitive period, I see only one difference of aspect: sympathy everywhere marks the passive, receptive side of the phenomenon—imitation, its active and motor side.[1]

[1] The psychology of imitation does not form part of our subject. Baldwin has made an excellent study of it (*Mental Development in the Child and Race*, pp. 263-366). He defines it as "a sensorimotor reaction, which finds its differentia in the single fact that it imitates; that is, its peculiarity is found in the locus of its muscular discharge. It is what I have called a 'circular activity' on the bodily side,—brain-state due to stimulating conditions, muscular reaction which reproduces or retains the stimulating conditions,—same brain-state again, due to same stimulating conditions, and so on." Imitation appears early in the child, at fifteen weeks (Preyer) or four months (Darwin). Are we to consider it as an instinct? Popular opinion is inclined to do so, as are also several psychologists—Stricker, James, and others. The contrary is maintained by Preyer, Bain, Sully, and Baldwin—a view I am myself inclined to take. Imitation does not present the true characteristics of an instinct; it is not

It manifests itself in animals forming aggregates (not societies), such as a flock of sheep, or a pack of dogs who run, stop, bark all at the same time, through a purely physical impulse of imitation: in man, infectious laughter or yawning, walking in step, imitating the movements of a rope-walker while watching him, feeling a shock in one's legs when one sees a man falling, and a hundred other occurrences of this kind are cases of physiological sympathy. It plays a great part in the psychology of crowds, with their rapid attacks and sudden panics. In nervous diseases, there is a superfluity of examples: epidemics of hysteric fits, convulsive barking, hiccup, etc. I omit the mental maladies (epidemics of suicide, double or triple madness) since we are only considering the purely physiological stage.

To sum up, sympathy is originally a property of living matter: as there is an organic memory and an organic sensitiveness, being those of the tissues and ultimate elements which compose them, there is an organic sympathy, made up of receptivity and imitative movements.

The *second phase* is that of sympathy in the psychological sense, necessarily accompanied by consciousness; it creates, in two or more individuals, analogous emotional states. Such are the cases in which we say that fear, indignation, joy or sorrow are communicated. It consists in feeling an emotion existing in another, and is revealed to us by its physiological expression. This phase consists of two stages.

1. The first might be defined as psychological unison. If, during this period of unison, we could read the minds of those who sympathise, we should see a single emotional fact reflected in the consciousness of several individuals. L. Noiré, in his book, *Ursprung der Sprache*, has proposed the theory that language originated in community of action among the earliest human beings. When working, marching, dancing, rowing, they uttered (according to this writer) sounds which became the appellatives of these different actions, or of various objects; and these sounds, being

adapted at the first attempt; it gropes its way, it is tentative, it fails again after success, it retrogrades, or progresses but slowly. It is an ideo-motor reflex; it takes its place above instinct (a blind and innate tendency inferior to the voluntary activity for which it prepares the way), because it is the first attempt at convergence towards an end.

uttered by all, must have been understood by all. Whether this theory be correct or not (it has been accepted as such by Max Müller), it will serve as an illustration. But this state of sympathy does not, by itself, constitute a tie of affection or tenderness between those who feel it: it only prepares the way for such an emotion. It may be the basis of a certain social solidarity, because the same internal states excite the same acts, of a mechanical, exterior, non-moral solidarity.

2. The second stage is that of sympathy, in the restricted and popular sense of the word. This consists of psychological unison, *plus* a new element: there is added another emotional manifestation, tender emotion (benevolence, sympathy, pity, etc.). It is no longer sympathy pure and simple, it is a *binary* compound. The common habit of considering phenomena only under their higher and complete forms often misleads us as to their origin and constitution. Moreover, in order to understand that this is a case of duality—the fusion of two distinct elements—and that our analysis is not a factitious one, it is sufficient to point out that sympathy (in the etymological sense) may exist without any tender emotion—nay, that it may exclude instead of exciting it. According to Lubbock, while ants carry away their wounded, bees—though forming a society—are indifferent towards each other. It is well known that gregarious animals nearly always shun and desert a wounded member of the herd. Among men, how many there are who when they see suffering hasten to withdraw themselves from the spectacle, in order to escape the pain which it sympathetically awakens in them. This impulse may go the length of aversion, as typified by Dives in the Gospel. It is therefore a complete psychological error to consider sympathy as capable, unaided, of delivering men from egoism; it only takes the first step, and not always that.

Third Phase.—Under its intellectual form, sympathy is an agreement in feelings and actions, founded on unity of representation. The law of development is summed up in Spencer's formula, " The degree and range of sympathy depend on the clearness and extent of representation." [1] I should, however, add: on condition of being based on an emotional temperament. This last is the source *par*

---

[1] *Principles of Psychology*, vol. iv. p. 565.

excellence of sympathy, because it vibrates like an echo; the active temperament lends itself less to such impulses, because it has so much to do in manifesting its own individuality that it can scarcely manifest those of others; finally, the phlegmatic temperament does so least of all, because it presents a minimum of emotional life; like Leibnitz's monads, it has no windows.

In passing from the emotional to the intellectual phase, sympathy gains in extent and stability. In fact, emotional sympathy requires some analogy in temperament or nature; it can scarcely be established between the timid and the daring, between the cheerful and the melancholic; it may be extended to all human beings and to the animals nearest us, but not beyond them. On the contrary, it is the special attribute of intelligence to seek resemblances or analogies everywhere, to unify; it embraces the whole of nature. By the law of transfer (which we have already studied) sympathy follows this invading march, and comprehends even inanimate objects, as in the case of the poet, who feels himself in communion with the sea, the woods, the lakes, or the mountains. Besides, intellectual sympathy participates in the relative fixity of representation: we find a simple instance of this in animal societies, such as those of the bees, where unity, or sympathy among the members, is only maintained by the perception or representation of the queen.

II.

Tender emotion marks an important stage in the evolution of affective life; with it we pass beyond the period of the purely egoistic emotions. The date of its appearance, as I have said, is not fixed with certainty; it may be at two months, according to Darwin, who noted at this age one of his characteristic modes of expression, the smile; more probably about nine months (Darwin) or twelve months (Perez), according to definite observations.

The physiological expression of tenderness, as far as movements are concerned, is reducible to a single formula —attraction. It shows itself either by elementary movements of approach, or by contact, or by the embrace which is its ultimate end, of which all the rest are but mitigated and arrested forms. It therefore stands in relation to the primordial sense, touch, of which Bain says, "Touch is both the alpha and the omega of affection."[1] The movements have a general character of relaxation, contrasting greatly with that of anger. One mode of expression which is specially, if not exclusively, appropriated to it is the smile. Is this the initial stage of laughter? or is it, on the contrary, only a weakened form of it, an arrest of development? This question has been discussed without much advantage. Darwin adopts the former view, which scarcely seems reconcilable with the general law of evolution; the child smiles before it laughs, whereas we should expect to meet with the inverse order of phenomena. Tender emotion approximates to joy; and its circulatory and respiratory modifications are analogous. There is acceleration, as in the case of pleasure, but to a less degree; tenderness suiting better with moderate and reposeful sensations.

It is also accompanied by an increase in the secretions, especially in that of the mammary glands in the woman. In the case of the lachrymal glands this symptom is more difficult to explain. It is known that tenderness often moistens the eyes; but tears are produced under conditions so varied, and sometimes so contradictory, that, even after all the recent work which has appeared on the expression of the emotions, the question of the causes seems to me very far from being exhausted. The pressure of the blood has a direct influence on this secretion, which is always accompanied by an increase in the circulation; but the simplicity of the mechanism is not incompatible with a diversity of causes. Tears may be provoked by mechanical or physiological acts: irritation of the conjunctiva, coughing, effort, vomiting; and by totally distinct psychic states, sorrow, joy, tenderness. In fact, all attempts at explanation relate to the painful states only; cases of this kind being, though not of exclusive occurrence, more frequent than others. Darwin admits that screaming, in infants, causes the vessels of the eye to become gorged with blood, and this produces a contraction of the orbicular muscles as a means of protection, whence a reflex action on the lachrymal glands; the shedding of tears continuing even after the sup-

---

[1] The point has been very well treated by this author (*The Emotions*, chap. vii. p. 127). See also Mantegazza, chap. xi. Lange does not mention it.

pression of the screams. Wundt rejects this explanation, seeing in the lachrymal glands *derivative* organs assuageing pain; this secretion, which is permanent, cleanses the eye from foreign bodies, such as dust and insects, etc. As the visual images are the most important of all, the shedding of tears would be an unconscious effort to drive away sad representations, having for its foundation an analogy between the painful sensations and the images. Whatever one may think of these hypotheses, they consider tears as signs of pain exclusively.

The augmentation of the lachrymal secretion depends on the increase in the pressure of the blood; now, the circulation is accelerated by joy and tenderness, as is proved by the shining of the eyes. The appearance of tears—not very abundant, however, in such cases—would be the natural consequence. Sorrow, on the contrary, is accompanied by a lowering of the circulation, and very often, in the early stage, tears are entirely wanting. The shedding of tears produces relief, it is a safety-valve; it would answer to a second stage—that of slackened tension—in which the return of vitality has begun. In other words, the tears of joy and tenderness would correspond to the stage of action, the tears of sadness to the stage of reaction.

The psychology of tender emotion seems to me reducible to a single question—that of its origin. The description of its varieties is without interest, and may be found elsewhere. We have stated it as simple and primary. Being the source of all altruistic, social, and moral manifestations, it will be worth our while to consider its nature at the period of its appearance.

In children, and the higher animals, the first manifestation of tenderness is towards the mother or the nurse.

"The relation involved in the sustenance of the child, a relation only a degree less close than that of the fœtus to the maternal organism, constitutes in itself the chief source of the feeling. Along with the supply of nutriment there goes that of warmth, support, or propping, which again is a continuation of the fœtal dependence. This first instinctive or sensuous attachment of the child grows into what we call fondness by the complication of this instinctive feeling with numerous "ideal" or transferred feelings, the product of the many pleasurable sensations, including those of the eye and of the ear, of which the mother is the source." [1] The primary tendency, therefore, is directed, in children and animals, to those who have been pleasant to them, or who have done them good, and from whom they hope to receive it again. This is an emotion which, in Herbert Spencer's nomenclature, might legitimately be called ego-altruistic, or even one with a marked preponderance of egoism. It must be so, for altruism cannot be innate.

The faculty of knowledge begins with an undifferentiated period, in which there is neither subject nor object, but only the consciousness of something without qualification. The separation of the ego and the non-ego in the order of cognition is the stage corresponding to the division, in the emotional order, between conscious egoism and altruism. How does this partial alienation from ourselves come about? How can it arise and be consolidated? These questions will be discussed later, when treating of moral emotion (Chap. VIII.). For the moment, I confine myself to a single question: Are we confronted with a veritable instinct—with an innate tendency incapable of being analysed, showing itself in the consciousness by the tender emotion or its varieties?

We know all the efforts made (especially in the eighteenth century) to reduce altruism by analysis to an extremely refined egoism, to a calculation; thus the tenderness of parents for their children was explained by the expectation of services to be rendered by them in the future. I think it needless to insist on this point.

In favour of inneity, the best argument that can be alleged, because founded on fact, is, that affection and attachment are met with even among animals, to whom we cannot attribute calculation or interested foresight. Apart from maternal love, which manifests itself energetically in very low stages of the animal kingdom, we find examples of benevolent and active sympathy between animals of the same species, and even (though this is rarer) of different species, [2] apart from any sexual attraction. Let us add, if necessary, in the case of human beings: "the instantaneous, unreflecting impulses of pity to creatures in distress, although

---

[1] Sully, *The Human Mind*, ii. pp. 104, 105.

[2] For these facts see Romanes, *Mental Evolution*, chap. xx., and Lloyd Morgan, *Animal Life*, pp. 397, 398.

strangers, enemies, criminals, noxious beasts, the absence of
all balancings of immediate loss with ultimate gain. . . .
Long-sighted selfishness does not explain the conduct of
the Good Samaritan. Again, the hosts of human beings
that in all ages have voluntarily given up their lives for their
country, could not be influenced by their own advantage.
For, although many of these have been taught the hopes of
a future existence, this has been by no means universal;
and there could be little certainty in the mass of minds
that the surrender of this life would receive a full compensation in another." [1]

The inneity of the altruistic instinct, therefore, seems to
me proved beyond the possibility of reply. It may be very
energetic in some individuals, or very weak in others; in this
it only resembles all instinctive tendencies. As a genus, this
instinct comprises several varieties, of a general character,
such as benevolence, affection, pity, etc. Finally, it is one of
the elements which make up several composite emotions—
veneration, admiration, sexual love, etc.

It remains only to inquire in what form it first made its
entry into the world, what was its earliest manifestation.
With regard to this matter, there are only three possible
hypotheses : those of maternal love, gregarious instinct, and
the very improbable one of sexual instinct. The value of
these hypotheses will be discussed later on, in the chapter
on moral emotion, which is the natural complement to the
present one. [2]

---

[1] Bain, *Emotions*, chap. vi. p. 111.
[2] The pathology of tender emotion does not offer sufficient interest
to detain us. The altruistic tendency may be totally wanting in certain
hypochondriac and demented patients, who, entrenched in an impenetrable egoism, have undergone a real "moral ossification."
Tenderness may become *sentimentality* towards persons, animals
(zoophily), and things (nostalgia), etc. Morel (*Études cliniques*, vol.
ii. sec. 4) quotes the case of a man of high intellectual capacity, in
whom the most futile and ridiculous causes excited absurd *accès de
sensibilité*. "The loss of domestic animals which he had reared
threw him into a state of bewilderment and convulsions of tears, as if
it had been the death of his best friends. I saw him one day almost
delirious with grief at the death of one of the numerous frogs which he
kept in his garden." This morbid emotivity, coinciding with congenital or acquired weakness, and with convalescence or other
adynamic states, throws into relief, by its exaggerated character,
that state of relaxation which is, as we have seen, one of the principal
marks of the tender emotion.

CHAPTER V.

THE EGO AND ITS EMOTIONAL MANIFESTATIONS.

Reducible to one primary fact: the feeling of strength or weakness—Positive form: type, pride. Its physiological and psychological characteristics. Its relation to joy and anger. Its evolution—Negative form: humility. Its semi-social character—Pathology, positive form: monomania of power, megalomania—Extreme negative form: suicidal tendency—Psychological problem of this practical negation of the fundamental instinct.

I.

THE English designate by the term of *self-feeling*, and the Germans by that of *Selbstgefühl*, a group of sentiments directly derived from the *ego*. I scarcely know what to call them: "personal" would be too vague a term, "egoistic" too ambiguous ("egotistic" would be better). To identify them with pride and its opposite would be to restrict them too far, for they have other forms. We might, for want of a better, include them under the term *amour-propre* (in its etymological meaning, *amor proprius*), *i.e.*, satisfaction or dissatisfaction with one's self, with its different varieties.

Whatever name we may give them, these emotional forms are reducible to one primary fact of which they are the embodiment in consciousness—viz., the feeling (well-founded, or not) of personal strength or weakness, with the tendency to action or arrest of action which is its motor manifestation. We can also, but in a less direct manner, connect them with the instinct of conservation, and say, with Höffding, that they result from that instinct "arrived at the full consciousness of itself and incarnated in the idea of the Ego."

This group has its peculiar characteristics. It is almost, if not quite, exclusively human, while the emotions hitherto studied have been as much animal as human. It is late in making its appearance (about the end of the third year), and is the last in chronological order, except the sex-instinct. This is because it soon assumes a reflective character, and because it implies that the *ego* is constituted and that the individual is conscious of himself as such.

The *self-feeling* has two forms, one positive, the other negative, of which pride and humility may respectively be taken as the types.

Under its positive form, it has a well-known physiological expression,[1] which consists of a series of movements tending to two ends—(1) Increase in size: the respiration is deep, the thorax greatly dilated, the gestures eccentric, and, as it were, aggressive, whence the popular expressions "puffed up" or "swollen" with pride. (2) Increase in height: the body and head are held more erect, the gait is assured, the mouth firmly closed, the teeth clenched; in megalomaniacs, who present, so to speak, the caricature of pride, these traits are still further emphasised. Some writers note, besides, as a specific character, the action of the *musculus superbus*, which everts the lower lip.

Psychologically, the feeling of strength is *sui generis* and irreducible. It is related on one side to joy, being the sthenic emotion *par excellence*, on the other to anger, because the feeling of superiority soon leads to contempt, insolence, brutality, and the exercise of strength under its aggressive form. Let us remember that we have, on a previous occasion, connected with this feeling the pleasure which frequently accompanies satisfied anger. As it depends, more than any other primary emotion, on reflection, its development is determined by intellectual conditions.

Is there any equivalent to it among animals? Certain facts allow us to suppose that there is. The courteous contests of pretended battle, the song, the dances by which the males attempt to captivate the females, the triumph of some and the defeat of others, must produce some states

[1] See Darwin (chap. xi.) and Mantegazza (chap. xiv.).

analogous to pride and humiliation. The arrogant attitudes of the cock and the turkey-cock, the ostentatious display of the peacock, are taken as symbols of *naïf* pride; and if the expression of an emotion is that emotion objectivised, we can easily suppose that it exists in some manner.   In children, the personal feeling is at first connected with the exercise of physical strength expended in struggling with each other and in games; later on, with personal appearance, clothes and ornaments, especially in girls.   In consequence of an increasing irradiation, the self-feeling envelops everything entering into its sphere of action which may help to swell its importance—house, furniture, relations. Later on comes the consciousness of intellectual force, and the advantages procured by it—fame, power, riches, etc.

As derivative, or different aspects of egotistic emotion, under its positive form, we find pride, vanity, contempt, love of glory, ambition, emulation, courage, daring, boldness, etc.   The special study of each of these feelings belongs rather to the moralist than the psychologist.[1]

Under its negative form, personal emotion cannot detain us long, as it would only be a repetition of what we have previously studied under the converse aspect.   It has for its basis a feeling of weakness and impotence.   It shows itself by diminution or arrest of movement; its gestures are concentric, and it consists in belittling instead of aggrandising, of lowering instead of raising.   It is related on one side to sadness, and on the other to fear; in short, it is the complete antithesis to the positive form.

From this source flow, with different adaptations, humility, timidity, modesty, resignation, patience, meanness, cowardice, want of self-confidence, etc.   Most of these manifestations are not simple, but result from the combined action of several causes, as we shall see later on.

II.

The positive or negative feeling of personal strength is a normal and healthy emotion when it remains within the limits of adaptation ; for it has an individual and even social utility.

[1] Consult James, *Psychology*, ii. 305, 329; Bain, *Emotions*, chap. x. xi.; J. Sully, *Psychology*, ii. 97 *et seq.*

For the individual, it is the instinct of conservation become reflective, and by the consciousness of his strength or weakness, it permits him to measure his pretensions by his degree of power.

Socially, it makes us in a certain measure dependent on others. Although strictly egoistic in its origin, *self-feeling* cannot develop unless it becomes ego-altruistic, or semisocial. According to Bain, self-esteem is a reflective sentiment which consists in judging ourselves as we judge others. This opinion has been criticised and scarcely seems tenable, in so far, at least, as it takes away from *amour propre* its instinctive and self-generated character and considers it as a return action. However, it is certain that the desire of approbation and the fear of blame are the *external* elements which count in the constitution and consolidation of the feeling of self-complacency; praise gives it extension, criticism impairs and mutilates it. This does not imply any great amount of reflection or culture. The child is extremely sensitive to the judgment of his equals. Primitive man is imprisoned in a network of custom, tradition, and prejudice which he cannot break without incurring excommunication; and those people are very rare who content themselves with their own approbation only.

But from a semi-social feeling, the love of ourselves can easily become an anti-social feeling. There is no emotion which passes so simply and definitely from the normal form to passion, and from passion to madness. At the bottom of the tendency of the *ego* to affirm itself there is a potentiality of limitless expansion and indefinite radiation. A man whose self-feeling is vigorous resembles those species of animals and vegetables which—prolific and of tenacious vitality—would, if left to themselves, cover the whole surface of the globe; his expansion is only kept in check by that of others.

Our path towards the pathology of the subject is already marked out. We have, first, the semi-morbid forms which have been called the monomania of power. Place a man in conditions where this tendency to unlimited expansion meets with no obstacle, and it will go to any extreme. This is the case with absolute power. No doubt this unique and, so to speak, superhuman position is not of itself sufficient. The madness of power (*folie du pouvoir*) is the resultant of two factors: first, the character, *i.e.*, the violence of the egoistic appetites, which, continually satisfied, continually increase; while the will, the antagonistic, inhibitive force, keeps on diminishing; and next, external circumstances—the absence of all restraint, of any equal power which might overawe by threats. A religious sanction, or the fear of a political catastrophe, has restrained more than one, and limited that unbridled tendency which is only the *ego's* feeling of its own power carried to the acute stage. It is needless to give examples from history, for they are known to every one.[1]

Self-feeling, under its positive form, has its ultimate incarnation in a well-known pathological manifestation—the delusion of greatness, or megalomania. Perhaps, indeed, in this case, the exaggeration produced by disease shows itself most clearly and without altering the original.

Megalomania is met with in general paralysis of the insane as a transitory phase; but especially in systematised chronic delusions (*paranoia*). We may pass over the period of incubation, which is often melancholic; thus, in a case of persecution-delusions, the patient is at first tormented by vague suspicions; he accuses no one in particular, he has as yet no accredited enemies; but one day he discovers them, and nothing will ever divert his thoughts from them again. Then, in some cases, the disease passing through another evolutionary stage, he arrives, by logical deduction, at the conclusion that it is his great merit, his high position, which are exciting jealousy. Thenceforth megalomania is fully developed; the subject thinks himself a millionaire, an unrecognised genius, a great inventor, a king, the pope, or even the Deity.

There is nothing more characteristic than such a description as the following, which has often been drawn up, and is yet another proof that emotion, its expressive and its physiological bases, are but parts of the same phenomenon. "He walks with head erect, with assurance; his speech is laconic and imperious, he seeks solitude, and is full of contempt for the society which surrounds him. His style

---

[1] For details on this point the reader should consult Ireland, *The Blot on the Brain*, p. 88 (where he will find a study of the Cæsars, the Hindoo Sultans, Ivan the Terrible, etc.), and Jacoby, *Études sur la sélection et l'hérédité*.

of dress is in accordance with the tendency of his aberration. Like the maniac, he is restlessly active; but, in him, no movement is fortuitous or without a motive; his will is always active, his actions have a definite aim; if he shows violence, it is in order to ensure the execution of his commands, to show that he has strength sufficient to annihilate everything; it is not a destructive spirit which animates him, but the necessity for showing his power. The functions of the assimilative life have undergone no alteration; they take place, as a rule, with perfect regularity. It seems as if the expansive form of their feelings, their contentment with themselves, the extreme and unbroken satisfaction surrounding their life, imparted to the organic vital apparatus a surplus of activity, resulting, in a manner, in an excess of health." Frequent cases of longevity among megalomaniacs have been noted. Finally, the following observation has its value, on account of the change—at once organic and psychic—there recorded:—"We have watched a patient who, after having suffered from melancholia for several years, suddenly became megalomaniac. His constitution had undergone great alterations, and his health was much weakened, so that he became a chronic melancholic; but so soon as his mental affection took on the character of megalomania he was not long in acquiring new vigour."[1]

We might add that the tendency of men is rather to pride, of women to vanity, which favours the views of those who maintain that madness is often only the exaggeration of the habitual character: it is sufficient to have shown that the feeling (though illusory) of personal strength in an extreme degree is only the normal state amplified, but not changed.

III.

It may seem strange to close this chapter by some remarks on a phenomenon which, both by its internal and external characteristics, belongs to the class of irresistible tendencies—the fatal impulse to suicide. Its affinity with homicidal obsession is undeniable, as is proved by the persons who are tormented, in turn, by the craving to kill

[1] Dagonet, *Traité des maladies mentales*, pp. 360 *et seq.*

others and to kill themselves. However, if self-love, in its positive form, reaches its culminating point in megalomania, it seems to me quite legitimate to maintain that self-feeling, under its negative form, attains its supreme negation in suicide.

Without insisting on a merely accessory point, it is certain that suicide, as a manifestation of emotional life, brings us face to face with a psychological problem as yet insufficiently noticed. If there is an incontestable fact—one which, even among the ancients, was familiar to triteness—it is that in every animal the fundamental, ineradicable instinct is that of self-preservation, of existing, and persisting in existence. Now, suicide, whether voluntary or unreflecting, deliberate or impulsive, is the negation of the fundamental tendency, not a theoretic or partial negation, or one in word only, but in deed and absolute. And the sacrifice of life is not subordinated to some other end which acts by superior attraction, such as devotion to a belief, to friends, to humanity, to one's country, it is a suppression pure and simple, a liberation desired in and for itself.

The ethnological, moral, and social study of suicide does not form part of our subject, having already been fully worked out.[1] Our aim is merely the psychological problem, which we must now define with more precision.

The act of suicide results from two very different mental states, that of reflection and that of impulsion.

In deliberate, reflective, voluntary suicide there is a struggle between two factors: the instinct of conservation and the insupportable state caused by pain (incurable disease, ruin, misery, grief, frustrated ambition, dishonour). Reflection decides, and as pain is always a beginning of destruction, it prefers a total and rapid destruction to a partial and slow one. The act is rational, since it tends

---

[1] Among the very copious existing literature on suicide I must mention Morselli's monograph, *Il Suicidio*, in which the various causes — cosmic, ethnic, social, biological, and psychological — are studied in great detail. His principal theoretical conclusions are—(1) Among all civilised nations suicide increases more rapidly than the geometrical ratio of the population and the general mortality; (2) suicides are in inverse proportion to homicides at any given time or in any given country. This last "law" has been strongly contested by Tarde and others.

towards the lesser evil, or at least what is judged to be such.

Impulsive suicide is harder to explain. A man throws himself suddenly out of a window, poisons himself, cuts his throat. In some cases death has been premeditated, but always appears as a compelling, inevitable force, inexorably claiming its victim; the epithet "irresistible" says everything. To the outside spectator the act appears motiveless, without reason, without cause. It is all the more surprising that the struggle, in this case, is no longer between instinct and reflection, but between two instincts, the conservative and the destructive, of which the one which usually is the strongest succumbs, and the individual turns against himself the destructive tendency originally destined to act on others.

Yet the psychology of deliberate suicide gives us the key to that of the impulsive variety. What in the first case results from conscious, clear, reasoned motives, results in the second from blind, obscure, unconscious states: it is an act of organic life, and its cause is found in cœnæsthesia. Impulsive suicide is the expression of the destructive process, slow, permanent, dimly felt, going on in the depths of the organism. Any one who presses in rage on an aching tooth, who rolls on the ground, strikes his head against the wall, or mutilates himself, is attempting an instinctive though absurd reaction in order to get rid of his pain. These are modified forms, it is true, but they will serve to show that the man who yields to an overmastering impulse to strangle or drown himself seeks a deliverance of the same kind.

Leaving degeneration (which is perpetually being dragged into this question) out of account, observation shows us that the difference between the two forms of suicide is reduced to that between psychic and purely organic causes. Impulsive suicide flourishes best on the soil of melancholia and hypochondria—*i.e.*, in states which involve deep dejection and a disorganisation of vital action. We may also notice the part played (as was long ago pointed out) by heredity, the descendants of suicidal ancestors often killing themselves at the same age and in the same manner as the latter;[1] now, psychological heredity is based on

[1] For further details see my *Hérédité psychologique*, Part I., chap. viii.

organic. Finally, the automatic character of these impulses approximates them to the class of reflex actions, attempts at suicide being repeated in the same form during a recurrence of the same circumstances—*e.g.*, somnambulism, intoxication, the menstrual period. All these character-istics assign to irresistible suicide an organic origin, which is equivalent to saying that its ultimate cause lies in temperament. The conservative instinct exists in all men, but it may exist in any degree. In some there is an innate joy of life capable of resisting all disasters; in others, a constitutional melancholy, or (which comes to the same thing) *the conservative instinct is very weak* and yields to the least shock. Impulsive suicide represents self-feeling at its last stage of regression, or, in other words, at its negative extreme.

CHAPTER VI.

THE SEXUAL INSTINCT.

Its physiology—Its evolution: Instinctive period—Emotional period (Individual choice)—Intellectual period (Platonic love)—Its pathology—How can sexual instinct deviate from the normal course?—Anatomical and social causes —Psychological causes: (a) unconscious, (b) conscious.

I.

THE sex-instinct, the last in chronological order with man and the higher animals, gives rise to the emotion of love with its numerous individual varieties. Most psychologists have been very sparing of details where it is concerned, and one might mention certain voluminous treatises which contain no mention of it. Is this through exaggerated delicacy? Or is it because the authors think that their place has been usurped by the novelists who have so obstinately confined themselves to the study of this passion? But the novelist's mode of analysis is different from the psychological mode, and does not exclude it.

Sexual love being an emotion whose evolution is complete, it is impossible to determine the physiological and psychical signs suiting all cases, from the blind instinct to the most refined and intellectualised forms. Nevertheless, there are certain specific characters which it always preserves, one special mark which is never effaced throughout its various metamorphoses, and that is, its origin. For the moment, let us take as typical the common and average forms which, as we shall see later on, are met with half-way, as we follow the evolution of sexual love from the lowest to the highest.

1. Though neither James nor Lange has cited it among his typical cases, love is certainly one of the emotions which express most clearly the state of the organism, and offer the clearest proof in favour of their theory. Let the reader suppress, in imagination, all the physiological manifestations which accompany it. What remains? not even the consciousness of a vague attraction, for that supposes an actual or nascent movement.

Love, as a sthenic emotion, presents physical characteristics which connect it on the one hand with joy, on the other with tenderness, which have already been described. The circulation is accelerated, sometimes to an extreme degree, the respiration likewise, and they react on the organic functions. (We have already seen how, in many animals, the period of love corresponds to deeply-seated chemical modifications—usually of a toxic character—in the organism.) We find, further, movements of mutual repulsion, or of mutual attraction, the dominant part played by touch resumed in its essential organ, the hand, caresses, embraces, fusion; the movements of attraction being all the more noisy and violent, in proportion as the instinct predominates. Finally, as the specific mark, we find a particular state of the sexual organs, varying from slight excitement to paroxysm. This disturbance,—whether strong or weak,—even when it has no echo in the consciousness, influences the unconscious activity.[1]

If from the organic, motor, and vaso-motor manifestations we pass to the nervous centres, where impressions are received and movements initiated, we can find scarcely anything but hypotheses. One point only has been fixed since Budge's researches: the existence in the spinal cord of a centre or an area on the level of the fourth lumbar vertebra, which governs the movements of the sexual act. Its psychological function is slight or non-existent: it is properly an

---

[1] M. Pierre Janet mentions the case of a woman in whom " the family feelings, the affective emotions, modesty, and the sensitiveness of the genital organs appeared and disappeared simultaneously." He adds: " Which of these phenomena brings the others in its train? Is genital sensibility a centre round which other psychological syntheses are constructed? I draw no conclusion."—*État mental des Hystériques,* i. pp. 217, 218.

instinctive centre, whose action is not obstructed by the removal of the cerebral hemispheres and the cerebellum, in the inferior vertebrates, and even in the dog, as proved by the experiments of Goltz and others.   Some authors admit, without precise localisation, a second centre, situated near the ganglia at the base of the encephalon, which they suppose to be the seat of the brute sensations and their corresponding movements, and in relation with the centres of olfactory and visual sensations.   This centre would have a psychological value.   Lastly, a third and last centre in the cortical layer, the organ of perception properly so called, and of the revival of images.   Nothing precise is known as to its position, whether it is localised in a certain area, or diffused.   On this point we find nothing but hypotheses— if so much as that.   The occipital lobes, the neighbourhood of the olfactory centre, have been suggested, but these are extremely doubtful.   We have to be content with the admission that, from the genital organs, impressions are first transmitted to the lower or spinal centre, which exercises a reflex action on the corresponding systems of vascular, motor, and secretory innervation, and thence— whether there is an intermediate centre, or not—reach the cerebral cortex, where they produce a more or less definite state of consciousness, according to circumstances.

Anatomy and physiology are not the only sciences concerned in this question; for if the existence of these superposed centres, connected with each other, though distinct in function, were thoroughly established, this would give us certain landmarks, and lay down fixed conditions, or stages, in the development of sexual emotion, which may result from a state of the organs (instinctive form) or from an external perception, or from a pure representation (imaginative love).   In the absence of an anatomical basis which might serve for the normal psychology of the subject, and still better for the comprehension of the pathological facts, let us follow the evolution of sexual love so far as observation enables us to do so.   It has already been sketched in the Introduction, but too briefly for our present purpose.

2. We have distinguished, in this psychological evolution, three principal periods : the instinctive, the emotional, and the intellectualised.

Taking the question at its remotest origin, some naturalists

and philosophers assert that the equivalents of sexual attraction exist in living beings devoid of nervous systems, in
vegetable or animal micro-organisms. "It is curious," says
Balbiani, "to find, in beings who from their small size, and
the external simplicity of their organisation, have been
placed by all zoologists at the furthest limit of the animal
world, actions denoting the existence of phenomena
analogous to those by which the sex-instinct manifests
itself in a great number of metazoa. . . . Thus, with
the paramæcids, at the moment of propagation . . . a
higher instinct seems to govern these little animals; they
seek and pursue each other, they go from one to another,
feeling each other with their cilia, cling to one another for
some instants in the attitude of sexual approach, and then
let go in order to seize each other again. These singular
games, by which these animalcules seem in turn to provoke
one another to the act of copulation, often last for several
days before the act becomes definitive." Other facts of the
same nature have been cited. Finally, it has been said that
"the coupling of the two sexual elements is analogous to the
coupling of the two animals whence these elements are
derived : the spermatozoid and the ovule do on a small
scale what the two individuals do on a large one ; the
spermatic element, in directing itself towards the ovule
which it is to fertilise, is animated by the same sexual
instinct which guides the complete being towards the female
of the same species." [1]

If we confine ourselves to the micro-organisms, these
facts of sexual attraction have been interpreted in two ways,
as we have already seen—one psychological, the other
chemical. Some, as we have just heard, admit a desire, an
elective action, a choice, quoting in support of this not

[1] This psychological thesis has been maintained, in all its rigour, by
Delbœuf: "That girl and that young man, in being attracted to one
another, obey the will, unknown to both, of a spermatozoid, an ovule.
But it may be taken as certain that this will is not unknown either to
the spermatozoid or the ovule; both know what they want, and seek it.
To this end they give their orders to their respective brains through the
medium of the heart, and the brain obeys without knowing why.
Sometimes it imagines that it has been convinced by reason and explains
its own choice to itself. At bottom it has been but an *unconscious*
instrument in the hand of an imperceptible workman who knew both
what he wanted and what he was doing." (*Revue philosophique*,
March 1891, p. 257.)

only the phenomena of generation, but several others: as the habitat, the use of a certain substance in the formation of the carapace, the movements of certain micro-organisms in seeking and seizing a determined prey. Others reject this psychology, which they call anthropomorphism, and maintain that chemical action is sufficient to explain the whole. Pfeffer had already shown, as far as generation is concerned, that the spermatozoids of the cryptogamia are attracted by certain chemical substances varying according to the vegetable species. More recently, Maupas and Verworn, who have successively studied the alleged cases of choice, eliminate all psychical elements and reduce the whole to a purely mechanical process. I am inclined to adopt the second opinion, while recognising that, as far as problems of origin are concerned, we decide by probabilities rather than proofs.

Above this chemical or organic attraction we find the sex-instinct properly so called, which, with its numberless adaptations, embraces the whole animal world. It is useless to prove that this instinct is fatal, blind, not acquired, anterior to all experience; but, as by its nature it consists essentially of motor manifestations, its psychology is scanty enough. Some remarks on this point may not be without advantage. In fact, as regards the problem of instinct, an entirely new position has been taken up.

During the first half of this century the inneity of instinct was placed in the order of cognition, while recent psychology places it in the order of movements, or, to be more accurate, in a fixed relation between certain states of consciousness and certain movements. According to the first hypothesis, stated in a masterly manner by F. Cuvier, instinct consists in images, or innate and constant sensations, which determine to action in the same manner as ordinary sensations; it is "a sort of vision, a dream, analogous to somnambulism." According to the second hypothesis, sensations, perceptions, and images excite movements determined by the organisation, as in the case of ducklings when they see the water, the kitten scenting a mouse, the squirrel laying up its winter store. There are no innate representations, or even innate movements, but a pre-established relation between some fortuitous impressions and a group of movements: instinct is the *innate motor reaction* to an external or internal excitement; it results from the nature of the animal. The impression only pulls the trigger and the shot is fired. Like every other instinct, that of sex consists in a fixed *relation* between internal sensations coming from the genital organs, or tactile, visual or olfactory perceptions on the one hand, and movements adapted to an end on the other. As far as it is an instinct, it is that and nothing but that. In the immense majority of animals, and frequently in men, it does not rise above this level; in plainer words, it is not accompanied by any tender emotion. The act once accomplished, there is separation and oblivion. More than this, in some cases there is not even indifference, but hostility: the males of the queen bee are put to death as useless, and it is well known that the mate of the female spider often runs the risk of being devoured.

Sexual *love* corresponds to a higher form of evolution. Over and above instinct, it implies the addition of a certain degree of tender feeling. It is not therefore a simple emotion, even in the tolerably numerous species of animals in which it can be studied. In man, more especially in civilised man, its complexity becomes extreme. The analysis made by Herbert Spencer is well known and somewhat lengthy, yet I do not hesitate to transcribe it, since I can find no other to equal it, nor any point which could be added or subtracted :—

". . . The passion which unites the sexes . . . is habitually spoken of as though it were a simple feeling ; whereas it is the most compound, and therefore the most powerful, of all the feelings. Added to the purely physical elements of it are first to be noticed those highly complex impressions produced by personal beauty, around which are aggregated a variety of pleasurable ideas, not in themselves amatory, but which have an organised relation to the amatory feeling. With this there is united the complex sentiment which we term affection—a sentiment which, as it can exist between those of the same sex, must be regarded as an independent sentiment, but one which is here greatly exalted. Then there is the sentiment of admiration, respect, or reverence ; in itself one of considerable power, and which, in this relation, becomes in a high degree active. Then comes next the feeling called love of approbation. To be preferred above all the world, and that by one admired beyond all others, is to have the love of approbation gratified in a degree passing every previous experience, especially as there is that indirect gratification of it which results from the preference being witnessed by unconcerned persons. Further, the allied emotion of self-esteem comes into play. To have succeeded in gaining such attachment from, and sway over, another, is a proof of power which cannot fail agreeably to excite the *amour propre.* Yet again, the proprietary feeling has its share in the general activity : there is the pleasure of possession; the two belong to each other. Once more, the relation allows of an extended liberty of action. Towards other persons a restrained behaviour is requisite. Round each there is a subtle boundary that may not be crossed—an individuality on which none may trespass. But in this case the barriers are thrown down, and thus the love of unrestrained activity is gratified. Finally, there is an exaltation of the sympathies. Egoistic pleasures of all kinds are doubled by another's sympathetic participation, and the pleasures of another are added to the egoistic pleasures. Thus, round the physical feeling forming the nucleus of the whole, are gathered the feelings produced by personal beauty; that constituting simple attachment, those of reverence, of love of approbation, of self-esteem, of property, of love of freedom, of sympathy. These, all greatly exalted, and severally tending to reflect their excitements on one another, unite to form the mental state we call love. And as each of them is itself comprehensive of multitudinous states of consciousness, we may say that this passion fuses into one immense aggregate most of the elementary excitations of which we are capable ; and that hence results its irresistible power."[1]

This evolutionary moment gives the complete type of love. As it goes on, a breach of equilibrium is produced at the expense of the physiological and instinctive elements, which gradually efface themselves before a more and more intellectualised image.

Certainly, there lies at the root of all love the unconscious search for an ideal, but for an ideal perceived in a concrete, personal form, incarnate for the moment in an individual. By a process of mental abstraction similar to that which draws from perceptions the most general ideas, the concrete image is transformed into a vague scheme, a concept, an absolute ideal, and we have a purely intellectual, Platonic, mystical love; the emotion is totally intellectualised. Let us remark that this last stage of evolution is not so very rare. Not only do we meet with it sporadically, but it has been

---

[1] *Principles of Psychology*, vol. i., § 215.

fixed and expressed, at certain moments of history, in institutions, such as the chivalric love, of which Geoffrey Rudel seeking the Lady of Tripoli is the most perfect example; the troubadours, the Provençal Courts of Love, deciding that true love cannot exist in marriage, and excludes all cohabitation, etc. We must not, however, allow ourselves to be misled by appearances. Platonic and mystic lovers have always maintained that their sentiment is perfectly pure, and has nothing in common with the senses; the contrary opinion seeming to them a profanation and a sacrilege. Yet how could love exist without physical conditions, however attenuated we may suppose them? If they are wanting, all we have or can have is a purely intellectual state, the representation of an ideal conceived but not felt. Besides, we have more satisfactory evidence than suppositions and arguments; facts of tolerably frequent occurrence show how rapidly we may fall from the ideal plane. It is only because all the circumstances are in its favour that the fall is so easy.[1]

In this ascending evolution from the instinctive to the idealistic form there is a decisive moment—viz., the appearance of the individual choice. This is the special criterion which differentiates instinct from emotion. Sexual instinct contents itself with a specific satisfaction; sexual love does not. And as choice manifests itself among the superior representatives of the animal kingdom, not only by sanguinary combats between the males, or by the more pacific tournaments which precede sexual selection, but, in the absence of all rivalry and competition, by the exclusive preference of one male for one female, chosen among many others whom he might possess, we may admit *a fortiori* that primitive humanity must very soon have left behind the stage of *Venus Volgivaga*. We know that Schopenhauer, and after him Hartmann, have tried to determine the reasons of choice; but such attempts must always be partial failures, because we can never be sure of discovering all the unconscious factors.

For the rest, the psychology of love contains many other mysteries. Whence comes the blind violence which astonishes and sometimes terrifies the calm spectator?

---

[1] For some curious observations on this point see especially Moreau (of Tours), *Psychologie morbide*, pp. 264-278.

Bain thinks it can be explained by the concentration of the attention on an individual, and by the fact that intensity and unity of object are associated in love. But this applies also to other passions, such as ambition and hatred. Herbert Spencer, in the analysis already quoted, attributes it to the complexity of the passion, love being an aggregate of heterogeneous tendencies all converging to one end and carrying the individual in the same direction. At bottom, the irresistible element is in the sexual instinct, and only exists in virtue of it; instinctive activity alone has such power. This is what Schopenhauer calls, in metaphysical terms, the Genius of the species, which makes of the individual an instrument for the furtherance of its ends. We might also call it, in biological terms, according to the hypothesis of Weismann now in vogue : the continuity of the germ-plasm which energetically manifests and affirms itself, safeguarding the rights of the species against individual fancies. But all these metaphors explain nothing, add nothing to the simple verification of the fact. Sexual instinct remains the centre round which everything revolves ; nothing exists but through it. Character, imagination, vanity, imitation, fashion, time, place, and many other individual circumstances or social influences give to love—as emotion or passion—an unlimited plasticity. It is the task of the novelists to describe all its various shapes, and one which they have not failed to perform.

II.

Though love, even in its average manifestations, is inseparable from obsession and impulsion, I see in these two characteristics no legitimate reason for placing it unrestrictedly—as some writers have been pleased to do—in the category of pathology.[1] It has its natural end, and tends to fulfil it by appropriate means. Every one knows that it sometimes reaches the confines of madness ; but in this it does not differ from the majority of the emotions. There are the impulsive and irresistible forms of love (erotomania), but they remain within natural limits ; the true pathology of love is elsewhere—outside nature.

[1] See Danville, *Psychologie de l'amour*, ch. vi., for a detailed discussion of this question, which the author also answers in the negative.

On the deviations and interversions of the sexual instinct so many observations have been published,—especially in our own day,—so many books written, so many medico-legal theses discussed, that we might think the psychology of the subject had thereby been cleared up. Nothing of the sort; and it is this alone which interests us.

Reduced to its simplest expression, the psychological problem is this: The sex-instinct having a clearly-defined and easily-verifiable end, how can it deviate therefrom? Other instincts—that of conservation under its offensive and defensive forms, that of self-feeling—have no mechanism exclusively appropriated to them, and are susceptible of various and multiple adaptations. This, on the contrary, is confined by nature within strict limits. No doubt every instinct has its oscillations; but it is only the means which vary, the end remains the same. The ant, the bee, the beaver, the spider, modify their manner of acting in accordance with their environment, because they are confronted with the dilemma that they must either adapt themselves or perish; but they always arrive at the same end. The nutritive instinct in man utilises animals and vegetables—the raw caterpillars of the savage or the scientific cookery of the civilised man—but the same end is always aimed at and attained. With the deviations—at least the extreme ones—of the sex-instinct it is otherwise: everything changes, means and end alike. The normal end, generation and the perpetuity of the species, is ignored or annihilated. This aspect of the question does not appear to me to have been sufficiently noticed. How can an instinct so solidly based, and having its own special mechanism, go astray?

This subject deserves a purely psychological monograph, a very difficult piece of work for which this is not the proper place. I would only seek to inquire into the principal causes of the alteration of this instinct. I shall cite no facts—they are sufficiently well known, or will suggest themselves; besides, the choice lies between excessive abundance and nothing. I pass over the extreme cases, those of necrophily, or of sexual erethism accompanied by a craving for violence, destruction, or blood. These are the equivalent of the animal manifestations already mentioned, in which the state of general excitement, so far from producing tenderness, awakens by preference the aggressive

17

tendencies. These are merely insane impulses. I am limiting myself to deviations and interversions—*i.e.*, to cases where the natural mechanism of instinct is falsified (excitations caused by impressions having nothing to do with sexuality, attraction towards the same sex, etc.).

We may pass over in silence the general causes, which are not particularly instructive: degeneracy, brought in, as usual, to serve as an explanation, and heredity, which is no explanation at all, being merely a repetition, and brings us back to the primary case, which states the question afresh. The inquiry can only be profitable when directed to particular causes.

1. One principal anatomical and physiological cause is found in the conformation of the genital organs: arrest of development, incomplete sexuality, hermaphrodism, malformations, etc. This is the simplest and most easily verifiable cause, and is found to be sufficient in some cases. The action, from below upwards, of the organ and its lower centre on the brain, is no longer normal; the conditions of existence of the instinct are absent or altered.

2. Other causes are not so easily assignable. One of a sociological order may be indicated: it is known what takes place when a number of individuals of the same sex are shut up together, as in boarding-schools, convents, prisons, barracks, ships on long voyages. But the most numerous causes are of psychological origin, and we may divide them into unconscious and conscious.

3. The existence of the unconscious, and therefore involuntary, causes is rather suspected than proved. They consist in strange associations of ideas formed at the period of puberty; whose ultimate reason eludes observation; they might be compared to certain cases of *audition colorée*, when a connection is formed between a sound and a colour, apparently fortuitous, but in reality resting on a common emotional basis. More than this, observation seems to show that, at a much earlier age, in the fifth or sixth year, there are apt to occur "unconscious genital impulses provoking associations of ideas which frequently serve, in later years, as a *substratum* to our sentiments and volitions. Most of these associations are unstable, and remain outside the consciousness. In the degenerate they take on the impulsive and overpowering character which distinguishes

their psychology; their intensity expresses the degree of consciousness which accompanies them, the recollection which is still connected with them, even the importance they assume in later existence. The existence of an unconscious sub-personality directing the conscious one manifests itself here rather than elsewhere with undeniable clearness."[1]

4. There remain the conscious voluntary causes which are the converse of the physical causes, representing an action from above downwards of the superior centres on the inferior centre and the organs. It is here that instinct finds itself in conflict with its most redoubtable enemy, the intense and persistent image. In predisposed subjects the creative power of the imagination works at some construction on an erotic theme, as in others it produces a mechanical invention, a work of art, a scientific discovery. Every vivid image tends to realise itself; in the present case it has the power to divert instinct from its natural channel if its motor power is stronger, and the sexual instinct has not in all men an equal stability.

I do not think, however, that these causes are sufficient to explain everything, even if we take account of imitation which fixes itself in custom, and of the contagion of example. If the facts were taken in detail, omitting nothing, we should meet with more than one embarrassing complication. Thus, sexual aberrations are found in animals, though of but moderate intelligence and living quite free from constraint. Can we, considering this, throw all the blame on imagination? They are also found among primitive races: the Huns, say ancient historians, had made of unnatural love a regular institution; can we blame civilisation? Many other difficulties of this kind might be raised; but I may remind the reader that pathology is only introduced into this work by way of elucidation, and it seems to me that, in the present subject, it receives from normal psychology more light than it throws on it.

[1] Dallemagne, *Dégénérés et Déséquilibrés*, p. 327.

CHAPTER VII.

TRANSITION FROM THE SIMPLE TO THE COMPLEX EMOTIONS.

The complex emotions are derived from the simple (1) by way of complete evolution; in a homogeneous form: Examples —In a heterogeneous form: Examples—(2) by arrest of development—(3) by composition; two forms—Composition by mixture; with convergent elements; with divergent elements—Composition by combination (sublimity, humour) — Modesty — Is it an instinct? — Hypotheses as to its origin.

HAVING studied in succession each of the tendencies which we look upon as incapable of further analysis, together with the simple emotion which expresses each, we now pass to the composite emotions. There is no need to point out that a simple emotion (fear, anger, etc.) is, in itself, a very complex phenomenon, and that "simple" means irreducible by analysis to any other emotion. All those which do not present this characteristic are complex. The problem to be stated, then, is this: How have the secondary and derivative emotions arisen from the primary or principal ones? Since it is admitted that these are typical emotions, and, on the other hand, the observation of human life shows us numerous emotional states, with their individual varieties and gradations, their transformations in the course of ages, how has this multiplicity been produced?

It is under this form that the masters of the seventeenth century had stated the question, and I take it up again, because this method seems to me far superior to that of classifications, which has since become prevalent. We know that Descartes admitted only six primary passions : admiration, love, hatred, desire, joy, and sadness. "All the others," he says, "are composed of some out of these six, or else they are different species of the same, and derived from them;"[1] and he goes on to describe about forty. Spinoza admits only three principal : desire, joy, and sadness, whence he deduces the others, which, after eliminating some repetitions, amount to forty-six. However, it is not very clearly shown by what method these philosophers determine their primary passions; it seems as though the criterion were their extremely general character, except in the case of admiration. As for the other passions, they are *deduced*, and in order to show this clearly, Spinoza always takes care in his definitions to connect the primary with the derived passion. Thus : " Fear is an ill-assured sadness, arising from the idea of some past or future thing of which we are in some doubt as to the result." In short, their method is geometrical and deductive, especially in the *Ethics;* but we can, with slight modifications, adapt it to the exigencies of experimental psychology. Thus we have determined the primary emotions by derivation, from the chronological order of their appearance, not by their extremely general character. As for the derivative emotions, we are about to seek to determine the very various conditions of their genesis, not by way of deduction, but by that of analysis or synthesis based on observation, *i.e.*, as far as possible by a genetic method. We have elsewhere spoken of classification and the insurmountable difficulties inherent in it; accordingly, the aim which we propose to ourselves is not, given a composite emotion, to determine its genus and species, but to know *from what primary emotion, and in what manner, it is derived.*

These natural methods of transition from the simple to the complex seems to me capable of being ranged under three heads: (1) evolution, (2) arrest of development, (3) composition (mixture and combination). These three methods may act separately or conjointly; the more complex emotions are usually the result of their co-operation. We shall examine them in succession.

[1] *Traité des Passions,* sec. 69.

I.

The transition *by evolution*, complete or incomplete, is the simplest and most general case. It consists, like all evolution, in the passage from simplicity to complexity, from the undifferentiated to the differentiated, from the lower to the higher. It depends on the intellectual development, and is based on the law of transference already described (Pt. I., chap. xii.), which is its active and unconscious instrument. However feeble the development of the emotions may be in any race or individual it is never entirely wanting (idiots excepted), because the events of national and individual life have always some variety and some changes of aspect, which influence the emotional life.

It is convenient to distinguish two cases, according as the evolution takes place in a homogeneous or a heterogeneous form.

I. *Evolution in homogeneous form.*—The primary emotion remains identical with itself, through the whole course of evolution; it only increases in complexity. Here are some examples : [1]

Æsthetic emotion has its origin in a surplus of activity expending itself in a particular direction, under the influence of the creative imagination; and it preserves this fundamental character from the drawings scratched on flints by quaternary man, or the symbolic dances of savages, through the classic ages, to the quintessential refinements of the decadents. It is true that all are not disposed to admit this: a person of delicate artistic temperament, brought up in a very cultured environment, and suddenly thrown into the midst of savage æsthetics, would deny any community of nature, but in this he would be mistaken. Those centuries which had no sense of evolution, of the continuity of development (the seventeenth and eighteenth), could see nothing in the origin of art but incomprehensible crudities, not worth notice. The transition from simplicity to complexity took place through the accumulation of knowledge, of ideas, and technical skill, and of causes or occasions of new ways of

[1] As all the emotions to be enumerated in this chapter have been already—or are about to be—studied separately, they will only be mentioned briefly, by way of example, and in order to illustrate the work of the mind in the creation of composite forms.

feeling: thus were formed juxtaposed aggregates acting by quality and quantity. This progress from simplicity to complexity is seen better than anywhere else in the development of the feeling for music, the most emotional of all the arts.

The religious sentiment is not of simple origin. It results: (1) from the fusion of two primary emotions—fear, and love in the larger sense (tender emotion); it is therefore a binary compound; (2) from a process of evolution which we shall have to follow in detail and which depends on intellectual conditions : predominance, first, of images, then of inferior concepts, then of superior concepts. Here, too, the continuity escapes the notice of many who do not see the bond connecting fetichism with the most idealistic of religions. How many travellers and ethnographers, after having ascertained the existence, among a given tribe, of magic, amulets, funeral rites, seriously affirm that these people are devoid of all religious feelings ! It is because for them complex and highly organised forms are the only ones that count, and because they are accustomed to think of religious feelings as formulated by the great established religions.

II. *Evolution in heterogeneous form.*—The primary feeling is transformed to such a degree as to become unrecognisable, and can, in many cases, only be recovered by laborious analysis. This case resembles that of the morphological development of animals: the forms of the adult give no hint of the forms of embryonic and fœtal life.

The best example I can give is the genesis of the benevolent emotions, which, however, will be more suitably placed in the next chapter. We can, however, examine another case.

The instinct of conservation is, as we have seen, a collective term, an abridged formula, used to designate the totality of particular tendencies which assure the persistence of the individual, and one of which, the craving for food, is fundamental. It manifests itself in all its simplicity in most animals and in savage tribes who live, strictly speaking, from day to day. Yet ants, bees, foxes, and many other animals put aside a reserve store of food for future needs. The human race has very rapidly acquired the habits of foresight and care for the future, even while still in the savage stage and living by hunting and fishing. With a nomadic or agricultural life, the need of possession affirms itself more and more. As social progress substitutes for exchanges in kind the use of the precious metals, first in ingots, then as coined money, and later still, of paper money, feeling follows the same course, transferring itself from things to the values which represent them and the representations of these values, in many cases with well-known tenacity; and we see people who prefer illness to the expense of a cure, the risk of being murdered to the unpleasantness of giving up their purses. So that those values and signs of values which represent the possibility of satisfying needs (food, clothes, lodging, etc.), become in and for themselves a cause of desire and pleasure, and, amassed as a security for life, remain useless—if, indeed, they do not cause death. Avarice is a passion very well suited to illustrate this evolution in heterogeneous form, which, in spite of a strictly logical development, undergoes so many changes that its extreme point seems the negation of its point of departure.

The feeling of strength, self-feeling in its positive form, is at first, as we have seen, the consciousness of physical energy ; but, with the intellectual development, it radiates in different directions, according to temperament and disposition. We can at least note two very different directions: (1) an evolution in the theoretical and purely individual sense, which leads a man to take up all questions, examine and criticise everything, form an independent opinion on every subject—in short, to have as his ideal an absolute liberty of thought, without any sort of restriction ; (2) an evolution in the practical and social sense, extending one's power over things and men ; the child who domineers over his playmates may, at a later age, impose his personality on a party, a nation, a number of nations (Cæsar, Napoleon). The quality of the emotions felt in the two cases is very different ; however, the original source is common to both, the divergence is the effect of character and intellectual evolution.

II.

The transformation of simple into derivative emotions, *by arrest of development*, is of less frequent occurrence.

While, in the preceding case, there was a forward movement in a straight line, intellectual evolution involving
emotional evolution according to the law of transference,
here the mental process is more complicated; it supposes
an antagonism between two states of consciousness, resolving itself into a compromise. There are, on the one
hand, emotional tendencies going in the direction of impulse; on the other, images, ideas, intellectual states of all
sorts acting by way of arrest, so that the resultant emotion
is composed at the same time of movements and inhibitions
of movement.

Except fear, all primary emotions imply tendencies to
movement, sometimes blind and violent, like natural forces.
This is seen in infants, animals, savages, the Barbarians of
the first centuries of our era as depicted by contemporary
chroniclers; the passage of emotion into action, good or
bad, is instantaneous, rapid, and fatal as a reflex movement.

Reflection is, by its nature, slow and inhibitory. How
can an image or a conception produce an arrest of movement? This is a very obscure question, the psychological
and physiological mechanism of which has had but little
light thrown on it; it is useless to treat it here in a cursory
manner; we need only remark that the arrest exists as a
matter of fact.

The intervention of this new factor, reflection, may result
in two ways. On the one hand, it may obstruct and finally
suppress; thus a passion kept in check ends, after various
oscillations backward and forward, in being altogether extinguished. The second is a transformation or metamorphosis by arrest of development; the passion is not
extinguished, but it has changed its nature.

The biological sciences have familiarised us with the notion
of arrested development and the morphological modifications resulting therefrom. We know that the parts of a living
being are so closely connected that none can change without
involving a change on the part of the others; such is the
formula of the "Law of Organic Correlations," and it has its
equivalent in the functional order. The "compensation of
development" exists beyond all doubt in psychology, though
it has not been as much studied as it deserves; thus
experience shows us that hypertrophy of certain faculties

entails as a consequence the hypertrophy or atrophy of certain others.

I have previously (Chap. III.) mentioned hatred as an abortive form of anger, the result of arrested development. I have only to add a few supplementary remarks on the two antagonistic elements. One is primary and tends to the partial or total destruction of the enemy, attacking him in his own person or in that of his friends, in his reputation, his honour, his interests. The other, made up of reflection and calculation, consists in the representation of consequences, in the fear of reprisals and of Divine or human laws. Hence arises an emotional state comparable to the movement of a body rotating on itself and incapable of passing certain limits; and it must be admitted that the metamorphic process is here very thorough-going, since many writers, so far from grasping the affinities between hatred and anger, set up the former as a primary emotion, the antithesis of love. Yet it is very clear that hatred, by the inhibitory character peculiar to it, is not and cannot be a primary emotion; it corresponds to a second stage. If it is objected that we might as well assert that anger is the developed form of hatred (*i.e.*, that the latter is primary), and not hatred an abortive form of anger, I should answer that this position is inadmissible, because in experience we have no example of the inhibitory form appearing *before* the corresponding impulsive form. What is primary is an instinctive, unconscious movement of retreat, of aversion (in the etymological sense), but this is no more the emotion of hatred than the instinctive and unconscious movement of attraction is the emotion of love.

Resignation, with its varieties and gradations, is an abortive form of grief. Its mode of expression has been described in detail by Darwin (Chap. XI.). This state is the resultant of two currents : on one side, moral pain, grief, which by itself and in its complete form shows itself in prostration, tears, etc.; on the other hand, an intellectual notion —that of the irreparable and irremediable, of the futility of all efforts. The intellect has its teleology, which is not that of feeling; if it prevails and asserts itself in the consciousness, we shall have, after a period of oscillation, a fixed state, in which the loss will be accepted and perceived in a mitigated form.

Mystic, platonic, or intellectual love (there is no advantage in distinguishing the exact shades expressed by these various epithets) is, as we have seen, an abortive form of sexual love. Predominance of the intellectual element, the conceived ideal; weakening of the physiological and emotional manifestations and the organic erethism, of the tendency to movements of contact and embrace, and everything which constitutes emotion in its plenitude : such are its characteristics. Here, more than elsewhere, the term "arrest of development" is strictly accurate, because mystical love results, not from a voluntary inhibition which mutilates or checks emotion, but from an impotence on the part of emotion to develop its complete form.

Experience furnishes the counterproof : let the antagonistic action of reflection, or of the intellectual state—whatever it may be—cease, and hatred will once more become anger, resignation grief, or despair ; mystical will change to sexual love, and the primitive form reappears under the ruins of the derivative.

To sum up, all the emotions of this group whose genesis depends on an arrest of development are reducible to a single formula : *intellectualised emotions*, because the intellectual element becomes dominant. We might also call them *attenuated* emotions, because they tend towards emotional weakening. The two contrary and reciprocally dependent tendencies peculiar to this group, determine, not a medium emotion, but a new form which, relatively to the primary emotion, and to the general quantity of emotional life, is a *loss*.

III.

Transformation *by composition* is a general term including two different cases : mixture and combination. This process consists of additions, and can be thus formulated : When two or more intellectual states coexist, each having its own peculiar emotional colouring, there arises a complete emotional state ; in other words, intellectual complexity involves emotional complexity. If we compare the primary emotions to the simplest perceptions of sight and hearing, the complex emotions will correspond to the perception of an extensive landscape or a symphony. It is thus formed by the addition or fusion of binary, tertiary, quaternary compounds, and so on, these terms implying the number of simple emotions which compose them. The composition may be brought about in two ways, which we shall distinguish by calling them respectively mixture and combination, in the sense in which these words are employed by writers on chemistry.

I. *Composition by mixture.*—In the emotions derived from this mental procedure, the constituent elements can be recovered from the compound; they embrace without interpenetrating one another, and a psychological analysis conducted with sufficient thoroughness is able to determine and enumerate them. For greater clearness, I distinguish two cases in the mixture of feelings.

(*a.*) The elements are homogeneous or convergent. If they are numerous, since they all tend in the same direction, the resultant emotion will be of great intensity. We have found one example of this in sexual love, an aggregate compound (according to Herbert Spencer's analysis) of physical attraction, æsthetic impressions, sympathy, tenderness, admiration, self-love, love of approbation, love of possession, and desire of liberty.

(*b.*) The elements are heterogeneous or divergent. As an example I take jealousy, which many authorities consider primary, perhaps because it is manifested by animals and infants, which simply proves that it is precocious,—quite a different thing. A contemporary writer tries to define it by saying: "It is a morbid fear passing from inert stupidity to active or passive rage." I greatly prefer Descartes' definition: "Jealousy is a kird of fear related to the desire we have of keeping some possession" (*Passions*, art. 167). This passion deserves a monograph to itself, and one will certainly be written when this style of work comes to be applied more frequently to the psychology of the emotions. Our task at present is not to study its gradations, from mild cases up to madness and homicide, but to inquire into its composition. There is, firstly, the representation of some good, possessed or denied—a pleasurable element acting by way of excitement and attraction; and, secondly, the idea of dispossession or privation (*e.g.*, of the lover with regard to his mistress, of the rejected candidate against his fortunate rival, and in general, of any who fail against all who succeed), an element of vexation which acts depressively; and, thirdly, the idea of the real or imaginary cause of this dispossession or privation, awakening, in various degrees, the destructive tendency (anger, hatred, etc.). In the passive or inert forms of jealousy this last element is very slight. This emotion is, therefore, a binary compound.

We might further mention the religious sentiment (a binary compound), the feeling of respect, composed of sympathy and a slight degree of fear, and the moral sentiment, which we are about to analyse in the next chapter.

I must remark that these derivative emotions, by reason of their complexity, ought logically to show as many shades of variety as they have constituent elements. In sexual love, where analysis discovers at least ten tendencies, whether primary or not, the predominance of one or more among these changes the aspect of the emotion according to times and individuals. The instability of the passions, of which we hear so much, is partly caused by their composite character.

II. *Composition by combination.*—The emotion resulting from this mental procedure differs, in its nature and characteristics, from its constituent elements, and appears in the consciousness as a new product, an irreducible unit. Here the analysis, uncertain and hazardous as it often is, cannot give us everything which we find in the synthesis— a psychological case which has well-known equivalents in chemistry.

A Danish psychologist, Sibbern, whom I believe to have been the first to point out this mode of composition of the emotions under the name of mixed sentiments, defines them as "Those in which the disagreeable excites the agreeable, and *vice versâ*, so that one is not antecedent to the other, but both act simultaneously, and the disappearance of the one involves the disappearance of the other."[1] In fact, there is not merely coexistence, but reciprocity of

---

[1] Sibbern's *Psychologie* (1856), having been published in Danish, is only known to me through extracts quoted by his compatriots, Höffding (*Psychologie*, 2nd German ed., pp. 330, 331) and Lehmann (*Hauptgesetze*, pp. 247 *et seq.*). These two authors may also be consulted with advantage on this question.

action; if you suppress a single term the emotion changes
its nature, as we shall see by the following examples.

In the emotion accompanying all forms of activity in
which we *seek* great difficulties to overcome, or risks to run
(as in hunting wild animals, dangerous mountain climbing,
exploring expeditions, etc.), if we suppress the unknown
element, the risk, the danger, there is no longer any
attraction. If we suppress this attraction and its accompanying pleasure we have nothing left but fear or disgust.
This particular emotion exists only through the inter-
dependence of its various elements. It can be produced in
a modified form, but without changing its nature, in the
spectators of bull-fights, wild beast tamers, violent struggles,
and thrilling dramas, and in a lesser degree by mere recita-
tion or reading.

I have already mentioned melancholy (in the ordinary,
not the medical sense) as one form of the luxury of grief.
It implies the calling up of pleasant states, past or distant,
plus a state of present sadness which surrounds them.
Suppress one or other of these elements and the melancholy
vanishes. If the pleasurable element, however slight, disappears, nothing remains but grief pure and simple. In
this combination sometimes the one element predominates,
sometimes the other, and the resultant feeling receives a
special emotional *timbre*, as the case may be.

The feeling of the sublime is usually considered as a
form of the æsthetic sentiment, and we shall have to return
to it later on. Whatever it may have for its object—
whether the spectacle of sullen glaciers, of a boundless
desert, or of a man who throws himself recklessly into some
great act of self-devotion,—it is composed of discordant
elements fused into a single synthesis: (1) a painful feeling
of oppression, of lowered vitality, of annihilation, which
drags us down and depresses us; (2) the consciousness of
an upward rush, of unfolded energy, of an inward lifting up,
of an increase of vital power; (3) the conscious or unconscious feeling of security in presence of a formidable
power. Without the last-named the emotion would
change its nature, and we should feel fear. These three
co-existent and interdependent elements enter collectively
into the consciousness, and present themselves to it as an
irreducible unit.

Höffding (*op. cit.*, p. 407) gives humour as an example of a combination, or, as he calls it, a mixed feeling. He defines it as "the sentiment of the ridiculous based on sympathy." This state consists in seeing simultaneously and indissolubly the petty side of great events and the great side of the most trivial things. It is the synthesis of two antithetic elements: the destructive and contemptuous laugh which makes us feel ourselves superior; and the indulgence, pity, and compassion which place us on a footing of equality with others. This emotional manifestation may be simply a passing whim, or it may be a permanent trait of character, a peculiar manner of understanding nature and human life, striking an average between optimism, which finds everything too bright, and pessimism, which sees the ugly side of everything. The school of "irony," which, with Solger, Schlegel, and others, played its part in German æsthetics at the opening of this century, proposed humour — negative and destructive in form, positive and constructive in reality — as its fundamental principle in the interpretation of the universe.

I am inclined to place in this group an emotional state which has given rise to many dissertations and discussions— I mean modesty. I look upon it as a binary compound capable of being resolved into two primary emotions: self-feeling and fear. Whatever may be thought of this explanation, the subject is worth the trouble of a little examination; it could scarcely be omitted from a treatise on the psychology of the feelings.

There is no lack of documents respecting the manifestations of modesty among different peoples; they may be found in the narratives of travellers, and in works on anthropology and ethnology. The psychological question of its nature and origin has been treated by Spencer, Sergi, James, Mantegazza, to mention contemporary writers only. The last-named even gives us a definition of it : "Modesty is physical self-respect."

It has a physical mode of expression peculiar to it, or at least only met with in the emotions related to modesty (shame, timidity, shyness), viz., the sudden redness of the face due to momentary paralysis of the vaso-constrictor nerves. We know Darwin's ingenious explanations of this point: a person who thinks others are looking at him directs his attention to his own face, whence results a flow of blood towards that part. These explanations are now rejected. The experiments of Mosso and others on the circulation of the blood rather justify the view taken by Wundt, who sees in the momentary relaxation of the vaso-motor innervation, causing the redness of the face, a compensation for the accelerated pulsations of the heart, produced by emotion.

Besides this special mode of expression, modesty shows itself by concentric, defensive movements, by a tendency to cover or disguise certain parts of the body. The means employed to this end are of the most various description, according to race, country, or period: some hide the whole body, some the sexual parts only, or the face, or the bosom, some paint the body, or the face, etc. It is impossible to determine the exact part played in this diversity by cir-cumstances, climatic conditions, the association of ideas, compulsion, fashion, imitation, and even chance.

So far as psychology is concerned, it is especially the question of origin which has been discussed: Is modesty an instinct? is it innate or acquired, primary or derived? Some writers, rather carelessly, assume that it is an instinct, on no other evidence than its quasi-universal character, which they deduce, legitimately enough, from its multiple manifestations. Most, however, adopt the contrary opinion, alleging the example of children, and of certain primitive races who seem totally devoid of it. This second view seems the more tenable, though it is difficult to find a categoric solution which is free from objections. Modesty, being an ego-altruistic feeling (and the same applies to shame and shyness), presupposes some degree of re-flection.

The conditions of its origin are little understood. H. Spencer, and, after him, Sergi, maintain that it results from the habit of wearing clothes, which began with men (not with women) from motives of ostentation and ornament. There are tribes where both sexes go naked, others where clothing is the privilege of the male sex: immodesty would thus be, in its origin, a lack of æsthetic feeling. Exclusively appropriated, at first, to the male sex, the feeling of modesty would then have transferred itself to the other. This ex-planation seems very precarious, not to mention the theory incidentally implied, that the feeling is not stronger in women than in men.[1]

W. James proposes another, which is less simple, but more acceptable.[2] Briefly, it is this : The emotional state which lies at the root of modesty, shame, and other similar manifestations, arises from the application in the second instance to ourselves of a judgment primarily passed upon others. The sight of certain parts of the body, and the ideas which they suggest, inspire repulsion, and "it is not easy to believe that even among the nakedest savages an unusual degree of cynicism and indecency in an individual should not beget a certain degree of contempt, and cheapen him in his neighbours' eyes." (In our opinion, this psychological state approximates to disgust, of which we have already seen the causes and the significance.) What is repugnant to us in others must be repugnant to them in us : whence the habit of covering certain parts and concealing certain bodily functions. Modesty cannot be considered an instinct in the strict sense of the word, *i.e.*, as an excito-motor phenomenon. Under the influence of custom, public opinion, civilisation, it passes through its evolution, till it reaches "the New England pitch of sensitiveness and range, making us say stomach instead of belly, limb instead of leg, retire instead of go to bed, and forbidding us to call a female dog by name" (James, ii. p. 437).

Taken as a whole, this emotion approximates most by its external symptoms to fear. It also contains elements derived from self-feeling. Must we add other elements derived from the sex-instinct? This is only admissible in certain cases. In short, its composition is variable. We cannot consider it as instinctive, primitive, innate. On the other hand, analysis cannot clearly resolve it into its constituent parts; we are inclined to see in it a particular case of mental synthesis, a combination.

To conclude, with regard to the emotions formed by combination :—

They are based on an association of intellectual states, which is, in most cases, an association by contrast.

They presuppose a fusion, in varying proportions, of

[1] Sergi, *Piacere e Dolore*, pp. 210 *et seq.*
[2] W. James, *Psychology*, ii. pp. 435-437.

agreeable and disagreeable states, which justly entitles them to be called mixed emotions.

The whole differs from the sum of its constituent elements.

Analysis ascertains and isolates these elements, but cannot boast of having discovered them all.

CHAPTER VIII.

THE SOCIAL AND MORAL FEELINGS.

AT the moment of beginning the study of the composite emotions which have had the most brilliant career, and played the most important part in human life, it will be well to indicate the course which will be followed, once for all. We cannot, in dealing with the social, moral, religious, æsthetic and intellectual sentiments, discuss the numerous questions which they suggest, and so lose ourselves in endless details. The allotted task of psychology seems to me to be quite clearly defined—viz., to take each feeling *at its origin* and try to determine its nature and follow its development, in its principal phases, by the help of the documents supplied to us by ethnology, and the history of morals, of religions, and of æsthetic and scientific culture, thus avoiding vagueness and *a priori* reasoning, without losing our way in an inextricable tangle of facts.

In conformity with this plan, we shall begin with the simplest forms of the social instinct in animals, passing from them to man, and thence to the evolution of moral tendencies.

Even if we admit the transformist hypothesis, zoological evolution has not proceeded in a straight line. This point, it is true, is contested, but it is all the more important to remember, because the development of the organisation and that of the social instincts do not always go on *pari passu.* Thus the social aptitudes of ants and bees are far superior to those of certain mammals considered of a far higher type of organisation. Without troubling ourselves, therefore, about the frequent disagreements between zoological taxinomy and sociological psychology, we shall follow the ascending march of the social instinct, no matter in what order or class or at what point of the genealogical tree it shows itself.

We thus find four principal forms of animal societies: at the lowest stage, those founded on nutrition; further on, those based on reproduction; then, unstable, gregarious societies; and finally, societies with a stable and complete organisation.[1] Some special question will be put with regard to each of them, so as to show us the social question under some one particular aspect.

" The idea of a society," says Espinas, " is that of permanent co-operation between separate living beings, engaged in the same action " (*op. cit.*, p. 157). The character of permanence even is not necessary for the inferior forms; there are temporary societies differing *in toto* from those

[1] For the general study of this question see Espinas, *Les Sociétés Animales*, 2nd ed. (1878), and Ed. Perrier, *Les Colonies Animales.*

heterogeneous, fortuitous, momentary aggregates which we call crowds. Reciprocity and solidarity are the two fundamental conditions, a fact which excludes from human and animal societies two forms somewhat approximating to them: parasites, in whose case there is no reciprocity, and who show a modified form of the struggle for life; and messmates, where community of life, though it involves no injurious action, likewise implies no helpful one.

I. In animal societies founded on nutrition, it is this function which constitutes the social tie; the individuals composing it are attached to one another in a permanent manner, from their birth onwards, and the nutritive liquid circulates from one to another, thus establishing a material community. It is found in the hydroid polypes, the Bryozoa and the Tunicata. As examples of the superior forms, we may quote the hydractinia, composed of individuals each of which has its own special and exclusive function: some, that of feeding; others, that of feeling and exploring; others, of defending the colony; others, again, of reproducing it—the last-named being divided into males and females. The siphonophora present an analogous division of labour, and the community, over a metre in length, suspended to a floating bladder, executes well co-ordinated collective movements.

Is there—at any rate in the higher forms of these colonies —a social instinct? Solidarity and reciprocity can indeed be perceived, in an objective, material way, in the form of adherence, and vascular communication; but nothing proves that there is anything more than an *organic* solidarity and reciprocity. Perhaps, in circumstances such as the nautical manœuvres just mentioned, in which a general obedience to one directing individual has been ascertained, there is a momentary consent—a certain unity of representation. To be accurate, the terms individual and community are diverted from their ordinary acceptation and used in an equivocal sense. Our notion of the individual is that of an organised whole living independently by itself: this no longer corresponds to the present case. Our notion of a community is an assemblage of individuals, and as these are, in the case under consideration, of a peculiar nature, it might thus be contended with equal force that these aggregates deserve, or that they do not deserve, the name of animal communities: it is a question of the point of view. On the one hand, one may regard the hydractinia or the siphonophora as a complex individual whose organs are the fishing, the piloting, the reproductive, etc., individuals. On the other hand, it may be maintained that the food-providers, pilots, etc., are true individuals whose aggregation forms a society. In short, it is an undifferentiated state, in which individuals and community are hardly to be distinguished from one another, and are only two different aspects of the same whole. The social instinct, also, if existing at all, is not yet differentiated from the conservative instinct under its simplest forms—the search for food, defence, attack. In fact, the two coincide. This stage has nothing more to teach us. Let us now pass on to social forms whose psychology is clearer.

II. These are the societies founded on reproduction—domestic societies, or families, under their various forms. I prefer to begin with these rather than with the gregarious state; first, on account of their universality; then because they are the first to appear in chronological order. Common opinion finds in them the first manifestation of the social sentiments, their origin, their source, and their moment of entry into the world. I reject this view in order to adopt that which connects the social instinct with the gregarious state.

If we take, one after another, the conditions of every aggregate founded on reproduction, we shall find three stages: that of sexual approach, that of maternal love, and lastly, but in the case of animals only exceptionally, paternal love. The social instinct—*i.e.*, the more or less vague consciousness of at least a temporary solidarity and reciprocity—does not, as we shall see, make its appearance at any of these stages.

1. Sexual approach results from one particular instinct; it unites two individuals only: can we consider it as the embryo of a society? "Around sexuality are co-ordinated the altruistic instincts of which the animal is capable." This formula of Littré's needs defining with more precision. First, in the immense majority of cases the connection is not lasting; the blind instinct satisfies itself, and all is over. Higher up there are more permanent forms, such as poly-

gamy and polyandry; but these small communities founded on sex-attraction are closed, and have no power of radiation or extension, no future. Higher still we find monogamy, as among wolves, many birds, etc.; but the monogamic aggregate is still more of a close corporation than the others. Let us note, in passing, that these two forms, polygamy and monogamy, are distributed through the animal world in an apparently fortuitous manner, having no relation to the intellectual development—as, for instance, the monogamy of the stork and the polygamy of the monkey.

Finally, this first stage yields us no result, tending rather towards social restriction than social extension.

2. Maternal love is of much greater importance. In domestic societies it is the universal and permanent element, the vital bond. This emotion is so widespread, so well known, we might say so trite, that it seems to involve no mystery, and yet, if we descend into animal psychology, we find nothing more enigmatical. The development of sympathy and intelligence partly explains it in the human species and the higher animals; but in the lower orders the difficulty becomes extreme. Yet it shows itself among the annelids, the crustacea, the mollusca, and even the echinoderms, which carry their eggs about adhering to their bodies. Frequently it shows itself as a feeling which, though vague, is tenacious, devoted, heroic. We do not indicate all the difficulties of the question, as for instance : How can an insect take such care of its eggs when it cannot recognise its own form in a creature which in nowise resembles itself, and has not even a living form?[1]

Most naturalists content themselves with ascertaining the fact, without inquiring into its origin. Darwin declares that it is useless to speculate on this subject. Others connect maternal affection with parasitism—scarcely a legitimate hypothesis, since the parasite is the enemy of its host and lives against his will at his expense. Romanes seems to have recourse to the principle of serviceable variations; an animal which takes care of its eggs or carries them about with it, has a better chance of preserving them; and if this way of acting becomes a fixed habit in its descendants, an

[1] For a detailed study of this question see Espinas, *Les Sociétés Animales* (2nd ed.), pp. 334 *et seq.*, 411 *et seq.*, 444 *et seq.*

instinct has been established. This explanation reduces itself to chance and to the hereditary transmission—an open question—of acquired modifications.

Excluding the insects and those analogous cases which, as Espinas has shown (*op. cit.*, pp. 334-339), require a special explanation, it is preferable to admit, with this author and Bain, the prominent part played by contact. " It seems to me that there must be at the foundation that intense pleasure in the embrace of the young which we find to characterise the parental feeling throughout. The origin of the pleasure may be as purely physical as in the love of the sexes; . . . [there is] an initial satisfaction in the animal embrace, heightened by reciprocation." [1] " The female, at the moment when she gives birth to little ones resembling herself, has no difficulty in recognising them as the flesh of her flesh; the feeling she experiences towards them is made up of sympathy and pity, but we cannot exclude from it an idea of property which is the most solid support of sympathy. She feels and understands up to a certain point that these young ones which are herself at the same time belong to her; the love of herself extended to those who have gone out from her changes egoism into sympathy and the proprietary instinct into an affectionate impulse. As sexual love implies the idea of mutual ownership, so maternal love supposes that of subordinated ownership. It is because this other self is so feeble that the interest felt for it takes the form of pity." [2] This last remark relates to an emotional manifestation which Spencer regards as the source of maternal love—tenderness for the *weak*. This seems to me rather one of its elements than its sole basis. On the other hand, Bain maintains that " an intensified attraction towards the weak is not merely consistent with the gregarious situation, but seems to be required by its varying exigencies. . . . An interest or solicitude about weak members would be almost the necessary completion of the social system " (Bain, *op. cit.*, pp. 138, 139). This granted, maternal love and social instinct would have an element in common, but they nevertheless remain distinct and mutually independent.

I have insisted to some extent on maternal love, because

[1] Bain, *The Emotions*, p. 140.
[2] Espinas, *Les Sociétés Animales*, pp. 444 *et seq.*

it is one of the most important manifestations of the emotional life. It is clear that it belongs to the category of the tender emotions, of which it is a well-determined form and remarkable by reason of its intensity; but it is not the source of the social instinct, because it implies neither solidarity nor reciprocity. It might be maintained that it is the gate by which the feeling of benevolence made its entrance into the world, and that its appearance is the earliest in date; but other conditions are needed for the social instinct to reveal itself.

3. The third stage, marked by the entrance of the father into the domestic community, does not affect our conclusion. In the animal world taken as a whole, paternal affection is rare and far from permanent, and among the lower representatives of humanity the feeling is a very weak one and the tie very loose. It exists, however, and its origin is much more difficult to assign than in the case of maternal love.[1] Though it may be maintained that in man it originates in pride and the feeling of ownership (Bain), this hypothesis is not applicable to animals; we cannot say, as in the case of the mother, that there is a material and visible relation, so that the offspring seems to be a separated portion of the parent. It remains to establish the significance of sympathy for weakness, as a primary cause of this feeling. We might add another element if we admit, with Spencer, that the life in common of the father and mother (paternal affection being only found where unions are permanent) creates a current of affection in proportion to the services rendered. Whatever origin we may assign to it, it adds nothing to our discussion, and has no efficacity in arousing the social instinct.

To sum up: what we find at the base of domestic aggregates is tender emotion, the genesis of altruism, but restricted to a closed group, without expansive force or elasticity.

III. The gregarious life—*i.e.*, that of the animals who live in troops or hordes—is founded on the attraction of like for like, irrespective of sex, and for the first time manifests the true social tendencies, through the habit of acting in common.

---

[1] For the theories on this matter see Espinas, pp. 401 *et seq.*

In its lowest degree it consists of accidental and unstable assemblages which are, as it were, an attempt at life in common. Every one knows that certain pelagic animals travel in vast numbers, their course being determined by the temperature of the water or the direction of the currents. We also know what happens in the migrations of processionary caterpillars, of crickets, and more especially of birds. Numerous species of animals assemble together in the morning and evening to sing, utter their various cries, pursue each other and gambol about, living dispersed at other times. This shows, says Espinas, "a latent social tendency, always ready to show itself when not combated by any other tendency."

Higher still, we find assemblages of variable duration, but voluntarily formed and maintained, in view of a common aim. They have all the characteristics of a society—community of effort, synergy, reciprocity of services. Darwin[1] has given many examples of this : Pelicans fish in concert, and close in round their prey like a living net; wolves and wild dogs hunt in packs, and help each other to attack their victims. These communities are to some extent accidental and unstable, and may come to an end in a final competition for the sharing of the spoil. Much more stable are those which have the common defence for their aim : rabbits warn one another of danger; many mammals and birds place sentinels (it is well known how difficult it is to approach a herd or drove of animals); monkeys remove vermin or take out thorns from one another's skins, form a chain to cross the gap between two trees, unite their forces to raise a heavy stone, and finally, gathered into bands under the direction of a leader, they defend themselves energetically and risk their lives to save their companions. We might enumerate endless facts of this kind. No doubt, we have not yet found the permanent organisation, the fixed division of labour, the continuity, which are peculiar to the higher animal societies; but the instability and intermittence of these social forms help us to understand why they exist and whence they originate.

Social tendencies are derived from sympathy; they arise in determinate conditions. The facts already given supply

---

[1] *Descent of Man*, chap. iii.   See also Espinas, *op. cit.*, sec. iv.

the answer to the questions: how do they arise? what is their source? They arise from the nature of things, from the conditions of the animal's existence; they are not based on pleasure, but on the unconscious affirmation of the will to live; they are auxiliary to the instinct of conservation. Society, as Spencer justly remarks, is founded on its own desire—*i.e.*, on an instinct.

The gregarious life, as this writer has shown in detail, predominates among the herbivora and graminivora, who, as a rule, being ill armed for strife and finding food in abundance, find it to their advantage to live in herds.

The contrary is the case with the carnivora; they are well armed, and need ample space in which to hunt down their prey, so that it is to their advantage to live in isolation, except in those cases already mentioned, where they associate together for a difficult chase, or for defence against a dangerous enemy.[1]

We may add that there are animals which, as they find it to their advantage or otherwise, live alternately in communities or isolated. "Certain sociable birds in Australia build bowers of branches, where they assemble in great numbers during the day. In pairing-time the society is broken up, and each couple retires by itself to construct its own separate nest. While the temporary families last there is no longer any assemblage, nor any life in common; it only begins again when the young are able to try their wings. This is only one of numberless examples which might be mentioned."[2]

In short, gregarious life depends on stature, strength, means of defence, kind and distribution of food, and mode of propagation. Derived from necessity, this habit of life in common creates a solidarity which is not mechanical and external, but psychological: the sight, the touch, the smell of his companions constitute in each individual a part of his own consciousness, of which he feels the want in its absence; the distressed state and the lamentations of an animal separated by chance from the herd are well known.

Here a disputed question suggests itself. It has been already settled by implication in the course of the statements already made, but it cannot be thus treated retro-

---

[1] Herbert Spencer, *Psychology*, ii. § 503 *et seq.*
[2] Houssay. *Revue philosophique*, May 1893, p. 487.

spectively and merely in passing. For the moment I may confine myself to indicating it. If we compare family societies and gregarious societies, what relation is there between them? We find ourselves in presence of two opinions or theories—one in favour of unity, the other of duality.

The first, the most ancient and widespread, derives social life from domestic life. The family is the social molecule : by its increase are formed aggregates of a more or less complex character, whose life in common creates a solidarity and an exchange of services—*i.e.*, the conditions of a community.

The second admits two groups of irreducible feelings and tendencies, mutually independent, though there are points of contact. The social instinct is not derived from the domestic feelings, while the latter are not derived from the social feelings. They are distinct by nature, having their respective sources in the attraction of like for like, irrespective of sex, and in the sexual appetite and the development of the tender emotions.

More than this: some writers, especially zoologists, have maintained that there is not merely dualism but *antagonism*. When the feelings of domestic life are strong, social solidarity is lax or non-existent. When social solidarity is close and rigorous, the family tendencies are transitory, effaced, or *nil—e.g.*, in ants and bees. The case of the Australian birds shows us this antagonism in an alternating form, the domestic and the social tendency predominating by turns. No doubt this antagonism is not irremediable and is compatible with various modifications and compromises ; but there is, in fact, a dualism not to be explained away. I shall return later on to this question, only remarking in anticipation that the dualist view seems to me the only admissible one.

IV. The higher societies are those in which the animal world has attained its loftiest degree of social development. In them we find division of labour, solidarity, stability, and continuity through several generations. Such are bees, wasps, ants, termites, beavers, etc. It is not part of our subject to study them, since our only aim is to follow the social tendencies to their highest point; but the problem already suggested again arises : On what foundation do these

higher societies rest? Espinas, who admits the view of the
family as the source of social life, classes them among
societies having reproduction for their purpose. For my
own part, I refer them to the gregarious state, in which
they mark the stage of the highest perfection. Let me
take this opportunity of pointing out the inconveniences of
a false position and the factitious difficulties arising from
it. The author draws out (pp. 370 *et seq.*) a detailed comparison between the societies of bees and those of ants; he
demonstrates the superiority of the latter, who, according to
circumstances, dig, carve, build, hunt, store up food, reap
harvests, keep slaves and cattle, and when they carry on
war against the wasps (the warlike representatives of the
bees) gain the victory. He also clearly shows that this
superiority is due to their terrestrial habits, in which every
contact, every march, leaves them a precise indication of the
nature of their surroundings. But he finds something perplexing in this superiority. As a matter of fact, a hive is
a perfect domestic society, since the queen-bee—*i.e.*, the
common mother—is the visible soul of social life among the
bees. An ant-heap is imperfect, "inferior" as a domestic
society, as containing several females. The apparent contradiction disappears, if we consider that in both cases,
especially in the second, the essential element is the
solidarity among the members, the mutual attraction between
similar beings, and that, consequently, we must refer them to
the gregarious, and not to the domestic type. For the rest,
in neither case does the family, in the true sense of the
word, exist: it is needless to demonstrate this at length, it
is quite sufficient to note the absence of maternal love.
And so certain writers have made use of this argument—as
I have already said—to prove that such a high development of the social tendencies has only been possible through
the suppression of the family tendencies.

II.

If we pass from animals to man, the situation remains the
same, and the tendency to social life, in spite of its manifold
adaptations, does not change its nature; it is always at bottom
a solidarity and a reciprocity of services, determined by the

conditions of human existence and variable as they. We need not come back to this; but the question already hinted at—that of the relation between the emotional manifestations serving as a basis to the family on the one hand, and those which are the foundation of social life on the other hand—presents itself anew. We cannot evade it, if we desire any light on the origin of the social feelings.

If we assume the family as the primitive fact which, by its increase, produced the clan, and afterwards, more complex aggregates, such as tribes, connected with each other by the memory of a common ancestor and at last subject to the authority of a patriarch-king, the social development is simply an expansion of the natural family. On this hypothesis, the domestic tendencies (founded on reproduction) are primary; the social tendencies are derivative and of secondary or tertiary formation.

If, on the contrary, we consider the smallest social groups (hordes, clans, or whatever other name they may be called by) as existing by themselves, independently of the domestic group, the tendency to live in societies must be considered as irreducible and self-determined; there is only one more general emotional phenomenon whence it could be derived, viz., sympathy.

Evidently, this question cannot be settled *a priori*, but only by the interpretation of facts. Now there is no lack of documents, supplied by ethnology from observations on actually existing primitive peoples, by the history of the remotest epochs, and by the literary monuments of the earliest ages, which are the echo of prehistoric times. There is no lack, either, of authorised works on the subject: MacLennan, Bachofen, Tylor, Sumner Maine, Starcke, Westermarck—to cite only a few at random. Although there is much disagreement, both as to the facts and the interpretation of the facts, the probability is very slight in favour of the priority of the family, very great in favour of two distinct developments with inevitable points of contact and interference.

Let us briefly recall the most generally admitted results of research into the evolution of the family and the progress of social development.

1. The evolution of the family has certainly not proceeded in all places in the same way, a circumstance which always

permits the critic to oppose facts to the view he is combating. A disease inherent in the human mind induces
most writers to try and refer everything to *one* formula,
to impose on facts that perfect unity which, in such matters,
does not appear very probable. Those who assign the
greatest length of time to the evolution of the family admit
three stages: promiscuity, matriarchate, patriarchate.

The period of primitive promiscuity (Bachofen, Mac-
Lennan, Girard-Teulon, etc.) is contested and rejected by
many authorities. In any case, it does not seem as if we
could establish the rule without a great number of exceptions. Not to speak, however, of archaic institutions
which have been interpreted in this sense, and as survivals,
there are still certain Tartar populations which approach
this stage. At Hawaii, the individual was related to the
whole horde, age alone determining the relationships: every
one called all the old people indiscriminately grandfather
and grandmother; all those who, as far as age went, might
be his parents, father and mother; all those of his own
generation, brothers and sisters; and so on for sons and
daughters, grandsons and grand-daughters. These five
terms expressed all known degrees of kinship. We may
note, in passing, that a very weak psychological argument
has been put forward in order to disprove the existence of
this period—viz., that the natural jealousy of man would
have rendered promiscuity impossible, at least for any
length of time. Those who have hazarded such reasoning
have been too ready to judge primitive man by civilised
standards. However this may be, such a mass, without
individual relationships, is rather a society than a family; or
rather, it is an undifferentiated state, which might be compared to the lowest form of animal societies (the nutritive),
which also is undifferentiated.

In the period of the matriarchate, which appears to have
lasted for a considerable time, the mother is the centre of
the family. This domestic form, coexisting with polygamy,
polyandry, and even with monogamy, has left so many
traces, and is still met with in so many different races and
countries, from the ancient Egyptians and Etruscans to the
present natives of Sumatra and some regions of Africa, that
there is no dispute on the subject. The woman gives her
name to the children, kinship is reckoned, and the inherit-

ance of property (though not always that of political
dignities) descends, in the female line; the position of most
importance is filled, not by the father, but the uncle—the
mother's brother. The causes of the matriarchal system
have been much discussed. Did it originate in an assumption that the true father was unknown, or in a common
opinion of his insignificance? Whatever view may be
adopted, it seems to me reasonable to compare the matriarchate with the predominating system among animals—*i.e.*,
maternal societies where the male is not admitted.

The patriarchate (*agnatio*) which makes the father the
centre of the family brings us down to the historic epoch,
to which it was even anterior in some parts of the globe.
Its appearance is saluted in lyrical terms by Bachofen as
the triumph of ideas over matter: "By the spiritual principle
of paternity the chains of tellurism were broken;" it was a
conquest of mind over material nature—over what can be
seen and touched.[1] It is not known how it came about,
whether by adoption or by a pretence of childbirth. In any
case, it corresponds with the admission of the male into
animal societies.

2. The development of social life is quite otherwise. It
would be foreign to our purpose to retrace its successive
phases; let us confine ourselves to the question of origin.
What was primitive man? On this point much has been
written by way of argument and conjecture. H. Spencer,
in his *Sociology* (vol. i.), has made a complete restoration
from prehistoric documents, burial-mounds, and more
especially from the condition of contemporary savages.
Nothing proves that this picture will suit all classes; there
have existed not one primitive man, but primitive men
differing considerably, according to race and environment.

However far we go back, the first form of life in common
seems to be the horde, an unstable, unorganised aggregate,
without recognised kinships, drawn together instinctively in
view of utility and defence. But the true social unit, which
arose at an early period in various parts of the globe, is the
clan (and analogous institutions), a fixed, stable, coherent,
closed aggregate, founded on religious or other affiliation

---

[1] *Mutterrecht*, pp. 17-19. See also his interpretation of the myths of
Orestes and Bellerophon as expressing the triumph of the patriarchate,
p. 85.

(but not on descent), independent of family conditions : a man cannot belong to two clans at once, and in most cases each of these groups is in a hostile attitude towards the rest. How has this social molecule been able to aggregate to itself others, and this closed organism to break its narrow limits, in order to extend itself by increase and fusion? This is a somewhat obscure question; perhaps by exogamy, *i.e.*, the imperative custom which forbade marriage within the group (yet in other groups the rule was endogamy, *i.e.*, the prohibition of marriage outside them); more probably the great agent of assimilation and fusion was war, followed by the assimilation of the conquered.

This simple comparison shows that the family and the clan are not similar institutions : the first is an autonomous group belonging to a master, and having for its end the enjoyment of property; the second is a group of another nature having for its end the common struggle for existence. "Where the interests defended by the family are less important than those of the clan, the family is influenced by the ideas which regulate the clan organisation; and this fact repeats itself in all primitive societies when defence against an outside enemy is the dominant necessity."[1] The family group and the social group have each sprung from different tendencies, from distinct needs; each has its special, independent psychological origin, and there is no possible derivation from one to the other.

III.

Life in common, even under the gregarious form, requires certain ways of acting, and habits founded on sympathy and determined by the concerted aim pursued by all. In order that it may become stable and constitute a society, an element of fixity must be added—the more or less clear consciousness of an obligation, of a rule, of what has to be done or avoided. This is the appearance of the *moral sentiment.* All conceptions of morality, coarse or refined, theoretical or purely practical, agree on this point; divergences exist, in practice, only as to the characteristics of the act reputed obligatory; in theory, only as to its origin.

---

[1] Starcke, *La famille primitive*, p. 116.

All *real* morality which has lived, *i.e.* governed a human society, large or small, which has existed, not in the academic abstractions of moralists, but in the concrete development of history, and has run its complete course, passes through two principal periods.

One of these is instinctive, spontaneous, unconscious, unreflecting, determined by the conditions of existence of a given group at a given moment. It expresses itself in custom—a heterogeneous mixture of beliefs and actions which, from the point of view of reason and of a more advanced culture, we consider sometimes as moral, sometimes as immoral, sometimes as unmoral, *i.e.*, puerile and futile, but all of which have been rigorously observed.

The other is conscious, reflecting, many-sided, complex, like the higher forms of social and moral life. It expresses itself in institutions, written laws, religious or civil codes ; and still more in the abstract speculations of philosophical moralists. Then, the apogee being reached, vague aspirations reach out towards a new, dimly apprehended ideal, and the cycle begins over again.

Most constructors of a scientific system of morality have forgotten or neglected the first period; but wrongly so, for it is the source of the second. This, too, is the reason for the two opposite views held with regard to the origin of moral development.

Some seek it in the order of knowledge, whence they deduce all the rest; they suppose innate ideas, or an adaptation acquired through a long process and fixed by heredity (Spencer), or the consciousness of a categorical imperative, or the notion of utility; all of which are intellectual solutions.

Others seek it in the order of instinct and feeling. They admit tendencies, impulses implanted in us by nature, *i.e.*, forming part of our organisation, like thirst and hunger, whose satisfaction produces pleasure and their non-satisfaction pain; this is the emotional view.

The two are not absolutely irreconcilable: each of them corresponds to a different period of evolution; the emotional view to the instinctive stage, the stage of moral chaos; the intellectualist view to the reflective stage of rational organisation; but it is clear that one alone can claim the mark of its origin. In other words, we may say : in the moral consciousness there are two elements—judgment and feeling. A judgment (approving or condemnatory) on our own conduct and that of others is the result of a deeper process— not an intellectual one—of an emotional process of which it is only the clear and intelligible manifestation in consciousness. It would be a psychological absurdity to suppose that a bare, dry idea, an abstract conception without emotional accompaniments, and resembling a geometrical notion, could have the least influence on human conduct. No doubt, we must admit that the evolution is rather that of moral ideas than of the moral sentiment, which, in itself, is no more than a tendency to act—a pre-disposition; but an evolution of *purely speculative* ideas, with no emotional accompaniment, will have no results in the practical order. We may note that the opposition between these two views is constantly reflected in the history of moral theory. In England, where psychology predominates, the doctrine of feeling has had numerous champions, from Shaftesbury down to the present day. In Germany, where metaphysics are predominant, the intellectualist doctrine, since Kant, occupies the first place, except with Schopenhauer and his adherents. It is quite natural that the metaphysicians, intellectualists by temperament and by profession, should have adopted this position.

For the rest we are concerned here with the moral sentiment, and with that alone; the other elements of morality do not form part of our study. It consists, at bottom, in movement or arrest of movement, in a tendency to act or not to act; it is not, *in its origin*, due to an idea or a judgment; it is instinctive, and herein lies its strength. It is innate, not like an alleged archetype, infused into man, invariable, illuminating him everywhere and always, but in the same way as hunger and thirst and other constitutional needs. It is necessary; it forces one to act (when not kept in check by counter-tendencies), as the sight of water forces the duckling to plunge into it. Thus we must say that the man who impulsively throws himself into danger to save another is more thoroughly moral than he who only does so after reflection; one must be blinded by intellectualist prejudices to maintain the contrary. *Natural* morality is a gift—theologians would say a grace; it is artificial, acquired morality, which is measured by the quantity of resistance overcome. Finally, like every other tendency, it results in satisfaction or dissatisfaction (*e.g.*, remorse).[1] In short, its innateness and its necessity place it in the *motor*, not in the intellectual order.

These characteristics being determined, let us follow the progress of its evolution. It presents two aspects: first, the positive, corresponding to the genesis of the beneficent feelings, or active altruism, an internal evolution—*i.e.*, one of the primary feeling, in and through itself; secondly, negative, corresponding to the rise of the sense of justice, an external evolution—*i.e.*, one produced under the pressure of conditions of existence and coercive means.

I. We include under the name of beneficence, or active altruism, such feelings as benevolence, generosity, devotion, charity, pity, etc.; in short, those foreign or contrary to the instinct of individual self-preservation. Their fundamental conditions are two psychological facts already studied :

1. Sympathy, in the etymological sense, *i.e.*, an emotional unison, the possibility of feeling with another, and like him. Could a society be based on this state alone? In extreme cases this might happen; but such a society would be transitory, precarious, unstable: we have found similar examples in the gregarious state, animal or human. Stability requires stronger ties, that is to say, moral ones.

2. The altruistic tendency, or tender emotion, which

---

[1] " The Australians attribute the death of their friends to spells cast by some neighbouring tribe; for this reason they consider it a sacred obligation to avenge the death of a relative by killing a member of the tribe in question. A native having lost one of his wives, announced his intention of going to kill a woman belonging to a distant tribe. The magistrate told him that if he committed this act, he would be confined in prison for the rest of his life. He therefore did not start on his journey; but, month by month, he wasted away: remorse preyed on his mind, he could neither sleep nor eat ; the ghost of his wife haunted him, reproaching him with his negligence. One day he disappeared; a year later he came back, having accomplished his duty " (Guyau, *Esquisse d'une Morale*, etc., p. 109). Here we have an example of instinctive morality and rational immorality. It should be noted that in this work Guyau has returned to the view of the moral instinct, adopted by him, after having previously criticised it, in his *Morale Anglaise* (III. chap. iv.).

exists in all men, except in those to be referred to at the end of this chapter. It belongs to our constitution, as much as the fact of having two eyes or a stomach.

Now the question put to us is this: How is active altruism developed, and by what psychological mechanism? How do disinterested feelings arise from primitive egoism? Setting aside all metaphysical solutions, such as Schopenhauer's theory of universal pity, compassion (*Mitleid*) for all beings, founded on a vague consciousness of community of being and identity of origin—a monistic conception,—I shall confine myself to a strictly psychological explanation.

Benevolence arises from a particular form of activity accompanied by pleasure: this vague and obscure formula will be explained presently.

The fundamental tendency consists, in the first place, of preserving, and then of extending one's self, of being and well-being, *i.e.*, expending activity. Man may devote this activity to things: he cuts, hacks, destroys, overthrows,— these are destructive activities; he sows, plants, builds, and exercises preservative or creative activities. He may apply it to animals or to men; he injures, maltreats, destroys, or he cares for, helps, saves. Destructive activity is accompanied by pleasure, but by a pathological one, since it is the cause of evil. Preservative or creative activity is accompanied by pure pleasure, leaving behind it no painful feeling; consequently, it tends to repeat and increase itself: the object or the person which is the cause of pleasure becomes a centre of attraction, the starting-point of an agreeable association. To sum up, we have (1) a tendency to the display of our creative activity; (2) the pleasure of succeeding; (3) an object or living being to play a receptive part; (4) an association between this being or object and the pleasure experienced; whence a continually increasing attraction towards this being or object. The conservative tendency in action and the law of transference (see Part I., Chap. XII.) are the essential agents in the rise of altruism.

This may be justified by several examples. If we reflect on the preceding, it will be understood that benevolence may well be the result of chance, and have, in its origin, no intentional character. A man, without paying any special heed to it, happens to throw some water on a plant which was drying up beside his door; next day he chances to notice that it is beginning to revive; he repeats the operation, intentionally; he becomes more and more interested in the plant, grows attached to it, and would not like to be deprived of it.[1] This is a very trivial, everyday occurrence, and there is no one who has not experienced something of the sort; this is all the better, as showing us the rise of the feeling in all its simplicity. If this happens in the case of a plant, how much more easily in that of an intelligent animal or a man!

It is an observed fact that a man attaches himself to another rather in proportion to the services he renders than to those he receives from him. There is, in general, a stronger current of benevolence passing from the benefactor to his *protégé* than *vice versâ*. Common opinion considers this illogical: from the point of view of reason, it is so—not from that of feeling; and the preceding analysis even shows that it *must be* so, because the benefactor has put more of himself into the recipient of his bounty than the latter can do to him. Thus, in many persons, gratitude needs to be supported by reflection.

If we are ill-disposed towards any one, the best and surest remedy against this incipient aversion is to render him some service. Conversely, the person who refuses all our benefits and obstinately avoids them becomes an object of indifference, or even hatred.

"During the proscriptions of Marius and Sulla," says Friedmann, "there were many sons who, out of fear, gave up their father, but it was never known that a father had denounced his son; a fact that somewhat startled the Roman moralists, who were unable to explain it." The explanation is involved in the constitution of the Roman family, by which the father could confer many benefits on the son, whereas the son was entirely dependent on the father, and could do nothing for him.

Many other incidents might be cited to justify the accuracy of the preceding analysis. Such is the mechanism

[1] Friedmann, "Genesis of Disinterested Benevolence," *Mind*, vol. i. (1878), p. 404.

by means of which our emotional self succeeds in external-ising, in alienating itself; but this could not be done were there not at the origin and starting-point a primary tendency, already studied under the name of tender emotion. It is clear, also, that beneficence is a generic term designating forms which vary according to circumstances: charity, generosity, devotion, etc.

The extension and heightening of the feeling of beneficence have taken place slowly, and owing to the work of certain men who deserve to be called *discoverers* in morals. This ex-pression may sound strangely in some ears, because they are imbued with the theory of an innate and universal knowledge of good and evil imparted to all men at all times. If we admit, on the contrary,—as observation teaches us to do,—not a ready-made, but a growing morality, it must necessarily be the discovery of an indi-vidual or group of individuals. Every one admits the existence of inventors in geometry, in music, in the plastic and mechanical arts; but there have also been men in moral disposition far superior to their contemporaries, who have initiated or promoted reform in this department. Let us note (for this point is of the highest import-ance) that the *theoretic* conception of a higher moral ideal, of a step in advance, is not sufficient; it needs a powerful emotion leading to action, and, by contagion, communicating its own impulse to others. The onward march is proportioned to what is *felt*, not to what is understood.

Were the human race, in the beginning, cannibals? Some affirm this, others deny it. What is certain is that the custom of eating one's fellow-men has existed in many places, and still exists in some. It has been explained by scarcity of food, by superstitious beliefs, by the intoxication of triumph in annihilating a vanquished enemy, by the idea of assimilating his strength and courage, and by a variety of other reasons; but it has not been sufficiently remarked that its extinction has not always been due to the inter-vention of superior races. It has sometimes taken place on the spot. In the Tahiti Islands it had disappeared shortly before the arrival of Bougainville; among the Red-skins, and even among the Fijians, parties had been formed in order to suppress not only cannibalism, but the tortures

inflicted on prisoners of war.[1] The promoters of this
abolition, whether individuals or groups, were certainly
inventors. The universality of human sacrifices is well
known; they are found still existing during the historic
period, from China to Judæa, from Greece to Gaul, from
Carthage to Rome. How did they disappear? On this
point we have nothing but ignorance or legends, but they
could not have disappeared without the agency of man.
Du Chaillu cites a case in which reform is, so to speak,
caught in the act—that of an African chief who was the
first to give orders that no slave should be killed at his
tomb.[2] Among the Aztecs, with their bloodthirsty religion,
a sect, formed before the arrival of the Spaniards, had placed
itself under the protection of a deity who abhorred bloodshed. All the great ancient legislators, whether historical
or legendary—Manes, Confucius, Moses, Buddha,—we might
say all founders of religions, have been discoverers in
morals; whether the discovery originated with themselves
alone or with a collectivity as whose summary and embodiment they may be regarded, matters little.

It would be easy to continue this historical demonstration, but the above is sufficient to justify the term discoverers. From causes of which we are ignorant, but
analogous to those which produce great poets or painters,
there arise men of indisputable moral superiority who *feel*
what others do not feel, just as a great poet does com-

---

[1] About 1820, during the time of scarcity consequent on Tshaka's
wars, certain of the Natal tribes (the natives say, at the suggestion of a
chief named Umdava) adopted the practice of cannibalism. It was
abandoned when food again became plentiful, and has always been
regarded with great horror; those individuals who had acquired such
a taste for human flesh as to prefer it to other food, fled into the recesses
of the Drakensberg and Maluti mountains. Moshesh, the great Basuto
chief, directed his efforts for years to the extirpation of the practice,
though unwilling to do so, as his advisers desired, by means of a
summary massacre of the offenders. The *Amazimu* (*Modimo*) are now
a myth to both Zulus and Basutos; indeed the word, as now used, is
frequently synonymous with "ogre." It is to be noted that Moshesh
was not in any way acting under European influence, in fact the last of
the cannibals had disappeared long before the country came under
British rule, and though the memory of their atrocities was still fresh
when the French missionaries arrived in 1833, the chief had already
been proceeding against them for some time. See Casalis, *Les Bassoutos*.

[2] Staniland Wake, *Evolution of Morality*, vol. i. pp. 427 *et seq.*
To be consulted for facts of this kind.

pared with ordinary men. And for one who has succeeded, how many have failed for want of a favourable
environment! A St. Vincent de Paul among the Kanakas
would be as impossible as a Mozart among the Fuegians.

In primitive societies there has been a long struggle
between the strongest egoistic tendencies, with their dis-
solvent action, and the weaker and intermittent altruistic
tendencies, which have progressed through the agency of
some more enlightened individuals, and also with the help
of force, of which we still have to speak.

II. Let us now examine the development of the moral
sentiment under its negative and restrictive aspect—*i.e.*, as
the sense of justice. Here the intellectual element evidently
preponderates, and its evolution involves the other.

"Justice," says Littré, "has the same foundation as
science." One rests on the principle of identity which
governs the region of speculation, the other rests on the
principle of equivalence and rules the sphere of action.
Justice, in its origin, is a compensation for damages. Its
evolution starts from an instinctive semi-conscious manifestation, rising by progressive steps to a universalist conception. Let us mark the principal stages.

The first, and lowest, is neither moral nor social, but
purely animal and reflex—"a defensive reflex."[1] The individual who suffers violence, who thinks himself attacked or
injured, immediately reacts. This is "the exasperated
instinct of conservation," or, to call it by its true name,
revenge. So the savage who, before Darwin's eyes, broke
his son's head for having dropped a store of shell-fish, the
fruit of a laborious day's fishing. This defensive reflex
frequently recurs in the psychology of crowds; it is needless
to give instances. It may seem paradoxical to take revenge
as a starting-point for the sense of justice; but we shall see
how it becomes mitigated and rationalised.

In fact, a second stage corresponds to revenge deferred
through premeditation, reflection, or some analogous cause.
It tends towards equivalence and reaches it under the form
of retaliation, so frequent in primitive communities. The
idea of equality, tooth for tooth, eye for eye, has won its
way; the instinct has become intellectualised.

---

[1] Letourneau, *L'évolution juridique chez les différents peuples.*

So far, the compensation claimed would appear to have only an individual character; but it must very early have taken on a collective character, by reason of the close solidarity uniting the members of the small social aggregate —the clan or family. An all-powerful opinion forces the injured party to pursue his revenge even when he does not wish it; and when a *vendetta* is in force as between clan and clan, the stage of collective responsibility appears, and the notion of the compensation due is enlarged.

However, revenge restores, in the social aggregate, a state of war, which has to be eliminated; hence a reaction on the part of the community tending to suppress or attenuate it. This is the stage of arbitration and peace-making. Many facts show that, in the beginning, the decision of the umpires is without binding value, and supported by no coercive means. It is a proof not so much of culpability as of an indemnity to be paid to those concerned; the criminal trial is as yet a civil action.

For this temporary and unsanctioned arbitration the social development logically substitutes a permanent and guaranteed arbitration, exercised by a chief, or an aristocracy, or the popular assembly. Compensation becomes obligatory and is forcibly imposed. The condemned person must submit or leave the community; if refractory, he is excommunicated, and in primitive societies the outlaw's life is intolerable; we see the equivalent of it in modern strikes. Let us also note the somewhat widely distributed custom of a division of the indemnity imposed, one portion being assigned to the injured party, the other to the state —*i.e.*, the chief. The notion of justice has taken on a definitely social character.

It only remains that it should become universal. It long remains enclosed within the limits of the social group. All that contributes to the material and moral welfare of the group is good, and conversely; outside the group, all acts are *unmoral*. We find in history, and even at the present time, many proofs of this dualism or duplication of the individual, according as he is acting within his own social environment or with regard to strangers. Such were the Germans of Cæsar's time.[1] In their earlier period, the Greeks con-

---

[1] " Latrocinia nullam habent infamiam quæ extra fines cujusque *civitatis* fiunt."—*De Bell. Gall.*, vi. 21.

sidered themselves as less under moral obligation towards
the Barbarians, and the Romans towards foreigners (*hostes*).
It is especially owing to the efforts of the philosophers—
Socrates, Plato, Aristotle, the Stoics—that justice ceased
to be national and became universal. It might be
added that at that period when the notion of justice remains a national one, it still varies within the group, according to caste; it is not the same for priests and warriors, for
free men and for slaves, for aristocrats and for merchants.
In the beginning, particularism was the rule.

It is evident that, on the negative side, the evolution of
moral life has been especially due to the progress of intelligence; the emotional element has only been incidental.
Compared with the sense of justice, the feeling of active
benevolence, if not evolved more quickly, at least appeared
sooner, because nearer to instinct and less dependent
on reason. A certain philosopher (Kant, I believe) was
surprised that there is so much kindness and so little justice
among men. He did not observe as a psychologist, or else
he was led astray by intellectualist prejudice. This must be
so, because tenderness is innate and spontaneous, justice
acquired and deliberate; because one springs directly from
an instinct, while the other has to undergo various metamorphoses. If man is sociable and moral, it is less because
he thinks than because he feels in a certain manner and
tends in a certain direction.

To conclude: moral emotion is a very complex state.
Those sentimentalists in the last century, or in this, who
have maintained the hypothesis of a "moral sense," have
erroneously considered it as a special sense with an innate
faculty of discriminating good and evil. It is not a simple
act, but the sum of a set of tendencies. Let us eliminate
the intellectual elements, and enumerate its emotional constituents only: (1) as basis, sympathy—*i.e.*, a community of
nature and disposition; (2) the altruistic or benevolent
tendency manifesting itself under different forms (attraction
of like to like, maternal or paternal affection, etc.), at first
weak, but gaining more expansion by the restriction of the
egoistic feelings; (3) the sense of justice with its obligatory
character—whose origin we have just traced; (4) the desire
of approbation or of divine or human rewards, and the
fear of disapprobation and punishments. As in the case

of all complex feelings, its composition must vary with the predominance of one or other of its constituent elements; in one case it is obligation (the Stoics), in another charity, in many the fear of public opinion or of the law, of God or of the devil. It is impossible that it should be constant and identical in all men.

IV.

The pathology of the moral sense cannot detain us long, its detailed study belonging to the department of criminal anthropology. Numerous works have been published on this subject within the last half-century; there would be no advantage in presenting a bald abstract of these. Lombroso's view of the "born criminal," with his physiological, psychical, and social characteristics, has been violently attacked, and sustained serious damage. Several successive theories have attempted to explain the existence of this moral anomaly: atavism, according to which the born criminal is a survival, a return to primitive man, who is assumed to have been violent and unsociable; infantilism, which has recourse, not to heredity, but to arrested development, and alleges that the perversion which is permanent in the criminal is normal, but transient, in the child; the pathological view which connects the criminal type with epilepsy, considered as the prototype of violent and destructive impulses; the sociological view (the most recent), which attributes a preponderant function to social conditions, and maintains that the criminal is "a microbe inseparable from his environment."[1] We need not enter into a detailed examination of these hypotheses, which have given rise to much passionate debate: one question alone concerns our subject, that of moral insensibility—a condition described, long before the days of criminal anthropology, under the names of *moral insanity* (Prichard, 1835), *folie morale*, impulsive insanity, in-

---

[1] It should perhaps be added that the more scientific writers on criminal anthropology do not regard the chief causes suggested above as rival theories, but rather as factors which may co-operate to produce criminality, the biological factor (heredity, arrest of development, infantilism, etc.) acting as predisposing cause, the sociological factor as exciting cause.—ED.

stinctive monomania, etc., and which will serve to show once more the independence and the preponderance of feeling in the moral life.[1]

"Moral insanity is a form of mental derangement in which the intellectual faculties appear to have sustained little or no injury, while the disorder is manifested principally or alone in the state of the feelings, temper, or habit." Such is the formula of Prichard, which has been but little modified since. Translated into the language of pure psychology, it signifies: a complete absence or perversion of the altruistic feelings, insensibility to the representation of the happiness or suffering of others, absolute egoism, with all its consequences. By a self-evident analogy, this state has been called one of moral blindness; and, like physical blindness, it has various degrees. It has also been compared to idiocy. Reduced to the vegetative and sensitive life, the idiot is, intellectually, opposed to the genius, while the moral idiot is the antithesis of the great benefactors of humanity (Schüle).

We may find numerous instances of moral insanity in works on mental pathology and criminal anthropology.[2] It shows itself in two forms: (1) the passive, or apathetic—*i.e.*, that of pure insensibility; if the temperament is cold and the circumstances favourable, there is no violence to be feared; (2) the active, or impulsive, where there is no check on the violence of the appetites. Taken as a whole, it consists in: complete insensibility, absence of pity, cold ferocity, absence of remorse after committing acts of violence, or even murder. On this last point statistics and figures have been given whose precision makes me somewhat suspicious;[3]

---

[1] According to Krafft-Ebing, *Lehrbuch* (vol. i., sec. 2, chap. iii.), Regiomontanus already maintained, in 1513, that depravity is quite independent of the accurate knowledge of good and evil; he attributed this anomaly to the influence of the planet Venus.

[2] Especially Despine, *Psychologie naturelle* (ii. pp. 169 *et seq.*), and Maudsley, *Pathology of Mind*.

[3] *Dictionary of Psychological Medicine*, art. "Criminal Anthropology." Here it is stated that, at Elmira, 34 per cent. criminals on admission exhibit entire absence of moral susceptibility; while (according to Dr. Salsotto, at Turin) in 130 women guilty of murder, or complicity in murder, genuine remorse was only observed in 6.

for it is very difficult to penetrate so far into the consciousness of a criminal as to be duped neither by the hypocrisy which simulates remorse, nor by the boastfulness which feels but will not acknowledge it. The absence of all maternal feeling, though rare, has also been observed.

Moral insensibility is usually innate, and coincident with other symptoms of degeneracy. Among several children of the same family, brought up in the same surroundings, having received the same care, a single one may differ from all the rest, be amenable neither to gentleness nor to force, and manifest a precocious depravity, which will only strengthen as he grows older.

This state may be acquired and momentary, its causes being epilepsy, hysteria, apoplexy, paralytic dementia, senile decay, blows on the head, etc. Krafft-Ebing, besides an observation made by himself (*loc. cit.*), quotes from Wigan the case of a young man who, in consequence of being struck on the head with a ruler, developed complete moral insensibility. When, by means of the operation of trephining, a splinter of bone pressing on the brain had been removed, he returned to his former state. We have met with other analogous cases in the course of this work.

The most difficult and fiercely debated point is whether this moral anomaly is strictly instinctive and emotional in its origin, intellectual activity being entirely unconnected with it. Most writers take the affirmative view of this question, others deny it. The different modes of mental activity are so interdependent, and their relations so close, that it is difficult to solve the question definitely. We cannot refuse to admit that the intellect sometimes suffers from a counter-shock; but observation shows that most of these persons are well acquainted with the requirements of morality, and have had the abstract ideas of good, of evil, and of duty instilled into them by education, though without the slightest influence on their conduct. They have moral *ideas*, not moral feelings—*i.e.*, a disposition to feel and act. The law is to them nothing but a police regulation, which they are conscious of having broken. Their intellect, often firm and clear, is only an instrument for weaving skilful plots, or justifying themselves by subtle sophisms.

It was worth our while to recall, if only in a cursory manner, the nature of moral insensibility, in order to show the importance of the emotional element. In these cases there is a lack of completeness, and the deficit comes, not from the intellect, but from the character.

CHAPTER IX.

THE RELIGIOUS SENTIMENT.

Importance of the subject—Its Divisions. First Period: origin of the religious feeling—Primitive notions of the Infinite (Max Müller); Ancestor-worship (H. Spencer)—Fetichism, animism; Predominance of fear—Practical, utilitarian, social, but not moral character — Second period: (1) Intellectual evolution; Conception of a Cosmic Order first physical, then moral—Function of increasing generalisation; its stages; (2) Emotional evolution; Predominance of love; addition of the moral sentiment—Third Period: Supremacy of the rational element; Transformation into religious philosophy; Effacement of the emotional element—Religious emotion is a complete emotion—Manifold physiological states accompanying it; ritual, a special form of the expression of emotion—The religious sentiment as a passion —Pathology — Depressive forms: religious melancholy, demonomania—Exalted forms: ecstasy, theomania.

IT must be confessed that psychologists have not troubled themselves greatly with the study of the religious sentiment. Some omit it altogether, while others content themselves with a brief reference in passing; they note the two essential elements whence it is derived—fear, and tender emotion (love)—without troubling themselves about the variable relations between these two elements, or the multiform changes undergone by them in the course of centuries, through the annexation of other emotional states.[1] As

[1] Since the above was written two lengthy and valuable studies of the psychology of religion, and more especially of the phenomena of

we cannot deny its importance, this abstention, or negligence, is not justifiable. To summon to our aid an ill-understood respect, to maintain that one religion only is true and all the others false, to allege that all are alike false,—these and other analogous modes of reasoning are not in any degree acceptable to psychology; for, even if we take up an extreme position, and admit that all manifestations of the religious sentiment are mere illusion and error, it remains none the less true that illusion and error are psychic states, and worthy of being studied as such by psychologists. To such, the religious sentiment is *a fact* which they have simply to analyse and to follow through its transformations without being competent to discuss its objective value or its legitimacy. Thus understood, the question bears on two principal points: primary manifestations and their evolution, *i.e.*, the different elements which have constituted the religious sentiment during the various stages of its existence.

In every religious belief there are of necessity two parts: an intellectual element, a knowledge which constitutes the object of belief, and an emotional state, a feeling which accompanies the former and expresses itself in action. To any one deficient in the second element, the religious feeling is unknown, inaccessible; nothing remains to such persons but abstract metaphysical conceptions. The study of the religious sentiment, in its evolution, cannot dissociate these two elements; and it is the degree in which the element of knowledge is present which renders a precise division possible. I trace three periods: (1) that of perception and concrete imagination, where fear and the practical, utilitarian tendencies are predominant; (2) that of medium abstraction and generalisation, characterised by the addition of moral elements; (3) that of the highest concepts, where, the emotional element becoming more and more rarefied, the religious feeling tends to be confounded with the so-called intellectual feelings.

"conversion," have been published by Leuba and Starbuck, largely inspired by Prof. Stanley Hall (*Am. Jour. Psych.*, 1896-97). Both these studies are founded on original data, in part obtained by a *questionnaire.* —ED.

I.

As usual, authorities are not agreed on the question of origin. Under what form did the religious sentiment first make its appearance? We must first put aside two extremely systematic answers, which, although differing in spirit, have this in common, that they are both purely intellectualist.

The first, a very ancient one, has found its latest and clearest interpreter in Max Müller, who thinks that the notion of the Divine, more especially under the form of the Infinite, preceded that of the gods. Our senses give us the finite, but "beyond, behind, beneath, and within the finite, the infinite is always present to our senses. It presses upon us, it grows upon us from every side. What we call finite in space and time, in form and word, is nothing but a veil or net which we ourselves have thrown over the infinite."[1] What, then, is the infinite, he asks, but the object of all religions? The religion of the infinite precedes and comprehends all others, and as the infinite is implied by the senses (*i.e.*, the limits to our sensory perceptions imply an unlimited region beyond), it follows that religion can, with as much right as reason, be called a development of our sensory perceptions. The earliest religion consisted in the adoration of various objects, taken, each in turn, and isolatedly, as incarnations of the notion of the Infinite. This is what Max Müller calls "Henotheism." For him, polytheism and even fetichism are later developments, resulting from the breaking up of the primitive unity, and due to a disease of language: each name becomes a distinct deity; words are raised to the dignity of things, having their life, their attributes, and their legends: *Nomina numina.*

This last view, though it has had a certain vogue among linguists, is worth nothing as a psychological explanation, for it is quite clear that the word is only a starting-point or a vehicle for the process of thought, which is the sole agent of the metamorphosis. If the *nomina* become *numina*, it

[1] Max Müller, *Origin and Development of Religion* (Hibbert Lectures), p. 227.

is by a disease of imagination or thought, rather than of language.[1]

As for the principal thesis, the alleged primitive notion of the Infinite, which is the source of henotheism, it is a metaphysical hypothesis of extreme improbability. Primitive man, enclosed within hard conditions of life, is practical and positive rather than a dreamer; he does not naturally tend towards the Beyond. But a better reason than this, and an entirely psychological one, is that he is incapable of attaining to even a medium degree of abstraction and generalisation. How could a savage, who cannot count up to four, form any idea whatever of the Infinite? Evidently, this notion of the Illimitable is far beyond him.

There is only one way of imparting a certain psychological verisimilitude to Max Müller's view, viz., to strip it of its intellectualist character, and admit as its origin a feeling rather than a notion, a craving, a tendency, rather than a cognition. Of these two factors, which make up all religious belief, one intellectual, the other emotional, which has the priority? Did the notion produce the feeling, or the feeling excite the notion? Such is the problem which lies at the heart of all debates on the origin of religious manifestations. Some place it in the region of instinct: so Renan when he compares religion in humanity to the nest-building instinct of the bird. Others maintain that every feeling presupposes an object. "At first sight this latter theory seems to have logic on its side. It is clear that, in order to love or fear any being, one must have conceived the notion of his existence. Yet, however indispensable it may be to assume an intellectual operation at the beginning of religion, we must recognise that the feelings set in motion by this operation must have long preceded the most ancient formulas of primitive theology."[2] For my own part, I am inclined to accept the priority of feeling, though unable to supply any arguments based on fact; the period of origins being also that of conjecture.

The second theory, that of Herbert Spencer, brings us down from the notion of the Infinite to the extremely terrestrial mental life of savages. It is well known that he

---

[1] For a discussion of this point see Goblet d'Alviella, *L'idée de Dieu*, pp. 60 *et seq.*

[2] Goblet d'Alviella, *op. cit.*, p. 50.

reduces all primitive religions to the cult of ancestors—to necrolatry. The primordial fact is the conception of a spirit, or rather, of a *double*. The savage believes that he has a Sosia, or, in other words, a principal *ego* and a secondary *ego*. He infers the existence of this double from a great number of facts, to him inexplicable: his shadow, his reflection in the water, echoes, apparitions in dreams, fainting, trances, epilepsy, etc. The world is thus, for him, full of wandering spirits which he tries to pro- pitiate. According to Spencer, fetichism and polytheism are only aberrant forms of ancestor-worship, and he tries to prove this by a series of arguments, through which we need not now follow him. Imperturbable in his systematic deduction, he even asserts that he can derive from the same root, by far-fetched and easily-controverted arguments, the adoration of animals, plants, and inanimate objects.[1] It is indisputable that a great number of beliefs have sprung from this root, but this conception, which is anthropo- morphism carried to its extreme, is found to be too narrow to include all the facts. Tylor and others have criticised it with some vivacity, and I do not think that it now claims many adherents.

These two systematic hypotheses being put on one side, we may remind the reader how religious development *seems* to have taken place during this primitive period; for the march of evolution has not been everywhere and always the same—a difficulty already pointed out with regard to the social instinct. According to the best authorities, the most frequent form has been the following.

The first stage is that of fetichism, polydemonism, natur- ism—terms which in the history of religions are not quite synonymous, but which answer to the same psychical condi- tion, the adoration of some object, living or not, which is *perceived*—i.e., apprehended as a concrete form, at the same time body and soul—or rather animated by a soul, judged to be benevolent or malevolent, useful or injurious; for there is scant justification for the opinion that the worshipper of a piece of wood or stone sees in it only a purely material object.

The second stage is that of animism or spiritism, "a

belief in spirits having no substantial bond or necessary connection with determinate natural objects." The spirit is conceived as independent, separable; it goes and comes, enters and departs; it is attributed not only to men, but also to animals: the savage tries to deprecate the wrath of the beast he has killed in hunting, the chief has his horses and dogs buried with him. Psychologically, this stage corresponds to a preponderance of the imagination over simple perception.

These primitive forms of religious belief originate in the tendency of the savage, and the child, perhaps also of the higher animal, to look upon everything as alive, to attribute desires, passions, will, to everything that acts, to form his ideas of nature from what he knows of his own nature. This anthropomorphism results from the awakening of reasoning thought under its baldest form: analogy, the first source of myth, language, arts, and even science. But those analogies, which to us are merely images, were realities to primitive man. It is needless to insist on so well known a point. We must remember, however, that this primitive god-creating operation is a projection from our activity rather than from our intelligence; it originates with man as a *motor* rather than as a thinking being.

So far we have considered nothing but the object of belief, perceived or imagined; but what does the believer feel? of what elements is the religious sentiment composed during this period? We may point out the following:

(1) First of all, the emotion of fear in its different degrees, from profound terror to vague uneasiness, due to the faith in an unknown, mysterious, impalpable Power, able to render great services, and, more especially, to inflict great injuries; for historians have always remarked that, in early times, it is always malevolent and terrible genii who are adored; the good and merciful ones are neglected; in the following periods this state of things will be reversed. During this period Power is the attribute of the gods.

(2) A second and much less marked characteristic con- sists in a certain attraction or sympathy which, though very slight, binds the worshipper to his deity. The saying " Primus in orbe Deos fecit timor" is not absolutely true; for fear has a tendency to withdrawal, flight, aversion, while in every worship there is at least some hope of moving

the most maleficent power and exciting its compassion,—
consequently an approach to it. Later on, this rudimentary attraction will become the essential point.

(3) A third characteristic resulting from the preceding
is that the religious feeling is strictly practical and
utilitarian; it is the direct expression of a narrow egoism.
It connects itself with the self-preserving instinct of the
individual or the group, and is in nowise, as Sergi has
maintained it to be, a pathological symptom. Quite on
the contrary, it is a weapon in the struggle for life; since it
is not a matter of indifference whether those in power
are for or against one. This by no means disinterested
character is shown in the worship which rests entirely on
the practical rule: *Do ut des.* Hence the oblations and
sacrifices proportioned to the worshippers' desires and
requests, for which the deity owes his faithful ones an
ample recompense. Hence incantations, magic, and sorcery,
which are methods not only of alluring and appeasing the
god, but of getting possession of him by stratagem and
holding him in one's power.

(4) Lastly, from this time forward, the religious feeling
has a *social* character, or rather, the religious and social
tendencies amalgamate into a whole. It strengthens the
principle of authority, often in favour of the altruistic
tendencies, which are still very weak. The chiefs, priests,
sorcerers, speak and act in the name of a higher power,
and keep up the social tie. The worship of the dead,
which Spencer has made the mistake of generalising too
much, is an element of stability, establishing a continuity
between different generations. The community of worship
and ritual is the objective and visible expression of social
solidarity. I do not consider as belonging to this period
institutions such as the religious oath, trial by ordeal, or
others presupposing the addition of a novel element, which
is still absent. But there are other customs, local or
general—*e.g.*, that of the *tabu*, existing in nearly the whole
of Oceania and elsewhere under different forms, in which
religion performs a social office, but a novel one (at least
according to our present ideas), and safeguards institutions
and conventions by terror, while still remaining outside the
region of morality.

II.

Except the intellectual feelings themselves, no emotional manifestation depends more on the intellectual development than the religious sentiment, because every religion implies some conception of the universe—a cosmology and a system of metaphysic. With the first period we have scarcely passed beyond the stage of imagination; with the second, reflection and generalisation, whose upward progress we are about to follow, make their appearance. The intellectual evolution and the emotional evolution must each be studied in turn during this second stage.

I. *Intellectual Evolution.*—We shall find it useful, more-over, to divide the study of the intellectual element into two questions : (1) the conception of a cosmic order, at first physical, afterwards moral ; (2) the progressive march of generalisation from an almost unlimited multiplicity up to unity. These two processes have not always coincided or kept pace with one another.

(1) We have seen that, for primitive man, everything is alive, full of arbitrary caprices, desires, intentions, and especially mysteries, because everything is unforeseen : it is the reign of universal contingency. The formula, "every-thing is alive," is, however, too absolute ; it only suits those things which were seen to move and change—*i.e.*, the majority, not the totality of things. It seems as if the absence of motion, stability, fixity, the want of reaction, had been a sort of revelation to a simple mind. Perhaps it was through the spectacle of the fixity of things that the notion of order or law made its very humble entry into the world. However that may be, it is certain that the deper-sonification of nature began early to mark the origin of science. In our present state of culture we find a difficulty in representing to ourselves a state of mind in which the idea of fixity in natural phenomena is almost *nil;* yet such a state of mind has existed, and there is no want of docu-ments to prove it. The expression, "the new moon," was not at first a metaphor : men wondered if the sun would always continue his course ; the Mexicans anxiously awaited his new birth every fifty years ; eclipses seemed to happen at random, and caused great terror, etc.[1] Gradually the

[1] For the facts see Goblet d'Alviella, *op. cit.*, p. 178.

spirit of observation and reflection arrived at constant relations, and introduced into the conception of Nature the
ideas of order and regularity, diminishing in so far the
domain of chance and contingency. This notion of a
cosmic order has influenced religious conceptions; the
government of the physical world was attributed to the
gods; they are its regulators; each has his department
where he is supreme. The co-existence of two opposite
principles has been remarked in the religion of several
nations in this period of their development: necessity being
personified in an abstract, mysterious, inaccessible deity
(Rita among the Aryans, Ma with the Egyptians, Tao with
the Chinese, Moira or Nomos with the Greeks, etc.[1]); while
contingency, or rather limited arbitrary power, was personified in more human gods having their legends, acting
within their own special sphere, as, for instance, the gods
of Greece. The latter are also sometimes divided into two
categories, which is the first step towards simplification,
one kind bestowing physical well-being—health, prosperity,
riches; the other inflicting physical ills—disease, famine,
tempest, shipwreck.

The notion of the cosmic order led to that of a moral
order; the gods have first the physical government, in a
later age the ethical government of the universe. The conception of higher powers, invested with moral attributes, has
been, as we shall afterwards see, an important stage in the
evolution of the religious sentiment. The very ancient
opinion, still prevalent among many believers, that the
crimes of men occasion epidemics, unchain the elements,
cause floods and earthquakes, shows that the human mind,
rightly or wrongly, has supposed an analogy between all the
forms of order in the universe. Hence also the change of
the physical dualism above mentioned into a moral dualism;
the genii of light and darkness become respectively moral or
immoral gods, good or bad counsellors, saviours or tempters;
and in this period a faith in the superiority and definitive
triumph of the good is firmly established. In short, the
gods have as attributes first power, then intelligence, and
lastly morality.

(2) Let us now see the part played by increasing generalisation in the constitution of religious ideas.

[1] Goblet d'Alviella, *ib.*, pp. 176-198.

When we wish to study the ascending degrees of general-isation, not *in abstracto*, but according to facts and documents, we may take as our guide the evolution of languages, or, better still, the progress of the scientific spirit (as, for instance, by following the methods of classification used in zoology, from antiquity up to the present day); we might also have recourse to the development of religion, for this is the same mental process applied to a different matter. It is sufficient to indicate the various steps in a very cursory manner.

It is a well-known fact that the various races of mankind differ greatly in their powers of abstraction and generalisation; some can scarcely get beyond the concrete, while others disport themselves, easily and swiftly, in the region of the abstract. This difference of aptitude is expressed in their religions. Many peoples have never passed beyond polydemonism—*i.e.*, the cult of individual genii; in other words, the realm of the concrete. Not to speak of savages, such was the religion of the ancient Chinese empire (Tiele); such the innumerable genii in the primitive religion of the Romans—a people not greatly inclined to abstractions.

Certain tribes have, even at the present day, words to designate every water-course in their country, but no general term for a river. To have found such a one is a step in progress. It is the same in the region of religious thought: by an analogous progress the spirit of each tree is subordinated to the deity of the forest, the various river-spirits to a river-god, etc. For a number of particular divinities is substituted one specific and pre-eminent divinity.

At a higher stage the mind seizes more remote resemblances and constitutes one god for water, one for fire, one for the earth, so that the spirits of the waters, the sky, and the earth are severally grouped under the dominion of one power, known in Greece as Zeus, Poseidon, or Hestia.

This generalising process which has taken place with regard to natural phenomena also goes on in the social order. There have been, successively, gods of clans, tribes, nations. We know how long religions—even complex and highly organised ones—have remained merely national: the god of a nation is its protector and guardian—watches over it and over nothing else; but his existence does not exclude that of other gods who are lords of other nations. The transition to the universal, extra-national religions was brought about by means of conquest and annexation, but also, and more particularly, by philosophical speculation.

At the point we have reached there are divine hierarchies, analogous, on one hand, to the ideal hierarchy of individuals, species, genera, on the other to the hierarchies of human society: they are conceived and constituted according to the human type. The anarchy of Vedic India is reflected in the mythology of the Vedas, the feudality of Egypt in its religion, Zeus resembles Agamemnon, the Peruvian Inca is descended from the sun, and applies to his empire the government of the solar deity; and "by an optical illusion, human society seems to be a copy of the Divine State." [1]

In its movement towards absolute unity, the human mind has still some stages to pass through before reaching the term. It conceives of a divinity far superior to the rest, who, however, act under him (Jupiter optimus maximus), and whom he does not suppress. This is "monolatry" but not monotheism. We still find accommodations and compromises in the conceptions of triads (trinities) and dyads (associations of masculine and feminine divinities). In fact, pure monotheism is a conquest of the metaphysical spirit, which traces back the series of secondary causes to discover the first cause, rather than an intuition of popular consciousness.

This survey of ascending generalisation is somewhat schematic, and has been presented as an ideal restoration, though all its elements have been taken from reality. Some nations have attained the first stages only; others have, with much difficulty, passed beyond them; others have passed through several at a bound. Perhaps the evolution of religious ideas has not been in any two cases identical.

II. *Emotional Evolution.*—It has been justly said that religious feeling consists of two scales. One, in the key of fear, is composed of painful and depressive states: terror, fright, fear, veneration, respect, are its principal notes. The other, in the key of tender emotion, is composed of

---

[1] For details, consult Tiele, *Manuel de l'histoire des Religions*, Goblet d'Alviella, pp. 153-163. "The divine feudality is the primordial fact in Egyptian religion, as political feudality is the primordial fact of Egyptian history" (Maspero, *Histoire Ancienne*).

pleasurable and expansive states: admiration, confidence, love, ecstasy. One expresses a feeling of dependence; the other of attraction, going even as far as reciprocal union.

One of the first changes produced during this period of evolution is the predominance of the second scale; in the combination of two elementary emotions the proportional relation has changed, whence a change in the nature of the resultant emotion. We have seen this in the progressive effacement of the worship of the evil gods, in the suppression of sanguinary sacrifices, first in the case of men, then in that of animals; in the tendency to substitute for them simple acts of homage.

A second change, and one of especial importance, consists in the coalescence of the religious and the moral sentiment, which contract a union so close that to many people it seems necessary and indissoluble. We have seen that this is not the case, and that there are religions without morality. Primarily, the religious feeling is a special emotional form, the moral feeling is another form. There are, first of all, the purely naturalistic religions, afterwards the moral religions. A mass of facts demonstrate that, in the beginning, the religious feeling is not only quite a stranger to morality, but even in conflict with it. We know the bitter criticisms directed by the Greek philosophers against the reigning religion, bearing, as it did, the impress of myths springing from a primitive naturalism and understood neither by orthodox believers nor by the philosophers themselves. Contemporary criminologists have shown that prostitutes and even ferocious criminals are most assiduous in their devotional practices. This is because the religious feeling, in its origin and taken by itself, is fundamentally selfish,[1] being nothing else but anxiety for one's individual salvation. This superposition of the moral sentiment has taken place in all the great religions—*i.e.*, all those which

---

[1] The theory of *do ut des* is expressed with naïve completeness in a Brahmanic hymn. "Well filled, O spoon [of the sacrifice], fly down; well filled, return. As having agreed on a price, let us make exchanges of strength and vigour. Give me, I give to thee; bring to me, I bring to thee." Better still: "If thou wilt injure any one, say to Surya: 'Strike such an one, and I will make thee an offering,' and Surya, to obtain the offering, will strike him." (Barth, *Les Religions de l'Inde*, pp. 25, 26.)

have had a complete evolution: in Brahmanism and especially in Buddhism when compared with the Vedic period, in the prophets of Israel, even among the Greeks, in the mysteries, etc. People end by believing that a right state of mind is the best of offerings.

For most religions, the supreme question is that of human destiny. Its history, having traversed two periods, the one naturalistic, the other moral, shows once more that the religious and the moral sentiment are, in their origin, two totally distinct feelings.

During the first period, we find no idea of retribution according to men's works. The life after death is a continuation or copy of the earthly life, sometimes resembling it exactly, sometimes better,—most often worse. We know the complaint of Achilles, in the *Odyssey* (xi), where Homer has left us a vivid picture of this primitive belief; men remain slaves, masters, chiefs, or kings, as they were during life. Nay, certain tribes, projecting their aristocratic prejudices into the other world, believed that the souls of chiefs alone were immortal.

During the second period there arises a belief in a preliminary judgment on men's actions, decisive of their future destiny. The conceptions of this future life are various: temporary or eternal penalties and rewards, transmigration upwards or downwards, total liberation (*Nirvana*), etc., but all resting on a moral idea. This notion appears at an early age among the Egyptians, in the judgment of Osiris and the weighing of the souls. In the " Book of the Dead," of which a copy was placed in the tomb with every mummy, the defunct addresses to the god a long enumeration of the good deeds he has done and the faults he has not committed; it is remarkable that he speaks, not of his oblations, but of his virtues.[1]

III.

At the point we have reached, the religious feeling has attained the height of its development, and can henceforth only decline, so that the third period need not detain us

[1] This prayer will be found in full in Maspero, *op. cit.* (4th ed.), p. 38.

long. It may be summed up in the following formula : an ever-growing predominance of the intellectual (rational) element, a gradual effacement of the emotional element as it tends to approximate to the intellectual feelings and to come under that category.

When the march of thought towards unity has reached its limit in pure monotheism, the work of theologians and especially of metaphysicians tends to refine the conception of divinity, assumed as First Cause, or moral ideal, or both at once, but always as an inaccessible ideal, visible only in occasional glimpses. The logical, necessary, inevitable consequence is the weakening of the emotional state. In fact, we may lay down the following principle :—

From the perception to the image, and from the image to the concept, the concomitant emotional element keeps on diminishing, other things being equal; for we must take into account differences of temperament and individual variations. This is only a summary way of stating what I have so often said in Part I.: emotional states, beyond all others, depend on physiological (visceral, motor, and vaso-motor) conditions. Now it is clear that perception is the operation which most rigorously demands complex organic conditions. Among images or representations there are two categories : the vivid and intense imagination approximates, by its hallucinatory tendency, to the percept; while the cold and dull imagination, which is a bare outline of things, approaches the nature of a concept. Finally, the pure concept, reduced almost entirely to a sign, a substitute for reality, is as much detached from organic conditions as it is possible for a psychic state to be ; it requires a *minimum* of physiology. In consequence, emotion, attacked at its source, flows very scantily; and of the religious feeling properly so called there remains only a vague respect for the unknowable—for the x—the last survival of fear and a certain attraction towards the ideal which is the last remnant of the love dominant during the second period.

We might say in clearer and simpler terms that religion tends to become a *religious philosophy*, which is an entirely different thing, for each corresponds to a distinct psychological condition, one being a theoretic construction of argumentative reason, the other the living work of a group of persons or an inspired great man, involving the whole man, his thoughts and feelings. This distinction is extremely important and throws light on our subject.

It would be easy to show that the great religions, at the height of their development, become transmuted into a subtle metaphysic, accessible to philosophers only. For the sake of impartiality, and not to shock any one, let us place ourselves in a remote period. In India, the religion which begins with the naturalism of the Vedas is organised, becomes social and moral with Brahmanism, and attains a transcendental ideality in the Bhâgavad-Gîtâ. Take the following passage, chosen at random among a hundred similar ones :—"I am [Krishna is speaking] incomprehensible in form, subtler than the subtlest of atoms. I am the light of the sun and moon ; beyond the darkness I am the brightness of flame, the rays of everything that shines, sound in the ether, perfume on the earth, the eternal seed of all that exists, the life of everything. As wisdom, I live in the hearts of all. I am the goodness of the good, I am the beginning, the middle and the end, eternity of time, the death and birth of all."

Is this religion, or metaphysics, or rather a beautiful philosophical poem, which moves us by the splendour of its images ? For such a doctrine to become a real religion it must be concreted and condensed. That we may not, however, seem to cavil and dispute about words, or come to an arbitrary decision that the one thing is a religion and the other a religious philosophy, we may state the question in an objective form. As soon as religious thought ceases to have a worship or a ritual, and indeed finds itself incompatible with such, it is a philosophical doctrine. Stripped of all external and collective character, of all social form, it ceases to be a religion, and becomes an individual and speculative belief. Such is the deism of the eighteenth century, with all analogous conceptions, where feeling is only present in a very slight, almost imperceptible, degree.

Let us note, however, that in these periods of intellectual refinement, feeling does not lose its rights: it has its revenge in mysticism. In all great religions which have reached their highest point, the antagonism between the two elements of belief, the rational and the emotional, shows itself in the opposition between dogmatists and mystics. History is full of their mutual antipathy: in Christianity we find it, from the Gnostics, through the schools of the Middle Ages and Renaissance, to the "pure love" of the seventeenth century and later. The same may be said of other religions: Islam, in spite of its dry monotheism and the poverty of its ritual, has not escaped the universal law; it has had, and still has, its mystical sects. When we study them we find that, for all the differences of time, place, race and belief, the mystics, caring little for rigorous dogmatism, all show a singularly strong family likeness to each other. In this case it is argument which divides and feeling which unites.

We have still to examine one question relating to the emotional element alone: is religious emotion a *complete* emotion? It is worth while lingering over this, since many writers (not to mention those who omit it altogether) set it down as a variety of the intellectual feelings—*i.e.*, of the coldest form of emotional life.

A complete emotion, as we know, includes, besides the purely psychic state, a somatic resonance, a vibration of the organism, consisting (*a*) of changes in the circulation, the respiration, and the functions in general; (*b*) of movements, gestures and actions which constitute its proper mode of expression. Without these, there is merely an intellectual state. Does religious emotion fulfil these two conditions?

(*a.*) It has its physiological accompaniment; it penetrates as far into the organism as any other. Since by its very nature it contains, though in varying proportion, two elements, depression and exaltation, let us very briefly survey their physiological relations.

Depression is related to fear and under its acute forms has been confounded with it. Does not the worshipper entering a venerated sanctuary show all the symptoms of pallor, trembling, cold sweat, inability to speak—all that the ancients so justly called *sacer horror?* Physical and mental weakness makes us religious through conscious-ness of human frailty. Austerities, macerations—in short, the asceticism which is an institution in the so-called pessimistic religions—though springing from a multitude of causes which need not here be inquired into, prove at least that the physiological factor is not regarded as indifferent.

The Hindoo ascetics of the early ages were able, by their insensate mortification, to dethrone the gods and take their places—gods in their turn. The widespread belief that austerities contribute to salvation is a very much modified form of this.

Exaltation is related to love and tends to union, to possession. The history of all ages abounds in physiological procedures made use of for the artificial production of enthusiasm in the etymological sense of the word, which implies having the deity within one's self.

There are inferior forms: the mechanical exaltation produced by dancing, or by the rhythmical music of primitive tribes, which excites them and places them in a favourable mental attitude for inspiration. Toxic exaltation: soma, wine, the Dionysiacs, the Mænads. The sanguinary means so widespread in the cults of Asia Minor: the Bona Dea and Atys, the Corybantes, the Galli, who mutilated and gashed themselves with sword strokes; in the Middle Ages, the Flagellants; and in our own day, Fakirs, dervishes, etc.

There are higher, less materialistic forms: the collective excitement of pilgrimages and revivals, where the emotion of each individual is increased by that of the rest; the artificial means, known from antiquity, of attaining ecstasy, i.e., full possession; the frequent confusion, which has so often excited the wrath of theologians, between the language of carnal and that of mystical love.[1]

All these facts are well known, and thousands of others are recorded in history. It is convenient to recall them in order to show that they have their psychological reasons; they are not aberrations, as might seem to be the case at first sight, but the necessary conditions of intense emotion. If it is objected that some of them border on madness, we may reply that every violent passion does the same, and sometimes crosses the border-line.

(b.) The religious sentiment, again, is attached to material conditions by its mode of expression, which is ritual. Ritual practices are not, as many think, purely

---

[1] For many original and quoted observations showing the close connection between the sexual and religious emotions, see the recent series of valuable papers by Vallon and Marie, "Des Psychoses Religieuses," *Archives de Neurologie*, 1897.—ED.

exterior and artificial, accessory and adventitious; they are a spontaneous creation, originating in the nature of things. Every religion, great or insignificant, is an organism constituted by a fundamental belief attached to percepts, images, or concepts, *plus* certain secondary notions which are sometimes mutually contradictory, *plus* an emotional state.   All this forms a living whole, which evolves, vegetates, or retrogrades.   This organic character distinguishes the positive religions from the purely theoretical and metaphysical conceptions, which are not alive, never have lived, and are nothing but pure speculation.   Now, as every animal organism, from the infusoria to man, has its relational life,—*i.e.*, relations with external agents,—so religion, as an organism, has its life of relations with the supernatural and mysterious powers on which man believes himself to be dependent.   This life is expressed by rites, which are means of action, methods of establishing a relation.

The history of ritual is a chapter of the expression of the emotions.   The only difference is this: emotional expression, in the sense given to the words by Duchenne, Darwin, their successors, and the world in general, has an individualist character, showing fear, anger, love, etc.; while ritual expression has a *social* character; being the spontaneous product of a collectivity, of a group, which has become fixed and permanent, erected into an institution by the influence of society, and safeguarded by tradition.   On this subject I cannot enter into detail; it is sufficient to remind the reader that ritual is psychic in its origin. There have been two principal phases in its development.

During the primitive period, ritual is the *immediate and direct* expression of the religious sentiment, and bears the stamp of the national character.   Among the Greeks, it was graceful and joyous, as is fitting for divinities who are merely superior and happy human beings.   Among the early Romans it has an agricultural and family character, is formalist and methodical; the omission of the minutest detail invalidates the sacrifice.   The Mexicans immolated human hecatombs to divinities who were intoxicated with blood.   Rationalist religions, being half philosophical, have little ritual and a dry liturgy; they resemble persons of phlegmatic temperament, whose gestures are rare and

21

322 PSYCHOLOGY OF THE EMOTIONS.

restrained. The religions of the imagination and the heart, on the other hand, manifest themselves by the splendour and exuberance of their ceremonies.

In the second period, we have the passage from the literal to the figurative; ritual becomes *symbolism*. Since it is a means of expression, a language, it is quite natural that this should be so, and this phase corresponds to that of metaphor in spoken language. Thus the offering of a lock of hair, or a figure made of dough, becomes a substitute for human sacrifice. Having reached this point, ritual can no longer be understood except through its history; but worshippers still use it, without fully knowing its meaning, just as they use metaphors without knowing their derivation, or being able to trace them back to their primary sense. Lastly, there are some rites which are simply survivals, analogous to a frown when we are perplexed, vestiges of certain ways of feeling and acting which have been, but have long ago disappeared.

The religious feeling is therefore a complete emotion, with its train of physiological manifestations, and those writers who have classed it among the intellectual feelings have only considered it under its higher forms, and when it is on the point of extinction. At the period of its fullest development, but rarely under either its primitive or its intellectualised form, the religious feeling may become a passion, yielding to no other in tenacity and violence, which has its own special name: religious fanaticism. It borders on madness without quite crossing the line. This passion would require a psychological monograph to itself; and there is no lack of documents whence to compose one. We may gather from these facts:

1. New proofs of the fundamental independence of the religious and of the moral sentiments. In religious wars, persecution, the torture inflicted on heretics, the murder of the chiefs of the opposite party, are held to be meritorious acts; all which seems inexplicable to persons of calm and deliberate sense. They would be less astonished if they would consider that religious emotion, when it reaches the point of a paroxysm of passion, becomes as uncontrollable as violent love, and, like it, must have satisfaction; that there is the firm belief in a right, superior to human obligations, because of higher origin (a belief attaining

its highest degree in theomania, of which we shall speak presently); and that the religious sentiment and the moral sentiment, though having numerous points of contact and moments of fusion, are yet, in their nature, essentially distinct, because answering to two totally distinct tendencies of human nature.

2. We find a proof of the tendency of the religious feeling to unite, group, *socialise.* Unity of belief creates the religious community, as community of external and internal interests creates the civil community. Both tend to expel dissidents (internal enemies), and to conquer external enemies—in this case, the heathen.

The distinct or vague consciousness of the conditions of a society's existence, *i.e.,* its instinct of conservation; determines its morality and its way of acting. National religions, therefore, which are the same thing as civil society, proselytise only slightly, or not at all: the Greeks never tried to convert the Persians, neither did the Romans the Gauls. The universal religions (Christianity, Islam, Buddhism) forming societies other than, and outside nationality, and transcending it, have aimed at spiritual conquest, *i.e.,* at their social extension.

IV.

The question whether there exist any tribes completely devoid of all religious belief has been extensively discussed. That there are any such seems doubtful, when we take into account, on the one hand, the reticence of the savage towards strangers with regard to his own feelings and beliefs; and on the other, the scanty psychological equipment of travellers, who frequently understand by religion only a developed and organised cult. The fact, even were it proved, would be but of slight value, since it could only be the case among the very lowest specimens of humanity.[1] A question scarcely ever asked is this : Are there *individuals* (not social groups) utterly without religious feeling ? We must eliminate idiots, imbeciles, and the uneducated deaf and dumb; we are speaking of normal

---

[1] For this discussion, Tylor, *Primitive Culture,* I. xi., and Réville, *Religions des Peuples non Civilisés,* i., pp. 10 *et seq.,* may be consulted.

men living in some society or other, all of which have a
religion. I am distinctly inclined to answer in the affirmative, though I find no decisive observation on this point.
The case would be analogous to those of moral blindness
already studied, to the absence, if it exists, of all æsthetic
feeling; it would denote a lacuna in the emotional life. It
should be noted that it is only in this department that such
a lacuna can occur. No normal man, living in a society,
can have his mind closed to religious *ideas*, can ignore
their existence, their object, their significance; but they may
have no hold on him, may remain within his consciousness
as a foreign substance, originating no tendency and exciting
no emotion; they may be conceived without being felt.

I have already reminded the reader that the religious
feeling may become a violent passion; it may even pass this
limit, take a chronic form, and enter the region of pathology.
For the alienist, religious madness is not a morbid entity,
but a symptom; it sometimes exists by itself, but is more
often associated with epilepsy, hysteria, and the forms of
melancholia. From a psychological point of view, it has to
be studied by itself, as a complement to the normal state.
Considered thus, from the purely psychological standpoint,
its manifestations, though very diverse, may be reduced to a
simple classification: the depressive, or asthenic; and the
exalted, or sthenic forms.

I. The depressive forms spring up and grow on the soil
of melancholia. Their physiological criteria are the symptoms so often described—lowering of the vital functions,
and so on. Their emotional criterion is fear in all its
varieties, ranging from the simple scruple to panic terror;
and the intellectual criterion, the possession by a fixed idea.
Religious madness follows a course depending on character,
education, environment, epoch, and form of belief. So
those who believe in predestination are tortured by the idea
of having committed the unpardonable sin. This obsession,
frequent among Protestants, is rare among Catholics, who
admit the possibility of absolution.[1]

One form, which we might call *subjective*, consists in
religious melancholy pure and simple, in which the patient
believes himself continually guilty, rejected, damned. In

[1] Hack Tuke says he has met with only a single case among
Catholics. (*Dict. of Psychol. Medicine*, Art. "Religious Insanity.")

its anxious form it is characterised by scruples about everything, lamentations over imaginary crimes or faults. This
state is connected with two primary emotions, both of which
have a depressive character : on one side fear, on the other
the self-feeling under its negative form of humility and
dejection. An unconscious or conscious course of reasoning leads the subject to a feeling of abjectness and self-
contempt ; he tries to weaken himself, to make himself·
worthy of pity. Asceticism, though, rightly or wrongly,
invoking moral reasons in its own favour, rests on the
fundamental desire of depreciating the individual, at least
in this life. This appears, even in its simple and mitigated
forms, but still more in its extravagances (the monasticism
of the fifth century, Simeon Stylites, etc.), in the cases of
castration, mutilation, partial destruction, and finally, in the
religious suicide of the Hindoos who threw themselves
before the car of Jaganath.

A second form, which for want of a better term may be
called *objective*, is demoniac melancholia—the delusion of
obsession or possession,—which, formerly superabundant
in all religions, has now become rarer.[1] In obsession, or
external demonomania, the patient is not in the true sense
possessed ; he hears, sees, feels, smells the spirits who are
obstinately determined on his ruin, but he does not feel
them *within* him. In possession, or *internal* demonomania,
they are inside him. There is doubling of the personality,
with sensory, visceral, and psychomotor hallucinations, these
last consisting of internal voices which the possessed person
hears speaking inside him and in spite of himself.

II. The morbid exaltation of the religious feeling is
derived from attraction and love, as depression springs from
fear. Related to joy, and sometimes to megalomania, it is
accompanied by partial or total augmentation of both the
physical and psychical life.

Ecstasy is a transitory and comparatively passive form.
Seen from without, it resembles catalepsy in the insensibility
to external impressions, and suspension of sensory activity.
It differs from it on the motor side. The ecstatic has not
the "flexibility of wax" and the complete immobility ; he
can move, walk, speak, and his face can assume any given

---

[1] For some recent observations see Krafft-Ebing, *op. cit.*, vol. ii. § 1 ;
Dagonet, *Maladies mentales*, pp. 321 *et seq.*

expression.   Seen from within, ecstasy is an intense state of
consciousness, of which the recollection remains after awaking, while catalepsy is attended by unconsciousness, or, at
least, complete oblivion.   Its psychology is simple enough,
if, neglecting details, we confine ourselves to the essential
conditions.   The confessions of ecstatics, which are tolerably numerous, agree in their principal features: (1) restriction of the area of consciousness, with one intense and
overmastering representation serving as the pivot and only
centre of association; (2) an emotional state—rapture—
a form of love in its highest degree, with desire and the
pleasure of possession, which, like profane love, only finds
its end in complete fusion and unification (ἐνῶσις of the
Alexandrians).   The declarations of the great mystics, however involved they may be in metaphor, leave us in no
doubt on this point;[1] and their critics, even theologians,
have reproached them with frequently being mistaken in the
nature of their love.

A more stable and active form of religious exaltation is
theomania—*i.e.*, "a mental state in which the subject
believes himself to be God, or at least inspired by Him
to reveal His will to men."   To draw a hard and fast line
between the founders of religions, the reformers, the promoters of religious orders, and pure theomaniacs, is as
difficult as to indicate the precise point at which a violent
love becomes madness.   We might make use of a practical
test, and say that the one has succeeded where the others
have failed, but this would be too simple, success and
failure depending on a variety of causes.   This discussion,
moreover, is out of place here.   It is sufficient to remark that
theomania is, in its psychical characteristics, the complete
antithesis to demonomaniac melancholia.   Instead of the
sorrow of the possessed person with the enemy lodged in
his own body, we find an unalterable joy, which can be
affected neither by persecution, nor misfortunes, nor tortures.   To the feeling of abjectness is opposed the delusion
of grandeur.   However modest a man may be by nature,

---

[1] For further details respecting ecstasy I refer the reader to my
Maladies de la volonté, ch. v., and to Godfernaux, *Le Sentiment et la
Pensée*, p. 49.   Purely medical works contain little that is instructive
with regard to the psychology of this state; the works of the mystics
themselves may be studied with far more profit.

or as a result of reflection, he cannot with impunity believe himself chosen by the Deity as His prophet, to speak and act in His name.

The preceding sketch, whence I have purposely eliminated details and observations (of which, as is well known, there is no lack), has but one object—viz., to show that the primary constituents of the religious sentiment may serve as a guide to its pathology, which rests entirely on fear and love. I may add that none among morbid emotions has —and still more, has had—a more marked tendency to rapid propagation in epidemic form: a further proof that, in its nature, it is not so much individual as social.

CHAPTER X.

THE ÆSTHETIC SENTIMENT.

Its origin: the theory of play, and its variants—Æsthetic activity is the play of the creative imagination in its disinterested form. Its instinctive nature—Transition from simple play to æsthetic play: primitive art of pantomimic dancing—Derivation of the arts in motion; of the arts at rest—Why was æsthetic activity evolved?—Art had, in the beginning, a social utility—Evolution of the æsthetic sentiment—Its sociological aspect: progression from the strictly social character towards individualism in the different arts—Its anthropological aspect: progress from strictly human character towards beings and things as a whole—The feeling for nature—The feeling for the sublime only partially belongs to æsthetics—Its evolution: it is not æsthetic in its origin, but becomes so—Why there are not two æsthetic senses—The sense of the comic—Psychology of laughter—It has more than one cause—Theory of superiority. Theory of discord—These correspond to two distinct stages, one of which is foreign to æsthetics—Physiology of laughter. Theory of nervous derivation—Theory of tickling—Pathology. Are there cases of complete æsthetic insensibility? Difficulties and transpositions of the subject—Pathological function of emotion: pessimistic tendencies, megalomania, influence of unconscious activity—Pathological aspects of the creative imagination; its degrees—Reason why the intense image, in artists, does not pass into action; ways in which it is modified—Cause of this deviation; its advantages.

WHILE all the emotions hitherto enumerated have their origin and their *raison d'être* in the preservation of the individual as an individual, or as a social being, the æsthetic feeling, as we know, differs from the rest by the fact that the activity which produces it, aims, not at the accomplishment of a vital or social function, but at the mere pleasure of exercising itself. The more directly a tendency is connected with life, the more necessary, urgent, and serious it is, and the less it paves the way for the æsthetic feeling, which must always have a surplus to expend. However, its inutility, which is only relative, has been exaggerated; for it tends in some measure to the conservation of the individual and the race, being, and especially having been in the past, a *social* factor, though an incidental and subordinate one, as we shall see afterwards.

In conformity with the plan adopted, we shall remain strictly within the bounds of psychology, avoiding any excursions into the history or theory of art, except for the purpose of seeking facts and illustrations. We shall thus have to study the origin of æsthetic emotion, the law of its development, and, subsequently, two forms of emotional life, rightly or wrongly, considered as related to it : the sense of the sublime and that of the comic ; and we shall conclude by some remarks on its morbid manifestations.

I.

On the origin of æsthetic feeling, and consequently on the character peculiar to it among all other emotions, writers belonging to all schools of philosophy are in agreement to an extent rarely found elsewhere. It has its source in a superfluity of life—a luxury of activity; in fact it is a form of play. Schiller is supposed to have been the first to state its formula: " Supreme art is that in which play reaches its highest point, when we play, so to speak, from the depths of our being. Such is poetry, and especially dramatic poetry. . . . As the gods of Olympus, free from all wants, knowing nothing of work or of duty, which are limitations of being, occupied themselves in taking mortal forms in order to play at human passions, so, in the drama, we play with the achievements, crimes, virtues, vices, which are not our own." [1] Kant referred the beautiful to the free play of the intellect and the imagination, and his immediate disciples follow him on this point. Schopenhauer says the same thing in other words, " Art is a momentary liberation." Finally, Herbert Spencer develops this thesis, from the experimental point of view, by connecting it with biological conditions.

The primary activity of our physical and mental faculties relates to proximate ends: the conservation of the individual, and his adaptation to his environment. The secondary activity is its own end, and is of somewhat late appearance in the animal kingdom. The lower animals are shut up in a narrow circle: they feed, defend themselves, sleep, and propagate their species. On a higher level appears "a useless activity of unused organs" (Spencer, *op. cit.*, ii. p. 630); as in the rat with incisors growing continuously in adaptation to the excessive wear they undergo; the cat, exercising her claws on the bark of a tree or the covering of a chair, etc. Higher still appears the true play-impulse; dogs pretending to hunt or fight, cats running after a ball which they catch, push away, catch again, and pursue, bounding as if after their prey. In children, we know the pre-eminent function of play, and how it differs according to sex, disposition, and age: it has its individual characteristics, and is often a creation.

Play is, however, a genus of which æsthetic activity is only a species, and in determining the peculiarities of this species, the authorities are somewhat vague. [2] The most

---

[1] This theory of play, however, appears, from recent researches, to be of English origin, and due to Home (1696-1782), so that, when taken up again by Herbert Spencer (*Principles of Psychology*, vol. ii., last chapter), it would seem only to have returned to its original home.

[2] In a recent book, very rich in observations on the play of animals (*Die Spiele der Thiere*, 1896, the only existing monograph on the subject), Groos substitutes for the thesis of a superabundance of energy that of a primary instinct, of which play, in all its forms, is the expression. I cannot see that the two theses exclude one another. Some base their argument on external manifestations. Groos connects them with an instinct—*i.e.*, a motor disposition *sui generis*. I am inclined to take Groos's view, the more so as the fundamental idea of the present work is that of finally reducing the affective life to the sum of a set of tendencies fixed in the organisation.

For the rest, the psychology of play is still awaiting treatment in its totality. The word, in fact, denotes several entirely different psychical

definite, Grant Allen, in his *Physiological Æsthetics*, has attempted a solution. For him play is the disinterested exercise of the *active* functions, as in racing, hunting, etc.; art, that of the *receptive* functions, as in the contemplation of a picture or a monument, the reading of a poem, listening to music, etc. This is definite, but quite inadmissible; for it is clear that æsthetic emotion requires a certain mental activity in the spectator, not to mention the creator.[1]

The peculiar characteristic of this superfluous activity, this form of play, is the fact of its spending itself *in a combination of images and ending in a creation which has its aim in itself;* for creative imagination sometimes has practical utility as its aim. It differs from the other forms of play only in the materials employed and the direction followed. We may say, more briefly, that it is the play of the creative imagination in its disinterested form.

This is not the place for a dissertation on the creative

manifestations. In its first stage, it is unconscious in its origin, spontaneous, an expenditure for the mere pleasure of spending; but, however disinterested in its source and its aim, it is useful; in children, play is often a form of imitation, often a form of experimentation, an attempt at easy and unconstrained exploration of beings and things. In the second stage, it has become reflective; pleasure is sought for its own sake, and with full consciousness of the reason; it is a complex state formed by the fusion of variable elements. In a special study, which, however, is merely tentative (*Die Reize des Spieles*, 1883), Lazarus adopts the following classification: (*a*) games connected with physical activity, (*b*) the attraction of all kinds of spectacles, (*c*) intellectual games, (*d*) games of chance. This last item alone might well prove a tempting one to a psychologist. It has a quasi-passive, somewhat blunted form, being what Pascal called a diversion (that which turns aside, distracts), a way of pretending to work, or filling up the blanks of existence, of "killing time." It has an active form, the gambling passion, whose tragedy is as old as humanity, and which is made up of attraction towards the unknown and the hazardous, of daring, of emulation, of the desire of victory, the love of gain, and the fascination of acquiring wealth wholesale, instantaneously, without effort. These and other elements show that, in play as in love, it is complexity which produces intensity. The absence of any complete first-hand studies on this subject shows once more the scarcity of monographs relating to the psychology of the feelings.

[1] For a detailed criticism of this view, see Guyau's *Problèmes de l'esthétique contemporaine*, p. 12. This writer, afraid of dilettantism, substituted for the theory of play that of life, as a source of art. I do not see what is to be gained by substituting a vague formula for a definite one. Moreover, are not all emotions connected with life?

imagination, which seems to have been somewhat neglected by contemporary psychology, so lavish in studies of what used to be called the passive imagination (*i.e.*, visual, auditory, motor, etc., images). I wish only to indicate, as belonging to our subject, its relations to instinctive activity.

When we have said that images, their association and dissociation, reflection, and emotion are the constituent elements of the creative imagination, it will be found that we have omitted an irreducible factor, the principal element, the *proprium quid* of this mental operation, that which gives the first impulse, which is the cause of creative work, and constitutes its unity. This *x*, which, for want of a better term, we may call spontaneity, is of the nature of an instinct. It is a *craving* to create, equivalent, in the intellectual order, to the generative craving in the physiological order. It shows itself at first, modestly, in the invention of childish games; later, and more brilliantly, in the budding of myths, that collective and anonymous work of primitive humanity; later still, in art properly so called. There always remains the craving for superimposing on the world of sense another world, having its origin in man, who believes in it, at least for the moment. If it should seem a mistake to compare instinct, which is fixed, with the æsthetic activity, which passes for absolute liberty, we must remember that we are dealing, not with their development, but with their origin; and in that point they coincide. *True* creative activity has the innateness of instinct, an innateness in this case to be rendered by the word precocity. This is proved by innumerable facts; at some unforeseen moment the spark flashes out; experience has hardly anything to do with it. It has its necessity and its fatality; the creator has his task to accomplish; he is fitted for one kind of work only; even when he has some adaptability, he is imprisoned within his own manner, and keeps his own individual style; if he leaves it, he fails altogether, or becomes a bad imitator of others. It has its impersonality; creation is not the child of the will, but of that unconscious impulse which we call inspiration; it seems to the creator as if another acted in him and through him, transcended his personality and made him a mere mouth-piece. What further is needed to show, as far as origin is concerned, the characteristics of instinct? In physiological creation the fertilised ovule assimilates to itself, according to its nature, the materials of its environment, and, following the laws of an inexorable determinism, becomes, in the end, a healthy individual or a monster. In the case of instinct, an external or internal excitation brings into play a pre-established mechanism, and the act goes straight to its end, or turns to a gross error. In æsthetic creation the process is identical; we know by means of numerous biographical documents, which I cannot here reproduce, that the creative moment with artists presents itself under one or other of two forms: either a rapid intuition, in which the generating idea appears as a whole, or a fragmentary, partial view, which gradually completes itself; unity established beforehand or arrived at afterwards; the intuition or the fragment. The intellectual ovule, too, is forced to this dilemma—revelation or abortion.

I do not insist on a subject which would require to be dwelt on at length, and which I propose to treat in another work where it will be more in place; but it was necessary to point out that under this superabundance of strength, this vaguely described useless activity, there is something more definite, an active tendency utilising this superfluous energy, and giving to it various directions, among others that of intellectual creation, with images for materials—a creative instinct having its type in primitive animism, the common source of myths and arts.

Let it not be objected that all this concerns the creator only, and that he alone feels this craving, this tendency, this inclination to act, which is the root of æsthetic emotion. He who experiences it in any degree, however coarse or however subtle—spectator, listener, dilettante—must perform over again, in a measure proportioned to his powers, the creator's work. Without some analogy between their natures, however slight, the spectator will feel nothing; he must live the artist's life and play his game, incapable of producing by himself, but capable of being, and even forced to be, an echo.

Now let us lay aside these theoretic considerations for a question of *fact*. Can we find the transition between play under its simple form of movement, expended for the sake of pleasure, and æsthetic activity, *i.e.*, creation-play? This transition must represent the origin and primitive form of art. This primordial art, now impoverished, dried up, like an old tree which has emptied all its sap into its suckers, is dancing, or rather the pantomime-dance forming an inseparable whole. In its origin it is "an expression of muscular force simulating the acts of life." No commentary is needed to show that here the junction between superfluous motor activity and æsthetic creation takes place: dancing includes both. Since we are at the source, it is as well to insist on this, all the more so, as the importance of this primordial art has in general either been forgotten or insufficiently emphasised by psychology.[1] Let us note its principal characteristics.

First of all, the artist finds his material in himself: a possibility of movements useful neither for seeking food, nor for defending himself, nor for attacking others, nor for his preservation, or that of his species, in any form whatever.

This art is primordial. We find it in the early stages of all peoples and tribes, even the most savage. The documents collected by ethnologists leave us in no doubt on this point, except, perhaps, with regard to the Arabs and the Fuegians; and, even in their case, there is nothing to prove that it is not our insufficient information that is at fault. We may therefore call it the natural art *par excellence*.

It is universal. It is found in all latitudes, all ages, all races, as much among the utilitarian Chinese and the grave Romans of the early ages, as among nations reputed artistic or frivolous.

It is symbolical, it means something, it expresses a feeling, a state of mind; that is to say, it has the essential and fundamental character of æsthetic creation. Originally, dancing had a sexual, warlike, or religious significance; it was appropriated to all the solemn acts of public and private life. Among the natives of North America there were dances for war, for peace, for diplomatic negotiations, for hunting expeditions in common; others, again, for each of the gods, for harvests, deaths, births, marriages. The

---

[1] We must except Sergi, from whom I have borrowed the above definition. In his *Psychologie Physiologique*, Bk. IV., chap. vi., sec. 374, he gives some interesting historical details.

negroes have a passion for it which almost reaches delirium. The ancient Chinese judged of the manners of a people from their dances; they had themselves a great number, bearing different names. This enumeration would be endless; it is simpler to say that dancing marks a phase of symbolism which all races of mankind have passed through.

Indubitably, in the genesis of the æsthetic sentiment, we have here the first stage, semi-physiological, semi-artistic, play becoming art. Let us further remark that primitive dancing is a composite manifestation, including the rudimentary form of two acts destined, later on, to separate in the course of their evolution—music and poetry. Poor music indeed, consisting sometimes of three notes only, but remarkable for the strictness of rhythm and measure, and poor poetry, consisting in a short sentence incessantly repeated, or even in monosyllables without precise signification.

Such is the original form of the arts aiming at motion. As for the arts whose result is repose, they are, with the exception of architecture, indirectly derived from the same source. Dancing, being a pantomime, has plastic qualities; it is living plasticity. Furthermore, as a social and ceremonial act, it requires ornaments which at first were applied to the human body: drawings, tattooings, or colours simply smeared on. Later on, the representation of forms and colours is externalised, passes from men to things, in order to fashion or modify them, becoming ornamentation, sculpture, painting.

We have just seen how æsthetic activity arose, and how humble was its origin. Another question still remains in debate: *Why* was it evolved? In fact, by its nature, by its definition, it seems to have had no utility as a stimulant, since it springs from superfluous activity and is not bound to the conditions of individual existence. The persistence and development of the individual social, moral, and religious emotions explain themselves through utility. The intellectual or scientific emotion, also, was at first entirely practical, and therefore useful: knowledge is power. The case of æsthetic emotion stands alone. How, amid the rough struggle for life in which humanity was involved, was it able, not merely to blossom, but to live and prosper? It is no answer to say that it resisted and grew, because rooted in an instinct, a craving; for this instinct, by reason of its biological uselessness, might have become atrophied, or disappeared, like functionless organs, and it is the contrary that has happened. Darwin's well-known explanation based on sexual selection, the preference of the females for the most skilful, the most graceful, the most brilliantly coloured, or the best singers among the males, is only partial, available for certain species of animals, not for all. More than this, the tendency dominant of late years to deny absolutely the heredity of acquired modifications cuts us off from the hypothesis of the transmission, consolidation, and increase of the æsthetic instinct in the course of generations. Hence the great embarrassment in which Weismann, Wallace, and all others who take this negative view, find themselves. They admit variation and selection only—not the fixing of variations by heredity. The first factor is sufficient to explain the appearance of the æsthetic activity, but the other two, selection and transmission, have nothing to do with it; so that, however frequently we may suppose this creative instinct to appear, it would always have to begin again at the beginning. The two above-mentioned writers have been much exercised on this point How could the aptitudes for mathematics, music, and art in general, so rudimentary in primitive man, take so marvellous a flight? "In the struggle for life these mental gifts may very possibly have proved serviceable from time to time, and even of decisive importance; but in most cases they are not so, and no one will pretend that a gift for music or poetry, ever, in primitive times, increased the chances of founding a family. . . . These are not qualities which favour the preservation of the species; they could not, therefore, have been formed by natural selection."[1]

[1] Weismann, *Essais sur l'hérédité* (French ed., p. 475); Wallace, *Darwinism*, chap. xv. Before these, Schneider (*Freud und Leid*, pp. 28, 29), an adherent of the English theory of the inherent uselessness of the æsthetic activity, has tried to connect it with the conservation of the individual and the species by an extremely bold and problematical hypothesis resting on heredity. If we experience different feelings before a stormy sea, or a calm, blue lake, covered with boats, or a vast plain, or snow-covered mountains, "it is because our feelings are those of primitive man, when he lived really in the midst of nature and had to wrest his daily bread from it. Through countless

There is only one possible answer: æsthetic activity, at its origin, had some indirect utility as regards conservation, being based on directly useful forms of activity to which it was auxiliary. Besides, to connect art with play, itself connected with an excess of nervous and muscular energy, is to place it in mediate relation with the vital functions. We have still to define the nature and the measure of its utility.

The arts which aim at motion, at their first appearance consisted entirely of dancing, accompanied by song. Weismann tells us that the musical sound is the complement of the sense of hearing, which itself is connected with natural selection, because it is not a matter of indifference, either for animals or men, that they should clearly hear and rightly distinguish the sounds of inanimate or animate nature, so as to act accordingly. This, however, explains nothing, acuteness of hearing and musical ear being two entirely distinct mental states, each requiring distinct cerebral and psychic conditions. It is in the dance accompanied by song and gesture that we must seek for the explanation; it had a *social* utility, it favoured concerted movements and common action, it gives unity, and the consciousness and visual perception of unity, to an assemblage of men; it is a discipline, a preparation for corporate attack or defence, a school of war. Hence the capital importance of *time*. The Kaffirs, in immense numbers, sing and dance with such precision as to resemble a huge machine in motion. Among several tribes the rhythm must be perfect, and any one who makes a mistake is punished with death.[1]

In the case of the arts whose result is repose, the explanation is more difficult. We have seen that there is a possible

generations our ancestors, on finishing their daily task, in the evening have thought with satisfaction of the work accomplished; it was in this frame of mind that they looked on the approach of evening and the sunset. Why does a landscape representing it produce on us an impression of repose and peace? We have no other answer than this : for countless generations past the evening sky has been associated with the consciousness of work finished and a feeling of rest and satisfaction." Apart from its extreme flimsiness, this hypothesis would not be applicable to all the arts.

[1] Wallaschek, *Primitive Music*, chap. x., which may be consulted for details.

transition from one group to the other,—dancing being a living picture,—but what utility is there in the ornamentation of utensils, in drawing, in sculpture? Wallaschek (*op. cit.*) supposes that savages drew or carved horrible figures on their weapons in order to frighten the enemy, as is still seen among the Dyaks. I prefer Grosse's explanation, as being at the same time more positive and more general.[1] In the first place, ornaments are signs, and have as such a social value. Besides, and more especially, primitive plastic art supposes two factors whose development must be favoured among savages by the struggle for existence: good visual memory and great manual skill. They are, like children, very acute observers; they do not pass beyond the narrow limit of their sensations; but within that limit they see, hear, feel, and smell with extreme precision; their existence depends on it. They have (as can be proved by numerous instances) an excellent memory for forms and figures. Lastly, they have few tools, but they know how to use them; they are skilful because their life also depends on their skill. The distance, therefore, between the practice of arts serviceable to life and the primitive practice of art is not so very great after all.

In the beginning, art is dependent on and auxiliary to the useful; the æsthetic activity is too wide to subsist by its own strength; but it will be emancipated later on. We shall return to the old question of the "relations between the beautiful and the useful," which cannot be cleared up unless we turn our attention from civilised ages and countries—where the divorce is already accomplished—to the remote epoch of their origin.

II.

Let us now, starting from its source, see how the æsthetic sentiment has, in the course of ages, come to specialise and differentiate itself. Its evolution presents two aspects—one

[1] *Die Anfänge der Kunst* (1894). This book, extremely lucid and interesting, full of ethnographic documents and general considerations, may be consulted with great advantage on the question of the beginnings of art. On the special point which occupies us, see pp. 191 *et seq.*

sociological, the other anthropomorphic—which in the nature
of things are inseparable, but which, for the sake of clearness in exposition, we shall study separately.

1. The æsthetic feeling, of a strictly social character in its
origin, tends progressively towards individualism. A division
of labour takes place in it, rendering its manifestations more
numerous and more complex.

2. The æsthetic sentiment, of a strictly human character
at its origin, gradually loses this in order to embrace the
whole of nature. It passes from human beauty in its
organic form to abstract beauty, loved for its own sake.

Let us consider its developmental progress under this
double aspect:

I. In recent times, especially in France, many writers
have occupied themselves with the relations between the
æsthetic feeling and social conditions. It is sufficient to
mention the names of Taine, Hennequin, Guyau,[1] but all
are studying the question under its contemporary, or at least
its civilised form; they place themselves at an epoch when
art has already to a great extent lost its social value. For
Hennequin, a form of art expresses a nation, because,
having adopted it, the nation recognises itself therein as
in a mirror. The famous theory (Taine's) of the work of
art as the necessary product of race, time, and environment
is much contested and very vague. Still more vague is
Guyau's view: "Art is, through the medium of feeling, an
extension of society to all natural beings and even to beings
conceived as transcending the limits of nature, or, in fact,
to fictitious beings, created by human imagination." It is
an abuse to words to apply the name of society in this way:
a society implies solidarity; every other use of the word is
merely arbitrary. The question is, therefore, Has art been
a co-operative factor in the establishment of solidarity among
men? It is in this sense only that it has or has had a
social character. Now, to find in it this characteristic in a
clear, positive, incontestable form, we must go back to the
beginning, to an epoch when æsthetic needs collaborated in
social unity and served a social end. This characteristic is,
as we have already said, so evident—at least as far as the
arts resulting in movement are concerned—that it seems

---

[1] For a historical survey of the question see Grosse, *Anfänge der
Kunst*, pp. 12 *et seq.*

preferable briefly to recapitulate how differentiation and individualism gradually came about.

We have seen that, in the beginning, dancing is everywhere and always a collective manifestation, regulated and safeguarded by tradition, later on by laws, as in the Greek republics, and later still subject to the influence of fancy and individual caprice—to the great scandal of the conservatives. But the evolution of this art has been poor enough when compared with its two acolytes, poetry and music. Poetry, even when separated from dancing, long remains inseparable from music; it is sung and accompanied by the playing of an instrument. It is at first anonymous; whoever the author may be, it is common property; it belongs to the clan, the group, as if it were the work of all. Later, —the first social differentiation,—there are found corporations of poet-singers: the ἀοιδοί, rhapsodists, jongleurs, minstrels, bards; among the higher Negro races of the Upper Nile these corporations are held inviolable, even in time of war.[1] Afterwards the poet's individualism, freed from its association with music, accentuates and asserts itself, and becomes the definitive form among civilised nations. It would not be rash to say that, in our day, poetry is tending more and more in the direction of pure subjectivity and absolute individualism. Stuart Mill even ventured to say, "All poetry is of the nature of soliloquy"; and according to him, "the peculiarity of poetry appears to lie in the poet's utter unconsciousness of a listener";[2] which proves how little he understood of its true origin. I do not inquire whether this sort of isolation in an ivory tower is a gain or a loss for poetry; but I observe its growing frequency as civilisation advances; the complete antithesis to its collective character in the earliest ages.

Indissolubly associated at first with dancing and poetry, music shares the common destiny; it is subject to inflexible rules, it is a State function, an instrument of education and order. Its function among the Greeks, especially the Dorians, is well known, as also its importance to philosophers who,

---

[1] Letourneau, *L'évolution littéraire chez les différents peuples*, p. 66, a work which may be consulted for documentary evidence.

[2] Quoted by Grosse (p. 48), who gives an acute criticism of this view, rightly pointing out that a strictly individualistic art is "neither thinkable nor discoverable."

like Plato, wished to reform or reconstruct society. In two other widely separated parts of the world, among absolutely different people, we find, in China, 2000 years before our era, a Minister of Music, whose importance is continually insisted on by the philosophers; and in Mexico, before the conquest, an official academy of music, regulating both that art and poetry. It is therefore regarded as being, in the first place, of social utility. It thus passes through a process of evolution similar to that already described in the case of poetry, slowly separates from it, and still more slowly takes its great flight to become the least imperfect mode of expressing the most refined and intimate feelings, and to admit of no rule outside itself. The separation which took place at the Renaissance between religious music, which is in its essence collective, and secular music, which tends towards individualism, would, if need were, supply other proofs in support of the regular march of æsthetic evolution.

In the group of plastic arts, the relation between æsthetic activity and individual or social utility shows itself less clearly, and rather under the form of a parasitical superfetation. Here the evolution has started from two quite distinct sources : the one, leading to no great results, is the ornamentation of the human body, which, however, has, as we have seen, a certain social value as a sign. The other, architecture, is for this group the equivalent of dancing, *i.e.*, the primordial and synthetic form whence differentiation started. As soon as man had passed the period of caverns and such shelters, and had learnt to construct durable buildings, he worked at first for gods and kings, who embodied the social order and were alone worthy of so great an effort, or for the assemblies and deliberations of the clan, as is seen even at the present day in the case of many savages, whose rudimentary architecture is only shown in the construction of the communal house. The work is at once architecture, sculpture, and painting, forming an inseparable whole, as do dancing, poetry, and music. Then the association was gradually dissolved, the independence of each art asserted itself, and each of these arts, at first exclusively reserved for kings or the community at large, afterwards entered the service of the rich and great, and, in time, of every one, thus becoming more and more individualised.

In short, the relation between disinterested æsthetic feeling, and practical, utilitarian ways of thinking, would be scarcely intelligible if we confined our attention to civilised ages. It has varied greatly, and in these variations we can distinguish three principal stages.

The first stage is that of close relation. Æsthetic pleasure, in its rudimentary form, co-exists with the useful, or rather, is involved with it in a common state of consciousness—the agreeable. To be felt, it must possess some individual or social utility. This mental state is still, at this very hour, that of many human beings, probably of the majority.[1]

The second stage is that of loose relation. Emerson's saying, that what Nature at one time provides for use she afterwards turns to ornament, is the formula which sums up this period. The æsthetic feeling has no fixed connection with the conservation of the individual; it is called up by occurrences which give its distant, disinterested echo, serving the purpose of pleasure only. The legends, the genii, fairies, mythological beings who have become mere material for poems, pictures, operas, were once a belief, a reality, a terror, of which we retain only the similitude in the shape of a game.[2] There are many reasons why the serf of the Middle Ages was not inspired with any sort of poetry by the Gothic castles or the donjons built on high rocks whose ruins we admire. It is possible that one day, under some entirely different civilisation, our factories, with their tall chimneys, may become material for art by calling up memories of a vanished past.

The third stage is that of complete liberation, which has its expression in the thesis of art for art's sake. My object is neither to defend it, nor to attack it, nor to pronounce judgment on it, but simply to ascertain its existence in

---

[1] Grant Allen (*Mind*, xx., Oct. 1880) points out that Homer describes beautiful districts as "fertile," "rich in wheat," "horse-feeding," etc. He heard a peasant in the neighbourhood of Hyères praising the magnificence of a cultivated plain covered with vegetables, while showing the greatest contempt for a picturesque bit of woodland. An American visiting England said, "Your country, sir, is very beautiful. In many parts you may go for miles together and never see a tree except in a hedge." Any one who has had much to do with the peasantry could quote hundreds of remarks similar to the above.

[2] See Spencer, *Essays*, i 434, 435.

theory and practice, and that it only makes its appearance at a late age and in mature civilisation.

To sum up: there is no more an innate and infused notion of the beautiful than there is an innate and infused notion of the good, but a system of æsthetics which comes into being just as morality does; and the history of the æsthetic feeling is that of its fluctuations during the process of coming into being.

II. The second aspect of its evolution consists in the progressive movement which sets it free from strict anthropomorphism, gradually withdrawing it from the purely human and extending it so as to embrace everything. The best way to follow this movement of extension is to put the question in a concrete form, as Grant Allen has done.[1] What objects did man at first consider beautiful, and in what order did he extend this judgment? In so doing we avoid the disadvantages of an *a priori* proceeding and the risk of confusion.

Human beings began by thinking that beautiful which resembled themselves; the Australian woman admired the Australian man, and the Fuegian man the Fuegian woman. Primitive æsthetics have a strictly *specific* character, and their relations with the sexual instinct are evident. At this stage they can scarcely be distinguished from animal æsthetics, if—which is a disputed point—animals are susceptible to the æsthetic sentiment. In any case their dances, their music, their tournaments, their ornaments, are only addressed to individuals of their own species, and have generation as their object. There is no fact to indicate that, for any species whatever, there has been any change or progress in this direction.

Man, on the other hand, rose out of this state, in the first instance, by ornaments added to his person. This addition may seem futile enough, but in reality it was the first step outside nature. It has been attempted to define man as a rational, or a religious animal; he might just as well be defined as an æsthetic animal.[2] In the

---

[1] *Mind*, 1880, p. 445.
[2] I shall be pardoned for introducing the following passage from Théophile Gautier; it is, under its humorous form, so just from a psychological point of view: " Ideals torment even the coarsest natures. The savage, when he tattooes himself, or smears his body with red and blue, or sticks a fish-bone through his nose, is only obeying a confused

colours and designs applied directly on the body, and at a later period fixed by the operation of tattooing, we already note a choice, a symmetry, a certain artistic arrangement.

From the human body the artistic instinct then extends to whatever comes in contact with it; it externalises itself, and is applied to weapons, shields, garments, vases, utensils. From the polished stone age onward we find a whole arsenal of ornament. In caverns and tumuli of a date anterior to the use of metals we find necklaces, bracelets, pins, and rings of pleasing shapes. There exist numerous and correct representations of various animals drawn or carved at a time when the reindeer was still living in Central Europe.

We may pass over architecture, an art which was useful from the first, and of which I have already spoken. It might, if necessary, be classed as an extension of clothing. Let us only note that, as far back as the epoch of the lake-dwellings, we observe the taste for symmetry; it is natural and innate, and probably derived from an organic source in the arrangement of the human body, the two halves of which exactly resemble one another.

The poetry of the earliest ages is as yet undifferentiated; being at once epic, dramatic, and lyric. The generic division was established later on, but all are characterised by the common trait of being exclusively human, being concerned with man, with human actions and human feelings only. Nature is absent, or nearly so, from the *Iliad*, the *Nibelungenlied*, the *Song of Roland*, etc. The poet is moved only by those whom Nietzsche calls *Ueber-menschen*, gods or deified men, kings, heroes; and it is only gradually that art descends to the middle classes or the populace, to the humblest representatives of humanity.

We need not discuss the origin of music, which has given rise to various hypotheses; but we find it associated with dancing, at first in vocal form, *i.e.*, translating human emotions by means of the human organ. Very soon it objectivises itself in instruments of percussion, extremely

---

sense of the beautiful. He is seeking for something beyond what exists; he is trying to perfect his type, guided by a dim notion of art. The taste for ornament distinguishes man from brute more clearly than any other peculiarity. No dog ever thought of putting rings into his ears; and the stupid Papuans, who eat clay and earthworms, make themselves earrings of shells and coloured berries."

rough, but sufficient to mark time or rhythm accurately, and also to produce a certain physical exaltation of the senses. Then comes the imitation of the human voice by means of the flute, and other wind or stringed instruments; and the ever-growing desire to give utterance by means of music to the most delicate shades of emotion has brought into existence instruments of increasing flexibility, number, and complexity, from the invention of the organ (in the Alexandrian age) up to our own day when instrumentation plays the preponderant part.

At an early stage the æsthetic activity was exerted to bring animals into its domain, especially the domestic animals, companions or servants of man, as is proved by the paintings or sculptures of India, Egypt, Assyria. The horses of warriors became characters in heroic poems; so do the dog of Ulysses and that of the Pandavas in the Hindu epic. They take their place in art by reason of their moral virtues—bravery, fidelity, etc.

At last we come to the stage where the æsthetic feeling is quite *dehumanised;* it is no longer attached to men or animals, but to the vegetable and inorganic world: it is the appearance of the "feeling for nature." Its late appearance is a recognised fact, and I think it needless to accumulate citations in proof. In primitive poetry, as we have just said, man occupies the foreground; nature is only an accessory. Very little description suffices in the beginning—a few lines, or a few epithets merely. Even at a later date, the Greeks, says Schiller, "artistic as they were, and blessed with so genial a climate, have some accuracy in the description of a landscape, but only as they might describe a weapon, a shield, or a garment. Nature appears to have interested their understanding rather than their feelings." The Greco-Roman period became conscious of some artistic communion with nature only in the so-called decadent epoch—*i.e.,* that of advanced civilisation (Euripides, the Alexandrians, the Augustan age, and especially the age of Hadrian). Landscape painting seems to have been almost unknown among the ancients. Humboldt, in his *Cosmos,* points out that, in the long catalogue left to us by Philostratus of the pictures of his time, we find, quite by way of exception, the description of a volcano. In the time of the Roman Empire mural paintings became a fashion, but they depicted only a tame and cultivated nature.

Without insisting on well-known facts, we may say that the æsthetic conquest of nature has passed through two very definite stages. During the first, art reproduces a smiling, cultivated, fertile nature, close to man, fashioned by him, bent to his needs, *humanised*. Such are the Pompeian paintings, and those found in the villas of the Roman Campagna or the shore of Pozzuoli. During the second, the taste for primitive, wild, untamed nature is developed, for the stormy sea, the boundless deserts, glaciers, inaccessible peaks. The taste for scenery of an abrupt or violent character only dates, it is said, from the time of Jean-Jacques Rousseau;[1] certainly, in the eyes of the ancients, and for centuries afterwards, such scenery consisted merely of horrible spectacles, to be avoided if possible. The Romans, who so often passed through Switzerland, found no beauty there; and it will be remembered that Cæsar, when crossing the Alps, composed a treatise on grammar to beguile the tedium of the journey. Even in modern times the revelation of tropical countries and their terrible grandeur has had but a tardy effect on poetry and art. In the present age, an immense majority of people feel only repelled by the wildness of nature. It is, therefore, only for the pleasure of the minority and within the last century that the relative positions have been inverted; the human *dramatis personæ* becoming accessories, and nature furnishing the main subject of the picture.

This lateness in the appearance of the feeling for nature has been accounted for in a variety of contradictory ways. Some consider that this feeling is awakened by contrast; the satiety of civilisation and disgust at its refinements drive man from it, at least in imagination, and lead him to seek another ideal elsewhere. Others (Schneider, Sergi) appeal to ancestral influences; primitive man feared nature more than he enjoyed her charms (as is still the case with peasants and children), wild nature, especially, inspiring him with a superstitious terror, and being, as he believed, full of maleficent spirits. This terror lasted for a long time, even after the conception of the world had been changed by the increased knowledge of physical phenomena, like

[1] Sully, *The Human Mind*, vol. ii. p. 144.

an echo from ancient times. Grant Allen points out that facility of communication implies an advanced state of civilisation; however practical the explanation may appear, it is not without value; the traveller who has to make his way across unexplored glaciers, or through virgin forest, is engaged in unceasing effort and struggle for mere life, which is incompatible with the disinterested character of æsthetic contemplation. One needs a certain security to be able to admire.

These explanations seem to me only partial. The true psychological reason lies in the natural extension of sympathy. We have elsewhere seen that it implies two principal conditions: an emotional temperament and a comprehensive power of representation. These conditions are most likely to be met with in a highly civilised generation, whose sensibilities are exceedingly acute and subtle, and their faculty of comprehension greatly extended.

The conquest of nature by intellect and emotion takes place through a process identical in both cases. There is an ascending movement of the intellect, which, by way of abstraction and generalisation, goes on to seek resemblances less and less obvious, and increasingly difficult to grasp. Certain races stop at the lowest stages: some ages never pass beyond a certain average of knowledge—*e.g.*, the first centuries of the Middle Ages. In the same way, there is a progressive movement of feeling towards analogies in nature of ever greater tenuity, and the same remark applies to races and epochs.

It has been said that the pantheistic tendencies peculiar to certain peoples, such as those of India, are favourable to a more rapid development of the feeling for nature. This is, in fact, the thesis of sympathy under another form, since the assumed community of nature among all beings involves a community of feeling.

Let us note, in conclusion, that this extension of the æsthetic feeling to inanimate nature is produced by a process analogous to that which explains the genesis of benevolence. The pleasures and pains belong to us, but we attach them to the objects which occasion them; what we call the soul of things is our own soul projected outside ourselves and imparted to the things which have been associated with our feelings.

By a few facts, chosen out of a vast number at our disposal, I have tried to show that the æsthetic feeling has progressed by evolution from the social form to that of individualism, and from man to nature. This mode of *objective* exposition has seemed to me preferable, because it allows us to seize in a concrete and verifiable shape the law of its development and increase in complexity.

III.

It is usual to include under the same heading as the æsthetic sentiment two other emotions, that of the sublime and that of the comic, though I can only perceive a somewhat vague analogy and partial affinities between them. We shall attempt to see wherein these three states approximate to and differ from one another.

"The feeling of sublimity is that peculiar emotion which is excited by the presentation or ideal suggestion of vastness, whether in space or time (Kant's 'mathematical' sublime), or physical or moral power (Kant's 'dynamical' sublime)."[1] The distinction generally drawn between the mathematical and the dynamical sublime appears to me quite secondary, as the two cases reduce themselves to the idea of a force in action. Current opinion asserts that the emotion of the sublime is simpler than the æsthetic emotion properly so called. If we understand by this that the latter is richer in its development, much more complex, much more varied in aspect, comprehending the pretty, the graceful, the purely beautiful, the pathetic, etc., the opinion cannot be disputed; but if we mean that the sense of sublimity is simpler as regards its origin, we cannot admit it. I have already given the emotion of the sublime as an example of a binary combination (Part II., Chap. VII.) formed by synthesis of (*a*) a painful feeling of oppression, dejection, lowered vitality, reducible to one primary emotion —fear; (*b*) the consciousness of a rush, of violent energy in action, of a heightening of vitality, reducible to one primary emotion—the sense of personal power, "self-feeling" under its positive form. Moreover, one negative condition is

[1] Sully, *The Human Mind*, vol. ii. p. 146.

necessary: the conscious or unconscious feeling of our security in the presence of some formidable power. Without this last all æsthetic feeling disappears.

The sentiment of the sublime loses the egoism which lies at its root by extending, through sympathy, to men and things. In participating, through the imagination, in the grandeur of a real or fictitious personage,—the Napoleon of history, the Moses of Michael Angelo, the Satan of Milton,—the *ego* is objectivised and alienated. It is the history of this development that we must now follow.

"Human might," says Bain, "is the true and literal sublime, and the point of departure for the sublimity of other things." This is, in fact, the starting-point. Grant Allen[1] has brilliantly illustrated this view, by trying to demonstrate that the feeling of the sublime has been evolved from a narrow anthropomorphism—the admiration for man's physical strength—towards the sublimity of moral and intellectual qualities, and that of mass and time in nature. This conception deserves to be given in a condensed form, though it is somewhat of an outline, and not without lacunæ: neither is it certain, whatever this writer may say, that the terror with which man was inspired by natural phenomena did not show itself at a very early period, in a form approaching to the emotion of sublimity.

According to Grant Allen, the earliest object of human admiration—*i.e.*, of a feeling of respect mingled with fear—is the strong man, the invincible warrior, whom none can resist. This feeling shows itself even among the higher animals, with regard to each other, and still more unmistakably among children: they admire physical strength. In the course of social progress, the chief or despotic king, with power of life and death over all, becomes the incarnation of power—the sublime object—and so the feeling is specialised. After his death, it is believed that his surviving "double," or ghost, is invested with the same, or even greater privileges. Thus the feeling hitherto enclosed within the world of experience is transferred to a supersensuous region.

The author might have shown that, at this stage of evolution, the idea of an intellectual power, proved by

[1] *Mind*, October 1878.

superior knowledge and foresight, and that of a great moral power, proved by courage and energy in effort, must have inspired the same feeling.

As, at this period, everything in nature is conceived as alive, man has necessarily assimilated natural forces to human power: as with thunderstorms, hurricanes, earthquakes, and volcanoes. Looking at mountains, he seems to see a superhuman power which has raised them. Finally, the movement of thought, continually going on, leads to the idea of a paramount or sole deity, considered as absolute and unlimited power, and the maker of all.

As for the sublimity of mass, it was probably first felt in presence of great monuments, temples, palaces, pyramids, tombs, constructed by the pride of kings, and suggesting the idea of their vast power and the enormous amount of human strength expended. As for sublimity in the immensity of time, it is not attached to the conception of empty and abstract time: it moves us because it appears to us as peopled by a myriad of past or possible events, of activities succeeding each other with unfailing prodigality.

Thus all these cases are reduced to an overwhelming force, conceived by analogy and felt by sympathy. Taking this evolution in its main lines, it has passed through two principal periods, one of predominant terror, which is not and cannot be æsthetic, and one of predominant admiration and sympathy, where the consciousness of personal safety gives the feeling a disinterested character: here emotion has *become* æsthetic. It is probable, says Sully, that this feeling passed from a disagreeable into an agreeable one, and became æsthetic "through the elimination of the gross element of personal fear." [1]

Attempts have been made to reduce the emotion of the sublime to a contrast; it rests rather on a harmony, a synthesis of contradictories (in the Hegelian sense); it is a case of *combination*, as we have tried to show in another part of this work. It is neither fear nor pride (consciousness of strength) felt directly or by sympathy, but a product of their coexistence in consciousness, and their fusion in a special state which can never be completely dissociated by analysis. In short, it is far more closely related to the two primary feelings already named than to the

[1] *The Human Mind*, ii. p. 148.

æsthetic feeling, to which it approximates, not by nature, but by accident.[1]

IV.

It is also through an abuse of language that the emotional state designated by the various names of a sense of the laughable, of the ridiculous, of the comic, is considered as a department of æsthetic emotion, for no other reason, as it seems, than because the comic enters into all the arts and produces a disinterested pleasure. Its domain, however, extends far beyond this. It has been closely studied in the general and special works of Darwin, Piderit, Spencer, L. Dumont, Hecker, Kräpelin, and others; and I do not propose to dwell on it at length, having very little to offer in the way of personal opinion on the subject. Yet this manifestation of the affective life, with its peculiar mode of expression, laughter, cannot be omitted from a complete treatise on the feelings.

This subject presents two aspects, one internal, subjective, psychological, the other external, objective, physiological. The latter presents no difficulties, being susceptible of an exact description; but to connect it with an internal cause, to say why one laughs, is a very difficult problem, which has been solved in various manners. In my opinion the error lies in thinking that laughter has *a cause*. It has very distinct *causes* which, seemingly, can be reduced no further,

[1] Æsthetic activity is that form of play which uses images as its creative materials. It is generally admitted that visual and auditory perceptions or representations are the only ones which provoke æsthetic emotion; yet Guyau (followed perhaps by others) has maintained that we must attribute this power to all external sensations, without exception (*Problèmes de l'esthétique contemporaine,* chap. vi.), heat, cold, contacts, tastes, and odours; but the facts he enumerates are in most cases referable to association, especially where odours are concerned. The so-called lower sensations do not act directly, they only revive the representations of sight and hearing. A delicious coolness, a soft contact, an intoxicating odour produce an agreeable state—*i.e.*, a physical pleasure, and nothing more, if there is no association. Besides, without entering into an idle and hair-splitting discussion, it is sufficient to observe that, as a matter of fact, there exists no art, in the æsthetic sense, based on any other sensations than those of sight and hearing, unless we are to look on perfumery and cookery as such.

Why is this privilege exclusively confined to two species of sensations? Various reasons have been given: because they

or, at least, their unity has not hitherto been discovered. If we were to recount only a few of the numerous definitions of laughter current in books, we should find none that was not in some way open to criticism, because there is none which embraces the question in all its manifold aspects. Thus L. Dumont, in a special work on Laughter, says, " It is an assemblage of muscular movements, corresponding to a feeling of pleasure." Is the laughter caused by tickling, by cold, or by the ingestion of certain substances, the hysteric laughter alternating with tears, the nervous laughter of soldiers in action, after the moment of danger is over—are all these to be put down to the account of pleasure? Even if we class these and analogous facts by themselves, as purely reflex actions, there still remain difficulties.

1. Considered from the purely psychological point of view, the mental state which shows itself in laughter consists, according to some, in the consciousness of incongruity, of a certain kind of contradiction; according to others, in a consciousness of superiority in relation to men and things on the part of the laugher.

The first view seems to number most adherents. It assumes as a fundamental fact the grasping of a contrast between two perceptions, images, or ideas. Yet all contradictory contrasts do not make us laugh; if they are to do so, they must fulfil certain conditions. In the first place, the

---

are more remote from the life-serving functions with which the sensations of touch, taste, and smell are closely connected (H. Spencer); or because their pleasures and pains have, in general, a moderate character, and their special nerves are rarely subjected to a violent shock (Gurney); or, according to Grant Allen, because the nerves of the lower senses are excited in mass, and those of the higher by isolated fibres (? ?). It appears to me that one of the principal reasons has been forgotten. If we refer back to the inquiries detailed in Chap. IX. (Part I.) as to the olfactory and gustatory images, we shall see that they have their own peculiar characters. For visual and auditory images, revival and association are easy, whether simultaneously, in groups, or successively, in series. For images of smell and taste, it is quite the contrary; their revivability is feeble or *nil*, their power of association with each other *nil*. (The tactile-motor images form an intermediate group, but nearer to the lower senses.) These psychological conditions render them quite unsuitable for a place in a constructive scheme. Called up with great difficulty by the memory, incapable of being grouped, either in simultaneities or in series, they can supply neither an art in rest nor an art in movement.

two contradictory elements must be given simultaneously as belonging to the same object, so as to induce us to think that a thing both is and is not at the same time. A monkey makes us laugh, because he reminds us of, but is not, a man; he makes us laugh still more if dressed in human clothes, because the contradiction is more striking. Next, the two states of consciousness must be very nearly of the same mass and intensity—a broken-down old man carrying a heavy burden does not make us laugh. " The two contradictory forces brought into play in laughter, being unable to attain to the unity of a conception, are forced to escape outwards by an expenditure of muscular energy" (L. Dumont).

The second theory, first formulated by Hobbes, but perhaps of still earlier date, is as follows: " The passion of laughter is nothing else but sudden glory arising from sudden conception of some eminency in ourselves by comparison with the infirmity of others or with our own formerly."[1] The partisans of this view have severely criticised the theory of incongruity, or discordance in things. " An instrument out of tune, a fly in ointment, snow in May, Archimedes studying geometry in a siege; . . . everything of the nature of disorder; . . . and whatever is unnatural; the entire catalogue of the vanities given by Solomon—are all incongruous, but they cause feelings of pain, anger, sadness, loathing, rather than mirth."[2] This view is quite as open to criticism as the preceding; and we might enumerate a long list of cases where the feeling of superiority, whether justifiable or not, does not make us laugh. In my opinion, both views ought to be admitted, as being partially true, and meeting distinct cases.

The second theory is suited to the primitive and lower form of that emotional state which shows itself in laughter. In the case before us, this state is directly derived from the sense of strength or power, or, as Hobbes calls it, glory; the contradictory contrast, if perceived at all, is in the background. The coarsest and most brutal, almost physiological, expression of this mental state, is the laugh of the savage after a victory, when treading his vanquished enemy under foot.

---

[1] Hobbes, *Human Nature* (2nd ed.), 1650. ·
[2] Bain, *The Emotions*, p. 257.

"It appears to be fairly certain, not only that laughter is a concomitant of brutality and cruelty among uncivilised races, and children, but that even in the cases of the more refined and benevolent, it is apt to accompany the recognition of any slight loss of dignity in another, when this loss does not evoke other and painful feelings." [1] It is a matter of common observation, that many people have a tendency immediately to burst out laughing at any accident, even if serious, happening to others; and this instinctive laughter certainly does not spring from the good side of human nature.   It is clear that, under this form, laughter has nothing to do with æsthetics.

The theory of discord suits well with the secondary and superior forms: the feeling of superiority becomes effaced and passes into the background.   It is an intellectualised manifestation, which has or may have an æsthetic value, the mental development permitting those fugitive and subtle contradictions which constitute the principal element of the comic to be caught on the wing.   It takes on an almost disinterested character, though never, perhaps, completely losing its original blemish.

Finally, laughter may take a still more elevated form in the humorous spirit we have already mentioned (Part II., Chap V., 3), in which the feeling of superiority is mitigated by a large proportion of sympathy.

2. The nature of laughter would be very incompletely known were we to confine ourselves to pure psychology, but the physiological study of this phenomenon has not been neglected.   The description will be found in special works on the expression of the emotions, especially in Darwin (chap. viii.).   Laughter is a strengthened expiratory movement; when prolonged, the excess of the expirations over the inspirations necessitates deep sighs in order to restore the equilibrium; there is a drawing back and raising of the corners of the mouth, the eyes become brighter through the quickening of the circulation.   According to Darwin, the uninterrupted gradation from violent laughter (which in all human races is accompanied by tears) to moderate laughter, a broad smile and a gentle smile, proves their common nature; but is laughter the

[1] Sully, *Sensation and Intuition*, p. 262; *The Human Mind*, i. p. 148.

complete development of the smile, or the smile a modified form of the noisy laughter of the first period? Evolutionists are, in general, inclined to consider noisy laughter as the primary form, connected with the brutal sense of superiority. Yet the early appearance of the smile in infants, at about two months, while laughter is not observed, as a rule, till the fourth month, seems, on this theory, to contradict the principle that the evolution of the individual reproduces, in an abridged and accelerated form, the evolutionary process of the species. On the other hand, animals do not give us any information on this point. Certain monkeys smile or laugh—*i.e.*, the corners of the mouth are drawn back, their eyes become brilliant, and they emit a certain sound approximating to a chuckle (Darwin, Wallace, Mantegazza, etc.).

But the important point is to know why this collection of physiological facts is connected with certain mental dispositions. If laughter were the constant and exclusive expression of joy and pleasure, the answer would be easy; as in addition to this it is sometimes morbid, sometimes futile and simply physiological, the explanation ought to be framed to include all these cases.

Herbert Spencer has proposed one, which, though published some time ago (1863), still remains one of the most satisfactory. In his view[1] laughter is due to a sudden diversion of nervous energy into a new path—an overflow-channel. The excitation of the nervous system existing at any given moment, especially if intense, can only be expended in three ways—either by transmission to some other part of the cerebro-spinal organism, exciting other feelings or thoughts; or by acting on the viscera, the heart, lungs, and digestive organs; or else by producing muscular movements; and, as the nervous discharge, especially if moderate, follows the line of least resistance, and the most easily moved muscles are the first to be shaken, it acts on the vocal organs, on the mouth, and on the face. Laughter is connected with this last line of action.

It may result from purely physical excitants : tickling, cold, toxic action, sudden relaxation after a long period of constraint.

[1] " Physiology of Laughter," *Essays*, vol. i. (1883) pp. 194 *et seq.*

It may be connected with representations—*i.e.*, have a psychical cause. Spencer admits the theory of incongruity, and defines it more precisely. He distinguishes the ascending incongruity, which goes from the less to the greater, and the descending incongruity between the greater and the less. The latter alone provokes laughter. There must be a sudden transition from one intense state of consciousness to one which is much less intense, while forming a complete contrast to it. Thus, while we are listening to a symphony, a sneeze on the part of one of the spectators may make us laugh. During a reconciliation scene, on the stage, between two lovers, after a long estrangement, a goat begins to bleat, and so introduces a comic element. The heightened attention of the first moment is suddenly transferred to a trifling incident which does not supply it with sufficient matter on which to expend itself; the surplus has to find an outlet, and this produces laughter.

The excess of emotion, when it does not give a shock to the whole frame, and is not the result of a contrast, takes another direction—*e.g.*, the automatic actions of certain barristers or other public speakers, of the embarrassed schoolboy twisting his pen between his fingers, etc.

Hecker, in a special work, propounds another hypothesis.[1] He connects everything with a typical fact—tickling, which explains the laughter arising from physical, and that arising from mental causes.

In tickling, there is, first, the effect produced by each cutaneous sensation : excitement of the vaso-motor and the great sympathetic nerves, dilatation of the pupil, brightness of the eyes, constriction of the vessels, as may be verified experimentally in the application of a mustard plaster or a sudden effusion of hot water. There is another necessary condition : intermittence; for tickling, there must be change in the rate or direction of the movements, or interruption.

The expiration corresponds to the moment of contact, the expiration to that of interruption ; in the first case the diaphragm is raised, in the second lowered. To sum up, tickling is an intermittent excitation of the skin producing

---

[1] *Physiologie und Psychologie des Lachens und des Komischen* (1873). For criticisms, see Léon Dumont, *Theorie scientifique de la sensibilité*, p. 211 ; Piderit, *Mimik*, pp. 138 *et seq.*

an intermittent excitement of the vaso-motor nerves and the respiration, and an alternation of pleasurable and uncomfortable states. But what is the use of laughter in this occurrence? Its function is protective, it compensates for the diminished pressure of the blood on the brain; the frequent expirations which compress the thorax, and consequently the heart, the larger vessels and the lungs, prevent the blood-vessels from emptying themselves.

As to intellectually-caused laughter, Hecker, who borrows his psychology from the æsthetician Fischer, and seems to fuse together the two theories of contrast and superiority, traces all manifestations of this kind to the comic. Now, in the comic there are two simultaneous states : one, pleasurable, the sense of our own superiority; the other unpleasant, the contradiction in the object. Hence a rapid alternation of pleasure and pain. The comic is an intermittent impression, which acts like tickling; it is a psychical titillation which, like the other, shows itself in laughter, and for the same cause. Such is Hecker's theory in its main outlines.

In conclusion, laughter manifests itself in circumstances so numerous and heterogeneous—physical sensations, joy, contrast, surprise, oddity, strangeness, baseness, etc.—that the reduction of all these causes to a single one is very problematical. In spite of all the work devoted to so trivial a matter, the question is far from being completely elucidated.

V.

The pathology of the æsthetic sentiment would require a work to itself.[1] We must here confine ourselves to some remarks on the most general physiological conditions producing it, and on the natural causes nearly always at work to produce deviation.

Can the faculty of artistic feeling be absolutely wanting? Are there cases of complete insensibility to every artistic manifestation, however humble? I do not think it in any wise rash to affirm this. *A priori* since the existence of

---

[1] The only attempt in this direction I am acquainted with is Nordau's book, *Degeneration* (*Entartung*), which is limited to the present day, and, moreover, treats of other questions as well.

moral blindness and religious indifference is certain, it is improbable that a superfluous emotion should have, in all men without exception, an indelible character. As a matter of fact, it is difficult to supply the proof; the insensibility passes unnoticed, having no injurious consequences to the individual or to society. However, partial cases, at least, may be observed. Total insensibility to music is not rare, and if this is a known fact, it is because it is the most easily verified.[1] Many people declare that the reading or hearing of poetry bores and wearies them to an extreme degree, and they cannot understand why poets take so much trouble, when it would be so much easier to express themselves in prose.

Leaving these extreme cases in order to consider pathology proper, we may first ask ourselves whether we really have here a subject for study, or whether we are pursuing a mere chimera. The question is not here put quite in the same form as elsewhere. Pathology signifies disorder, deviation, anomaly; now, in æsthetic activity, where is the rule? It has often been repeated that the essence of art is absolute liberty. I see no objection to this statement; art has its end in itself, and is subject to no other requirement than that of creating works able to live, accepted by contemporaries, and, if possible, by posterity also. By what method, then, can we decide that any given æsthetic manifestation is normal or abnormal? Such a decision can be merely arbitrary. We have not even the resource of saying that everything belonging to beauty is healthy, and everything belonging to ugliness unhealthy; for—not to mention that the line of demarcation between the two is frequently very vague—the ugly is admitted

---

[1] There is, with regard to this point, a very complete observation of Grant Allen's (" Note Deafness," in *Mind*, iii. 1878). The subject, a young man of great intellectual cultivation, had studied music during his childhood without result. It was discovered, later on, that he was incapable of distinguishing one note from another, except at intervals which were sometimes as much as an octave, or even more. He was quite unconscious of harmonies and discords, or the *timbre* of instruments. The distinctive features of the latter were, for him, only clearly perceived noises of different kinds—a sound of wire-work for the piano, a scraping for the violin, a puff of air for the organ. He was very sensitive to the rhythm of poetry. It is not known whether anomalies of this kind originate in Corti's organs or in the cerebral centres.

into all the arts by way of ingredient or foil, and one author (Rosenkranz) has even written on the "Æsthetics of the Ugly." I see only one way of escaping from the difficulty, viz., transposing the subject, studying, not the pathology of the æsthetic feeling itself, but that of the source whence it emanates; in other words, considering it merely as a symptom. This requires some explanation.

Every failure of harmony between the tendencies which constitute a healthy human being shows itself in a disturbance of equilibrium, an anomaly in the affective life. This deviation from normal life may be considered under two aspects: one general, the other special; one human, the other professional.

If we consider it under its general form—*i.e.*, as simply inherent in the human constitution—the want of equilibrium expresses itself in many ways, following different directions according to temperament, character, and circumstances, such as melancholia, phobias, sexual aberrations, irresistible impulses, etc.

If we consider it under its special, particular form, as peculiar to a given individual carrying on a given occupation and having given habits of life—an artisan, a labourer, a tradesman, a lawyer, a physician, etc.—the disturbed balance will appear to us as setting its mark on the individual's professional activity and its products. The artisan will pass from a fury of work to excesses of idleness or drink; the merchant from exaggerated caution to a reckless daring in his enterprises; and the same in every trade or profession. Now art is a profession like any other, and the artistic *product* must bear the mark of the craftsman—a mark of disequilibrium in the present case. Consequently the anomalies of the æsthetic sentiment may be studied by comparison, not with an imaginary norm, not with any alleged regulative principles of art with which we are unacquainted, but with a psychological criterion; they may be studied as the effects and the revelation of a morbid diathesis. To speak more simply, we have to deal, not with æsthetics, but with psycho-pathology in connection with æsthetics.

Even thus transposed, the subject still presents inevitable difficulties, the principal being as follows. With regard to the psycho-physiological constitution of the creative artist, there are two theories. (We must not forget that, in the amateur, or mere taster of works of art, the same psychological conditions are required, though in a less degree, being more strongly accentuated in proportion as he feels more acutely.)

One of these theories, set forth in many well-known works, maintains that æsthetic superiority is incompatible with health of mind and body. The facts in support of it have often been very uncritically collected, and among the characters mentioned as typical we find all sorts. Among creative artists there are vigorous men and puny ones, tall and short, handsome and deformed, weak-willed and enterprising, slowly-developed and precocious, misanthropists and men of pleasure, the morose and the cheerful. In short, we can only conclude, at most, that they have a tendency to depart from the average—whether to rise above it or fall below it.

According to the other theory, all this is secondary, accessory, physical and psychical defects being by no means a necessary condition of genius. It grows equally well on a sound stem or a rotten one; it bears the marks of its origin, but this is quite a matter of accident. There are also facts in support of this view, though it must be acknowledged that they are less numerous than those on the other side.

We may also generalise the question, and ask whether æsthetic activity is not always a deviation. Nordau has maintained the affirmative: "Art is the slight beginning of a deviation from complete health." Thus presented, the question is equivocal. If we understand by mental health the *ataraxia* of the ancient philosophers, it is clear that creative and even æsthetic enjoyments are incompatible with it. To demand that we shall create or enjoy without excitement, remaining all the time in the level, prosaic calm of every-day life, is to expect the impossible. On this showing we might say as much of any emotion whatever and allege it to be a deviation from health. Some intellectualists, Kant among others, have ventured to make this claim, which is as much as to say that man is, by nature, an exclusively reasonable being—so enormous a psychological error that we need not discuss it. Besides, even supposing this to be the ideal, the mission of psychology is not to study an ideal man, but the real one.

After this somewhat lengthy preamble, rendered necessary by the ambiguity of our subject, let us investigate the part played by the two essential factors, emotion and imagination, when their activity is pathological, and in clearly-defined cases.

I. The necessity for vividness and sincerity of feeling in the artist is so obvious that I need not insist on it. This disposition, however, is not in all cases identical. Acute emotion may be intermittent, appearing only at moments of inspiration and creation, and then, the crisis over, disappearing to let the emotional life take its normal course. This is the characteristic of healthy genius or talent, which, descending from the heights, returns and adapts itself to the groove of ordinary life. A more frequent case, if we may judge by biographical documents, especially as we approach our own day, is the state of permanent excitement or hyperexcitability. Artists and dilettanti are exceedingly delicate instruments vibrating continually to every sound. Here our triple criterion of pathological activity comes again into use: we find (apparent) disproportion between cause and effect, violent and prolonged shock to the system, chronicity. This physiological state is one of continual loss; not a combustion, but a series of explosions; not a life, but a fever. Hence the craving for artificial excitement so frequent in emotional natures of this kind; they seek it under all its forms, and the remedy aggravates the evil. It is needless to multiply examples, we need only recall the great contingent of melancholiacs, hypochondriacs, alcoholics—persons subject to hallucinations, insane, or merely *déséquilibrés*—furnished by artists or passionate lovers of art. Besides these general characteristics, we may note as particular pathological symptoms of æsthetic emotion:

1. An obstinate tendency to pessimism—the persistent and exclusive taste for gloom in art predominating in certain epochs of history, especially in our own. Its contagion is not sufficiently explained by imitation and fashion; it springs from deeper causes—from a general state of depression, enervation, and debility. Art is the expression of this secret uneasiness, both among those who create and those who enjoy. This pessimism is not a disease of art, but of the individual and the age, which can bring forth no other fruit. We know that the nature of the ground

modifies the flowers of plants and gives to their fruits a peculiar taste—the flavour of the soil; the human soil is subject to the same necessity, and at certain stages of civilisation it can produce nothing save a melancholy crop of flowers with strange and acrid odour. The constant love and complacent enjoyment of the mournful and morbid, of all connected with death, is the æsthetic form of the *luxury of pain* which I have already (Part I., chap. iv.) tried to analyse, and to determine its pathological causes.

2. The tendency to megalomania under the form of pride, and still more of excessive vanity. The remark on the *genus irritabile vatum* is of old date; but at various epochs the insanity of greatness has raged like an epidemic in the domain of art. It has found its supreme expression in this century in the doctrine of "the divinity of art" proclaimed by the school of Schelling, and surviving among contemporary "æsthetes." "The beginning of all poetry," said Schlegel, "is to suspend the march and the laws of reason, to plunge us once more into the beautiful maze of fantasy, the primitive chaos of human nature. The good pleasure of the poet suffers no law above him." We have gone still farther since then, and an interesting collection might be made of the folly written on this subject. When, sincerely and without prepossessions, we ask ourselves what are the grounds of these high pretensions, of this apotheosis, they are not very evident. Is it because art yields enjoyments far superior to those of the senses? But scientific research, and the love of travelling and exploration, do the same thing. Is it because of its creative function? But we find creation everywhere—in science, mechanic art, politics, commerce, industry: artistic creation is only one form among many others. Is it because it adds an ideal world to the real? Religions do as much, with the advantage that they do not work for the few, the elect, but for the whole world. Malherbe used to say that a good poet is no more useful to the State than a good skittle-player. This is an extreme statement on the other side, for the poet, after all, has a social value; he can foresee, instruct, express the confused feelings of the mass of human beings who arrive through him at the consciousness of life.

If, accepting this form of megalomania as a fact, without discussing its legitimacy, we seek for its psychological causes, we shall find two principal ones.

The first is in the character of the individual, the hypertrophy of his *ego*. The self-feeling breaks out under an æsthetic mask, as it might do under any other. " Egotist" art is the sincerest expression of this impulse of pride (be it noted in passing that it is the very antipodes of primitive art, which is collective, social, anonymous); but it is an ephemeral form destined to die of inanition. Besides, its expansive force would be, if necessary, limited by the expansion of rival individualities. The production of monsters is a necessity of civilisation. By means of the division of labour, it imposes, in all positions and occupations, an excess of unilateral development, of tendency towards a single aim; it requires specialisation. In primitive times, art was not a profession; the artist, while all the time going on with other work, produced naturally, spontaneously, as a rose-tree gives its roses; it was a superabundance of mental activity which thus found vent. Gradually he fell into the professional track, and now, a victim to his own glory, he is *forced* to produce, *nolens volens*, as he can, consciously fabricating works of art as others do articles of commerce, reckless of over-production. It is a hypertrophy of the creative function.

The second cause must be sought in a deeper region than that of consciousness, in that unconscious part of us (whatever opinion may be entertained as to its nature) which produces what is vulgarly called inspiration. This state is a positive fact accompanied by physical and psychical characteristics peculiar to itself. First and foremost, it is impersonal and involuntary; it acts like an instinct, when and as it pleases, it may be solicited but not compelled. Neither reflection nor will can supply the place of original creation. We have numerous anecdotes relating to the habits of poets, painters, and musicians when composing : striding up and down, lying in bed, seeking complete darkness or full daylight, keeping the feet in water or ice, and the head in the sun, the use of wine, of alcohol, of aromatic drinks, of haschisch or other poisons acting on the intellect. Apart from some oddities not easy to explain, all these proceedings have the same object—viz., to bring about a particular physiological condition, and increase the cerebral circulation in order to provoke or maintain the unconscious activity. The ancients saw in inspiration a supernatural state, a divine action, a possession in which they firmly believed. Certainly, we now look on the Muses, and the various mythological gods of music and poetry, merely as superannuated fictions; yet there remains an impression of mystery, of a superior power, of a rare inborn gift bestowed on a man, which is his special privilege, which acts through him and is unknown to others, something analogous to what we have already met with in the case of theomania. From the vague consciousness of this state of election, this exceptional favour on the part of nature, it is for the artist an easy step to the affirmation of his greatness.

II. The pathology of the creative imagination does not belong to our subject; it is only connected with it through the influence of feeling on its operations. The power of constructing an imaginary world is a human attribute of which no one is devoid, since without it we could never take one step out of the present into the future and form for ourselves an image, however inadequate, of the latter. Observation shows that, from this universal level upward, there are all gradations, from the dry, clear, coherent imagination to incoherent, impalpable reverie and disordered exuberance : now, the increasing predominance of the imagination involves the danger of living entirely in the world of the unreal, which frequently happens. Biographical documents permit us to note the stages in this ascent towards the suprasensible.

There are artists who divide their lives into two parts and keep them distinct; they keep their accounts in double entry; they have their hours of unbridled imagination, and their hours of practical good sense. Ariosto was one of these; it was said of him that he had put his folly into his books and his wisdom into his life.

Others are, for the moment, caught by their own creations, and so violently carried away by them that they are near the state of hallucination. According to the constitution of their minds, they either see their characters or hear them speak; the sounds are in their ears, they breathe odours, taste flavours. On this last point, Flaubert's declaration, reported by Taine, has been doubted, but without sufficient reason.

There are some who appear to be in an almost continuous state of hallucination. Such seems to have been the case of Torquato Tasso. "At certain moments," Gérard de Nerval used to say, "everything would assume a new aspect to me: secret voices rose from plants, trees, animals, to warn and encourage me. Formless and life-less objects had mysterious ways, whose meaning I under-stood." The "symbolists" of various countries—French, Belgian, English—are now telling us the same thing with more to the like effect. I do not think, however, that we can be deceived by them. They are returning, through a sharpened and refined sympathy, to the primitive period of naïf animism, in which everything in nature has life, sight and voice, in which, as one of them says, the real world assumes the air of fairyland.

Beyond this there is only one step, that of complete and permanent hallucination, such as is to be found in lunatic asylums; the total substitution of an imaginary world for the real, without intermission, doubt, or consciousness of unreality.

This is the clearest part of the subject, but there is one obscure point which must detain us, the more that it is connected with the fundamental phenomenon of emotional life: *tendency*. If there is one psychological law more firmly established than another, both by facts and argument, it is that every intense representation of an act tends to realise itself; which is inevitable, since the vivid image of a movement is the beginning of a movement—a re-vival of motor elements included in the image. A man who, standing on the top of a tower, is fascinated by the idea of a possible fall, runs the risk of throwing himself over; the attraction of the abyss is nothing else but this. On the other hand, artists naturally have intense representa-tions and feel things violently; they dream of orgies, love adventures, sanguinary dramas, self-devotion, virtues and vices of all sorts. How comes it that all this is merely imagined, and never passes into action, or becomes a reality?

It is because in their case the law is subject, not to an exception, but to a *deviation*. The intense representation *must* be objectivised—*i.e,* from being internal become external, and it may arrive at this result in two ways:

by a real action, as in the case of ordinary people, or by the creation of a work of art which delivers one from the haunting idea : this is the peculiarity of artists. If, besides this, a physiological reason is required, it might be admitted, merely as a hypothesis, that in these cases the motor centres have not, usually, sufficient energy for practical realisation, whence it comes that their satisfaction is a purely æsthetic one.

To keep strictly to our subject, we have a large body of testimony to show that many have only been delivered from their haunting ideas by creative production, as I have already mentioned when treating of memory. It is fixed in a poem, a novel, a drama, a symphony, on the earth, or in stone; we may remember Michelangelo and the sculptures of the Medici chapel, Schiller's early manner and the "Robbers." Is not Byron, whose psychological state has been so well analysed by Taine (born for action and adventure, returning, perhaps, to his true vocation when he went to die at Missolonghi), the poet of pirates, of strange and doubtful enterprises? The reader will think it needless for me to enumerate further instances.

This rule, however, is not without exceptions. The law which requires that the intense image shall be actualised is always satisfied; but sometimes this happens in two ways, artistically and practically, at once. Many have lived out their dreams of love, orgies, adventures, violence, and have produced a work of art besides ; a double stream has flowed from the same source. Some of the romantic school have revived the aspect of past ages in their houses, their furniture, their lives. Artistic sovereigns have been able to realise their imaginations to the full : Nero, Hadrian, Ludwig II. of Bavaria, and others.

An Italian anthropologist, Ferrero, has pointed out, with some justice, that, in spite of our complaints of the pessimistic, satanic, *macabre*, or neurotic character of contemporary art, this evil is not without its accompanying good; it is a safety-valve, an overflow channel. Morbid art "is a defence against abnormal tendencies, which, otherwise, would tend to transform themselves into action." Many content themselves with a literary, plastic, or musical satisfaction. This seems to be indisputable. We may also grant to this author that the suggestion of a work of art has not the power of direct suggestion, that of the actually perceived fact, and that, so far, it is less dangerous.   But as it is more widely diffused and acts especially on subjects predisposed to it, it may be questioned whether, in the long run, the gain is serious.

This is a sociological question which it would be out of place to discuss here, and which, consequently, we may dismiss with a bare reference.   Our conclusion is that the pathology of the æsthetic sentiment has no independent existence.   It is one among many forms of expression (of which we have already pointed out several) of a morbid predisposition which can only follow this track in a small minority of persons—those possessed of the power of creative imagination.

CHAPTER XI.

THE INTELLECTUAL SENTIMENT.

Its origin: the craving for knowledge—Its evolution—Utilitarian period: surprise, astonishment, interrogation—Disinterested period: transition forms—Classification according to intellectual states—Classification according to emotional states: dynamic forms, static forms—Period of passion: its rarity—Pathology—Simple doubt—Dramatic doubt—"Folie du doute"—Mysticism in science: deviation comes, not from the object, but from the method of research.

I.

THIS name stands for the emotional states—agreeable, disagreeable, or mixed—which accompany the exercise of the intellectual operations. Intellectual emotion may be connected with images, ideas, reasoning, and the logical course of thought; in a word, with all the forms of knowledge. Except in some rare cases, which will be pointed out later on, it scarcely ever rises beyond a medium tone, especially in its higher manifestations.

After having traced it to its origin, we shall have to follow its evolution, which passes through three principal phases: the first, utilitarian and practical; the second, disinterested and scientific; in the third, which is much less frequent, it attains the power and exclusiveness of a passion.

I. This feeling, like all the others, depends on an instinct, a tendency, a craving; it expresses in consciousness its satisfaction or non-satisfaction. This primitive craving—the craving for knowledge—under its instinctive form is called curiosity. It exists in all degrees, from the animal which touches or smells an unknown object, to the all-examining, all-embracing scrutiny of a Goethe; from puerile investigation to the highest speculations; but whatever may be the differences in its object, in its point of application, in its intensity, it always remains identical with itself. Those devoid of it, such as idiots, are eunuchs in the intellectual order.

Assuming this innate craving, how is it developed during the first period?

The first stage is that of *surprise*. It appears early in the child; quite clearly, at latest, in the twenty-second week, according to Preyer. It is a special emotional state which cannot be traced back to any other, consisting of a shock, a disadaptation. In my opinion, its special and peculiar character lies in its being without contents, without object, save a relation. Its material is a *relation*, a transition between two states—a mere movement of the mind, and nothing more. The mode of expression and the physiological accompaniments of surprise are very clearly defined. The description of these will be found in Darwin (*Expression of the Emotions*, ch. xii.); the eyes and mouth are wide open, the eyebrows raised, the sudden shock is followed by immobility, the pulsations of the heart and the respiratory movements are accelerated, etc.

The second stage is that of *wonder*. I think with Bain and Sully,[1] that the distinction between these two stages is not a vain subtlety. Surprise is momentary, wonder is stable; one is a disadaptation, the other a readaptation; one is without objective material, the other has for its material some strange or unaccustomed object. It is this second stage, no doubt, which Descartes called admiration, and which he placed among his six primary passions:—
"Admiration is a sudden surprise of the soul which leads it to consider with attention the objects which appear to it rare and extraordinary."[2] In fact, wonder is the awakening of the attention, of which it has the principal characteristics —unity of consciousness, convergence towards a single object, intensity of perception or representation, adaptation

---

[1] Bain, *The Emotions*, ch. iv. pp. 85, 86; Sully, *Psychology*, vol. ii. p. 126.
[2] Descartes, *Traité des Passions*, Part ii., § 70.

of movements.[1]   In the beginning, before wonder is accompanied by pleasure (or pain, as the case may be), it has a peculiar character approximating to what we have called the neutral state, or that of simple excitation.

The third stage is that of *interrogation*, of reflections succeeding to the consternation produced by the first shock. This is the stage of curiosity properly so called, which consists in two questions, put implicitly and explicitly: What is that? What is the use of it? What is the concrete nature of this object? and what can be its utility? Primitive peoples, children, animals, incessantly put to themselves this double question; not, certainly, in clear and analytical terms, but instinctively and by their actions. The dog, brought face to face with an unknown object, looks at it, smells it, approaches, withdraws, ventures to touch it, returns, and begins again; he is pursuing this investigation after his own fashion; he is solving a double problem of nature and utility.[2] The interrogation consists in assimilating the new object to our former perceptions or representations—classing it, in fact.

Is primitive man curious? Herbert Spencer alleges a large number of facts in proof of his distaste for novelty.[3] However, the craving for knowledge seems to be very unequally distributed among the various races; the only universal fact appearing to be that primitive curiosity is limited to very simple things, all of which have, or seem to have, some practical utility. Curiosity and the emotional state which accompanies it have no other end than the preservation of the individual—just as we have seen with regard to the tendency to live in communities, or to revere the gods, in this same initial period of evolution. To be wide awake, to make inquiries as to what will help or harm one, in a word, knowledge in the practical order, is a powerful weapon in the struggle for life; a cause of selection in favour of the curious, and at the expense of the incurious. It is the survival of this entirely utilitarian curiosity which explains why, at the present day, uncultured and even

---

[1] I have given further details on this point in my *Psychologie de l'attention.*

[2] See for facts as to the curiosity of animals, Romanes, *Mental Evolution*, pp. 283-351.

[3] *Principles of Sociology*, i. pp. 98, 99.

semi-civilised peoples object to the entrance into their country of travellers from a distance for the purpose of geological or other scientific explorations; they are always suspicious of a search for treasure, of espionage, or of some unknown ill deed on the part of the strangers.

II. How did the transition to the disinterested period come about? We may admit, with Sully,[1] that this took place through the natural, innate inclination of the human intellect towards the extraordinary, the strange, the marvellous. The same tendency which, under its creative form, engenders religious, poetical, social myths, attempts under the form of research to discover instead of imagining causes.[2]

We are here at the point of junction between the æsthetic and the intellectual sentiments, which will presently bifurcate, and pursue each its own course. This inquiry is only half disinterested, however, for if man tries to penetrate the mystery of things it is in the hope of profiting thereby.

For the rest, however this transition may have come about, it took place when the struggle for existence became less keen, and it was possible to cultivate disinterested research for its own sake. Next, curiosity became scientific emotion, and gradually extended itself to every kind of investigation: the intellectual sentiment was formed in all its fulness.

It has been studied with a certain favour by psychologists,

---

[1] *Psychology*, vol. ii. p. 131.

[2] In the following, reported by a traveller, we have an instance of this spontaneous transition to disinterested curiosity, in the case of an intelligent Basuto. " Twelve years ago " [the man himself is speaking] " I went to feed my flocks. The weather was hazy. I sat down upon a rock and asked myself sorrowful questions; yes, sorrowful, because I was unable to answer them. Who has touched the stars with his hands? On what pillars do they rest? I asked myself. The waters are never weary; they know no other law than to flow without ceasing,— from morning till night, and from night till morning; but where do they stop? and who makes them flow thus? The clouds also come and go, and burst in water over the earth. Whence come they? Who sends them? The diviners certainly do not give us rain; for how could they do it? and why do I not see them with my own eyes, when they go up to heaven to fetch it? . . . I cannot see the wind; but what is it? Who brings it, makes it blow? . . . Then I buried my face in both my hands."—Quoted by Vignoli, *Mito e Scienza*, p. 63. This passage is from *The Basutos*, by the French missionary Casalis (p. 239).

especially those of the school of Herbart, or those who have felt his influence, under the name of "feelings of relation," "feelings connected with the cause of representations." I do not intend to follow them through their tedious and uninstructive task of divisions, subdivisions, and distinctions worthy of the schoolmen of the fourteenth century. Besides, the alleged classification of the intellectual feelings varies from one writer to another—one giving fifteen, another sixty. It is an artificial method, a labyrinth, a source, not of clearness, but of obscurity. I defy the subtlest psychologist to note and fix the delicate gradations of feeling which, *ex hypothesi*, should answer to this endless enumeration.[1] But its most serious defect lies in its including only the intellectual and not the emotional states.

I can only admit one division, which has the advantage of simplicity, and, more especially, of being based on the very nature of the emotional process. This is, into the pleasures and pains accompanying research or the acquisition of knowledge, and those which are attached to its possession, or the state of being without it. The former are *dynamic*, the second *static*.

Intellectual emotion, under its *dynamic* form, depends on the quantity of energy expended. In fact, it is only a particular case of the emotional state accompanying every form of activity directed towards an end compatible with success or failure; it is only one form of self-feeling, differing only in its object, not in its nature, from the feeling of the explorer or the hunter. The search for knowledge is a hunt like any other, truth being the game, and just as many sportsmen find more charm in the vicissitudes of their expedition than in their spoils, so many truth-seekers will accept as their own, Lessing's well-known saying: "If I were

---

[1] I give a specimen, choosing a classification which is neither one of the longest nor one of the shortest : (1) Emotions arising from logical relations (reasonable, unreasonable, contradictory, logical satisfaction, ignorance, the unknown, the hypothetical; possibility or impossibility of coming to a conclusion). (2) Emotions arising from relations of time (present, past, future, anticipation, hope, presentiment; feeling of the irremediable, of opportunity, of routine, etc.). (3) Emotions arising from relations of space (size, nearness, distance, etc.). (4) Emotions arising from relations of coexistence and non-existence, quantity, identity, etc. This is a much abridged catalogue; there are thirty-two subdivisions in all.

offered the choice between already ascertained truth and the pleasure of finding it out, I would choose the second."

Under its *static* form, intellectual emotion is still a particular case of self-feeling, whose principal manifestation is the sense of power, or its opposite. It is one form of this sense, by the same right as the pleasure of physical strength, the pleasure of riches, or their opposites. It approximates especially to the feeling inspired by possession or property; it is felt, under its positive form as augmentation, under its negative as diminution and poverty; ignorance is a retrenchment, a limit.

To sum up, intellectual emotion is simple enough; it is only the transfer of the emotional manifestations already known to us, to a group of mental operations. There is no need, therefore, to insist further on the matter.

III. We have still to follow it into a third stage, which it rarely attains, because pure ideas have little attraction for average human beings—viz., the cases in which it becomes a *passion*. It is evident that the intellectual passion cannot exist outside the dynamic group, possession being, in the nature of things, a calm pleasure, or, as the ancients said, a pleasure at rest.

We might find numberless instances in the biographies of scientific men and philosophers. Some names suggest themselves at once: Kepler, Spinoza, and many others who devoted their lives strictly and exclusively to the pursuit of truth. It may be objected, however, that, in certain cases and with certain men, nothing proves that the intellectual passion has not been fed or sustained by foreign elements; that the love of learning, though the principal motive, has been the only one; that it has not been adulterated with others—*e.g.*, desire for position, influence, riches, fame, glory, in short, ambition under its manifold aspects. It is not easy to find absolutely pure cases; for, besides the rarity of the intellectual passion, the terms in which the demand is framed are almost contradictory, since the men we want to find must be unknown to fame. The following instance, however, seems to me to answer perfectly to all the conditions. Descuret, in his *Médécine des Passions*, gives a brief biographical sketch of a Hungarian named Mentelli, a philologist and mathematician, who, without a definite end in view, simply for the pleasure of learning and to satisfy his intellectual cravings, consecrated his whole life to study, having apparently no other want. "Living at Paris, in a filthy lodging, the use of which was allowed him out of charity, he had cut off from his expenditure all that was not absolutely necessary to sustain life. His outlay— apart from the purchase of books—amounted to seven sous a day, three of which went for food and four for light; for he worked twenty hours a day, without intermission, except on one day in the week, when he gave lessons in mathematics, on the fees received for which he subsisted. All he needed was water, which he fetched for himself, potatoes which he cooked over his lamp, oil to feed the latter, and coarse brown bread. He slept in a large packing-case, into which, during the day, he used to put his feet wrapped in a blanket or a little hay. An old arm-chair, a table, a jug, a tin pot, and a piece of tin roughly bent into a convex shape, and serving as a lamp, formed the rest of his furniture. Mentelli saved the price of washing by wearing no linen. A soldier's coat bought at the barracks and only replaced in the last extremity, a pair of nankeen trousers, a fur cap, and huge *sabots* composed his entire costume. In 1814 the cannon-balls of the allies fell all round the lodging he was then occupying, but failed to disturb him. . . . During the first epidemic of cholera at Paris, it was necessary to employ armed force to compel this scientific anchorite to interrupt his studies, so as to clean out his pestilential cell. He lived thus, uncomplainingly, and indeed happily, for thirty years, without a day's illness. At last (on December 22nd, 1836), at the age of sixty, having gone as usual to fetch water from the Seine, his foot slipped, he fell into the river, then in flood, and was drowned. Mentelli left no work behind him, in fact there remains no trace of his long researches." [1]

Other instances might be quoted, but they would appear trifling by comparison with this. Great anonymous collaborations, like those of the Benedictines, have certainly enlisted the services of enthusiasts of this kind; thus Dom Mabillon was the type of a worker animated with passionate fervour, modest, unknown, punctually fulfilling his religious duties, and when free from these, travelling about the world on foot to collect historical documents.

Thus we find cases where the love of knowledge alone,

[1] Quoted by Letourneau, *Physiologie des Passions*, p. 23.

untarnished by other motives, has all the characteristics of a fixed and tenacious passion, filling the whole of life, and expressing the whole nature of a man.

II.

The intellectual feeling also has its pathology, in connection with which I have to point out two principal cases : the extreme forms of doubt, and the introduction of mysticism into science.

1. Doubt is a state of unstable equilibrium in which successive contradictory representations neither mutually exclude nor conciliate each other. I distinguish simple doubt, dramatic doubt, and the insanity of doubt.

In simple or limited doubt, intellectual indecision has as its emotional accompaniment a slight uneasiness, a state of discomfort resulting from an unsatisfied desire, a tendency which comes to nothing. Under this form doubt is normal, legitimate, and even necessary; it becomes morbid when it takes a chronic, permanent, and aggressive form, when it produces a violent shock and a long reaction.

This is the doubt which I call dramatic, because it is an internal convulsion, a crisis which often lasts a long time and repeats itself. It precedes great conversions and then subsides, but sometimes lasts through life, as with Pascal. There is nothing surprising in its violence, since it is, in the intellectual order, the equivalent of an intense, incurable, and hopeless love; in the two cases the situation and effects are identical.

The insanity of doubt takes us further into the intricacies of pathology. It is "a chronic disease of the mind, characterised by constant uneasiness." It presents numerous varieties, which have been classified by alienists. Some do not pass beyond the region of every-day trivialities, as the man who will return twenty times to see whether he has really locked his door. Others exhaust themselves in abstruse and insoluble questions, never able to satisfy themselves or stop, like an ever-turning wheel. Others, the timid, lose themselves in endless scruples and puerilities. But, whatever be the matter to which the mind applies itself, the psychological process remains the same. It is a questioning without pause or limit, accompanied by distress, constriction of the head, epigastric oppression, vaso-motor troubles, etc. There is the ardent desire to find a fixed state for thought without the ability to do so.

Under its gravest form it is "the complete loss of all notion and feeling of reality." It is absolute scepticism, not theoretic and speculative, after the manner of the Pyrrhonians, but *practical,* bearing not only on ideas, abstract conceptions, memories, reasonings, but even on perceptions and actions; the exercise of the intellect is not accompanied by any belief—*i.e.,* any state of mind which presupposes a reality. "I exist," says one of these patients, "but outside real life and in despite of myself . . .; something which does not seem to be in my body impels me to act as I formerly did, but I cannot succeed in believing that my actions are real. I do everything mechanically and unconsciously. My individuality has completely disappeared; the way in which I see things makes me incapable of realising them, of feeling that they exist. . . . Even when I see and touch, the world appears to me like a phantom, a gigantic hallucination. . . . I eat, but it is a shadow of food entering the shadow of a stomach; my pulse is only the shadow of a pulse. . . . I am perfectly conscious of the absurdity of these ideas, but cannot overcome them."[1] This state belongs, in fact, to the category of conscious madness.

But it is not essentially a disease of the understanding: the intellectual element is secondary; this perpetual doubt, these endless questionings are merely the effects; the cause lies in a weakening of the emotional life and the will, rendering them incapable of arriving at a belief—*i.e.,* an affirmation—and, more deeply still, in a disturbance of the organic life, as demonstrated by sensory perversions, motor enfeeblement, and the melancholic state of the patient with its physiological accompaniments, and lowering of the vital functions.

2. The introduction of mysticism into science, though particularly prevalent just now, is an intellectual disease incident to all ages. In the beginning, scientific research

[1] See Hack Tuke's *Dictionary of Psych. Medicine,* article, "Insanity of Doubt." Analogous cases have been reported by various authors, Griesinger, Clouston, etc.

had no clear consciousness either of its method or its object.

The earliest Greek philosophers speculated at once on first causes, second causes, and practical applications, without drawing any hard and fast distinction between these subjects. Thales constructed a cosmology and calculated eclipses; Pythagoras reduced the universe to numbers, but he also greatly advanced the study of mathematics, and founded a communistic society on his own principles. By slow degrees the proper domain of science became recognised: the determination of second causes, of natural laws. At the Renaissance, alchemy, astrology, and the occult sciences were discredited, in spite of their provisional services, and some positive discoveries due to them. At present, the methods are fixed, in their main lines; a fact which permits us to determine the anomalies and deviations of the intellectual sentiment.

How does it deviate from the normal track? It is needless to remark that it is not by seeking the unknown, since this is its fundamental task, for every day and for all time. Is it by pursuing the unknowable? This view is scarcely tenable, for how can we determine where the unknowable begins? Let us admit, for the sake of argument, and in order to simplify matters, that this word covers the whole region of first causes, taken as inaccessible; but, having eliminated these, only by an arbitrary act can it be decided that this or that thing is unknowable. The history of science supplies us with proofs in abundance. To give but one example, which is closely connected with psychology: one of the greatest physiologists of the century, J. Müller, declared that the time necessary for perceiving a sensation is not measurable and can never be determined; this, however, did not prevent Helmholtz from measuring it some years later, and it is well known what successful experiments have since been made in that direction.

It is not so much in the object pursued as in the method employed that the love of science may go astray. Scientific mysticism consists in replacing regular methods by intuition and divination; in expecting everything from an inward revelation, a supernatural illumination; in substituting the subjective for the objective, belief for demonstration and verification, individual for universal validity. True, it would be a great mistake to assert that intuition and divination have not played an important part in the discoveries of scientists; they lie at the origin of nearly all, and there is a certain point where the psychological conditions of scientific and of artistic creation coincide; but no scientist worthy of the name will confound the vision of a truth with its demonstration. He does not allow it to rank as scientific till he has furnished his proofs. Mysticism is the reintegration, in science, of the love of the marvellous, and the illusory desire of acting on nature without preliminary research, work, or trouble.

Intellectual emotion, therefore, has two principal morbid forms : doubt, which, at the last extremity, ends in dissolution; and mysticism, which is only a deviation, and whose essence consists in substituting imagination for logical methods.[1]

To sum up, the intellectual emotion moves between two

---

[1] Two American psychologists, without mentioning the principal forms we have just studied, reckon among contemporary aberrations of the intellectual feeling some tendencies which appear to me to be very slight infirmities by comparison : (1) "A more subtle form is that distinctively nineteenth-century disease, the love of culture, as such. When the feeling is directed, not towards objects, but towards the state of mind induced by the knowledge of the objects, there originates a love of knowing for the sake of the development of the mind itself. The knowledge is acquired because it widens and expands self. Culture of our mental powers is made an end in itself, and knowledge of the universe of objects is subordinated to this. The intellectual feelings are separated from their proper place as functions of the integral life, and are given an independent place in consciousness. Here, as in all such cases, the attempt defeats itself. The only way to develop self is to make it become objective ; the only way to accomplish this is to surrender the interests of the personal self. Self-culture reverses the process and attempts to employ self-objectification or knowledge as a mere means to the satisfaction of these personal interests. The result is that the individual never truly gets outside of himself" (Dewey, *Psychology*, pp. 305, 306). This criticism is just. We might say, more simply, that the pursuit of intellectual emotion for its own sake borders on scientific dilettantism—*i.e.*, a superficial disposition and a tendency of the mind to run in every direction without going very deeply into anything. But we cannot reckon as morbid the love of abstract and purely speculative research ; for in this the intellectual feeling remains faithful to its nature, *i.e.* curiosity, and its mission, *i.e.* the pursuit of truth. Besides, the speculations which in appearance are the most useless and merely theoretical, may some day show themselves in results susceptible of practical application. (2) Ladd, *Psychology*

poles : one, where it involves a confused knowledge and plays a preponderant part under that instinctive form which may be called *flair*, or intuition ; the other, where it is only the pale shadow of the exercise of abstract thought.   Under this last form it is the type to which all other emotions approximate, when the affective element is impoverished— viz., moral emotion in rationalistic theorists (the Stoics, Kant), æsthetic emotion in critics, and religious emotion in metaphysicians and dogmatic theologians.

Descriptive and Explanatory, pp. 566 *et seq.*, considers as a morbid form of the intellectual sentiment the personification of Science, which is so popular at the present day (in my opinion, it is rather a disease of thought, an instance of the incurable tendency of the human mind to realise abstractions and bow the knee before idols of its own fabrica-tion), and also criticises the growing love of minutiæ and the obstinate pursuit of small facts.   It must be acknowledged that this tendency sometimes becomes a nuisance in sciences founded on observation, experiment, or documents, and that those whose attention has been confined to this kind of work have a natural disposition to exaggerate its importance ; but it is nevertheless necessary, and is the price paid for all progress in science.   Each individual contributes in his degree and according to his strength ; there is no architecture without labourers.

CHAPTER XII.

NORMAL CHARACTERS.[1]

*Necessity of the synthetic point of view in psychology—
Historical summary of theories of character: physiological direction, psychological direction—Two marks of
the real character: unity, stability — Elimination of
acquired characters—Classificatory procedure: four degrees—Genera: the sensitive, the active, the apathetic—
Species—Secondary function of the intellect: its mode of
action—Sensitives: the humble, the contemplative, the
analytical, the purely emotional — Active type: the
medium, the superior—Apathetic type: pure type, intelligent type, calculators—Varieties: the sensitive-active,
the apathetic-active, the apathetic-sensitive, the temperate
—Substitutes for character: partial characters; (a)
intellectual form, (b) emotional form.*

SEVERAL writers have on various occasions pointed out,
with some reason, that the great analytical work carried on
in our day, in the domain of psychology, ought to be completed by studies of a directly opposite character; *i.e.*,
analytic and abstract psychology has as its indispensable
complement a synthetic and concrete psychology. Like
every other science, ordinary psychology proceeds by means
of generalities. Whether it is concerned with percepts or
concepts, with the association of ideas or with movements,
with the attention or the emotions, it takes these manifestations, wherever it finds them, in men or in animals, and
attempts to explain them by tracing them back to their

---

[1] This chapter was published as an article in October 1893; it has
been left unchanged as far as the main argument is concerned.

most general conditions. It starts with the implied assumption that instincts, habits, intellectual, emotional, voluntary phenomena are to be found in every man. But in what proportions are these elements combined in order to constitute the various psychological individualities? What complex assemblages can they produce? Is there a preponderance of emotion, intelligence, or action? Has the preponderance of one any influence on the development of the rest? These questions, and many other analogous ones, are not put by analytical psychology, and justly so, because they do not come within its province. Yet it is worth while to put them, were it only for the sake of practical utility.

It has been said with regard to medicine that "there are no diseases, only diseased persons." This is why pathological treatises, describing the general characteristics of a disease in the abstract, are necessarily supplemented by those clinical studies which describe concrete, particular cases. In the same way, in psychology, it might be said that there is no such thing as humanity, but only human beings. It is not sufficient to describe the manifestations of the mind in general, we must also take into account the individuals in whom they are incarnated and the varieties which they reveal to us. The synthetic point of view is neither visionary nor negligible, and less so in psychology than elsewhere.

A very widespread error consists in believing that when we have resolved a complex whole into its elements we have *all* the constituents. We are apt to forget that the greater number of combinations resemble rather chemical *combinations* than simple mixtures, that they are not formed by simple addition, and that there is *more* in the synthesis than there can be in the analysis.

The elimination of the synthetic point of view becomes less and less admissible as we rise from inorganic nature to life, consciousness, society. Even in the inorganic world, which contains only the general properties of matter in the rough, certain composite bodies already show a sort of individuality—*i.e.*, a way of acting and reacting peculiar to themselves. This is best seen in crystals; their growth may be interrupted and go on again; when broken or mutilated they can repair their losses; they may undergo disaggregation or profound modification, but so long as one portion remains unaltered it still has the power of growing and escaping "senility." Two totally different substances, even, may be almost inextricably intertwined, while preserving each its own individuality. In the world of life the cell and the ovule have a very definite individuality; then come aggregates of a vague, unstable, and precarious unity, such as those of vegetables, hydrozoa, and those fixed or wandering animal colonies which have been called federations; but after passing through these stages of evolution, the higher animal forms assert their individuality so decidedly that argument is needless. The same may be said of psychology. What has not been said of the unity and utility of the *ego*, considered as a simple and indissoluble entity? The present writer will not be suspected of an inclination towards this view. Yet it must be acknowledged that we have been so much occupied of late years with disturbances, alterations, disaggregations, and dissolutions of personality, that the triumph of the analytical method has been complete, and the synthetic side of the subject somewhat neglected.

Without insisting on a question of too great extent to be treated incidentally—viz., the opposition between analytic and synthetic psychology,—we may say that there are two equally legitimate ways of considering all things in nature: the analytic, abstract manner, which recognises only laws, genera, species, generalities; and the synthetic, concrete manner, which sees only particular facts, events, individuals. Each one presupposes and completes the other: they are two stages of the same method.

So far it is clear that, in the new psychology, the analytic process has prevailed. In spite of these unfavourable conditions, some valuable work has been done in the other direction, the principal being the determination of certain types of imagination, visual, auditory, motor, and other varieties. But the chief problem proposed to synthetic psychology is elsewhere, in the region of action, not of knowledge. It is practical, and consists in determining the principal types of individuality from the kind of action and reaction which has its source in the feelings and the will. This is called by a name slightly vague, but consecrated by usage—character.

I.

The aim of the present chapter is not to treat this difficult subject, but simply to attempt a classification of characters, and to show their relations with affective psychology.

I shall pass by in silence the history of the question; it would be long and monotonous. It seems to me that it has developed in two directions, one especially physiological, the other especially psychological.

The physiological theory is very ancient, and was for centuries the only one current. It is summed up in the classical doctrine of the four temperaments, which dates from the Greek physicians. These great observers had deduced it from their long experience, adding, it is true, chimerical hypotheses as to the predominance of the liquids of the organism or the cosmic elements. Criticised, defended, abandoned, taken up again, modified, increased by Cabanis by the addition of the nervous and muscular temperaments, reduced by others to three, it has remained substantially the same up to the present day. Psychology has been content with adapting this arrangement to its own use, and translating the terms into its own language. For the rest, this work was, so to speak, done in advance; for the description of each temperament enumerates not merely physical, but also psychical characteristics. The *sanguine* is reputed to be light, versatile, superficial, accommodating; the *melancholic*, deep, self-involved, hesitating; the *choleric* has an active imagination, and intense, tenacious passions, difficult to supplant; the *lymphatic* (or phlegmatic) is soft, cold, with slow reactions and dull imagination. The detailed description of these four types may be found almost anywhere, so that I need not dwell on them. I notice that, during the present century, it is mostly in Germany that this psycho-physiological theory has been dominant. Kant adopted and developed it (*Anthropologie*, Bk. III.). Lotze substitutes the term "sentimental" for that of "melancholic," as being less equivocal; while Wundt, in his *Physiologische Psychologie*, reproduces Kant's divisions almost unchanged.

The psychological theory is more recent, and, I believe,

of English origin.   We know that J. S. Mill demanded the
constitution of a science of character ("Ethology") to be
deduced from the general laws of psychology.   Bain seems
to have attempted a response to this appeal in his book
On the Study of Character (1861).   This is not the place
to analyse his work.   Half of it is devoted to a criticism
of the phrenologists, who also, in their way, were making
an examination of our subject without paying much
attention to the temperaments.   It is only of importance
to note that Bain's position is strictly, rigorously psychological; he admits three fundamental types : the intellectual,
emotional, and volitional or energetic.   More recently, M.
B. Perez [1] has proposed a classification of characters, based
solely on an objective phenomenon—viz., the movements,
their rapidity and energy.   He distinguishes, in the first
place, the lively, the slow, and the eager; further, as mixed
types, the lively-ardent (*vifs-ardents*), the slow-ardent, and
the deliberate (*pondérés*).   Paulhan traces back the law
explaining the formation of character to a more general law :
that of "systematic association—*i.e.*, the aptitude inherent
in every element, desire, idea, or image of exciting other
elements which may associate themselves with it in working
towards a common end."   He has given a very detailed
description of the numerous and varied forms to be met
with in ordinary life, illustrating it with a vast multitude
of instances.   Fouillée makes a separate study of temperaments and characters, and divides the latter into three
categories : the "sensitive," the "intellectual," and the
"voluntary," with several subdivisions. [2]

If we now try to take up the question again at our own
risk, the first thing to be done is clearly to determine the
essential marks of a true individuality, a real character.
This will permit us to eliminate at once all that resembles it,
but is not: appearances, *simulacra*, phantoms of individuality.

In order to constitute a character, two conditions are
necessary and sufficient : unity and stability.

[1] B. Perez, *Le caractère de l'enfant à l'homme*, chap. i.   With this
objective classification may be compared the work of graphologists
and of those who have devoted themselves to the expression of the
emotions.

[2] Paulhan, *Les caractères* (1894) ; Foullée, *Tempérament et caractère
selon les individus, les sexes, et les races* (1895).   These two works
have appeared since the first publication of the present chapter.

Unity consists in a manner of acting and reacting which is always consistent with itself. In a true individuality the tendencies are convergent, or at least there is one which subdues the others to itself. If we consider man as a collection of instincts, cravings, and desires, they form, here, a tightly fastened bundle acting in one direction only.

Stability is merely unity continued in time. If it does not last, this cohesion of the desires is of no value for the determination of character. It must be maintained or repeated, always the same in identical or analogous circumstances. The special mark of a true character is, that it shall make its appearance in childhood and last through life. We know beforehand what it will or will not do in decisive circumstances. All this is as much as to say that a true character is *innate*.

This disposition might be found fault with as being too ideal. In truth, invariable characters, all of a piece, are rare enough; yet some exist, and it is the conscious or sub-conscious notion of this type which influences our judgment. There is an instinctive craving for this ideal unity in our psychological, moral, æsthetic conception of character. It does not please us to see a contradiction between a man's beliefs and his acts. We are annoyed if an ascertained rascal should show a good side, or a very good person some weakness. Yet what more frequent? On the stage, or in a novel, undecided or contradictory characters do not attract us. This is because individuality appears to us as an organisation which must be governed by an inner logic following inflexible laws. We are very ready to put down to duplicity and hypocrisy what is often only a conflict between incoherent tendencies; and it is not the least important among the practical results of recent investigations into personality to have shown that its unity is merely ideal, and that, without going the length of mental dissolution and madness, it may be full of unreconciled contradictions.

These reserves being made, our definition of character has the advantage of supplying us with a criterion which remarkably simplifies our task; for it is clear that, among the innumerable individuals of the human species, there must be some, and these by far the greater number, who have neither unity nor stability nor personal characteristics

25

peculiar to themselves. This immense number of defective cases, which are ruled out of our study, may be divided into two categories—the *amorphous* and the *unstable*.

The *amorphous* are legion. I understand, by this term, those who have no special form of their own, the acquired characters. In these there is nothing innate, nothing resembling a vocation; nature has made them plastic to excess. They are entirely the product of circumstances, of their environment, of the education they have received from men and things. Some other person, or, failing that, the social environment, wills for them, and acts through them. They are not voices, but echoes. They are this or that, according to circumstances. Chance decides on their occupation, their marriage, and other things; once caught in the machinery of life, they act like every one else. They represent, not an individual, but a specific, professional character; they are copies, to an unlimited number, of an original which once existed. It has been said that the production of amorphous people is the speciality of civilisation, to which we owe their present abundance. This is only half true. It is certain that excessive culture rubs down the angles of character, and that, by raising some and lowering others, it tends to a general dead level. But we must not forget that, at the other extreme of social life, in the savage state, where the manners, customs, ritual, traditions of the tribe or clan, which can neither be discussed nor infringed, weigh heavily on each individual, where every innovation is rejected with horror (this is what Lombroso calls misoneism), the conditions are also very unfavourable to individual development. It seems, if we may judge from history, as if the period best suited for the growth of true characters were the half-civilised ages, such as the first centuries of the Roman Republic and of the Middle Ages, or epochs of disturbance like the Italian Renaissance, and, in general, all periods of revolution.

The *unstable* are the *disjecta* and scoriæ of civilisation, which may justly be accused of multiplying them. They are the complete antithesis of our definition, having neither unity nor permanence. Capricious, changing from instant to instant, by turns inert and explosive, uncertain and disproportionate in their reactions, acting in the same manner under different circumstances, and varying their actions in the same circumstances, they are indefiniteness itself. These are, in different degrees, morbid forms, expressing the inability of tendencies and desires to attain cohesion, convergence, unity. We shall return to these in the next chapter.

These two categories being excluded, the first because they are simply a product of their environment, and the second as being only an incoherent bundle of almost impersonal impulses, there remain the self-existent characters, which we must attempt to classify. Like every good classification, this must be systematically conducted—*i.e.*, descending, step by step, from the general to the particular. It must determine genera, species, varieties, and thus, at last, reach the individual. The principal defect in the doctrine of the four temperaments (adapted to psychology, as we have already seen) is that of being too general: it remains, as it were, suspended in air, without intermediary, without middle term, or anything to connect it with the individual. It states the genera, nothing more. For the rest, some writers appear to have perceived this lacuna, having described mixed temperaments, but they are far from being agreed as to the nature and number of the latter.

The attempt at classification I am about to make includes four degrees of increasing definiteness and diminishing generality. On the first stage, we have the most general conditions, a mere framework, almost empty, and not corresponding to any concrete reality, but analogous to the zoological and botanical genera. In the second degree (corresponding to species), we have the fundamental types of character, pure forms, but real, this time, and, later on, justified and verified by observation. In the third degree, the mixed or composite forms (corresponding to varieties) are less clearly defined than the preceding. In the fourth degree, we have those substitutes or equivalents for character (they might also be called *partial* characters) which depart more and more widely from the pure type, but, in many people, take its place.

II.

We may begin by laying down the most general conditions for the determination of character, the main guiding lines, the dominant traits which impress on it a clear and decisive mark.

As the psychic life, considered from the most general point of view, can be reduced to two fundamental manifestations: feeling and acting, we have in the first place, broadly speaking, distinguished two types : the sensitive and the active.

1. The *sensitive*, who might also be called the affective or emotional, have as their special characteristic the exclusive predominance of sensibility. Impressionable to excess, they are like instruments in a perpetual state of vibration, and their life is for the most part inward. The physiological bases of this type of character are not easy to enumerate ; but if we admit what seems to me incontestable—viz., that the internal organic sensations of vegetative life are the principal source of the affective development, as external sensations are the source of the intellectual development,— we must admit also that here the balance inclines in favour of the first. It may be known by the extreme susceptibility of the nervous system to agreeable or disagreeable impressions. In general, this type may be said especially to include the pessimists ; for experience as old as the world itself proves that sensitive subjects suffer more from a small misfortune than they enjoy a great happiness. Uneasy, timid, fearful, meditative, contemplative, such are the very vague terms in which they may be for the moment characterised, without passing beyond the region of generalities.

2. The *active* have as their dominant characteristic a natural and continually renewed tendency to action. They are like machines always in motion, and their life is mostly directed outwards. The physiological basis of this type of character consists in a rich fund of energy, a superabundance of life,—what Bain calls spontaneity,—which is very different from the intermittent and explosive reaction of the unstable, and which, in the end, amounts to a good state of nutrition. Taken in mass, and under their pure form, they are optimists, because they feel strong enough to struggle with obstacles and overcome them, and take pleasure in the struggle. Gay, enterprising, bold, daring, rash—such words describe their principal characteristics.

H. Schneider, in an interesting article on zoological psychology,[1] has attempted to show that all special move-

[1] *Vierteljahrsschrift für wissenschaftliche Philosophie*, vol. iii.

ments in the higher animals are only differentiations of two simple, primary movements : contraction and expansion. The tendency to contraction is the source of all impulses and reactions, including flight, by which the animal acts in a manner tending towards its own preservation. The tendency to expansion shows itself in impulses and instincts of an aggressive form : feeding, fighting, seizing on a female, etc. The antithesis between the sensitive and the active connects itself also with this fundamental contrast between contraction and expansion, between the tendency towards the inward life in some and that towards the outward life in others.

3. The above classification is not sufficient. No doubt, if we confine ourselves to theory, there is nothing to be taken into account beyond feeling and acting ; but observation teaches us that it is necessary to form a third class, that of the *apathetic*, corresponding, on the whole, to the lymphatic temperament of physiology. Its general characteristics are very well defined ; they consist in a state of *atony*—a lowering of the powers of feeling and acting beneath the ordinary level. The two other classes are positive ; this is negative, but very real. The apathetic characters must not be confounded with the amorphous, the first being innate and the second acquired : the special mark of the pure type of apathetic is *inertia*. He is not plastic, like the amorphous type : there is no hold over him. He cannot feel enough to induce him to act. He is neither an optimist nor a pessimist, but indifferent. Idle, sluggish, inert, careless : such are the epithets which usually describe him. The physiological basis of his character is the often-described lymphatic constitution—lowering of the nervous tension, increase of the lymphatic circulation according to some, weakening of the circulation of the blood according to others. However, we must not conclude that it is only a barren soil, on which nothing will grow. Add a third element,—which till now we have purposely refrained from mentioning,—intelligence, and the apathetic character assumes an individuality, as we shall see presently.

In this definition of the genera, of the fundamental types reduced to their most general form, are we to admit a fourth type—the *temperate?* We might say that when we have (*a*) predominance of feeling, (*b*) predominance of action, (*c*) apathy in the absence of both the foregoing, there is required, as a complement, a fourth state of perfect equilibrium between sensibility and action. This type exists, but I cannot admit that it should be included in a primary definition. It is a mixed, composite form, whose study is consequently out of place here. Besides, we must not allow ourselves any illusions; every character is hypertrophied or atrophied; the "perfectly balanced" character is an ideal analogous to the *temperamentum temperatum* of physiologists; or else it approaches the amorphous.

III.

Leaving this very general classification, let us enter upon our definition of the second degree. Let us pass from genera to species. Here there enters on the scene a new factor : the intellectual dispositions.

The term *feeling* is applied to two distinct groups of psychic manifestations, originally confounded—the affective and the representative states. So far, in employing this term we have taken account of the affective states only, because they and the movements are the sole primary constituents of character. They form the lower stratum, which is the first to make its appearance : the intellectual dispositions form a second layer, superimposed on the first. What is fundamental in the character is the instincts, tendencies, impulses, desires, and feelings; all these, and nothing else. This fact is so easily verified, and so obvious, that there would be no need to insist on it if the majority of psychologists had not confused the question by their incurable intellectualist prejudices—*i.e.*, by their efforts to connect everything with intelligence and explain everything by means of it, to lay it down as the irreducible type of mental life. This view is quite untenable, for just as, physiologically, the vegetative life precedes the animal life based on it, so, psychologically, the affective precedes the intellectual life, which is based on it. The groundwork of every animal is "appetite" in Spinoza's sense, "will" in Schopenhauer's — *i.e.*, feeling and acting, not thinking. I do not wish to insist on this point, which would require to be developed at great length; I forbear, not on account of the scarcity, but of the superabundance of proof.[1]

Let us confine ourselves to some decisive remarks which belong, in the strictest sense, to our subject. As the character expresses the inmost qualities of the individual, it can only be composed of essentially subjective elements, and these must not be sought among the intellectual qualities, since the intellect, in the ascending evolution from sensations to perceptions, images, concepts, tends more and more towards the impersonal.

We might in addition prove, by means of numerous examples, that the excessive development of the intelligence frequently involves atrophy of the character, clearly establishing their independence. The great manipulators of abstractions, confined to pure speculation, tend to reduce their ordinary life to a monotonous routine, whence emotion, passion, the unforeseen in action, are as far as possible excluded (Kant, Newton, Gauss, and many others). Schopenhauer was right in saying that many men of genius are "monsters by excess," *i.e.*, by hypertrophy of the intellectual faculties. "If normal man," he says, "is made up of two-thirds will and one-third intellect, the man of genius consists of two-thirds intellect and one-third will."[2] There are exceptions, as we all know. They prove, not that the development of the intellect favours that of the character, but that *in some cases* it does not fetter it. Is it not also a matter of common observation that these two factors, character and intellect, are often discordant? Men think in one way and act in another; they write sublime treatises on a morality which they do not practise; they preach action and remain inactive; they have the tenderest hearts in the world, and dream of plans for universal destruction.[3]

Intellect, then, is not a fundamental constituent of the

---

[1] I refer the reader to the brilliant chapter of Schopenhauer entitled "On the Primacy of Will," while reminding him that, with this writer, "will" signifies tendency or feeling. (*Die Welt als Wille und Vorstellung*, supplement to Book II., chap. xix.) I shall return to this subject in the Conclusion of this work.

[2] *Op. cit.*, supplement to Book III., chap. xxxi.

[3] Need we recall the often-quoted cases of Francis Bacon, D'Alembert, etc.? On this point see Dr. Le Bon's article in the *Revue philosophique*, vol. iv. p. 496.

character; it is its light, but not its life, nor, consequently, its action. The character sends its roots down into the unconscious—*i.e.*, into the individual organism: this is what makes it so difficult to penetrate and modify. The intellectual dispositions can only exercise an *indirect* action in its constitution. We have now to see by what mechanism they do so.

We know that the various emotions (fear, anger, love, contempt, etc.) show themselves in certain spontaneous movements and attitudes of the body, which constitute their natural expression. Emotion is the cause; the movements are the effect. It is less generally known that movements and attitudes of the body, artificially produced, are capable (in some cases, and to a slighter degree) of exciting the corresponding emotions. Remain for some time in an attitude of sadness, and you will feel sad. By mingling in cheerful society and regulating your outward behaviour in accordance with it, you may awaken in yourself a transient gaiety. If the arm of a hypnotised subject is placed, with clenched fist, in a threatening attitude, the corresponding impression spontaneously appears in the face and in the rest of the body; the same holds good for the expressions of love, prayer, contempt, etc. Here the movement is the cause and the emotion the effect. The two cases are reducible to a single formula. There is an indissoluble association between a given movement and a given feeling. Emotion excites movements, movements excite emotion; but with this very important difference: that movements are not always capable of exciting emotion, and when they do succeed, the states they bring about are neither intense nor permanent. In a word, the action from without inwards is always inferior to the action from within outwards.

It is exactly the same psychological law which governs the relations between the affective and the intellectual dispositions in the manifestations of the character.

Let us (merely in a metaphorical way, and for the sake of making the matter clear) call the action of the feelings on the ideas, action from below upwards, and that of the ideas on the feelings, action from above downwards.

The action from below upwards is solid, tenacious,

energetic, efficacious; it has its strength within itself, drawing it from the region of the unconscious—*i.e.*, from the organisation. When it reaches the consciousness, it merely becomes sensible. Thus what is at first a vague sense of discomfort, asserts itself in the consciousness as hunger, and may lead to theft, murder, and all sorts of excesses. Another state of the organism shows itself in floating, indeterminate desires, then asserts itself as love for some particular being, and may in the end break out like a thunderstorm. It would be superfluous to review in like manner the whole of the passions, making the same comments. Whether simple or complex, their evolution is the same. The moral, religious, or æsthetic vocations have their periods of incubation, of revelation, and of action. The saying of Correggio, on looking at the painting of a master, whether true or false historically, is psychologically true.

On the other hand, the action from above downwards is unstable, vacillating, variable, weak, and of doubtful efficacy. It has only a borrowed, extrinsic force. The psychological (and often pedagogic) problem stated is the following: How to bring about intellectual states, ideal images, so that they may, if they can, provoke, by way of reaction, the corresponding feelings. The action is mediate, indirect, and usually fails or shows very poor results. The sensibility produced is entirely intellectual; and who does not know that intellectual passions are mere phantoms, which a real passion sweeps away like a gust of wind?

In conclusion, the action of the emotions on the movements resembles that of the feelings on the ideas; the action of the movements on the emotions is like that of the ideas on the feelings.

Having thus briefly established the secondary and superficial part played by the intellect in the formation of character, let us return to our classification. We are now face to face with real individuals, unequally endowed with energy, sensibility, and intelligence. Let us now take our three great skeleton divisions, and fill them up, one by one.

I. *The Sensitive.*—In this genus I distinguish three principal species, which I am about to describe, taking the simplest first, and consequently departing more and more from the pure type as we approach the mixed characters.

1. The first species cannot be designated by any proper name; it is that of the *humble*. Excessive sensibility, limited or moderate intelligence, no energy — such are their constituent elements. Every one knows such persons, for they are frequently met with. Their dominant note is timidity, fear, and all paralysing modes of feeling. Like La Fontaine's hare, they live in perpetual uneasiness. They are afraid for themselves, for their families, for their small position or business, for the present, for the future. They worry themselves about everybody's opinion, even that of unknown passers-by. They tremble for their salvation in the other life, and in this they feel their own nothingness, and the weight of the social organism pressing upon them, which, in most cases, they cannot understand. The smallest misadventure gives them a severe shock, because they are conscious of being weak, and without springs of action or the spirit of initiative.

There is no one who cannot affix one or more names to this portrait; but I need mention none in particular, just because they are humble. I have eliminated all pathological cases from this study; but I may point out, by way of illustration, that many hypochondriacs belong to this type, and show it in an exaggerated form.

2. The second species is that of the *contemplative*, distinguished from the preceding by a much higher intellectual development, so that their constituent elements may be enumerated in the following order: acute sensibility, sharp and penetrating intellect, no activity.

A tolerably large number of varieties may be grouped under this heading; they all resemble one another by having the above three marks in common:

The irresolute, like Hamlet, who feel and think deeply, but cannot pass to action.

Certain mystics, not the great ones, who have acted, and whom we shall find later on, but pure adepts of the Inner Life, such as may be found in all ages and countries— Hindu Yogis, Persian Sufis, Therapeutæ, monks of all creeds—plunged in the beatific vision, writing nothing and founding nothing, and, always in pursuit of their dream, passing through life without leaving a trace behind them.

The analysts, in the purely subjective sense—*i.e.*, those who assiduously and minutely analyse themselves, who keep diaries, noting down from hour to hour the small changes of their inner life, the variations of their feelings according to the prevalent atmospheric influences. Such were Maine de Biran among psychologists and Alfieri among poets. For the rest, it is needless to mention particular names, since this mania for personal analysis has, in recent times, under the influence of excessive nervous excitement, of intellectual refinement, and the enervation of the will, become a disease. It should be noted that these sensitives are nearly all pessimists.

3. There still remains the third species, whom I shall call the *emotional* type, though not in the wide sense in which the word is used by Bain, who makes them into a class. In this type, which abounds in great names, the category of the sensitives attains its apogee. Activity is here added to the extreme impressionability and the intellectual subtlety of the contemplatives. But their activity has its own special characteristic : it is intermittent and sometimes spasmodic, because arising from an intense emotion, not from a permanent reserve of energy. The purely emotional character, says Bain, is inclined to indolence. Nothing can be juster, under an appearance of paradox. He only acts under the momentary influence of powerful motives, then he falls back into the inaction which is his essential nature; he alternates between impetuous energy and sudden collapse.

To this group belong many great artists: poets, musicians, and painters, capable of feverish activity when sustained by inspiration—*i.e.*, by an unconscious impulse ; then undergoing periods of exhaustion and impotence. We may cite, at random, Jean Paul Richter, Mozart, Rousseau. This last, as has frequently been demonstrated, should be regarded as a pathological case. The same may be said of certain orators, those who have "temperament." It is only on certain occasions that they put forth their full power, when there is a cause, in which their feelings are deeply engaged, to be defended, or enemies to be overthrown.

II. *The Active.*—I divide this type into two species, according as the intellect is mediocre or powerful.

1. The species of the *mediocre active* shows us more clearly the distinctive traits of this form of character and the points in which it differs from the *sensitive*. "The active man does his work better [than the sensitive] because he can do the uninteresting drudgery, while the other neglects whatever has not an intense and sustaining interest. One man can take a walk without any object in view more engrossing than the prospective warding off of ill-health; the other cannot move abroad without a gun, or a fishing-rod, a companion or something to see." [1]

The *active* are strongly constructed machines, well supplied with vital force, and still more with potential energy. Look at a small shopkeeper belonging to this type, a man without talent or education; he wears himself out in continual goings and comings, in offers of service, in talk without end or cessation. It is not the love of gain alone which impels him, it is his very nature, he *must* be active. Put a sensitive in his place, he will do nothing but what is absolutely necessary, or what interests him. To this first group belong all those who have an abundant supply of physical energy and need an outlet for it: sportsmen, those who love an adventurous life without other aim than action, globe-trotters, who hurry about the world as fast as steam will take them, not for the sake of business or of acquiring knowledge, making no attempt to study the countries they pass through, either at the time, or before, or afterwards, hurrying to the end of their journeys in order to begin again. We may add those fighters who are actuated by no resentment or ill-feeling, but are merely letting off their superfluous energy. The mercenary armies of former times must have been recruited almost entirely among men of this type.

2. Let us now take the ordinary *condottiere*, such as the Italian republics had in their pay by the thousand, fine types of physical energy and mindless activity. On this robust stock, graft an intellect, powerful, penetrating, supple, refined, unscrupulous, thoroughly skilled in diplomacy, and the ordinary *condottiere* becomes Cæsar Borgia, and we pass from the lower to the higher form of the active character.

[1] Bain, *Study of Character*, p. 214.

The latter, the *great active* types, abound in history, and play prominent parts in it. Unhappily, the line of separation between these and the mixed forms which we shall encounter later on is so vague that I hesitate to name any individuals. Julius Cæsar seems to belong to this pure type; Lucan's line *Nil actum reputans si quid superesse agendum*, is the complete formula for the active. Nothing either in his life or his style indicates an acute sensibility, unless we reckon certain well-known passions, and his epileptic fits, which, however, prove nothing. We may also cite the Conquistadores of the sixteenth century (Cortez, Pizarro), those Spanish captains whose expeditions read like romances, who, with a handful of men as daring as themselves, overthrew the great empires of Mexico and Peru, and appeared to the vanquished as gods.

III. *The Apathetic* (lymphatic, or phlegmatic, in the ordinary classification of the temperaments).—I use this word in the etymological sense, to denote, not a complete absence of feeling, which is impossible, but a slight degree of excitability and consequently of reaction. We should be disposed to think, *a priori*, that this type of character never rises above mediocrity; experience, however, shows the contrary. It is here that intellect is paramount. In the silence of the passions, and the absence of physiological activity, it finds a medium suitable for its development.

Nowhere can we better see the influence of the intellectual powers on the constitution of the character, and the exact limits imposed on them by nature.

In this class, too, I distinguish two species:

1. The first is the pure apathetic type: slight sensibility, slight activity, slight intelligence, a negative state. There is little to add to what has been already said. They are at once above and below the amorphous: above, because they have their own special character, their indelible mark, inertia, which the amorphous have not; and below, because they meet external occurrences with a passive resistance. They are only slightly influenced by education or suggestion, not plastic, equally incapable of good and evil.

2. With a powerful intellect, the case is quite different; but we have to distinguish two cases, according as the intellectual tendencies are speculative or practical.

The first case is outside our subject. If a lymphatic

temperament coincides with a lofty speculative intellect, which has occurred in a tolerably large number of mathematicians, metaphysicians, and scholars generally, we have to do with pure intellect only: these are Schopenhauer's *monstra per excessum*, and I have nothing further to say of their character.

The second case, that of practical intellect, deserves attention, because it shows us a very special form of character, that which is the result of the action from above downwards, of the influence of ideas on feelings and movements. I call this group of characters the *calculators*. The ideas give the first impulse, and thus we observe a lack of spontaneity; the tendencies are only excited indirectly, the will is not a *laisser faire*, but an alternation of effort and inhibition: of effort, because the motor power of ideas is always very weak compared with that of desires; of inhibition, not because there are any violent movements to check, but because reflection is dominant and only allows of action at proper times and places. These characters might also be called *reasonable*, and they are the work of art much more than of nature. If this chapter were not exclusively devoted to individual psychology, I should point out that this form of character has been predominant among certain races, in certain tribes, and at certain epochs.

Benjamin Franklin is an excellent example: he is "the great genius of prudential calculation." In his letter to Priestley entitled "Moral Algebra, or method of deciding doubtful matters for one's self," [1] the reasons *pro* and *con* are entered opposite one another every day, after reflection for a sufficient, frequently a long, period; they are then compared, cancelled, balanced, and, this arithmetical operation concluded, we proceed to action.

Among the great names of history bearing this mark we may mention William the Silent; Louis XI., who, considering his epoch, was so devoid of the chivalrous spirit; Philip II., who would not be interrupted in his vespers by the news of the victory at Lepanto, and, shut up in that cold bare room which is still to be seen at the Escurial, concocted plots involving the fortunes of both worlds.

[1] Reproduced *in extenso* in Bain, *The Will*, p. 413 (chap. vii.).

In more modest circumstances we may observe the same character in cold-hearted speculators, tenacious of purpose, who leave nothing to caprice, imagination, or chance— neither uplifted by success nor dejected by reverses.

To sum up: the three classes include great names. The celebrated sensitives have acted through the intensity and contagion of their feelings; the celebrated actives by the force of their energy imposing itself upon others; the great calculators by their power of reflection, which leaves nothing to chance. They are strong, because wise; but their glory is lustreless, unsympathetic, without prestige. They are, however, *true* characters, because they have reactions peculiar to themselves—coming from within, not from without.

IV.

I cannot enter on my definition of the third degree without some preliminary remarks. We pass from species to varieties—from relatively simple to composite characters. The doctrine of temperaments attempts a similar definition when it undertakes the description of the mixed temperaments (lymphatico-sanguine, nervous-sanguine, etc.), which has given rise to many discussions. Instead of one dominant characteristic—sensibility, energy, or reflection—we have *two*, in juxtaposition and coexistent, sometimes in harmony, sometimes in contradiction. We are departing from unity. Those who, treating this subject as logicians, reason on pure concepts, have said: There are states of being which are mutually exclusive; we cannot, *e.g.*, be at the same time apathetic and active; *ergo*, mixed forms must be rejected. We need pay no attention to this: our business is to observe, not to reason. Has experience established the existence of mixed characters, whether contradictory or not? This is the whole question. And it is not this point which perplexes me, but the difficulty of finding clear, and, above all, legitimate and incontestable differences between the second and third degrees of definition—between the species and the varieties of character. I have already pointed out that the higher forms of the sensitive, active, and apathetic types tend to shade away into the mixed types.

Without undervaluing possible objections, I would propose the following groups:—

1. The *sensitive-actives*. Nothing contradictory in this form of character. An acute sensibility, without excess or morbid hyperæsthesia, is easily reconciled with an active and energetic temperament, because there is a natural connection between feeling and acting. These characters result from a synthesis of the sensitive and the active types, having all the qualities not mutually exclusive found in both. In short, as shown in its most brilliant representatives, it seems to us one of the richest and most harmonious varieties of character.

I find it in its lowest degree in those who, without much intellectual scope, live a life of pleasure, have a purely egoistic craving for enjoyment and action. These specimens of the sensitive-active character are without marked features and have no originality; it would not always be easy to distinguish them from the amorphous on the one hand, or the unstable on the other.

On a higher plane are the martyrs and enthusiastic heroes who feel the need of action, of self-devotion, of sacrificing themselves for their country or their faith : the great mystics, founders or reformers of orders : St. Teresa, St. Francis of Assisi ; the great religious preachers : Peter the Hermit, Luther ; and men consumed by love for others, as St. Vincent de Paul ; in short, all those who may be called, in the widest sense of the word, apostles.

Further, we may include warriors like Alexander and Napoleon ; many great leaders of revolutions, like Danton ; such poets as Byron ; and such artists as Benvenuto Cellini and Michelangelo. I mention only well-known names, and of these only just enough to make my meaning clear.

2. The *apathetic-active*. This variety closely approximates to the species just described as "calculators." It seems to me, however, to be rendered more complex by the addition of a certain quality of feeling or passion which allows them to act, but rather defensively than offensively. The dominant element is the idea which gives to this character an unalterable fixity, and subjects their somewhat weak sensibilities to its sovereign power. It is the "*moral temperament*," *par excellence*, but its morality is cold, has been hardened by habit, and inspires respect rather than

sympathy. The moral ideal which is the groundwork and support of this form of character may be either true or false: it varies according to time and place, consisting now of public health, now of the general advantage, or belief in some dogma, religious or other, or duty in the abstract, or the categoric imperative. It is found among martyrs and *passive* heroes, who do not run to meet danger, or challenge tortures and death, but without enthusiasm, and equally without fear or hesitation, do their duty to the end.

Current language calls them stoics. We may add to them cold-blooded fanatics of all sorts, the Jansenists and others.

3. The *apathetic-sensitive.* This is a contradictory synthesis, which, nevertheless, exists. It must be recognised that if "character" signifies an essential, fundamental, invariable mark, this variety is not so much normal as semi-pathological. I reduce it to the following formula: atony and instability. We meet with people (this is not a fancy portrait, but one taken from nature) of lymphatic temperament, passing their days in inaction and torpor, who, flung into action by some unforeseen circumstance, spend themselves with as feverish an energy as the sensitives; but this only happens by way of episode. A man of this sort, whom I knew as leading a sedentary life and disliking locomotion and change, suddenly started for Australia, fascinated by some very hazardous project, and returned as quickly as possible, vowing he would never do such a thing again. The dominant note of this variety is apathy, though it approximates to the unstable.

4. If we admit the existence of the *temperate* character, it ought to find its place here. Can we admit it, or ought it not rather to be looked on as a purely ideal category? Though we may admit that persons are actually to be found in whom feeling, thought, and action are present in strictly equal proportions, ought we not to consider this as the absolute suppression of character, *i.e.*, of any marks of individuality? Such perfect equilibrium belongs to a being favoured by nature, and is a pledge of happiness, no doubt; but the constitution of a character requires something other than this. We might say that the *temperate* come under our definition of character as complying with its two fundamental conditions, unity and stability, and that they have a

26

system of action and reaction peculiar to them and consistent with itself, so that it can be foreseen.   But we
should need to know whether this initiative does not come
from circumstances rather than from themselves, and
whether their personality is not above all things an adaptation.

I do not intend to dwell on an ambiguous problem,
which would become a mere debate about words.   In any
case, it is a fugitive, indecisive form, without marked traits,
and bordering on the amorphous.

I can find no names of mark to place under this heading.
Goethe has often been cited as a fine example of a balanced
character; but is he to be reckoned as a character or a
genius?

V.

Departing more and more from simple, clear, and definite
forms, we come at last to a group of what I have called the
substitutes, or equivalents for character.   The shortest and
most suitable appellation for them seems to me to be "partial
characters."   Their formula is: amorphousness *plus* an
intellectual disposition, or a well-marked affective tendency.
The complete character expresses the whole individual; the
sensitive, active, and apathetic are respectively sensibility,
energy, apathy to the backbone; all their reactions, or
failures to react, show it.   The partial character only acts on
one point; but on this one point the reaction is energetic,
invariable, consistent with itself, foreseen.   In all other
ways, he thinks, feels, and acts like the rest of the world.
He is an imitator, a copy, an impersonal product of his
education and environment.   This state of being takes the
place of a character in many persons, and many take it for
such.

The partial characters resulting from intellectual aptitudes
are the simplest.   If we suppose an innate aptitude for
mathematics, mechanical arts, music, painting, etc., it tends
to develop itself and to mask all the rest of the character,
to become the mark of the individual as a whole, and to
produce the illusion of a character which, after all, does
not exist, *i.e.*, is impersonal.   Current speech applies to
this sort of hypertrophy an expression borrowed from the
phrenologists: "He has such or such a bump."

Partial characters of an affective form consist in the exclusive predominance of some one passion—*e.g.*, sexual love, gambling, avarice, etc. Anything which excites this, whether near or far off, causes an energetic and identical reaction. Outside this ruling passion there is either slight reaction, or indifference. It should be noted that this form of partial character has not much stability, because it is in the nature of passion to extend its influence, gradually to invade the whole individual, and to bring about in him a pathological transformation.

Lastly, as nature is fertile in combinations, and we must try not to forget any, we find composite forms—*e.g.*, an amorphous character *plus* an intellectual aptitude and a passion.

However incomplete, the classification just detailed may have seemed over minute. I have no apologies to make for this, my aim being to follow the natural method—viz., carefully to distinguish the dominant from the subordinate elements, to descend from the general to the particular by an uninterrupted derivation, adding new characteristics as we proceed. Is this a practical method? can it serve to guide us amid the multitudinous manifestations of character? If not, it ought to be rejected.

What, at any rate, is apparent from this classification is the diversity and heterogeneity of those individual modalities which we designate under the collective name of character. The unity of the word disguises the multiplicity of the cases. This permits us to reply, in conclusion, to a very important question frequently debated from the practical point of view: Is character immutable?

Two opposite answers have been given, both equally sweeping.

Some think that character is acquired, and, consequently, indefinitely transformable by appropriate culture. This is the theory of the *tabula rasa* transferred from the region of the sensations to that of the tendencies and feelings. It was held by some of the eighteenth century philosophers, and is implied in the views of all who have blind faith in the omnipotence of education.

Others look upon character as innate and immutable. All acquired gradations are borrowed garments, or a superficial and fragile coating which falls off at the least shock.   With a vast superfluity of metaphysical distinctions, Schopenhauer has maintained this view with much spirit and vigour.

The problem, therefore, seems to be reduced to this dilemma : innate or acquired.   I cannot, however, accept it under this form; it is not so simple.   Character is an abstract entity — there exist only *characters*.   For this ambiguous term, which has only an abstract and factitious unity, let us substitute the multitude of species and varieties already described, and perhaps forgotten.   Let us place at one extreme the clear and definite forms which I have called the pure types.   Nothing modifies them, nothing impairs them; good or bad, they are solid as the diamond. At the other end of the scale let us place the amorphous, who, by their very definition, are plasticity incarnate.   Between these two extremes we may arrange *seriatim* all modes of character, so as to pass by imperceptible gradations from one end to the other.   It is clear that, as we descend towards the amorphous, the individual becomes less refractory to the influences of his environment, and the proportion of acquired character increases in the same ratio.   This is equivalent to saying that *true* characters never change.

CHAPTER XIII.

ABNORMAL AND MORBID CHARACTERS.

Are all normal characters mutually equivalent?—Attempt at classification according to their value—Marks of abnormal character: absence of unity, impossibility of prevision—Class I. Successive contradictory characters: anomalies, conversions; their psychological mechanism. Alternating characters — Second class: Contradictory coexistent characters. Incomplete form: contradiction between principles and tendencies. Complete form. Contradiction between one tendency and another—Third class: Unstable characters. Their physiological and psychological characters—Psychological infantilism.

In the works already quoted—those of Perez (1892), Paulhan (1894), and Fouillée (1895)—and in the preceding chapter, the various forms of character have been classified, described, traced back to explanatory principles. In spite of divergent interpretations and differences of nomenclature, there are types universally accepted: the active, the sensitive, the apathetic. But are they equivalent? Such is the question put in the first instance when we pass from normal to morbid characters. It seems to be implicitly admitted that, each type having its qualities and defects, its advantages and disadvantages, they ought to be placed on the same level. The writer who confines himself to classification and description may, by going no further, avoid the difficulty. But as soon as we enter the region of frankly morbid characters, we are led to ask, in the first place, whether the characters reputed normal are all so in the same degree, or whether some are not, by their very nature, nearer to pathological forms, and more apt to undergo a retrogressive metamorphosis; in other words, we have now to establish, not a classification, but a hierarchy, a valuation often disputed, and difficult to fix.

A Russian anthropologist, N. Seeland, is the only writer, so far as I know, who has taken up the question from this point of view. In fact, the ancient authors, when classifying temperaments, and consequently characters, only divided them into strong (the choleric and melancholic) and weak (the sanguine and phlegmatic).

This division (recently accepted by Wundt) is not at bottom very clear, and might give rise to numerous objections. Seeland has once for all broken with tradition and abandoned the quadripartite division; he "does not look upon all temperaments as having the same value, some approximating more to the idea of perfection, some less." [1] His classification is, therefore, in fact a hierarchy; and, beginning with the most perfect forms of character, may be briefly stated as follows [2]:—

I. The *strong* or *positive* temperaments, including—

1. The gay temperament, a type of which the classic "sanguine" is only a variety; it comprehends three species: (*a*) the strong sanguine, vegetative life predominant, reactions rapid but appropriate, adapted to their end, without agitation; (*b*) the weaker sanguine, resembling the preceding, but with a mixture of the nervous type, the reactions are less moderate and controlled; the French and the Poles belong to this division; (*c*) the serene temperament which stands midway between the strong sanguine and the phlegmatic, uniting the advantages of both.

2. The *phlegmatic* or calm temperament never rises above medium intensity, and presents a singular uniformity; it is a mass whose movement can neither be accelerated nor retarded: but calm does not exclude the possibility of strength; on the contrary, it presupposes it. As nations, the English, the Dutch, the Norwegians belong to this type.

---

[1] "It has been asserted that every temperament is equal to every other, and that all are equally necessary to the progress of humanity: I do not believe this."

[2] "Le tempérament au point de vue psychologique et anthropologique," a paper published (in French) in the *Bulletins du Congrès International d'Anthropologie*, iv. St. Petersburg, 1892, pp. 91-154.

II. We descend a degree lower with the *medium* or *neutral* temperament, "unknown to science, though that of the majority of men." It corresponds to the "balanced natures" of Paulhan, and to those whom elsewhere we call the amorphous, because they have no definite characteristic peculiar to themselves.

III. Lastly, we descend another step with the *weak* or negative characters. "Their reaction may be quick or slow, but what characterises them is the irregularity, the superfluity, and even the perversity of their manifestations. There are three varieties: (*a*) the pure melancholic, distinguished by sadness and apathy, without nervous symptoms, or at any rate, without dominant ones; (*b*) the nervous, versatile, with alternations of normal activity, and dejection, or excitement; (*c*) the choleric, which is not a genus, is tolerably rare and distinguished by irascibility, and may be combined with the melancholic or the weaker sanguine; the serene and the phlegmatic are incompatible with it."

In support of this classification follows a long anthropological inquiry, drawn up in six tables. Its subjects were 160 men and 40 women belonging to the four principal types, gay, phlegmatic, neutral, and melancholic. It includes comparative statistics of stature, chest measurement, neck and arm measurement, cubic capacity of the lungs, respiration, pulse, temperature, dynamometric pressure, cephalic indices, state of the senses, etc. The results are decidedly favourable to the gay and unfavourable to the melancholic temperament (see especially Table V., p. 114), the latter being ascertained to have less strength and less delicate senses, except as regards sensitiveness to pain. In women, the nervous group, which takes the place of the melancholic group in men, is the only one presenting any anomalies.

In his conclusions, this writer combats the "rooted tendency to seek the essence of the temperaments in the phenomena of the circulation and its satellite, the activity of tissues." Eight soldiers in good health, four of whom belonged to the gay, and four to the melancholic type, were kept by him on the same diet and carefully watched for three days: the result of the analysis of weight, secretions, and excretions "does not show that a more

rapid change of tissue took place in the case of the
sanguine than in that of the melancholic subjects."

Can so limited an experiment, and one of such short
duration, be called decisive?

However that may be, rejecting the chemical theory,
Seeland prefers a physical explanation. In his view, "the
nervous tissue, besides its general activity, possesses an
elementary life which is the basis of temperament and
character." Everything depends on the way in which the
nervous system responds to external or internal excitation.
The gay temperament would correspond to rapid and
harmonious molecular vibrations; the phlegmatic to vibrations less rapid, but of imperturbable regularity; the
neutral to slow but constant vibrations, and the negative
forms to slow and discordant, or rapid and interrupted
vibrations.

This arrangement in order of precedence is not free from
objection. I give it merely as an instance of a classification
according to the presumed value of characters, and as an
introduction to the study of the morbid forms which we
are about to commence.

I

In the first place, it is necessary to know by what signs
we can recognise whether a character deviates from the
normal types. Not to return to a subject already treated in
the preceding chapter, we may briefly say:

1. A true character is reducible to one characteristic, one
preponderant tendency which ensures its unity and stability
throughout life. This conception is somewhat ideal, but
definite characters tend, in varying degrees, to approximate
thereto.

2. In practice, a clearly defined character always (except
in rare cases, which explain themselves) permits us to foresee and foretell. We know beforehand what an active,
a sensitive, a phlegmatic, or a contemplative will do
under given circumstances. Neutrals, who are, properly
speaking, not characters at all, are acted on by events or
by other people, and calculations as to their future must
start from a point, not within, but outside them.

One, if not both of these marks, is wanting in abnormal

characters, and the further they depart from these two constituent conditions—unity and the possibility of foresight—
the further they depart from the typical forms, to become
at last unmistakably morbid.

We might be tempted to believe that the anomalies of
character, as observed, are so varied in aspect, so manifold,
as to elude all classification, so that it is impossible to
find our way through the chaos.   I think, however, that
the determining characteristics given above will supply us
with a clue.   It is scarcely necessary to say that I exclude
from the group of anomalies those slight, temporary, and
intermittent deviations which are only passing infractions of
the unity of character.   Cæsar, Richelieu, Napoleon were
well-defined types; yet, at certain points in their lives, they
ceased to be themselves.   On his journey to Elba, in face
of the fury and the insults of the populace, Napoleon had
moments of strange timidity.   Facts of this kind prove,
once more, that the complete character only exists as an
ideal; but an indisposition lasting a few hours cannot be
called an illness.   Having made this reserve, we may, in our
classification, follow the retrogressive march from co-ordinate
unity to multiplicity, from stability to dissolution, and we
thus have three groups departing more and more widely
from the normal forms: (1) successive contradictory
characters; (2) simultaneous contradictory characters; (3)
unstable or polymorphic characters: the last stage of
disaggregation.   It only remains to study them, one by
one, in their order.

By *successive* contradictory characters, I understand two
opposite forms or manners of feeling and acting, so that the
life taken as a whole seems to be that of two individuals,
one preceding, the other following the crisis.

Before dealing with the genuine cases, we must eliminate:

1. The apparently contradictory characters abounding
in political history, such as the triumvir Octavius and
emperor Augustus.   Cromwell, by turns an illuminated
mystic and a practical joker, retained, under these appearances, the fundamental tendencies of an entirely practical
nature.   So far from contradicting themselves and being unstable, the character is single and homogeneous throughout:
there is perfect unity in the aims: it is only in the means that
contradiction appears.   The moralist has a perfect right

to call them false characters, because they wear masks; for the psychologist they are quite normal and well marked. They may frequently be met with in ordinary life, and there one need not be an actor on a great stage to appear to contradict one's self; it is enough to be faithful to the end in view and unscrupulous in the choice of means. Those whom, in revolutionary times, fear makes suddenly cruel belong to the same category; their unity lies in the instinct of self-preservation.

2. The transformations produced by the evolution of life and the change of circumstances. Thus an active character may show itself successively in love, in dangerous adventures, in ambition, and in the pursuit of riches.

Having got rid of doubtful cases, we may divide the successive contradictory characters into two classes: the first including anomalies, the second pathological forms.

I. As, in our classification, we start from the normal state and gradually leave it behind us, we must begin with the modified forms which are simple deviations from the ideal of the character—*i.e.*, from a constant and undisturbed unity. Apart from all ideals, the successive characters are exceptional with regard to the generality of people; for even neutrals have throughout their lives a kind of unity, that of their perpetual plasticity.

In this first class I distinguish two cases. The reader may find these divisions and subdivisions excessively minute, yet they are necessary. There is no classification without distinctions, and it is impossible to follow a retrogressive order without marking every step on the way to dissolution.

1. The simplest case, and the nearest to the normal condition, consists in a change of direction in one and the same predominant tendency in the individual. Such is the case of Raymond Lulli, the change of the profane loves which occupied the first part of his life into the platonic and chivalrous love which filled the second; while the converse case, too, is not rare, and examples might be found among the mystics. Such are sincere conversions in religion or in politics (St. Paul, Luther). The same may be said of the cases where the fire of the temperament, having previously expended itself for good, now does so for evil,

or conversely.   All this, from the moralist's point of view, is a complete change—*i.e.*, there are two men ; from the psychologist's, it is simply a change of direction, and there is only one man.   It is easy to see that, under the two contrasts, there is a common foundation, a latent unity, the same quantity or the same quality of energy directed to different ends ; but we can recognise the chrysalis in the butterfly without difficulty.

2. These last are the modified forms ; the clear cases, which depart further from the rule, imply a fundamental and genuine duality—*e.g.*, the passage from a life of orgies to a *lasting* ascetic one (if it does not last, the change is only a passing accident), from active to contemplative life (Diocletian), from contemplative to active life (Julian the Apostate); in short, all the cases where men burn what they have worshipped and worship what they have burnt, where we find two individuals in the same person.   The common language calls this "a conversion."   It may be religious, moral, political, artistic, philosophical, scientific, etc., but it always consists in the substitution of one tendency or group of tendencies for the contrary, of one belief for its opposite, of one form of unity for another form, synonymous expressions which express the different psychological aspects of transformation.   We may note, in passing, that in men who have passed through two opposite phases, common opinion is only cognisant of one, usually the final, or else the one of longest duration and the most conspicuous, the other being overlooked.   We understand by St. Augustine, the man of the post-conversion, by Diocletian, the man of the pre-abdication period.   This judgment is founded on the need for simplification and unity of mind as applied to character.

How does this change, dividing life in extreme cases into two contradictory phases, come about?   It is impossible to reply in general terms ; each particular case supposes special conditions.   We may try, however, to determine, approximately, the causes oftenest in action.

First, the physical causes.   A serious illness may, by changing the constitution, transform the character, thus showing how far it depends on cœnæsthesia.   It is im- material whether we suppose the ultimate condition to consist of chemical (or nutritive), or of physical modifications, the latter being the view of Henle and Seeland. There are violent shocks, more especially injuries to the head, of which we shall take occasion to speak later on. Azam gives some examples of these metamorphoses.[1]   A steady, industrious man sustains a complicated fracture of the leg and subsequently becomes impulsive and ill-tempered; the author supposes that there must have been cerebral ischæmia.   Another, under similar circumstances, exchanges a cheerful disposition for incurable melancholia. Persistent facial neuralgia has transformed a thoroughly kind-hearted man into a spiteful and morose being.

We now come to the moral causes.   They appear to act like a shock whose effect is either immediate or falls due some time later; hence the change is either sudden or consequent on a long incubation.   The type of the former is found in conversions following an unforeseen crisis: St. Paul and his vision, Pascal and his accident, Raymond Lulli and the revelation of one of his mistresses; the Spanish nobleman, Maraña, whose story has so often been told, who, for half his life, was a Don Juan, and was suddenly changed by listening to church music.   The "sudden conversions" of theologians involve a psycho-logical truth.   Those of the second type do not take place all at once, but after a struggle between the old and new tendencies.   St. Augustine, Luther, Loyola, Francisco de Borgia, who, on seeing the corpse of his empress (Charles V.'s wife), resolved to renounce the world, but did not do so for many years after.   To these illustrious names each reader may add for himself less known ones from among his own acquaintances.

We may ask whether even the most sudden changes are, in truth, as much so as they seem, if they have not their antecedent conditions in the life of the individual in question, and are not the accelerated result of a sub-conscious process.   Whatever we may think, the psycho-logical mechanism of conversions is very similar to that of irresistible impulses.   In its complete evolution it passes through three stages: (1) the conception of an opposite aim or ideal; this may happen to any one without lasting or leading to action; this state will produce no effect if it merely passes through the mind.   (2) This conception must

[1] *Le Caractère dans les Maladies*, p. 188 *et seq.*

become a *fixed* idea, with the permanence, the predominance, the overmastering possession, which are the peculiarities of such ideas. (3) The action takes place because already
included in the fixed idea, and because the fixed idea is a
belief, and all beliefs presuppose something existing or
about to exist. In short, there is no result till the idea
becomes an impulse. In the cases where the individual is,
so to speak, struck by lightning, the impetuous movement
of the passion springs up suddenly and triumphs immediately. This is yet another point of resemblance to the
irresistible impulses which pass into action, sometimes after
a period of struggle, sometimes in a sudden ecstasy.

There is, in any case, this difference, that the new
character—*i.e.*, new ways of feeling, thinking, and acting—
is lasting. This could not be, if in both stages, incubation
and eruption, a profound change had not taken place in
the individual constitution. Conversions do not create a
new tendency, but they show that the greatest antitheses
are latent in us, and that one may replace the other, not
by an act of the will, which is always precarious, but by
a radical transformation of our sensibility.

2. This division includes the *alternating* characters,
whose phases sometimes succeed one another with such
rapidity and frequency as to approximate to the simultaneous contradictory characters. Instead of two different
characters, one before and one after the crisis, whose
formula for the whole life of the individual would be
A, B, we have the alternation of two forms of character,
with or without intermediary crises, and the formula would
be A, B, A, B, and so on.

This alternation is found in the normal or quasi-normal
state, but is too fugitive or too difficult to fix, to be
distinguished from the unstable characters; but the case is
not the same with the morbid types which show it in an
exaggerated form. Such are the phenomena so much
studied in our own day, under the name of alterations,
diseases, disorders of personality. They will be known to
the reader, but they are not altogether germane to our
subject, and I only touch upon them in order to elucidate
a particular point, the variations of character.

In cases of alternating personality we may consider either
the physiological changes, which are rather obscure, or

the intellectual changes, which have been referred, on the whole, to the memory, or the emotional changes, which have been somewhat neglected and in some observations omitted altogether. It is these last alone which interest us, because they may be summed up as alternations of character.

If, in fact, we take complete observations, it will be seen that the two personalities (there are sometimes more) do not consist merely in the alternation of two memories, but also in that of two distinct and usually opposite affective dispositions. Azam's celebrated Félida is, in her first state, gloomy, cold, and reserved; in her second, cheerful, talkative, lively to the point of coquetry and boisterousness. In the case of Mary Reynolds, reported by Weir Mitchell, we have first a melancholy, silent, retiring woman; then, in her new personality, "her disposition is totally and absolutely changed," she is fond of pleasure, noisy, always seeking company, except when taking long rides and walks through the woods and over the mountains, delighting in the spectacle of nature and absolutely unconscious of fear. These alternations lasted for sixteen years, after which "the emotional opposition between the two states seems gradually to have effaced itself," and resolved itself into a medium state between the two—"a well-balanced temperament," which for a quarter of a century coincided with her now permanent second state. We may also recall the well-known case of L. V., who *spontaneously* showed at the same time two opposite forms of character : at one time, talkative, arrogant, violent, brutal, insubordinate, a thief, ready to kill any one who gave him an order; at another, gentle, polite, silent, sober, of an almost child-like timidity. I say, spontaneously, for MM. Bourru and Burot have *artificially* produced physical modifications in V. which are accompanied by some modifications in his character; but I am only speaking of natural changes. For other instances I refer the reader to special works on the alteration of personality.

I am inclined to believe that alternations of memory, though the strongest and most disturbing phenomena, result from an alternation of the affective dispositions (in other words, of the character), which themselves result from physiological changes, so that, in the last resort, we arrive at cœnæsthesia as the ultimate cause. When we see, *e.g.*, that in L. V. the violent character always accompanies hemiplegia and anæsthesia on the right side, and the gentle character, hemiplegia and anæsthesia on the left side, not to mention the partial modifications accompanying the paraplegia, total anæsthesia, etc., artificially produced in the hypnotic state, it is difficult not to admit that changes in memory, in character, and in physical habit form an almost indissoluble whole, which is also the conclusion drawn by Bourru and Burot from their experiments.

In default of positive proofs that the change of cœnæsthesia is primordial in these alternations of character, we may compare them with a mental disease, where the alternation, being still simpler, allows us more easily to detect its physiological conditions. This is that duplex form of madness, sometimes called *folie circulaire*, or "alternating insanity," etc. It consists in the regular alternation of two periods, that of depression and that of exaltation. The transition from one to the other is instantaneous, or takes place by imperceptible gradations, but nothing can be clearer than the contrast between the two periods.

During the depression, the affective symptoms are: melancholy, feeling of fatigue, torpor, indifference, vague terror, uneasiness with regard to everything. Physically, the patient is emaciated, aged, broken down, the temperature is lowered, and there is an enormous decrease in the pulse, the secretions and excretions, and the weight of the body, the latter going down as much as ten pounds in one week.

During the period of excitement the reverse takes place, point for point : a feeling of well-being, joy, pride, exuberant activity; the patient looks younger, grows stout, and his organic functions go on extensively and regularly. "This contrast," says an alienist, "is one of the most curious and interesting peculiarities of mental medicine."[1]

Here the connection between the affective disposition and the somatic state is quite clear, and seems to be referable to a tropho-neurosis of the brain (Schüle, Krafft-Ebing). It must be recognised that this disease, which is the extreme form, and the alternations of personality, which are modified forms, supply us with none but pathological

---

[1] Régis, *Maladies mentales*, p. 200.

examples; but the germs of morbid manifestations are present in normal life. Unfortunately, these alternations are only perceptible where strongly marked, and therefore none but exaggerated cases can be quoted. Compared to the successive characters, where the second has destroyed the first, the alternating characters mark a new stage on the road to dissolution, and form a transition to our second group—the *coexistent* contradictory characters.

II.

They consist in the coexistence of two opposite tendencies of equal force and mutually incompatible; there are two characters, two contradictory springs of action, and, tested by our practical criterion, there are, in any given circumstances, two possible and equally probable courses to be foreseen. They differ, both from the successive characters, in which the second man has eliminated the first, and from the alternating characters, which occupy the stage, in turn, *exclusively*, and for some time. They present themselves under two principal forms.

1. The first form is not a pure or complete type. It is the result of a contradiction between thought and feeling, between theory and practice, between principle and tendency. Nothing is less rare, and I need scarcely adduce examples: the contrast between a man's private and public life, between his aspect as a scientific man and his aspect as a believer. One who, in a question of scientific proof, is quite intractable, will show, in religion or in love, an unparalleled simplicity and ingenuousness. As for those who loudly profess any given doctrine, and contradict it by their actions, there is no lack of them. Schopenhauer, in theory a pessimist and misogynist, penetrated with compassion for all living beings, a professed ascetic, was nothing of the sort in practice. He is an instance of unreconciled contradiction, to which we may oppose the perfect unity of a Spinoza.

A man who was, *ex hypothesi*, entirely intellectual, and yet (if that were possible) capable of acting, would, by his constitution, escape this contradictory duality. The magistrate, observed by Esquirol, who, though perfectly lucid in mind, had lost all sensibility, and was "as indifferent to his family and everything else as to a theorem of Euclid," approximates to it. We find modified forms of the same in the apathetic-intellectual division.

But this contradictory duality is so common that we should not venture to insist on it were it not that it completely exposes the inanity of the widespread prejudice that it is sufficient to inculcate principles, rules, and ideas, in order to make them result in action. No doubt, authority, education, law, have no other means of influencing men; but these means, by themselves, are not efficacious; they may succeed, or they may fail. The question which the experiment is intended to solve amounts to this: Do the intellectual character (if there are, as some writers admit, such things as intellectual characters, properly speaking) and the emotional keep an even rate of progress?

2. The second form is pure and complete; it involves a deeper contradiction because subsisting between two ways of feeling, two tendencies, two modes of action, one of which is the negative of the other. These characters bring us to our last group, the unstable; there are incoherent beings who will not or cannot resolve the contradiction in them. One of the commonest instances is that of those men who carry to an extreme degree both religious sincerity and licentiousness of conduct. Popular opinion judges them severely and considers them hypocrites, thus confounding two very distinct cases, that of voluntary dissimulation and that of incurable contradiction. The religious and the sexual sentiment, both deeply rooted in their natures, act on them, each in its turn; and they make no attempt to reconcile the two. We may also mention those men who are divided between the craving for activity and that for repose, passing incessantly from the one to the other; the lover who feels for his mistress at the same time an ardent love and a violent contempt. In towns and countries where the monarchical sentiment is still deeply rooted we find an analogous state of mind in some subjects, who feel an unutterable loyalty to the throne and a profound contempt for the person of the king. In studying the "composite characters," Paulhan reminds us that Rubens, calm, tranquil, and of decent behaviour in practical life, became a prey to a tragic fermentation as soon as he seized his brush. It has been said of a celebrated contemporary

(Wagner) that he had in him "the instincts of an ascetic and of a satyr, cravings for love and hatred, an appetite for enjoyment and a thirst for the ideal, a haughty dignity and a cringing courtiership, a mixture of devotion and base treachery." This portrait might suit many others. It denotes something more than a contradictory duality, for it cannot be reduced to two essential points; but it is not yet the genuine type of the unstable.

If we might trust certain authors, the cause of simultaneous contradictory characters would be very simple, being due merely to the dual form of the brain. It is known that the two cerebral hemispheres, even when normal, are asymmetrical, differing in weight, in the distribution of the arteries, and in functional importance, the left having the preponderance; that hallucinations may be unilateral or bilateral, vary in character, etc. In short, cerebral dualism is undeniable; but that it should suffice to explain the duality of character is a hypothesis of such exceeding *naïveté* that I am unwilling to waste any time in discussing it.

An explanation drawn from psychology is less simple, but also less easily overthrown. To understand how characters are constituted, the following process seems to me the best. Let us take as our starting-point the well-balanced, "completely unified" characters, which present a graduated co-ordination of the various tendencies. The first step towards a break is marked by the predominance of a single tendency: the character is active, contemplative, sensitive, etc. It is still a unity; but, instead of a convergent unity which may be compared to a federation, we have a unity of preponderance reminding us of an absolute monarchy. A second decisive step is marked by the appearance of two dominant tendencies, but, to fulfil the conditions, they must be contradictory. Thus, Miguel Cervantes, who, after a life of chivalrous adventure, became the great novelist, gives us an instance of a complex and composite but by no means contradictory nature. The contradiction is found in cases analogous to that of the devout libertine, because, while asserting in words the rule of morals prescribed by his religion, he denies it by his acts. Hence two un-coordinated tendencies. Yet this is only the exaggeration of a perfectly normal occurrence. A man of grave demeanour may have sudden fits of mad spirits; another may be seized upon by a passion at variance with all his habits. If this transitory, episodic state becomes stable and permanent, the contradictory character is established. This transformation may be assigned to circumstances. I believe that it is still more dependent on innate tendencies inherent in the individual constitution, which are only developed by opportunity.

Speaking decisively, we may maintain, without paradox, that these characters are or are not contradictory, according to the point of view adopted. They are so for the logic of the intellect, but not for the logic of the feelings.

When we judge a contradictory character, whether our own or another person's, we are apt to proceed *objectively ;* we ascertain in the individual the simultaneous existence of two governing ideas, one of which negatives the other; we rationally declare this to be illogical, because the principle of contradiction is the pith of all our affirmations, and the logic of the intellect rests on it.

The logic of the feelings is *subjective ;* it is ruled by the principle of finality or adaptation. The individual, as a purely emotional being, aims at one end only, the satisfaction of his desires; and in him every special tendency makes for its own special end, its own special good. If, therefore, the scholar, moved by the love of truth, strives after strict truth, and moved by a strong religious sentiment, satisfies himself with childish beliefs, there is not and cannot be any contradiction between these two desires; the discrepancy exists only objectively, in the region of ideas.

The logic of the feelings also has its illogicalities, but of another sort, and I can only find two: (1) when an isolated tendency, in attaining its end, is the cause of injury or ruin to the whole individual; and (2) when the individual is quite content with his own destruction, as in the case of the "luxury of grief," which we have studied elsewhere, and whose highest term is the fascination of suicide.

III.

Unstable or polymorphic characters cannot be called "characters" except by an abuse of that word, for there is neither unity, stability, nor possibility of prevision. How will they act? Every fresh moment brings us face to face with another enigma. In fact, we have here to do with the decay of character, and all the specimens given in this group are pathological.

It is needless to describe them, for they are self-evident. Their principal types are to be met with in the hysterical, whose Protean psychology has so often and so thoroughly been studied that we need not dwell on it; in the adventurer, whose history, with its numberless variations, is, in the main, always the same, and may be summarised thus: precocity, insubordination at home or at school, frequent flights, inaptitude for all sustained work; he passes suddenly from enthusiasm to disgust, tries everything in turn and drops it, drifting at the caprice of impulse or circumstance, till some final catastrophe lands him in the prisoner's dock or the lunatic asylum.

The causes of this instability are either congenital or acquired.

The spasmodic diathesis, as Maudsley calls it, is most usually innate. It is characterised by the various symptoms comprised under the name of degeneration, grouped as physical and psychical stigmata; they are too well known to need enumeration.

The instability acquired in the course of life is left behind by certain maladies, especially injuries or shocks to the brain, and above all, lesions of the frontal lobe. Such is the conclusion resulting from the observations of David Ferrier, Boyer, Lépine, and others. More recently, Allen Starr,[1] out of forty-six cases, has ascertained that, in twenty-three, the only symptoms were mental obtuseness, impossibility of attention, irritability, un-coordinated and impulsive acts, absence of voluntary control and the loss of inhibitory power, phenomena specially coinciding with lesions on the left side of the frontal region.

M. Paulhan, in his book on Characters, when studying those whom he calls the unquiet, the nervous, and the contradictory (*contrariants*), gives several instances; among others, Alfred de Musset, from his own portrait, confirmed by that given by G. Sand. Let us listen to each of them in turn.

" When these frightful scenes were over, a strange love,

---

[1] *Brain*, No. 32, p. 570, and *Brain Surgery* (1863), chap. i.

an exaltation carried to excess, made me treat my mistress as a divinity. A quarter of an hour after I had insulted her I was at her knees; as soon as I ceased to accuse her I asked her pardon; the moment I was no longer uttering bitter words I burst into tears" (Musset). "His re-actions were sudden and violent in proportion to the acuteness of his joys. . . . One might have thought that two souls were engaged in a desperate contest as to which should animate his body. . . . It was an invariable rule, unheard of, but absolute in this strange organisation, that, sleep changing all his resolutions, he would go to rest with his heart full of tenderness, and awaken in the morning eager for battle and murder; but if he had left in the evening cursing, he returned next morning to bless" (G. Sand). Hence, and from analogous cases, Paulhan concludes that "these types result from the predominance of association by contrast." It seems to me impossible to refer the psychology of the unstable, and of the contra-dictory characters which come nearest to them, to this single fact. In the first place, association by contrast is not a primary fact. Psychologists are right in connecting it in-directly with association by resemblance, sometimes mixed with elements of contiguity. Furthermore, contrasts only exist in couples, and in the "nervous, unquiet, and contra-dictory" there is not merely a transition from contrast to contrast, but from difference to difference—they traverse the whole scale. Lastly, association by contrast only has a precise form as an *intellectual* phenomenon, and it could not be maintained that love, as a representation, would suggest the *representation* of violence, or the *idea* of jealousy that of indifference. Here the association of ideas is only an effect, a result, a rendering to the consciousness of deeper occurrences belonging to the emotional or even the organic part of us. If Musset, having represented George Sand to himself as a divinity, rages at her immediately afterwards, as a brutal planter might at a slave, his change of attitude is in his feelings, not in his thoughts. I see rather the effect of a rapid but partial exhaustion,—a frequent occurrence in unbalanced natures. If we insist on retaining the word contrast, it will have to be taken, not in its psychological sense, but in that given to it by physiologists when they speak of "successive contrast," and attribute it, rightly or wrongly, to the fatigue of certain portions of the retina.

The formula which, in my opinion, sums up and explains the unstable is this: *psychological infantilism.* We might also call it arrest of development, but this latter expression would not be applicable to all cases.

If, in fact, we consider the distinctive marks of the character of children, apart from exceptions, we find, first, mobility. They wish for one thing, and then another and another; they pass rapidly from one extreme to the opposite, from eagerness to disgust, from laughter to tears; the character is an un-coordinated bundle of appetites and wishes, each of which, in turn, drives out the rest. Then there is weakness or total absence of will under its higher inhibitory form, which rules and co-ordinates. Are they impulsive for want of inhibition, or incapable of controlling themselves through the excess of their impulses? Both these cases are met with, and the result is the same. The formula of their character, which we need not enumerate in detail, is the same as that of the unstable—*i.e.,* there is no constituted character.

The term *infantilism* is equally applicable to the congenital and the acquired forms. The former have never left their childhood behind, the latter return to it; they are on the same level, the first through not having climbed high enough, the second through having descended too far. In the one case we have arrested development, in the other retrogression. It is no objection to say that this instability has often been met with in minds of a superior calibre; genius is one thing, character another, and we are here dealing with character only. The populace, who, struck by the incoherence of their conduct, call these people "grown-up children," have hit on the right expression, without any subtleties of analysis.

In short, beginning with the *true* character (*i.e.,* the affirmation of a personality under a stable form consistent with itself), which is never completely realised, or free from transient eclipses, there are all possible shades of deviation from unity and stability, till we reach that stage of un-coordinated multiplicity at which character has either not come into being or has ceased to exist.

CHAPTER XIV.

THE DECAY OF THE AFFECTIVE LIFE.

Law of Decay: its formula, and its general application in psychology—Difficulties where the affective life is concerned — Successive disappearance of the disinterested emotions (the æsthetic and intellectual), of the altruistic (moral and social), the ego-altruistic (religious feeling, ambition, etc.), and lastly, the egoistic—Converse proof: cases of arrested development—Theory of degeneration —Its relation to decay.

AT the opening of this work I gave a general survey of the evolution of the affective life; at its close we have to undertake a task of an opposite nature: the survey of its decay. Does this take place at haphazard, varying from one man to another? or does it follow a regular and ascertainable course? Is it reducible to any formula which can be referred to a law?

The law of decay, in psychology, consists in a continuous retrogression, descending from the higher to the lower, from the complex to the simple, from the unstable to the stable, from the most to the least organised; in other words, those manifestations which are the latest in date of evolution are the first to disappear; while those which were the first to appear are the last to vanish. Evolution and decay follow opposite courses.

I have already shown that the slow and continuous disappearance of memory verifies this formula, and, as a converse proof, that, in the rare cases where this faculty is recovered, the restoration proceeds, step by step, in the opposite direction, up the path previously descended. The methodical process of decay is still better seen in motor psychology. I may perhaps be permitted, by way of elucidation and preparation, to recapitulate briefly what I have detailed at greater length elsewhere: motor retrogression in the well-known case of drunkenness. There is, first, a period of excitement, even of exuberant spirits, which is the very antithesis of reflection; that is to say that attention under its highest form, as the result of a motor convergence, can no longer exist. Next, a man can no longer control his tongue, he tells all his secrets; the will, under its higher, inhibitory form, has disappeared. After this, he becomes incapable of any continuous plan or action: the will, even under its lower or impulsive form, remains powerless. Then the most delicate voluntary movements, those of speech and of the hands, cease to be co-ordinated. One degree lower, he loses the semi-automatic movements, those of walking: he staggers and loses his balance. Still lower, the muscular tonicity is weakened, he falls from his seat under the table; then the reflex movements are abolished; and finally, if the condition is continued long enough, there is cessation of the automatic movements—those of respiration and of the heart. Here is a well-marked, easily determinable retrograde process, the psychological function of the movements being comparatively simple.

The object of this chapter is to prove that the disappearance of feelings, when it takes place gradually and continuously, in consequence of age or of some slowly evolved malady (general paralysis, senile dementia, etc.), conforms to the same law. But, by reason of the complexity of the affective life, the question presents some difficulties which we must first of all point out.

The first is this: May not affective retrogression be simply the consequence of an intellectual retrogression? or must we take it as primary, independent, and self-determined, not secondary and consequent upon the decay of intellect? Or else—and this view appears to me the most probable—do both cases occur? It is impossible to give a categorical answer; the two elements, the intellectual and the affective, being closely associated. Yet, as retrogression is irremediable and results from organic decay or waste, the presumption is rather in favour of a gradual extinction of the tendencies.

The second difficulty is at least equally important. We have admitted that in every normal person all the primary tendencies exist; but their coexistence does not imply their equality. Experience proves this. The individual character results from the preponderance of one or more tendencies: the æsthetic or the sexual, the moral or the religious; one man is constitutionally timid, and another choleric. It follows from this that all cases of retrogression are not strictly comparable with one another; for it is evident that the dominant tendency is better able than the rest to withstand shocks and assaults, and to resist destructive action. This, in my opinion, explains how it is that—as in a case mentioned below—the æsthetic sentiment, one of the most delicate and latest in formation, is of very late extinction in an artist. This apparent exception is, in fact, a confirmation of the law.

The ideal case for illustrating our subject would be this: An average man, all of whose tendencies are nearly equipollent, is struck down by a disease involving slow retrogression, so that the order in which the feelings are weakened and extinguished can be noted; then the decadence stops short, and is followed by a restoration of the affective life, which can be followed, step by step, in its gradual ascent, so as to ascertain whether it is or is not the repetition, in reversed order, of the period of dissolution. The search for such a case, however, would be no less than the pursuit of a chimera. The only practical method would be to collect a great number of observations on different patients, and thus draw up a schematic table of decay, analogous to Galton's composite photographs—formed by the accumulation of resemblances and the elimination of individual differences. This is what I shall try to do, as far as the extreme scarcity of material and the difficulties of an unexplored subject will permit. I shall first examine dissolution properly so called; then, by way of converse proof, the arrest of development.

I.

As the decay of the feelings progresses from the higher to the lower, from complex adaptation to simple adaptation, gradually narrowing the area of the affective life, we may, in this decadence, distinguish four phases, marked by the successive disappearance of (1) the disinterested emotions, (2) the altruistic emotions, (3) the ego-altruistic emotions, and (4) the purely egoistic emotions.

(1.) I class under the first head the æsthetic emotions and the higher forms of intellectual emotions, which aim at no practical or utilitarian end, but are luxuries, not necessaries of life. Æsthetic and scientific cravings are so slightly marked, and so far from imperative in the majority of men, that it is impossible to demonstrate with certainty that they are the first to disappear; but it may be indirectly inferred.

It cannot be denied that those who have a passion for art or science, and for whom these are necessary conditions of life, are extremely rare compared with those who are moved or possessed by love, the desire for riches, or ambition. In the mass of men the æsthetic and intellectual feelings remain in a rudimentary condition, or attain only a slight, at most a medium development, and it cannot be said with certainty when they become extinct, seeing they have never really existed. Compared with the higher forms, they resemble a case of arrested development, *i.e.*, of retrogression; and this arrest of development is the rule, as it must be for all tendencies beyond the bounds of the mere necessities of life.

To this negative proof I may add other positive proofs.

Age and diseases whose effect is retrogressive diminish, if they do not annihilate, zeal, enthusiasm, the impulse towards creation, discovery, or the simple enjoyment of art, and the curiosity which is always on the alert. I omit some very rare exceptions, each of which would require individual examination. In the majority of men weakened vitality at once destroys all taste for the superfluous.

We must also note the decided hostility to all innovations—new forms of art, new discoveries, new ways of stating or treating scientific questions—which comes on with old age. The fact is so well known as to make proof unnecessary. As a general thing, in art especially, every generation rejects that which follows it. The usual explanation of this "misoneism" is that there is a fixed cerebral constitution, organised intellectual habits. Yes—but if the proposed new scientific or artistic ideal caused a true, deep, intense emotion, it would break down and sweep away the barriers of habit. There would be a shock, a turning upside down, a conversion. Cases of a rupture with the artistic or scientific past sometimes occur, but rarely, as they presuppose the possibility of a violent shock and the revival of an imperious passion, but turned in another direction. This repulsion for novelty is rather of emotional than of intellectual origin; it is a sign of the weakening of the affective life, and of a tendency towards diminished effort, repose, inertia.

(2.) The altruistic feelings (social and moral emotions) having a practical value, and being reckoned among the conditions of human existence, it is much easier to fix the moment of their partial or total decay. Now, the preceding groups apart, they are the first to disappear. They may have been altered or extinct for a long period, while the ego-altruistic, and still more the egoistic tendencies, are still intact. We have seen, again and again, how quickly persons become unsociable and ungovernable through dementia, general paralysis, melancholia, epilepsy, hysteria, shock, and injuries to the head.

But their retrogression takes place by gradations to be determined by observation alone.[1]

Case 1. "F—— entered the asylum December 20, 1889, suffering from general paralysis, which took the form of dementia. He was an intelligent, well-educated man, capable of filling a brilliant position in society. Being a gifted musician, he became well known as a violoncellist and his playing was long an attraction at the most frequented concerts. What especially struck one in this patient on his admission was his utter indifference to all about him—doctors, nurses, and patients alike. When shown an aged dementia patient who was dying he was neither touched nor disturbed, but simply remarked, 'There's one of 'em going to croak' ('*En voilà un qui va claquer*'). To suggestions that he should leave the asylum and mingle again in society, he never returned any other answer than 'I like my own comfort too well—I wish people would leave me in peace.' The more general altruistic feelings, therefore, would seem at this date to have vanished; but family affection, especially filial love, is still intact. F——

[1] I owe these observations to the kindness of Dr. Dumas, who collected them with a view to a special study of the decay of feeling.

incessantly speaks of his father, wants to write to him, to see him. On being shown his picture he burst into tears. The personal feelings are still intact, the love of liberty, and the instinct of self-preservation in all its forms.

"Jan. 15, 1891 (a year and a half later). F—— is now in the *gâteux* ward. The feelings already ruined or destroyed have not reappeared. Retrogression has gone on almost uninterruptedly. F—— no longer speaks of his father, and if spoken to about him he replies with indifference. One day, all his family being assembled at the foot of his bed, he recognised each of his relations and spoke to them by name, but showed no emotion whatever; the moment of separation left him as indifferent as their arrival had found him.

"Even the egoistic feelings are now impaired; he no longer demands freedom of movement. Eating is the only thing that interests him; he devours ravenously, and, after his meals, picks up the crumbs which have fallen on the bed-clothes. The nutritive instinct is the last surviving.

"Yet, in this patient, the artistic feeling long remains unimpaired, for the reason indicated above, viz., that it is the direct expression of his temperament, and an essential part of his *ego:* because he is an artist.

"Two months after his admission into the asylum, though devoid of social tendencies and generous feeling, he was still able to co-ordinate his movements and play his old tunes on the violoncello. One day, in the garden, he was found gazing ecstatically at the blue sky, flecked with small white clouds; he was saying, 'How beautiful it is! how beautiful it is!' Nothing else, by-the-bye, could be got from him that day. Chance having brought the famous violinist X—— as a visitor to the asylum about a month before F.'s death, he was asked to play to the latter. The patient had been, for some time, in the last stage of insanity and was past understanding anything, yet he understood this, and when he heard the familiar airs of old times played on the violin his eye became clear, and for a minute the mind seemed to have found itself again under the influence of art."

Case 2. "Ph. R——, aged 70, suffering from senile dementia, was up to this age an intelligent, peaceable, respectable citizen. At the last elections he presented himself as a candidate for the Chamber, and, in spite of the protests of his family, placed himself at the head of an Anarchist group, and drew up a programme which we will not inflict on the reader. He claimed to have received 700 votes. However that may be, it became necessary to place him in seclusion. His political and social tendencies perished in the first catastrophe, but his domestic feelings still remained intact. He spoke of his family with a touching simplicity. A letter written to his brother-in-law (too long for reproduction here, but very sensible) furnishes through-out irrefragable proofs of this. Gradually these feelings became weaker, the disease progressed rapidly, he became dirty in his habits, and the only function now remaining is the genera-tive instinct in its simplest form, as masturbation."

In the following cases intellectual retrogression seems to precede and determine the affective evolution :—

Case 3. " D——, a general paralytic, on his admission into the asylum, is fond of talking of the 3000 francs he has invested ; he is much occupied with the dividends and coupons now due which he ought to have received. On inquiries being made all this was found to be accurate. He had, therefore, a tolerably clear idea of property, since this idea was suggested by the image of certain papers representing the values involved. At a later period, when spoken to about his 3000 francs, he had forgotten everything and did not understand. When reminded of what he had himself said, and that he possessed the values guaranteed by the receipts, he understood no more than before. But D—— carries money about with him, and knows very well how much he has at the time. ' For ten centimes,' he says, ' I can have a cup of coffee every day, and I have three francs.' The sight of a white, shining metal is sufficient to awaken in him the idea of possession represented by the pleasure to be bought with it." Three months later he no longer understands even this third degree of possession : possession with him means having something to eat ; the piece of bread which he is holding in his hand and greedily devouring is the only thing he cannot be induced to give up.

Case 4. " M——, formerly employed in the *octroi;* paralytic dementia. During the first few days after his admission he gave himself up to political divagations, spoke much of universal suffrage, and especially of liberty. When asked for a defini-tion of this word he gave the following explanation : ' Liberty is the right to do what one wishes.' A short time after this he ceased to make speeches and seemed to collapse. He was no longer capable of giving his definition, or of understanding it ; when pressed with questions he said at last, ' Liberty is being able to walk about in the yard.' The abstract idea is replaced by a concrete idea indicating an assemblage of movements. Later still, a few days before his death, he answered the same question with, ' Being free is when any one is in bed ; I shall be free when I am in bed.' The idea of liberty, therefore, was at last confused in his mind with that of a vague state of comfort."

These observations show how the group of altruistic

sentiments dissolves piecemeal, and the affective sphere narrows itself more and more. The first to disappear are the vaguest and weakest of all the forms of benevolence—those embracing the whole human race; then the family emotions, which are more stable, more restricted, more frequently repeated; finally, there is absolute indifference to every one.[1]

(3.) The ego-altruistic emotions (to employ H. Spencer's terminology) form a group whose limits are vague, floating, and indecisive. It is even uncertain whether it exists as a distinct group or simply corresponds to a particular "moment" in the evolution of complex emotions. Without arguing this point, or attaching any importance to it, I employ this formula, because it is a convenient one in following step by step the retrogression from pure altruism to pure egoism.

Sexual love is a fairly good representative of the group. Need we say that, appearing later than the other instincts, it disappears before them, thus being in strict conformity with the law of retrogression. It does not belong to childhood, but neither does it to old age. We must eliminate the survivals and *simulacra*, which are only a factitious product of imagination; we are dealing with the tendency under its normal and complete form, with *all* its physiological and psychological conditions.

The religious sentiment in its medium forms, neither too coarse nor too subtle, belongs also to this category, plunging

[1] "When the mind undergoes degeneration, the moral feeling is the first to show it, as it is the last to be restored when the disorder passes away; the latest and highest gain of mental evolution, it is the first to witness by its impairment to mental dissolution. . . . In undoing a mental organisation, nature begins by unravelling the finest, most delicate, most intricately woven, and last completed threads of her marvellously complex network. Were the moral sense as old and firmly fixed an instinct as the instinct to walk upright, or the more deeply planted instinct of propagation,—as many people in the presumed interests of morality have tried to persuade themselves and others that it is,—it would not be the first to suffer in this way when mental degeneration begins; its categorical imperative would not take instant flight at the first assault, but would assert its authority at a later period of the decline; but, being the last acquired and the least fixed, it is most likely to vary, not only . . . in the pathological way of degeneracy, but also . . . in physiological ways, according to the diversities of conditions in which it is placed." (Maudsley, *Body and Will*, p. 266.)

its roots deeply into the individual, but in order to rise beyond him. Of its two constituent elements, love tends towards the dispossession of the individual; the other, fear, towards strict egoism; with retrogression, the latter becomes exclusive. The believer, especially in the melancholic state, at first complains of being wanting in pity, fervour, love of God; he no longer finds consolation in prayer. Thus, as decadence increases, or simply in consequence of age and the approach of death, the egoistic anxiety about personal salvation becomes imperious. This was the time of life when the kings, princes, and lords of the Middle Ages multiplied pious foundations—monasteries, churches, and hospitals; and the same thing still takes place, in our own day, in religions which admit of the efficacy of works in purchasing salvation, and of prayers for the dead. The religious feeling thus comes back to fear, its primary form in evolution. We might also note the frequent survival of observances and rites when the *true* feeling has disappeared, *i.e.*, the solidity of the organic and automatic element. In a retrograding religion, dogma dissolves before outward acts of worship, which, as we have seen, is the inversion of the evolutionary process.

Ambition is the type of the higher form of egoism; but as it must take into account the nature of other men and employ them in carrying out its designs, it is a modified form of egoism. We know how tenacious and durable is this passion in its numerous forms—the pursuit of power, honour, renown, riches; in it we have a foretaste of the stability of egoism after the ruin of all other tendencies. It disappears when the stage is reached when man sincerely declares himself disgusted with everything, and speaks like the author of Ecclesiastes. The greatest of the Cordovan Caliphs, Abderrhaman III., who noted down the principal events of this life, wrote: "I have reigned fifty years in peace and in war, loved by my people, feared by my enemies, respected by my allies, seeing my friendship sought for by the greatest kings on earth. Nothing have I lacked that the heart of man could desire—neither glory, nor power, nor pleasures. Yet, having counted the days in this long life in which I enjoyed unalloyed happiness, I found that there were fourteen." But this contempt for human interests comes late, and springs rather from weak ness than from wisdom. Men renounce the world, not so much because they have weighed it and estimated it at its true value, as because they no longer have the courage to conquer or keep it. Except in the case of philosophers, the disappearance of all ambition is the first symptom of the decadence of the egoistic tendencies: it indicates weariness, exhaustion, and a want of faith in one's self.

(4.) The last group, that of the strictly egoistic feelings, the most general and most firmly organised of all, is the last to disappear. The threefold group formed by the offensive instinct (anger), the defensive instincts (fear), and the nutritive cravings, persists in men and animals up to the farthest limit of consciousness. We know that anger makes its appearance later than fear; does it vanish earlier? I have no data to enable me to reply to this question. What is certain is that the affective states associated with nutrition last to the end, and that all remaining activity is concentrated in them, as shown by the cases above quoted. The fact, moreover, is so well known that there is no need to dwell on it.

II.

We have just seen how the process of decay, beginning at the top of the building, gradually destroys all its storeys, one after another, as it descends to the foundations. It would be interesting to ascertain whether the work of restoration would follow, as it ought, the inverse order; but, when decay has fully accomplished its task, all is over, without hope of recovery. We only meet with partial and fragmentary cases of restoration. In the absence of this converse proof we may proceed from below upwards, not to retrace the normal evolution of the affective life, which has already been done, but to consider the cases in which this evolution remains in a rudimentary state, or becomes abortive at various stages of its ascending progress, *i.e.*, in idiots, imbeciles, feeble-minded persons, human beings of incomplete development.

In the lowest stage, that of the complete idiot, all instincts are wanting, even that of nutrition. In infancy idiots only learn to take the breast with difficulty. At a more advanced age, there are some who feel neither hunger nor thirst; the sight of food fails to awaken them from their torpor, and without the help of others they would perish of inanition. Ordinary cases, on a higher level than this, show unbounded voracity. Idiots may be capable of feeling nothing but the nutritive cravings, and giving no signs of pleasure or pain except inarticulate growls, shrill cries, or strident laughter.

The complete idiot shows no sign of fear; he cannot fear, because he feels and comprehends nothing. Those less devoid of sensibility dread punishment, especially blows.

With regard to anger, there are the apathetic and insensible, and, above them, in imbeciles, fits of bestial rage, with convulsions, suffocations, violent impulses, and destructive cravings.

Those who pass the purely egoistic stage and do not remain totally indifferent to those about them, show a vague and transient affection for the person who takes care of them. Others, less destitute, "seem amiable and affectionate, and we may compare these patients to the dog who fawns on those who caress him" (Schüle). The highest step attained by them, and that rarely, is a certain sense of injustice. Itard observed this in his famous "savage of the Aveyron," whom he had purposely punished without cause.[1] In short, the social and moral tendencies are rudimentary or non-existent.

With regard to the sex-instinct, it is either entirely absent or there are various perversions and unrestrained erethism.

Lastly, there are some who can rise to a rudimentary manifestation of the superfluous or disinterested feelings. The idiot, as a rule, does not play; he is self-centred, isolated, and has no surplus vitality to expend. That activity which seems to live on itself and costs no effort, but is a source of pleasure without fatigue, is almost, if not quite, unknown to him. Even when invited and induced to play, he does so with little enthusiasm. We find, however, a rudiment of artistic tendency in those who have some taste for drawing or music. We may note, in passing, that the musical faculty being, as we know, one of the first

---

[1] Itard, *Mémoire sur le sauvage de l'Aveyron*, éd. Bourneville, pp. xlviii. *sqq.*

to appear, ought also to be one of the last to disappear.[1]
But all this is very poor and reduces itself to mere imitation,
and even this natural and simple tendency is wanting
among the lower grades of the feeble-minded.

Such, briefly, is the balance-sheet of the affective life in
these disinherited ones. It is generally admitted that, in
this abortive development, there are two main periods: the
first lasting from birth till about the third or fourth
year, when, if arrest of development takes place, the
psychic state remains almost *nil;* the second, from the
fourth year onwards, allows of a less scanty, but a discordant
and perverted psychology. In both cases, the evolution,
however incomplete, reproduces in all its stages the contrary order to that of decay.

It will be necessary, in concluding this study of decay, to
say a few words about a doctrine, much used and abused in
these days, and often alluded to in the course of this work,
which stands in direct relation to the pathology of the
feelings, and, in short, permits us to return some sort of
answer to the question put at the begininng of this
chapter: the Theory of Degeneration.

When we review the abnormal or morbid forms of the
affective life: destructive impulses, phobias, incurable
melancholy, sexual perversions, failure of the moral sense,
insanity of doubt, etc., and seek their causes, we at once
find some which are proximate or immediate. Among the
most frequent are physical maladies, injuries to the head,
sudden shocks, as in railway accidents; sorrow, whatever its
origin, whether love, ambition, ruin, separation; intellectual
overwork, and excesses of all sorts. A little reflection,
however, shows us that the alleged causes are not the

---

[1] Ireland (*Journal of Mental Science*, July 1894) has published
some observations which tend to favour the idea of this slow retrogression in dementia. He gives the case of a patient, sinking into
dementia, who not only retained her musical ability, but could even
pick up new tunes ; and mentions cases where the patient, seated
before a piano, could play old melodies though incapable of anything else.
A girl, aged fourteen, became demented through brain fever and had
ceased to speak, save a few words, but was still fond of music and
would play fragments of tunes. Two lady patients, though incoherent
in speech, played with great accuracy on the piano—one by ear only,
the other from musical notes, although she was quite unable to read a
book, etc. (Perhaps in this last case there was " word-blindness "
applying to words *only.*)

whole cause—that, in fact, they are often, rather, accidental and occasional.   One man bears courageously or even cheerfully a loss under which his neighbour succumbs.   Many are able to give themselves up with impunity to excesses of pleasure or work, physical or mental.   Of the passengers in the same train, at the time of an accident, the greater number will suffer nothing worse than fright, while one perhaps may on this account become insane, or permanently subject to phobias.   To explain this difference of results under identical conditions, we must seek a supplementary cause in the constitution of the individual himself.   When he offers only a slight resistance, and succumbs to the least shock, we say that he is a degenerate.

The conception of degenerescence as a fundamental cause is due, as every one knows, to Morel, and has flourished famously since his day.   Unfortunately, it has been called in to account for occurrences so numerous and so dissimilar that, in the end, it has brought down on itself the suspicions of some writers, who have recently stigmatised it as a " metaphysical," *i.e.*, vague and transcendental explanation.   In fact, different writers seem to understand by this word totally different things.   The original propounder of the doctrine had a clear if not a correct notion of degenerescence.   " The clearest idea," says Morel, " which we can form of human degenerescence is by representing it to ourselves as a morbid deviation from a primitive type.   This deviation, however simple we may suppose it at its origin, nevertheless contains such elements of transmissibility that he who carries its germ in himself becomes more and more incapable of performing his functions as a member of the human race, and progress, already impaired in his person, is threatened in those of his descendants. . . . Degenerescence and morbid deviation from the normal type of humanity are therefore, in my idea, one and the same thing."   This is quite clear. Morel, as a Christian, believed in a typical man, perfect as he came from the hands of the Creator: such a belief simplifies many things.   This position has been given up. At present, we understand by degenerescence, a morbid predisposition, having its peculiar signs, its physical and psychical " stigmata."

The physical stigmata, which have been enumerated at

great length by specialist writers, consist in anomalies of the skeleton, the muscular and the digestive system, of the respiratory, circulatory, and genito-urinary apparatus, of the skin, the special sense-organs, of speech, and especially of the central and peripheral nervous system. The detailed lists contain about sixty items.

The psychic stigmata are more vaguely defined. The principal are: irritability, showing itself in a marked disproportion between action and reaction; instability of character, absence of unity, of consent, incessant changes, eccentric conduct, painful haunting by fixed ideas, irresistible impulses, or extraordinary apathy.

It has been objected to this doctrine that, of a thousand individuals taken at random, there is perhaps not a single one who does not show one or more of the stigmata, so that the whole human race would be included in the alleged class of degenerates. No stigma, it has been said, is specific by itself; neither is any group of symptoms, at least in a clear and indisputable form; so that one can come to no conclusion from them.

This and other difficulties have supplied matter for many discussions, into which this is not the place to enter. Degenerescence, whatever its value as an explanation, and the abuse to which it has been subjected, is not a mere word; it expresses a reality: it sums up in itself a number of characters. This is sufficient for us, and allows us to eliminate one hypothesis: that the decay of the feelings is necessarily dependent on intellectual decay.

To say truth, the question stated above: Is the retrogression of the feelings a primary, and that of ideas a secondary fact? or the contrary? is, under this form, somewhat factitious. It is only by analytical artifice that we separate thought and feeling, which, by their nature, are closely connected. The law of retrogression is generally valid in biology, and probably also in psychology; it does not act on isolated points, it gradually surrounds and saps the whole building, no matter on what side it begins. It is clear that all weakening of the intellect, such as that produced by old age and disease (difficulty in understanding general ideas, loss of certain groups of recollections, etc.), involves the disappearance of the corresponding affective states: one of the observations already quoted (Case B.) is

an instance in point.   But we must not thence conclude
that the retrogression of the affective life *is, by right*,
always subordinated to that of knowledge.   Most cases of
degenerescence prove the contrary; it is essentially an
organic decadence, a state of physiological poverty, showing
itself first of all by alterations in the range of the emotions,
tendencies, actions, and movements.   The intellect, for its
part, is better able to stand the shock, and sometimes
remains uninjured.   More than this, the adherents of this
doctrine have shown that the degenerate are sometimes
endowed with brilliant intellectual faculties; while some
have even maintained that degenerescence is a necessary
condition of high mental originality ("genius a neurosis,"
etc.).

Apart from all exaggeration, the mass of facts permits us
to make the induction that decadence is primarily (not exclusively) that of the affective tendencies and manifestations,
since it is on them that degenerescence (taking the word in
its least vague sense) first and principally acts.

CONCLUSION.

The place of the feelings in psychic life—They come first—Physiological proofs—Psychological proofs.

THROUGH the multiple aspects of our subject and the diversity of questions we have dealt with, the fundamental idea of this book has been to show that the foundation of the affective life is appetite or its contrary—that is to say, movement or arrest of movement; that at its root it is an impulse, a tendency, an act in the nascent or complete state, independent of intelligence, which has nothing to do with it and may not even be present. It is unnecessary to inflict upon the reader any new variations on a theme so often repeated. I only desire, in conclusion, to add some remarks on the place of the feelings in the total psychic life, and to show that that place is the *first*.

This statement must be made precise. To compare "sensibility" and "intelligence," as some authors have done, to see which of these two "faculties" is inferior to the other, is an artificial and unreasonable task, since there is no common measure of the two, and there can be no solution of the question which is not arbitrary. But we may proceed objectively, and ask if the one is not primary and the other secondary, if the one is not grafted on the other, and in that case which is the stock and which the graft. If the feelings appear first it is clear that they cannot be derived, and are not a mode or function of knowledge, since they exist by themselves and are irreducible.

Thus stated the question is simple and the reply evident.

The physiological evidence in favour of the priority of the feelings need only be briefly recalled; it all centres in one point: organic vegetative life always and everywhere appears before animal life; physiologists constantly repeat that the animal is grafted on the vegetable which precedes him. Now organic life is directly expressed by the needs and appetites, which are the stuff of the affective life; animal life by the sensations, the stuff of the intellectual life. The primordial part played by organic sensibility has been shown in the Introduction. We may remember also the myriads of animals which are only bundles of needs, their psychology consisting in the search for food, in defence, and in propagation; their senses (often reduced to touch alone) are only tools, coarse instruments, teleological weapons in the service of their needs; but closed in as they may be from the external world, appetite in them is not less intense. Even in man is not fœtal life, and that of the first months after birth, much the same, almost wholly made up of satisfied or unsatisfied needs, and consequently of pleasures and pains? From the purely physiological point of view, knowledge appears not as a mistress but as a servant.

The psychological evidence is not difficult to supply, and has indeed already been presented by Schopenhauer in so brilliant and complete a manner that it would be a bold task to present it afresh. The chapter entitled "The Primacy of Will in Self-Consciousness"[1] is a long argument in favour of the priority of impulse over knowledge. We need not be duped by the equivocal use of the word "will," since for Schopenhauer "to will is to desire, to aspire, to flee, to hope, to fear, to love, to hate; in a word, all that directly constitutes our good and our ill, our pleasure and our pain." Nor need we occupy ourselves with his metaphysics nor his antiquated physiology, nor his personal hatred of intelligence, which he treats as an enemy and usurper, "because all the philosophers up to to-day have made it the intimate primitive essence of their so-called soul;" and having made these eliminations we may find many of his pages full of penetrating and consummate psychology. I recall his chief arguments.

Will (in the sense above indicated) is universal. The basis of consciousness in every animal is desire. This fundamental fact is translated into the impulse to preserve life and well-being, and to propagate. This foundation is common to the polypus and to man. The differences

[1] *Die Welt als Wille und Vorstellung,* Part III., chap. xix.

among animals are due to a difference in knowledge; as we descend in the series intelligence becomes weaker and more imperfect; there is no similar degradation in will (or desire); the smallest insect wills what it wills as fully as man; will is everywhere equal to itself. Relatively to intelligence it is the robust blind man carrying on his shoulders the paralytic who sees clearly.

It is fundamental. The will to live, with the horror of death which results from it, is a fact anterior to all intelligence and independent of it. In it is the basis of identity and of character; "the man is hidden in the heart and not in the head." It is the source and the bond of all stable associations, religious, political, or professional. It makes the strength of party spirit, of sects, and of factions. Compare the fragility of friendships founded on similarity of intelligence with those that spring from the heart. Thus religions have had every reason to promise eternal recompense to man's moral qualities, and not to the gifts of the mind.

Its power is sovereign. It is not reason which uses passion, it is passion which uses reason to reach its ends. Under the influence of intense desire, the intellect sometimes rises to a degree of vigour of which none would believe it capable. Desire, love, fear render the most obtuse understanding lucid. And besides, if will and intelligence were identical in nature, their development would proceed side by side, whereas nothing is more frequent than a great intellect united to an inferior character, and "we sometimes find violent desires, impassioned and impetuous impulses, joined to a feeble intellect, that is to say a small brain badly enclosed in a thick skull."

Memory, which is commonly considered a purely intellectual phenomenon, often depends—as we have seen—on the state of the feelings. This had not escaped Schopenhauer. "Even a weak memory sometimes retains perfectly what concerns the passion dominant at the moment; the lover never forgets a favourable opportunity, the ambitious nothing that serves their projects; the miser never forgets his losses, nor the proud man a wound to his honour; the vain remember every word of praise and every distinction they receive. . . . That is what might be called the heart's memory, more intimate than the mind's."

How is it that facts of common observation, so clear and so numerous, requiring for their discovery neither experiment nor special research, nor even long reflection, have been so generally misunderstood ; and that the contrary opinion has always predominated, reducing the manifestations of feeling to "qualities of sensation," to "confused intelligence," and other oft-repeated formulas? The only reason I can find is that during centuries this subject has been treated philosophically, not psychologically, and the method of philosophy is necessarily intellectualist. Only the adult and complex forms of the affective life were considered, without regard to their evolution, which alone brings us to their origin. The parts played by movements as psychological factors, and by unconscious activity, were forgotten or misunderstood. Pleasures and pains in their manifold forms were regarded as the essential phenomena in place of the hidden springs which give rise to them.

To sum up, the psychology of the emotions has its point of departure in those complex feelings which daily life brings beneath our eyes every moment. Their complexity is the work of our intellectual nature, which associates and dissociates, mixing and combining perceptions, images, ideas, each of which, in so far as it relates to the individual or social conditions of existence, to the physiological needs, to the offensive and defensive instinct of conservation, to the social, moral, religious, æsthetic, and scientific tendencies, produces in the organism variable effects which, translated into consciousness, impart an affective tone to intellectual states. Analysis shows that these complex forms are reducible to a few simple emotions. The simple emotion itself is a complexus made up of impulses, that is of motor elements, and agreeable, painful, or mixed states of consciousness; these two factors form a whole apparently indissoluble. Finally, the fundamental motor or dynamic element manifests itself under two forms : conscious impulses or desires, unconscious impulses or appetites; there is identity of nature, the first possessing consciousness in addition. Hence for the desires (the psychological form), thanks to consciousness, there is the possibility of manifold adaptations and indefinite plasticity. Hence for the appetites (the physiological form) there is stability, fixity, automatism, the absence of invention, and of that state of indecision arising simultaneously with consciousness.

If we include all the primitive conscious impulses beneath the name of *desire* (or its opposite, *aversion*), we find two apparently contradictory theses concerning its origin. According to one, desire is a primitive phenomenon, anterior on the one hand to all knowledge, and on the other to all experience of pleasure or pain. According to the other, desire is a secondary phenomenon, the anticipation of a known pleasure to seek for, a known pain to avoid; the latter counts most partisans, and is also condensed into well-known axiomatic sayings and formulas : "We cannot desire what we do not know," "We can only desire what seems to be for our advantage," "Desire is founded on a proved pleasure." Both theses are true, each for a separate moment, and the first alone relates to the question of origin.

At the first moment desire is anterior to all experience, to every consideration of pleasure or of pain; it acts as a blind force; it is a *vis a tergo*, a propulsion only explicable by the physical and mental organism. It must necessarily act at once without knowing whither it goes, else it would act too late or not at all.

At the second moment, it is guided by experience and rests on proved pleasure or pain, seeking one and avoiding the other. It is to this moment that the sayings above quoted apply. That is the final form, and it embraces the immense majority of cases. Even in the adult, however, we have noted examples of vague desire, without object or determined aim.

Blind impulse, when it reaches its end, finds its satisfaction there, and seeks it anew because it is pleasant. But the pleasant and the unpleasant are relative qualities, varying in individuals, and at different moments in the same individual. If the physical and mental organisation changes, the impulses, the position of pleasure and pain change also; pathology furnishes us with unquestionable proof.

Impulse, therefore, is the primordial fact in the life of the feelings, and I cannot better conclude than by borrowing from Spinoza a passage which sums up the whole spirit of this book : "Appetite is the very essence of man, from which necessarily flow all those things which seem to preserve him. . . . Between appetite and desire there is no difference, save that desire is self-conscious appetite. It follows from all this that we desire and follow after nothing because we deem it to be good, but on the contrary deem that to be good which we desire and follow after." [1]

[1] *Ethica*, iii. prop. 9, schol.

INDEX.

THE WALTER SCOTT PUBLISHING CO., LTD., FELLING-ON-TYNE.